Turkey's Entente with Israel and Azerbaijan

With the end of the Cold War came a new political instability in Turkey and a shift in relations with the West, leading Turkey to adopt new foreign policies and forge alliances with neighboring states. This book offers a detailed and comprehensive analysis of the evolution of the trilateral relationship between Turkey, Israel and Azerbaijan.

Drawing both on first-hand interviews and on research not previously available in the English language, Alexander Murinson brings a new perspective to the study of the relationship between the three countries. In particular he examines the commonalities of state identities that brought the countries together, the role of state institutions, the security dimension and the influence of globalization. In a period of growing concerns about European energy security, the book provides an extensive discussion of the activities carried out by various think tanks, especially in Washington, regarding the regional and domestic politics of the three countries.

An original contribution to study of regional processes in the expanded Middle East after the end of the Cold War, this book is a welcome addition to the literature on the regional politics of the Middle East and the Caucasus. As such, it will be of great interest to anyone studying international relations, security studies and Middle Eastern politics.

Alexander Murinson is an independent researcher. He received his Ph.D. from the School of Oriental and African Studies, University of London, and has written a number of articles on Turkish foreign policy and the entente with Israel and Azerbaijan.

Routledge Studies in Middle Eastern Politics

Turkey's Entente with Israel and Azerbaijan

State identity and security in the Middle East and Caucasus

Alexander Murinson

R Routledge
Taylor & Francis Group

LONDON AND NEW YORK

First published 2010
by Routledge
2 Park Square, Milton Park, Abingdon, Oxon OX14 4RN

Simultaneously published in the USA and Canada
by Routledge
711 Third Avenue, New York, NY 10017

Routledge is an imprint of the Taylor & Francis Group, an informa business

© 2010 Alexander Murinson

Typeset in Times New Roman by
Florence Production Ltd, Stoodleigh, Devon

British Library Cataloguing in Publication Data
A catalogue record for this book is available from the British Library

Library of Congress Cataloging in Publication Data
Murinson, Alexander.
  Turkey's entente with Israel and Azerbaijan: state identity and
  security in the Middle East and Caucasus/Alexander Murinson.
      p. cm.—(Routledge studies in Middle Eastern politics; 19)
    Includes bibliographical references and index.
    1. Turkey—Foreign relations—Israel.   2. Israel—Foreign
  relations—Turkey.   3. Turkey—Foreign relations—Azerbaijan.
  4. Azerbaijan—Foreign relations—Turkey.   5. National security
  —Turkey.   6. Security, International—Middle East.   7. Security,
  International—Caucasus.   I. Title.
  JZ1649.A57T95 2009
  355'.0310956104754—dc22   2009025728

First issued in paperback 2013

ISBN13: 978–0–415–85318–7 (pbk)
ISBN13: 978–0–415–77892–3 (hbk)
ISBN13: 978–0–203–86280–3 (ebk)

To Beth, with love and affection

Contents

Preface

This book evolved from my Ph.D. dissertation undertaken at the School of Oriental and African Studies, University of London between 2002 and 2008. The book's main premise that an innovative approach is needed in order to analyze alignments that emerged after the end of the Cold War. The formation of two informal Eurasian strategic alliances in the expanded Middle East in the last decade of the twenty-first century is not widely appreciated in the international relations literature. One is the US-supported informal alliance of Azerbaijan, Turkey and Israel (possibly Georgia); and this is counterbalanced by that of Russia, Armenia, Iran (possibly Greece and Syria).[1] The original contribution of this book represents a study of regional process in the expanded Middle East after the end of the Cold War. As no literature exists that analyzes an attempt to forge a trilateral strategic axis or an entente between Turkey, Israel and Azerbaijan, this work intends to fill this lacuna. In my view, more specifically, a Turkish–Israeli axis was extended to include Azerbaijan.

The proposed analytical framework straddles three disciplinary domains, namely, International Relations, Security Studies and Transnational Studies. The methodology for the book was borrowed from the field of Comparative Foreign Policy. This field specializes in comparing the foreign policies of different states in order to establish general empirical connections between the characteristics of the state. Specifically, I studied the entente of Turkey, Israel and Azerbaijan (1992–2005) and its ideational make-up. In view of the fluidity of the ideational content of state identity, I sought general tropes or matching patterns by using discourse analysis of narratives, ideology and connotations of political rhetoric. Under conditions of globalization, another important set of non-state interactions became crucial for the understanding of alignments in the twenty-first century, known as the transnational factor. In my attempt to elucidate its role, I pay attention in the book to the role(s) of transnational corporations, and ethnic diasporas as agents of political and economic networks and reconstruction of "individuals' journeys" and their written and oral utterances.

The interpretive methodology presents a host of methodological difficulties, such as the manipulation of records and the omission and distortion of facts.

My proposed model of alliance formation in the post-Cold War era also requires a lot of adjusting and testing. So the end result of my research, I hope, will not only stir a healthy debate abut also produce criticism of the proposed model that will enable the creation of a more adequate model of alliance formation in the twenty-first century.

Lastly, I note that all misconceptions and erroneous views presented here are the responsibility of the author.

Note

1   Bulent Aras, *The New Geopolitics of Eurasia and Turkey's Position*, London: Frank Cass, 2002, p.34; Svante Cornell, "The Conflict in Nagorno-Karabagh," in Dmitry Furman (Ed.), *Azerbaijan and Russia*, Moscow: Letny Sad, 2001, p. 471; Zeyno Baran, "The Caucasus: Ten Years After Independence," *The Washington Quarterly*, Winter Section: Eurasia after ten years, Vol. 25, No. 1, 2002, p. 223.

Acknowledgments

I would like to acknowledge the help and advice of many people who made completing this book possible. First, I would like to acknowledge the invaluable guidance and friendly advice of Professors William Hale and Shirin Akiner, my Ph.D. supervisors at SOAS. A special "thank you" is extended to William Hale for setting my sail for Turkish Studies. The indomitable faith of Shirin Akiner in my ideas was a constant source of inspiration. I would like to express my sincere appreciation of insights into the history and society of Turkey gained in private conversations with Andrew Mango and Jacob Landau, Senior Dragomans of Turkish Studies. I am also grateful to Soner Cagaptay and Keith Weissman for introducing me to many influential Turkish policymakers and diplomats. Sabri Sayari, Alan Makovsky, Barry Rubin and Efraim Inbar, Gareth Jenkins, Suha Bolukbasi, Gareth Winrow, and Soli Ozel have my appreciation for their thoughtful advice. Ambassadors Feridun Sinirlioglu and Engin Soysal, Turkish diplomats, deserve special credit for devoting their valuable time to help me understand the central preoccupation of Turkish foreign policy today, i.e. entry into the European Union. I would also like to thank Anna Zelkina and Nariman Gasimoglu for their introduction to the modern political realities of Azerbaijan. My gratitude is extended to Robert Freedman of the Johns Hopkins University, and to Charles Fairbanks, formerly of SAIS, the Johns Hopkins University, for pointing me to important analytical sources.

Thanks are due to James (Joe) Whiting, Acquisitions Editor, Middle Eastern and Islamic Studies, Routledge, who brought the fruit of my labor to the publication stage. I also would like to thank Sarah Enticknap, Production Editor, Social Sciences, Routledge, for overseeing the publication process. My special thanks to Suzanne Richardson, Editorial Assistant, Routledge, and Sue Leaper, Florence Production Ltd., for their attention to all details involved.

My sincere thanks are also due to my Turkish friends, especially to Yucel and Guldan Kalem, and friends in Azerbaijan, especially Qanimat Zahidov, editor-in-chief of the *Azadliq* daily. Finally, I would like to express my utmost gratitude to my wife, Beth, for the gift of unflinching faith and inspiration that she shared with me throughout this work.

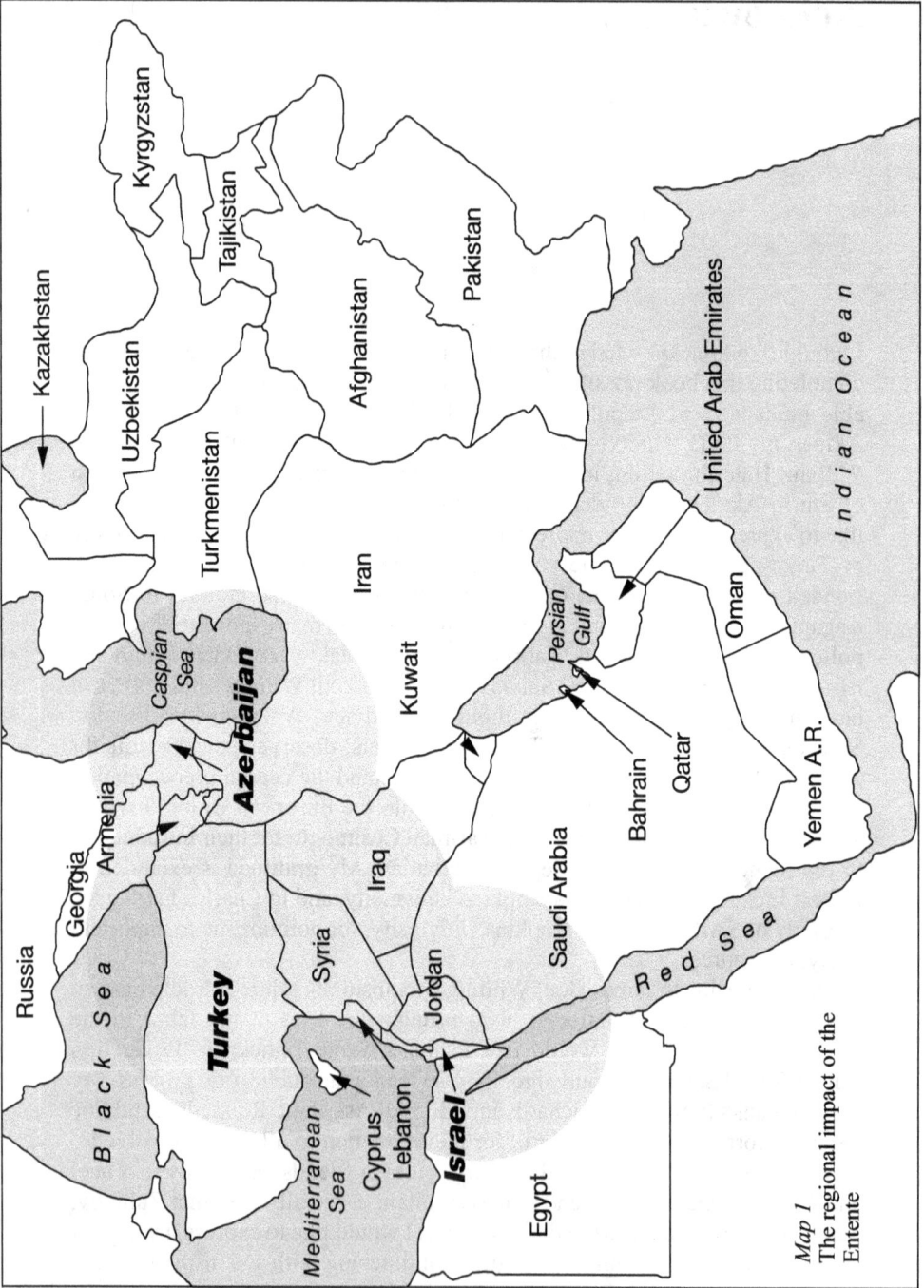

Map 1
The regional impact of the
Entente

Map 2
The Transcaucasus

80 miles

1   The entente of Turkey, Israel and Azerbaijan

A new type of alliance in the post-Cold War era

Introduction: the tripartite entente

The end of the Cold War brought confusion and new sources of instability into geopolitical calculations of the Turkish foreign policy elite. In the early 1990s, Turkey was hard pressed to replace its relationship with the West based on the security aspect of the transatlantic community. With the end of the Cold War, what were the Turkish geo-strategic options? The new trend in Turkish foreign policy was to replace reliance on the West with an extension of Turkish influence into areas that were historically part of the Ottoman Empire, and to penetrate the Turk Dunasi ("Turkic world") building upon historical, cultural and ethno-linguistic ties. Ottoman and Azeri Turks, for example, are connected by bonds of common descent and language, and supported each other throughout the centuries, especially, during the dramatic period of the short-lived independent republic of Azerbaijan (1918–20).

The traditional Turkish policy was based on the principle of non-involvement in regions to the north (formerly under Soviet control) and to the east (the countries of the Middle East region), practiced by the foreign policy elite of the Republican Turkey since the collapse of the Baghdad Pact in 1958.[1] If, in the previous four decades, Turkey had a clear-cut role of the "frontier state," embedded in the North Atlantic Treaty Organization, the future seemed less predictable.[2] Thus, the emergence of a Turkish–Israeli entente, which later included Azerbaijan in the post-Cold War era, was a major geopolitical departure in Turkish foreign policy. This book presents an analysis of this tripartite entente using a novel approach that utilizes the core concepts of the Constructivist School in international relations and the theory of Trans-nationalism. The time framework of my research will be limited to the period between 1992 (the independence of Azerbaijan) and 2005 (the beginning of consolidation of AKP's power in Turkey).

The term *entente* is used in this work in its conventional meaning reminiscent of the *Entente Cordiale* among France, Great Britain and Russia in the period of World War I. *Entente* means, in other words, an arrangement or understanding between nations to follow a particular policy with regard to affairs of international concern.[3] However, entente is more a tenuous arrangement than an alliance, since it more susceptible to fluctuations in domestic politics and shifts in the foreign policy calculations of its members.

Turkey, since the foundation of the Turkish Republic, had an ambivalent relationship with regional neighbors in the Middle East. The Republic has a Muslim population, but it chose to align itself with the Western alliance. Because of the half-hearted support of the West for its desire to join Western regional organizations such as the EU in the beginning of the 1990s, Turkey sought other strategic options. The new post-Cold War reality dictated a search for a replacement of Turkey's role as a "Northern Tier" state. With the collapse of the Soviet Union, Turkey changed its foreign policy rather creatively. So new factors, such as cultural and historical links, emerged to drive Turkish foreign policy. If earlier it was a Western alliance within NATO that defined Turkish state identity, the post-Cold War reality transformed Turkey into a frontier state of a different kind. Because new threats arose, namely militant Islam and Kurdish ethno-national separatism as well as other ethnic conflicts in the Turkish frontier, Turkey needed to reinvent itself and find a new strategic vision in response to the new challenges.

The history of the Israeli–Turkish diplomatic romance goes back to the late 1950s. It was then, after the dissolution of the Baghdad Pact, that Israel extended a secret alliance with Turkey as part of its "peripheral strategy."[4] However, only with the dissipation of the Soviet threat did Turkey and Israel realize that their strategic interests in the Middle East and Eurasia strongly overlap. Turkey also sought to re-energize its relationship with the Jewish people, both in the United States and Israel. This linkage was rooted in the historical amity and mutual appreciation between the Ottoman Turks and the Jews who fled the Christian persecution on the Iberian Peninsula in the late fifteenth century. Jewish refugees from Spain and Portugal became permanently interwoven in the fabric of Ottoman society as the Sultan's physicians, diplomats and financiers in subsequent centuries. Israel's relationship with Azerbaijan is also embedded in the history of the long co-existence of two people. The core territory of modern-day Azerbaijan, i.e. Shirvan, Quba and other Azeri Khanates in the Caucasus, served historically as place of refuge for Persian and later Russian Jews.

After the collapse of the Soviet Union, Turkey sought to develop its ties with the former Soviet Turkic republics. At the same time, it sought to reinvigorate relations with the "unseen or invisible member" of the Western alliance, Israel. It also turned its gaze to its Near Eastern neighbors in the Balkans as an alternative to its role as purely an East–West corridor, concurrently pursuing its policy of integration into Europe. Success of the Turkish journey to its European vocation is not guaranteed; moreover, the process of European integration is a long and complicated one. Membership in the European Union is based on *acquis communautaire* and the fulfilment of the Copenhagen criteria.

This trilateral axis of Turkey–Israel–Azerbaijan flourished very quickly after its inception in 1992, but after reaching its peak in 1999, the entente began to unravel. The entente encountered important limitations of domestic and structural nature. The rise of "Islamic politics" (election of Islamist Refah and "moderate" Islamist AKP) gained mass support in Turkey as the country began the process of liberalization. Turgut Ozal's economic and political reforms of the 1980s unleashed the pent-up discontent of conservative religious strata against the secular regime. The newly urbanized class of former peasants of Central Anatolia underwent political mobilization and provided an electoral base for the Islamists' success. The considerations of Turkish domestic politics weighed heavily against further improvement of Turkish–Israeli relations, which were seen by civilian authorities as an entanglement with the enemy of Islam. The Turkish government's verbal attacks on Israel and accusations of "state terrorism" further cooled the atmosphere of bilateral relations. Especially damaging in this regard was the invitation extended by AKP's leadership to Khaled Mashal, a Hamas leader in Damascus, to visit Turkey on February 16, 2006.[5]

In the case of Azerbaijan, the particularistic interests of the Aliyev clan began to dominate domestic and foreign policy in 1999–2005. These interests necessitated rapprochement with Russia. The failure by the American Jewish lobby to strike down Section 907 in Congress during its 1998–9 session exposed the limits of its power. Azerbaijani authorities realized that an Israeli "connection" does not guarantee desirable outcomes in the high echelons of American government, and the value of an informal relationship with Israel has declined. Since 1999, Israelis, in their turn, encountered the policy of evasion on the part of Azerbaijanis and a lack of progress in the diplomatic sphere.

There have been few comprehensive works addressing this new foreign policy strategy of Turkey. My work is an attempt to fill this lacuna. This book will attempt to answer questions about the causes of the formation of this entente or axis. Some scholars call this relationship a strategic relationship,[6] a security relationship,[7] axis,[8] alignment or pact.[9] The multiplicity of terms used to define the relationship between the countries in question suggests a lack of clarity about its nature or its novelty. My argument is that there was a brief period of convergence of foreign policy interests among the three countries, but that it was not strong enough to support a lasting relationship as Turkey reasserted its Muslim identity following the election of an Islamist AKP in 2002. We cannot explain this relationship exclusively by power politics or economic interests, as other forces were clearly at work. The subject of this book is to explore these forces. I propose that this relationship can be better understood as a manifestation of shared state identities actualized through subnational agents and transnational networks in the globalized international polity. The conventional wisdom in IR focuses on *realpolitik* explanations for the formation of alliances. The earlier assumption that alignments are driven exclusively by rational calculations of power balances is insufficient to explain the complex dynamics that characterize the new types of alliance in the post-Cold War era. These new combinations of states that do not correspond to classical alliances require elaboration in the alliance formation theory. Which forces brought this entente into existence? Why is the formation of the triple entente intimately linked with the issue of the state identities of the three nations? What in the ideational make-up of these states compelled the three nations to realize the complementarity of their interests? How did transnational factors affect the shape of this alignment? How did shared traditional security concerns bring these countries together in the 1990s? What are the ideational forces in the three countries that counteracted or limited the maintenance of the entente?

Central to this book is the examination of such social constructs of state identities of Azerbaijan, Turkey and Israel as (1) garrison-states, i.e. states whose political and territorial integrity is threatened by internal ethno-national conflict or secessionist movements (the Nagorno-Karabagh Armenians, the Kurds, the Palestinian Arabs); (2) secular and Western-oriented states; (3) constitutionally nationalist states; and (4) "lonely" states—states rejected by their neighbors due to religious, ideological or ethnic differences.

Next, state "drivers" of the entente will be identified, and their structural role explicated. Another integral aspect of this study is the investigation of the role played by epistemic communities and transnational actors, including transnational corporations (TNCs), religious networks and ethnic diasporas, in shaping this trilateral relationship. According to Colonomos, it is the "intermediate actors in international relations with various forms of autonomy-business firms, NGOs, and indeed networks of professionals which occupy a significant place in a number of supranational spaces" in the new international system.[10] The transnational networks function as the essential conduits of what Wendt called the "two systemic processes" of interdependence and transnational convergence of domestic values in the international system.[11] In particular, it is important to elucidate the roles of TNCs, which, acting in para-diplomatic roles, operate at the intersection of "state logics and transnational dynamics."[12] Many trajectories of these transnational networks converge on the United States as their meeting point. So it is essential to highlight the role the United States plays, not only as an instigator of transnational processes, but as their target or their political arena. Colonomos notes that "the logics of networks in their transnational variant very often includes a 'stopover' in the US."[13] Consequently, it is crucial to elucidate the impact of the ethnic lobbies, in particular the Jewish lobby, in the United States on the formation and maintenance of this strategic alliance.

The blind men and the elephant: identity politics, transnationalism and security as factors in international relations in the post-Cold War era

The end of the Cold War and globalization are the quintessential features shaping the international environment in the twenty-first century. The formation of two informal Eurasian strategic alliances in the expanded Middle East in the last decade of the twentieth century is neglected in international relations literature. They are the US-supported informal alliance of Turkey, Israel and Azerbaijan (and possibly Georgia), which is counter-balanced by the Russian-backed alliance of Armenia, Iran and Syria (and possibly Greece).[14] After the removal of the Soviet threat at the end of the Cold War, both Turkey and Israel faced a dilemma concerning the role they should play in the US-dominated unipolar world. The new geopolitical realities of the post-Cold War era compelled both countries to reinvent themselves as "pillars" of the American strategy in the expanded Middle East.

The depth and scope of the ongoing trilateral cooperation between Azerbaijan, Turkey and Israel requires special mention. An Israeli scholar recently commented that the "Israeli friendship with Azerbaijan (allied with Turkey) dovetails with Israel's deepening relationship with Turkey."[15] According to the *Turkish Daily News*, "The Turkey–Israel partnership has silently been expanding to include one of the most important countries in the region, Azerbaijan."[16] Neill Lochery quotes Turkish international relations experts noting "the role of Azerbaijan in the new regional strategic structure," adding that, "There is an obvious intersection between the Turkey–Israel, Israel–Azerbaijan and Turkey–Azerbaijan partnerships."[17] Several Iranian scholars also point to the strategic cooperation between Turkey, Azerbaijan and Israel.[18] According to Eldar Namazov, a former chief advisor of Azeri President Heydar Aliyev, the idea of an informal alliance between Turkey, Azerbaijan and Israel was quite popular among the military–political elites of the three countries in the mid-1990s. This strategic amalgamation not only reflected the logic of the budding Azerbaijani–Turkish strategic alliance, but also purported to reinvigorate the Azerbaijani historical relationship with the Jewish people.[19] This idea also had strong backing among the Israeli foreign policy elite and the Jewish lobby in the United States.

Attempts to explain the genesis of this tripartite relationship by focusing exclusively on one aspect (e.g. security) seem to this author off the mark. It would be the paradigmatic tale of the Blind Men and the Elephant.[20] There is a dearth of analysis in international relations of a new type of alliance formed in the post-Cold War period. Ian Lesser identified this new type of alliance as the "new security geometries" in critical regions.[21] It is noteworthy that two examples of these informal strategic alliances came into being in Eurasia in the early 1990s.[22] A multi-causal model of this relationship seems more appropriate and useful in shedding light on a parallel Near Eastern counter-alliance of Russia, Iran, Armenia, and Syria (and possibly Greece). This study of the trilateral relationship intends to contribute to the field of international relations on substantive and theoretical levels. By advancing a multi-causal model, the book aims not only to contribute to the study of particular post-Cold War geopolitical alignments, but also to expand the theoretical debate in international relations. Traditional "neorealist" accounts of strategic alignments fail to produce multidimensional representations of interactions that generated post-Cold war alignments due to their preoccupation with "hard" security issues. Radical Constructivist accounts suffer from their detachment from the concrete and present dangers inherent in the possession of WMDs by totalitarian and unstable regimes, and from the absence of realistic scenarios of the use of primitive makeshift nuclear devices, such as "dirty bombs," by terrorists.

The proposed model emanates from a symbiosis of the constructivist approach and the transnational studies approach. The model provides a more adequate description of alliance formation in the international system under conditions of globalization. I would like to elucidate the causes of the formation of this relationship, and to examine one set of domestic and transnational agents that reinforce/maintain this relationship, and another set that has the capacity to undermine it. The proposed study will also be of practical value to international security studies because, as Efraim Inbar succinctly notes: "In the Middle East, where the dominant prism for understanding international relations is power politics and informal alliances are at least as important as formal explicit coalitions."[23]

An alternative view

Taking a new approach, I would like to contribute to the debate about the nature of multilateral alliance formation in the post-Cold War era. The study investigates the post-Cold War identities of three states: Turkey, Israel and Azerbaijan. The model is contingent upon state identities and the social and political practices through which these identities are reproduced, as well as the understanding of foreign policy as a function of the international context (structure) and the identity and interests of other states (agents). Under conditions of globalization, transnational and subnational actors have come to play a greater part in reproduction of state identities, hence I would like to trace the interaction between these factors and state identities. I propose to combine a modified constructivist theoretical framework proposed by Alexander Wendt with the transnational studies conceptualization of transnational networks in order to elucidate the trilateral relationship between Azerbaijan, Turkey and Israel.

The systemic structural change affects also sub-systemic structures, i.e. geographical regions; hence the end of the Cold War had profound effects both in the Middle East and the Caucasus. The first Gulf war and the start of the Arab–Israeli peace process at the Madrid Peace Conference, not to mention the creation of an independent Azerbaijan within the same year (1991), had been inconceivable before the end of the Cold War. This systemic shift (the end of the Cold War) produced a shift in the social identities of the states in question. In other words, the reconstitution of the regional environment (structure) precipitated structural changes that allowed the formation of this strategic relationship. However, Wendt's theory is insufficient to explain the reproduction or maintenance of alliances or collective identities. Wendt replaced neorealist interests with Constructivist identity. To his critics, it is still a state-centric conceptualization.[24] State as an agent in Wendt's view is a homogenous, unitary entity. This conceptualization should be challenged by introducing more sophisticated and multivariate understandings of state identity. One can observe that state identity is the subject of competition by sub-national actors such as foreign policy elites, the military, and ethnic, religious and business actors. State identities can be challenged also by popular identities. Whether these states succeed in reproducing the actor identity favored by their political elite depends on the congruence or non-congruence of elite identity with popular identities. Generally, elites are severely constrained in reproducing pro-Western secular identities when mass identities favor an Islamist Refah Partisi (Welfare Party), in the case of Turkey, or Shas, a Sephardi religious party, in the case of Israel. Viewed from a Constructivist perspective, for example, the authoritarian rule of Heydar Aliyev's clan, massive illegal flight of capital and labor migration to Russia, massive tax evasion and pervasive corruption may all be viewed as social practices that undermine and constrain efforts by the Azerbaijani elite to reproduce an international identity as a Western, liberal and democratic state. So state identity can be understood as a product of this competition or inter-action. To add another dimension to this conceptualization, under conditions of globalization, supranational actors also participate in the reproduction of state.

In this context it is interesting to investigate the historical trajectory of this strategic trilateral relationship[25] and its future potential with reference to the concept of state identity. A number of salient properties of the states in question can be highlighted and demonstrated to be complementary vis-à-vis each other. Such properties include garrison-states, pro-Western orientation, democratic and secular societies,[26] commonality of geopolitical interests, commonalities of language[27] and civic culture, geographic proximity, and complementary national economies.[28] Several geopolitical factors distinguish these countries, creating natural tensions between each of the three and its immediate neighbors on the one hand, and a sense of commonality of interest, if not common destiny, on the other. They include competition with such powerful neighbors as Russia and Iran for control over Caspian Sea oil reserves; the pivotal geopolitical position of Turkey;[29] a general desire to integrate fully within Western (European?) security, political and economic frameworks;[30] and security issues with and the fear of penetration by radical Islam from Iran and neighboring Arab nations.

Review of chapters

This book has the following structure. In the first chapter, I introduce the questions the book will attempt to answer and the issues it addresses; define key terms; review current scholarship on Turkey's entente with Israel and Azerbaijan; and describe the case studies, methodology and sources. In the second chapter, I will review the existing literature on theoretical debates in the field of international relations relevant to the book's subject matter. A multi-causal model is advanced for testing the hypothesis of the formation of the new type of post-Cold War alliances. Chapters 3, 4, 5 and 6 comprise the empirical core of the book. In Chapter 2, I will present the main argument, that it was the commonality of state identities that brought these three countries together to form an entente after the Cold War. In Chapter 3, I will analyze state institutions that became the drivers of this relationship. Chapter 4 deals with the transnational forces and agents that emerged under conditions of globalization after the 1980s. In it, I will address the question how these factors affected the trilateral relationship. The fifth chapter addresses the heart of the entente, i.e. the security dimension of this relationship between the three countries. Here I pay special attention to the shared threats emanating from the particular identities that Turkey, Israel and Azerbaijan assumed in the 1990s. Chapter 6 addresses the domestic factors that limit and are capable of eventually undermining the triple entente. Given the fluid nature of the regional environment in which these nations exist, the convergence of their interests might dissipate. In the final chapter, I will reiterate my main conclusions, summarize empirical findings and indicate directions for future research.

2 State identities as building blocks of the relationship, 1992–9

Introduction: the return of identity

The importance of state identity and of cultural/institutional constructions of national security, as well as values and norms in international relations, has gained wide acceptance in IR theory.[1] The Constructivist school, in particular, espouses this view. Baruch Kimmerling also argues that the notion of state identity has been ignored by many social scientists. Kimmerling defines it as the "unique fingerprint" that distinguishes each state–society complex and is created through state–civil society interactions.[2]

Even before the creation of the Jewish state, its founder, David Ben-Gurion, paid tribute to the achievements of Ataturk's Turkey as a model of development in the Middle East. In the introduction to the first monograph about Turkey in Mandate Palestine he wrote: "Turkey is the largest, the most independent and most advanced country in the Near East. The creator of the modern Turkey, Mustafa Kemal, knew how to turn the political destruction of the Ottoman Empire in World War II into the source of renewal and awakening."[3] Identifying the Turkish Republic as a potential ally in the region, Ben-Gurion added, "Our people have an obligation to assist the progressive forces that operate in this part of the world, and, among these forces, Turkey occupies the first place."[4] A deep thinker and outstanding leader, David Ben-Gurion recognized the profound transformation that Turkey had undergone as a result of the sweeping and fast-paced political and institutional reforms of Mustafa Kemal.[5] The future Israeli leader, architect of the "Periphery Alliance" of the 1960s, captured the fundamental spirit of the Republican Turkey that made it the natural ally of the young Jewish democracy apart from corrupt and backward regimes in the neighborhood. His vision bore fruit when Turkey became the first Muslim country to recognize the State of Israel after its creation in 1949.

From the foundation of the Turkish Republic by Kemal Ataturk, the country defined itself as a secular state that aspires to join Western civilization. Recognition of the State of Israel was a manifestation of Turkey's commitment to Western democratic values. In the post-Cold War period, this relationship evolved in the direction of an informal Turkish–Israeli alignment.[6] Azerbaijan became a strategic partner to both countries in the post-Soviet space shortly thereafter.[7] The commonality of interests between the three countries was described by the Azerbaijani deputy foreign minister, Araz Azimov: "These three [countries] are close to each other in this piece of the world in terms of their geopolitical and geo-economic interests, closer approach to the United States, realistic approach to the problems between Arabs and Israelis."[8] Another Azerbaijani former state official reflecting on the strategic partnership between Turkey, Azerbaijan and Israel commented: "For Azerbaijan, this concept was attractive because Turkey, the strategic ally of Azerbaijan, had a similar relationship with Israel. While in Azerbaijan there is great respect for Israel and Jews in general."[9] For Azerbaijan, foreign policy initiatives aimed at Israel and Turkey served to promote its image as a "Western" country as well as to manifest the explicit commitment to a pro-American orientation in its foreign policy. As a result, the Azerbaijani political elite realized that Turkey and Israel shared with their country, "if not enemies, then opponents, but also . . . mutual allies."[10]

This chapter will explore the importance of shared norms and values that contributed to the creation (or rather, the revival) of a strategic entente between Turkey and Israel after the dissolution of the Soviet Union, with later involvement of the Republic of Azerbaijan. Turkish academics Ali Carkoglu, Mine Eder and Kemal Kirisci introduced the concept of "like-minded" states when they described Turkey and Israel in their book in 1998.[11] A corollary premise of this chapter is that the Republic of Azerbaijan, a junior partner in this axis, also espoused the shared values of Westernism, secularism and nationalism. Heydar Aliyev, an ex-KGB general who ruled Azerbaijan between 1993 and 2003, admired Kemal Ataturk and adopted the authoritarian methods of Turkey's founder in his domestic politics.[12] Barry Buzan advanced the concept of "Westernistic" states to describe such states as Turkey, Israel and Azerbaijan. Buzan acknowledges that these states can "never be purely Western or European by definition," hence their political structure must deviate from the Western liberal model.[13]

According to Stephen Walt, shared "ideology" plays a role in alliance formation.[14] Although Walt's thesis asserts that states form alliances based on shared threat perceptions, my research demonstrates that this is an effect rather than a causal explanation. Threat perceptions are in large part determined by the identities or self-definitions of the states. They are based upon explicit or implicit understandings, norms and values. Specifically, General Çevik Bir, one of the chief architects of this axis on the Turkish side, indicated that Turkey and Israel share common threats, including religious fundamentalism, terrorism, illicit trafficking of arms and drugs, transfer of weapons of mass destruction, proliferation of nuclear weapons and mass movements of refugees.[15] Contrary to the neorealist "billiard balls" conceptualization of interactions between states, the foreign policy of a state represents a normative expression of identities within the international system. For example, Iran is perceived as a major threat by Israel not because it is a large and powerful state in the Middle East, but because of its radical Islamic regime, which has the avowed goal of exporting Islamic revolution and destroying the Jewish state.[16] In fact, General Çevik Bir stressed that it is the "commitment to democracy" that underlies the strategic understanding reached between Turkey and Israel in 1996. General Bir pointed to the Iranian support for PKK and Hizballah as "one fact among many that illustrates the need for greater cooperation between Turkey and the *region's other democracy*, Israel."[17]

With the beginning of the Cold War, the United States, under the Truman doctrine, promoted a pro-Western alliance or security system in the Middle East. The Eisenhower administration took concrete steps to realize its intention to build an alliance of the "Northern Tier" countries.[18] US Secretary of State John Foster Dulles wrote in his recommendations of June 1, 1953 that in the Northern Tier, "there is a vague desire to have a collective security system. But no such system can be imposed from without. It should *be designed and grow from within out of sense of common destiny and common danger*" [emphasis added].[19] In other words, in this region, only countries that embrace Western norms and values would also share the Euro–Atlantic preoccupations and threat perceptions. This dictum continues to animate the broader American strategy in the expanded Middle East in the post-Cold War period. Another implication of Dulles's recommendation is that the United States would not be willing to impose directly a system of alliances in the Middle East, but expected that such a system would emerge naturally based on perceptions of "common danger." Indeed, such a "security regime" was envisioned by American, Turkish and Israeli top security echelons to include Jordan and Azerbaijan (and Georgia) in 1996.[20] What is noteworthy about this post-Cold War axis in the Middle East is that the Turkish side initiated it.[21]

Examining the foundation of the strategic understanding between Turkey and Israel, Faruk Logoglu, then ambassador to Washington and a senior Turkish diplomat, said: "In other terms, Turkey and Israel espouse similar values and principles, and the relations between the two countries are based on mutual political and economic benefits. Both countries aim at enhancing democracy and improving welfare in the region, with a view to provide a stable, secure and peaceful environment."[22] An Azerbaijani diplomat explained that special relations between Azerbaijan and Israel are a reflection of the particular status of Azerbaijan, distinct from the majority of Muslim states, as a secular state albeit with a Muslim population.[23]

This chapter will focus on features of state identity common to Turkey, Israel and Azerbaijan. These essential features include (1) "garrison-states"— states that are marked by the high securitization of all important functions of their polities due to perceived or real external and internal threats. In particular, deep internal cleavages characterize these states based on ethno-national (the Palestinian Arabs, Kurds and the Nagorno-Karabagh Armenians) and religious (Jewish/Muslim, Sunni/Shia, Christian/Muslim, secularist/radical Islamist) sections of the population and contending claims to sovereignty (autonomy) and territory; (2) "like-minded" or "Westernistic" states—strongly pro-Western, secular and constitutionally nationalist states with a non-Western history, religion and culture; and (3) the "lonely" states—states rejected by their neighbors due to religious, ideological or ethnic differences.

The garrison-states

For Western European countries, the collapse of the Soviet Union and the reunification of Germany (1990) marked the end of the Cold War. The Soviet bloc as the key security threat disappeared.[24] The three countries under investigation, however, experienced a new constellation of security threats. Turkey, Israel and Azerbaijan exist in a highly charged regional environment. The Middle East and the Caspian regions both suffer from endemic political instability and transborder conflicts.[25] Since their founding as modern states, Turkey and, to even a greater extent, Israel have had to contend with the open animosity of Arab neighbors and with the power play of the great powers in the Middle East.[26] While Israel was involved in five major military confrontations with Arab states, Turkey had to contend with diplomatic estrangement rooted in its antipathy toward pan-Arabist regimes and irredentist claims by Syria over the province of Hatay (Iskanderun) and the issues related to distribution of the water resources of the Tigris and Euphrates rivers.[27] Anti-Arab inclinations certainly color the atmospherics of the Turkish–Israeli alignment.[28] In fact, the Ottomans, like the Persians, perceived Arabs as inferior in their intellectual achievement, military organization and state-building efforts.[29] This historical attitude was described as "immunity to Arabism."[30]

Turkey's regional rivals, Iran and Syria, supported anti-Turkish terrorist organizations such as the Kurdish PKK and the Armenian Secret Army of Liberation of Armenia (ASALA). Both countries armed, trained and provided basing facilities to PKK guerrillas who have conducted raids into Turkish territory since the early 1980s.[31] With the end of the Cold War, Turkey was exposed to the "fragmentation" of the geopolitical environment given the emergence of new independent states in the Caucasus and the Balkans and the ethno-national conflicts that ensued.[32] A Kurdish insurgency led by the PKK flared up in the same period and presented a serious challenge to Turkey's stability, until suppressed by Turkish Armed Forces in 1995. Israel had to contend with two Intifadas ("Shaking Off" in Arabic) in 1987 and 2000, due to the elevated nationalist expectations of Palestinians, particularly following the failed Peace Process of 1993. Meanwhile, Azerbaijan, which declared independence only at the end of 1991, was embroiled in a conflict with Armenia over Nagorno-Karabagh starting in 1987. Armenian forces occupied the Nagorno-Karabagh region and seven Azerbaijani regions that constitute 20 percent of Azerbaijani territory, causing a million ethnic Azeris to flee their homes. The psychological and humanitarian wounds inflicted by the war in Nagorno-Karabagh (and the internationally unrecognized secession of this predominantly Armenian region) form the core of the collective identity of the Azerbaijani state today. Since gaining independence, Azerbaijan has faced threatening diplomatic démarches and irredentist claims by the Islamic Republic of Iran.[33]

These three cases deviate from the original concept of the garrison-state introduced by Harold Lasswell. In the classical "garrison state," a non-democratic militaristic state is ruled by "experts of violence," and the state functions solely to contend with security challenges.[34] However, these states can be designated "garrison-states" because of the primacy of security in their international personalities. The omnipresence of the military–security apparatus and its percolation through the fabric of society are the historic features of this region. A historian draws our attention to the two historical factors that have left an indelible mark on the state tradition in what has become identified as the "Northern Tier" region.[35] The military and security forces lay claim like ancient monarchs to "their usefulness to the state" and proclaimed "benevolence, paternalism, justice and concern for the welfare of the people" as their tenets.[36] The proclivity for the military–security complex to intervene in the civilian sphere is also embedded in the ancient state tradition of the region, where the rule of even quasi-divine autocrats perceived not to be serving the common good was interrupted by assassination or palace revolutions.[37] As a natural outcome, the securitization of all important functions of the state, including foreign policy, is the distinct characteristic of the three countries considered.[38] In our case, the elevated status of the military is embedded in the broader state ideology, at least in Turkey and Israel. Historically, the military and security apparatus (MSA) has occupied a prominent place in the institutional make-up of these three states. MSA operates through formal and informal networks to shape policy outcomes under formally democratic regimes in these countries.[39] The senior ranks of the military traditionally were over-represented in the ruling elites in Turkey and in Israel. The security apparatus of the former Soviet Union was conspicuously represented in the top leadership of the independent Azerbaijan by the late President Heydar Aliyev (1993–2003), a former KGB general.

Turkey as a garrison-state

Scholars argue that the elevated status of the military in Turkish society is rooted in the history and culture of this land.[40] Jenkins contends that "not only is Turkish society still dominated by the values, attitudes and traditions which underpin the role of the military but, to the vast majority of Turks, the military and military values still lie at the heart of any definition of what it means to be Turkish."[41] In the foundational myth of the Turkish Republic, the army occupies a privileged position. It is widely recognized that the Turkish army played a critical role in gaining independence and creating the Turkish state.[42] After the foundation of the Republic, former officers occupied many key positions in government. During the critical period between 1921 and 1922, newly appointed Chief of General Staff Fevzi Cakmak served as prime minister. Later, Ataturk appointed a chief of general staff in the cabinet on par with the minister of defense. The Turkish leader saw a broader role for the army in his nation-building vision. It was to be a fountainhead of progressive practices: in short, an organ for the spread of reforms Ataturk considered vital. In the first decades of the Kemalist revolution, many former generals and other military officers joined the political establishment or pursued parliamentary careers.[43]

The Turkish army built the Republic and subsequently contributed to its modernization and Westernization. Following Kemal's death in 1938, Turkish politicians attempted to build a democracy based on multi-party elections. Yet Turkish democracy has been repeatedly fractured by periods of instability and military rule. While military rule is traditionally associated with ruthless and arbitrary terror, the Turkish military stands out as an exception in one important respect. It has a pronounced secular orientation and emphasizes the need to separate the state from religion.[44] When a political vacuum appeared in Turkish society due to political deadlock as in 1960, 1971 and 1997, or the endemic violence of militants of the 1970s, the military took steps to restore order based on Kemalist ideological foundations.[45] In the 1982 Constitution, the Turkish military institutionalized its privileged position in the power structure by introducing Article 118. Under this article, the National Security Council (NSC), an advisory body established in 1933, was vested with the power to make political decisions regarding matters of high politics. Article 118 stipulates that the government must give "priority consideration" to NSC decisions.[46] Through this constitutional arrangement, the Turkish Armed Forces (TAF) were able to retain control over final decisions on a variety of political matters, including the passage of legislation in parliament.[47]

The Turkish general staff reserves the highest prerogative in the Turkish Republic, i.e. to serve as the guardian of Kemalist ideology. The internal legal code of the Turkish Armed Forces explicitly stipulates this responsibility of the army. Article 35 of the Turkish Armed Forces Internal Service Law of January 1961 states: "The duty of the Turkish Armed Forces is to protect and preserve the Turkish homeland and the Turkish Republic as defined in the constitution."[48] This mission turned the army into the political symbol of nationhood and the instrument of preserving the nation. Kemalism's two fundamental principles are territorial integrity and secularism. The main function of Turkish foreign policy, according to Kemalist principles, was to enhance the internal cohesion of the nation.[49] Kemalist preoccupation with maintaining national unity in the face of divisive forces such as radical Islam, sectarianism, and separatist Kurdish nationalism eventually led to an expansion of the role of the military into political and social spheres.

In fact, the military in Turkey stepped in to protect a fragile secular democracy from the authoritarian policies and Islamist tendencies of the Demokrat Party in 1960 and radical militancy in 1980.[50] The late President Turgut Ozal's (prime minister 1983–9, president 1989–93) outstanding political skills and active personal involvement in shaping Turkish foreign policy allowed him to impose civilian control over this sphere.[51] After his death in April of 1993, Turkish politics again entered a phase of domestic turbulence, while the Turkish foreign ministry lost interest in pursuit of a dynamic policy vis-à-vis the Turkic republics, in particular Azerbaijan. The TAF took a leading role in shaping the strategic direction of Turkish foreign policy from 1994 until the November 2002 general election of Adalet ve Kalkinma (AK) Party (Justice and Development party).[52] This was done in the name of Kemalist principles, counteracting a perceived deviation from the Western orientation by the Islamist-led coalition government.[53] The military embraced one of the main vectors of Turgut Ozal's foreign policy, namely the pursuit of energetic engagement with the broader Turkic world, i.e. former Soviet Turkic-speaking countries. A prominent role in this policy was fulfilled by the relationship with Azerbaijan.[54] Çevik Bir, Turkey's deputy chief of general staff, articulated this new foreign policy vision: "Turkey is one of the rare countries the importance of which increased after the Cold War" because, as he put it, Turkey is "both European and Asian." He indicated that Turkey was perfectly placed to undertake a "leadership mission" in Central Asia owing to its historical and cultural links to the region."[55]

When the Islamist Refah (Welfare) Party led by Necmettin Erbakan came to power in 1996, the new prime minister shifted the focus of Turkish foreign policy from allegiance to the Western alliance to pursuit of improved relations with the Muslim world. By pursuing "Islamic-centered" diplomacy, Prime Minister Erbakan immediately alienated the military.[56] In the foreign policy sphere, the Turkish military convinced Prime Minister Erbakan not to block three comprehensive military agreements, which, however, excluded a formal defense alliance with Israel. This led to the concluding of a military–strategic agreement with Israel in 1996.[57] In the domestic political arena, the military (through the mechanism of the National Security Council recommendations) warned the prime minister against the "re-Islamification" of the country. A Turkish media campaign, orchestrated by the military, also served to remind Erbakan that he was testing the patience of the Kemalists. This political campaign by the military led to dissolution of the Erbakan government in June 1997. As the only public institution to have maintained its status above party politics, populism and especially endemic civilian corruption, the army continues to serve as the final arbiter on contentious issues of security, politics and education.[58]

The cult of the military in Turkey is preserved to this day. A contemporary account of youth in Turkey illustrates how, for many young men from poor shantytowns and villages across the country, the army is a "vessel of hope." Navaro-Yashin observes that "becoming a soldier gives them the sort of communal respect, show of affection, and a high regard of the kind they in no way otherwise could hope to obtain." And she concludes about army service in Turkey: "It has been a rite of secular statist initiation to masculine adulthood."[59] She explains that army service in Turkey, beyond its direct function as a military organization, also serves as the main mechanism for socialization into the values of the Kemalist state. She illustrates this in her description of a farewell party for young enlisted Turkish men in contemporary Turkey: "The language, symbols, and feelings—the whole experience of the soldier's farewell—has been transformed, at least to a certain degree, into a show of veneration for the state. The state is exalted, celebrated, and reified in the soldier's farewells."[60] The Turkish public appreciates this commonality of national culture with Israel.[61]

Israel as a garrison-state

> Even when the wolf lies down with the lamb, it's still better for us to be the wolf.
>
> (Popular Israeli Army saying)

If in Turkey, the concept *devlet* connotes "the strong and sacred state, whose rights transcend those of individuals,"[62] Israeli society also reifies the state and state security.[63] Israeli society also shares with Turkey a heightened sense of threat that emanates from the state's neighbors.[64] Israel is a militaristic society par excellence; universal military service is considered a basic part of young adulthood, something that defines Israeliness. Describing Israeli society, Yigal Yadin (the second army chief of staff) said on numerous occasions, "the civilian is a soldier on eleven months' annual leave."[65]

The process of creation of the Israeli state carries noteworthy historical parallels to the creation of the Ottoman Empire and later of the Turkish Republic. Hagana ("Defense" in Hebrew), an underground Zionist military organization, was founded during the period of the British Mandate in 1929.[66] The organization evolved into the core of the Jewish military force that fought in the 1948 War of Independence.[67] The war on Israel was unleashed even before the proclamation of its independence on May 14–15, 1948.[68] The conjuncture of events of the creation of the Jewish state as a result of the War of Independence conducted by Labor Zionist Hagana in alliance with right-wing military groups (Etzel and Lehi)[69] is perfectly captured in the following description of an army's role in the foundation of the Ottoman Empire: "The Ottoman Empire too was 'an army before it was anything else,' created through conquest and, particularly initially, administered along military lines."[70] Israel has fought five regional interstate wars since its establishment (1948, 1956, 1967, 1973 and 1982) in addition to waging a constant struggle with Arab insurgents in the occupied territories and Israel proper, the result being a state of war as the status quo, and universal military service as a sine qua non of citizenship. The educational system, public commemorations of military victories and acceptance of the "security imperative" even by the left-wing sections of society—all these factors generate the militaristic, or "Spartan," culture of Israeli society.[71] According to Feige, national holidays and military service itself insert the militaristic ethos into society and construct a subject to whom war is a "normal" experience.[72]

The complex of insecurity, which grew out of the recent experience of the Holocaust and the history of persecution and status deprivation, fostered the Israeli fixation on issues of defense and preservation of territory. Beyond a purely military role, the Israeli Defense Forces serve a symbolic role as a representation of the new Israeli society, where Jewish religious symbols and Biblical prophecy are fused into a new national culture. This culture is based on the primacy of force and an ability to defend the Jewish community. The army serves also other essential social functions in Israeli society. Since its foundation, Ben-Gurion envisioned that the army would serve to socialize and educate the young generation.[73] In particular, in a society made up of immigrants, the Israeli army serves as a means of social integration and acculturation into Israeli values, mores and attitudes. The Israeli Defense Force also places an emphasis on high educational standards and Hebrew acquisition. As in the case of Turkey, the values of secularism and republicanism inherited from the French Revolution also conferred upon the Israeli military a nationalist and "messianic" mission.[74] An Israeli sociologist concludes: "All these conflicting primordial and civic values have been absorbed into the Jewish Israeli collective identity and condensed around the cultural code of a civilian militarism."[75]

Due to the existential threat perceived to be posed by its neighbors, a military ethos penetrates all layers of society in Israel.[76] In the Israeli case, the military also serves as one of the central symbols of the new nation. Since the Hagana (later reorganized into Tzava Hagana LeIsrael or TZAHAL, the Israeli Defense Forces) played a critical role in the foundation of the Jewish nation-state, its myth is intimately intertwined in the national consciousness with the creation of the State of Israel. As Itzhak Laor points out: ". . . army is the one player in Israeli society whose motives are never questioned. Israeli militarism is about Israel's faith in this huge benevolent apparatus."[77]

Membership in the political and military elites in Israel closely overlaps. This phenomenon serves the expansion of the role of the military into the Israeli political domain. This process is known in Israel as *tzniha* or "parachuting"—when retired senior officers easily transfer from the military elite into the political elite. Such leading personalities of Israeli politics as David Ben-Gurion (an unofficial head of Hagana) and Shimon Peres (a former head of the Ministry of Military Procurement) led the Israeli defense establishment as civilians, but many Israeli generals see their political career as a continuation of their military career by other means.[78] Yitzhak Rabin (a former chief of staff and defense minister), Benjamin Netanyahu (a former senior officer of Special Forces unit), Ehud Barak (a former chief of staff), and Ariel Sharon (a highly accomplished general and former defense minister) were directly involved with the military–security apparatus in their careers. In Israeli society, according to Ben-Eliezer, this process allows legitimization of the government actions by having cabinet ministers with a military "background" involved in decision-making. "Parachuting" also has a moderating effect on relations between the government and the army. Some authors point to this unique pattern of military–civilian relations that deviates from the classical separation of civilian and military personnel in top state bureaucracies of Western democracies.[79] However, penetration of the "civilian" values and modes of operation into the institutional realm of the military resulted in a military "civilianization" that alleviates to some degree the tendency to become a garrison- or praetorian-state.[80]

Azerbaijan as a garrison-state

Hostilities with the Soviet-supported Armenian militants over the Nagorno-Karabagh enclave (1988–93) and its continued occupation by Armenia have been the major factors in Azerbaijan's domestic and foreign policy arena between 1992 and 2005. The intimidating posture and irredentist statements of Iranian clerics and politicians further aggravated the threat perceptions of Azerbaijani policymakers.[81] Azerbaijan was also concerned about the designs of Russian politicians intent on subjugating Azerbaijan as a satellite state in the Caucasus.[82]

During the short-lived Azerbaijani Democratic Republic (1918–20), Turkish divisions led by Nuri Pasha formed the nucleus of Azerbaijani armed forces. In the modern era, Azerbaijan endeavors to create the most powerful army in the South Caucasus region, and the Turkish military is again at the forefront of building up, equipping and training a nascent Azerbaijani army and Special Forces. The Azerbaijani army has adopted the essentials of Turkish military ideology, and its doctrine conforms in many respects to Kemalist principles.[83] During his tenure as president, Heydar Aliyev acknowledged the critical assistance Turkey provided in the Nagorno-Karabagh hostilities: "Approximately from the end of 1987, hostile forces, which are trying to dismember and destroy Azerbaijan, artificially created the 'Karabagh problem.' From that period on the Armenian aggression against Azerbaijan continues. And throughout this period Turkey always has been assisting us. We always feel its moral support, its aid in state building, in the international arena and other spheres."[84]

Turkey has consistently supported the formation and Kemalist ideological indoctrination of the Azerbaijani officers' corps.[85] The Turkish military assisted in organizing and staffing the only military academy in Azerbaijan. As a result, a new generation of officers has been raised in Azerbaijan on the ideals of the Turkish Republic. The college-educated Azerbaijani youth share pan-Turkist aspirations and manifest militant tendencies, especially toward a solution of the Nagorno-Karabagh conflict.[86] The main opposition parties, i.e. the Azerbaijani Popular Front, Musavat, AMIP (The Party of Azerbaijani National Independence) and Social Democratic Party of Azerbaijan, all strongly advocate a military solution to the conflict. But due to the economic deprivation of a significant part of the population and the politically repressive regime in Azerbaijan, 3.2 million people, many of military conscription age, have permanently or temporarily left Azerbaijan.[87] This factor undermines the military potential of Azerbaijan.

While Azerbaijan is in the process of building armed forces, its military doctrine is still ill defined. In 1994 Heydar Aliyev acknowledged that the Azerbaijani army was in the process of formation and Azerbaijan lagged behind Armenia in its defense capability.[88] Even after ten years of self-rule, the official national military doctrine was not promulgated.[89] In fact, the interests of the clan-based elites in Azerbaijan create a particular pattern of relations between the state and security apparatus wherein threats to regime survival are perceived as threats to national security.[90] This creates a situation of chronic insecurity in a country ruled by an autocratic regime of the Aliyevs. This pattern is paramount in the identity of the new Azerbaijani republic.

After the return to power, in June of 1993, of the penultimate Azerbaijan President Heydar Aliyev, a former KGB General, the security forces infiltrated all institutions of power, political parties and community organizations. In this clan-based society, it is the Aliyev clan that holds all reigns of power in the state.[91] Concerned about challenges to the authority of his Nakhichevan clan, Heydar Aliyev pursued a policy of marginalizing political opposition organizations. A Council of Europe report describes abuses of power in Azerbaijan such as "authoritarian practices like intimidation of voters, pressures on elections commissioners or clear bias of the media in favor of the ruling party's [formerly led by Heydar Aliyev, currently led by his son Ilham] candidate."[92] The twelve years following the 1993 bloodless coup, in which Abulfaz Elchibey was deposed, were characterized by arrests and "politically motivated" employee dismissals. The Azerbaijani security apparatus used torture and threats to intimidate political parties and human rights activists. This policy was reinforced by "spontaneous" campaigns of violence and murder against members of the opposition and the independent media.

There exist several challenges to the cohesion and unity of the Azerbaijani state. These challenges are primarily of an ethno-religious character. The predominant cause of insecurity in Azerbaijan remains the unresolved Nagorno-Karabagh conflict that has resulted in 20 percent of Azerbaijani territory still occupied by Armenian forces. Azerbaijani security structures also perceive a threat emanating from Iran's support for underground Islamist networks in Nardaran, Lenkoran and Baku. The security situation is further complicated by ethnic strife in the Lezgin-dominated northern[93] and Talysh-dominated southern regions. The failed Talysh-Mugansk secession attempt of 1993 was also linked to Russian security forces and possibly to Iran, since Talysh are a Farsi-speaking minority. The Russian link is more likely, given demands by Talysh rebel leader Ali Akram Gumbatov to restore Russian-backed Ayaz Mutalibov to power in Azerbaijan.[94] In response, the Azerbaijani state securitized all institutions of society as well as its domestic and foreign policy. There are persistent rumors that the security apparatus employs alienated Kurds, refugees who fled the Nagorno-Karabagh war zone, as agents of influence, informers and agent-provocateurs.[95] The Azerbaijani Republic began to conform to the most outdated Orientalist stereotypes of state in Islam becoming, in the words of Navaro-Yashin, "a bit of caricature of that predominant approach to Muslim societies, where an absolutist, all-seeing, and all-controlling state was constructed as definitive of Islam."[96]

The main institution of national security in Azerbaijan is the Ministry of National Security (MNB), a successor to the Azerbaijani KGB. It was founded during the rule of the Azerbaijani Popular Front in 1992. After the return of Heydar Aliyev, MNB experienced a revival of stature and effectiveness. The peak of MNB activity was reached between 1993–6. Heydar Aliyev expanded MNB staff and provided the organization with badly needed funding. Namik Abbasov, Aliyev's KGB colleague, headed the MNB from October of 1994 to August 2004. The Azerbaijani opposition accused Abbasov of introducing corrupt practices into the security apparatus. According to these sources, Abbasov sold senior posts in the ministry for financial gain.[97]

The Turkish Intelligence Service (MIT) has assisted in modernizing and developing the Azerbaijani security apparatus since the first years of independence. The main channel for cooperation between the security organizations of Turkey and Azerbaijan is membership in Azerbaijani branches of *Boz Kurtlar* ("The Grey Wolves"), an ultra-nationalist Turkist organization.[98] Israel has also been involved in cooperation with Azerbaijan in the area of security after the establishment of diplomatic relations in 1992. Israeli security forces have trained and equipped the Azerbaijani elite Special Forces and Azerbaijani intelligence.[99] Israeli security systems firms provide services and technological expertise in Bina airport and at the border terminals.[100]

According to an anonymous Russian source, during the same period MNB uncovered a network of militant Islamist organizations funded primarily by Iran. Since 1989, the Iranian regime planted agents of influence and began creating Islamist networks, print organs and mosques. In 1993, pro-Iranian political forces founded a political party, the Islamic Party of Azerbaijan (AIP).[101] By 1995, AIP became a formidable force that could have influenced the outcome of presidential elections. In that year, 100 AIP activists led by Ikram Aliyev were arrested and pleaded guilty to cooperation with Iranian security forces.[102] A plot to overthrow Heydar Aliyev's government, organized by former President Ayaz Mutalibov and Suret Guseynov, was uncovered in March 1995. Shortly after this, President Aliyev brutally suppressed opposition to his brokered ceasefire in the Nagorno-Karabagh conflict.[103] A number of generals who opposed the cessation of hostilities with the Armenians were arrested and put in jail.[104] As a whole, political instability and repression by security forces, accentuated by Islamist militancy in segments of the population, generate an atmosphere of a "police" state, while the military play a "subaltern" role in Azerbaijani society.[105]

In August 2000, Heydar Aliyev instituted a set of reforms in order to stem corruption in the national security apparatus. During that period, President Heydar Aliyev appointed people from his inner circle into the top echelons of MNB to reassert his hold on the security apparatus. In October 2003, Heydar Aliyev's son Ilham became the new Azerbaijani president as the result of fraudulent presidential elections. After his consolidation of power, Ilham Aliyev relieved Namik Abbasov from his post as MNB head in August of 2004.

Like-minded or "Westernistic" states

Turkey, Israel and Azerbaijan are Western-oriented states or "Westernistic states." What characterizes these countries is the particular make-up of their political system, i.e. the secular nature of the state counter-poised by the religious and ethno-nationalist ideology of the masses (Sunni Islam in Turkey, Shia Islam in Azerbaijan, Judaism in Israel).[106] In particular, Turkey and Israel share a special niche in world affairs.[107] Former Israeli Foreign Minister Shlomo Ben-Ami states that "Both Turkey and Israel see themselves as 'different,' because they are the only secular democratic states in the region."[108] Azerbaijan is located in the Caucasus, an area that serves as a natural border between Europe and Asia. As a result of this geographic location, Azerbaijan is included both in the "European neighborhood" project of the European Union and the greater Middle East project promoted by the United States. An Azerbaijani diplomat highlighted three causes of the strategic partnership between Azerbaijan and Israel: (a) Azerbaijan belongs in a "broader sense" to the Middle East, but is at the same time a European country; (b) Azerbaijan is a secular Muslim state; and (c) Azerbaijan is located in a "sizzling hot" region that, "if not of strategic importance for Israel, is still constantly under the special purview of Israeli leadership."[109] This borderline or "bridge" identity of the three countries produces the natural commonality of geopolitical interests. Despite this Western commitment, the three countries were considered marginal in the contemporary concept of "Europe." Turkey, Israel and Azerbaijan have expended great efforts to be included in the powerful European regional organizations. These efforts, in particular the Turkish drive for admission to the European Union, so far have been only partially successful.[110] European Union membership is capable of bringing not only democratic liberal order to Turkey, but also the safety net of the European welfare state. Without the Cold War to bind them together, Euro–Turkish relations fluctuate between confrontation and cooperation. In the Middle East, Turkey and Israel are also perceived as members of the Western Euro–Atlantic community.[111] Stephen Kinzer notes about the two countries: "[Turkey] is also a European nation, and its central ambition, reiterated endlessly for more than a century, is to move ever closer to the West. In this respect it is like Israel, a country geographically in the Middle East but with democratic aspirations that are profoundly European."[112] Even before the emergence of the Turkish–Israeli strategic relationship in 1996, many Iranian Islamic ideologues and journalists denounced Turkey as a "Westoxicated" country.[113] In comparison with neighboring Muslim countries, Turkey is

perceived by the Iranian leadership as an important threat due to its membership in the Western military alliance, NATO. As a Western "proxy," Iranian
strategists believe that Turkey is a hostile neighbor "with great potential to
intervene in Iran on behalf of the United States."[114]

Turkey as a like-minded state

By the time of the Tanzimat of 1839, Ottoman Turkey had firmly established
itself as a member of the European system of balance of power and there was
no trace of Turkey's principle of "unitary action" in the international arena.
Ottoman Turkey maintained a strategic doctrine that allowed the flexibility to
choose which military–political bloc to join. This doctrine took its final shape
during the Young Turk revolution.[115] Some Turkish historians emphasize that
the conquest of Byzantium and adoption of its institutions and mores forever
changed the political outlook of Turks and set the course for their Western
orientation.[116] The Western orientation of Turkey became an integral part of
the Kemalist revolution.[117] Following World War I, the pursuit of an alliance
with the West reflected Ataturk's desire to transform Turkish society into a
modern, progressive and civilized nation.[118] However, the Western orientation
of Turkey has been molded not only by Kemalist ideology, but also by the ethnic
origins of significant portions of the Turkish population. The portion of
Turkey's population known as Beyaz Turkler ("White Turks") has Albanian,
Armenian, Bosnian, Bulgarian, Hungarian, Macedonian and Greek or Slavic
ancestry. Family history connects many Turkish citizens with southern and
eastern regions of Europe.[119] At the same time, penetration of Western values
into broader Turkish society has been a slow, painful process. A Turkish
diplomat writes that "the Turks adopted Western concepts—the most contemporary, advanced and modern ideas of the age. Yet Turks never forgot that they
had come from Asia. They adhered to an Asian set of values and age-old Asian
traditions."[120] Until the the late 1980s, a majority of the Muslim population of
Turkey, especially in rural areas, had hardly embraced Western values and
norms disseminated by the state elites.[121] Many scholars point to the Turkish
identity as a bridge between civilizations.[122] Yuksel Soylemez provides an
enlightening description of the complexity of Turkey's identity:

> Turkey is both a Mediterranean and a Middle Eastern country—
> historically, geographically, strategically, economically and, last but not
> the least, culturally. Turkey has a European identity also, again historic-
> ally, geographically, economically, politically and strategically. It is a
> well-known fact that Turkey has been a historic bridge across the
> continents. Consequently it has a historic claim to a multiple, schizoid
> and most unique and colorful identity.[123]

The ideology and policies of Mustafa Kemal's Republican regime only
reinforced the notion that Turkey belonged to the European "region." If many

national liberation ideologies were forged in opposition to Westernization, Turkish nationalists proclaimed Westernization as one of the goals of Ataturk's revolution.[124] The process of modernization and nation building was carried out through the formation of the new Turkish identity. Westernization, in the Turkish context, combines such norms as modernism, emphasis on positivism, "this-worldly" knowledge and pragmatism.

Another aspect of the "Western" orientation was the security imperative. From the foundation of the Republic, Turkey's Western orientation reflected a geopolitical imperative of being embedded in the Euro–Atlantic security system aligned against Communist Russia. With the emergence of the Soviet threat to Western Europe in the aftermath of World War II, the geopolitical weight of Turkey's position as a "flank state" increased substantially. The Republic's geographic position played an increasingly crucial role in relations with Western European institutions and the incorporation of Turkey into the Atlantic security system. During his years of leadership, Ataturk stipulated the European vocation of Turkey. The long struggle for entry into the European Union is essentially the realization of Kemalist aspirations for Turkey to become a full-fledged European nation and for "participation in the one universal civilization."[125] Since the 1980s, the desire to join the Common Market (the European Union of today) has evolved into the Kizil Elma ("the Red Apple," or the mythical Ottoman "Great Dream") of the modern Turkish Republic.[126] A majority of the population strongly embraces the notion of Turkish membership in the EU today, even though the political elite's aspiration to join the Common Market, a predecessor of the EU, dates back to the 1960s. In 1963, Turkey and the European Community entered into an Association Agreement hinting at possible future membership. In 1995, Turkey entered into a customs union with the EU, thus strengthening the economic cooperation between the two entities. In 1999, the Helsinki European Council granted Turkey the status of a candidate for accession. The June 2004 European Council in Brussels reaffirmed the prospects for future Turkish EU membership, provided that the country meets all EU accession criteria.

After the Cold War, however, when Western (more specifically European) security burdens were alleviated by the collapse of Soviet military power, Turkey had to reinvent itself and find a new role in the Western security architecture.[127] In pursuit of this new role, Turkey sought rapid improvement of relations with Israel, the main US ally in the region.[128] Bulent Aras argues: "Turkish foreign policy makers' cooperation with Israel served to maintain an image of 'political correctness' and 'cultural correctness'—in Western terms—during and after the Cold War era. In a sense, improving relations with Israel has been a holdover from the radically pro-American attitudes of the Cold War era and of a deepening identity crisis thereafter; these relations served, in the eyes of official Turkey, as reinforcements for Turkey's modern Western identity."[129] The breakup of the Soviet Union at the end of 1991 created new foreign policy possibilities for Turkey in the Caucasus and Central Asia. These two regions were tied to Turkey by history, ethnicity and religion. Turkey's political elites desired to maintain the Western orientation of Turkey, while simultaneously pursuing an active policy toward the Turkic states of the Soviet Union. At the same time, Turkish policymakers realized that Turkey had an opportunity to become the central power in the "Turkic" region. As a promoter of Western orientation among Muslim former Soviet republics, Turkey solicited the United States to provide "a new Marshall Plan," but the United States was not interested in this project.[130] As an alternative, Turkey pursued a US-inspired policy of encouraging the "Turkish model" as the most fitting for the post-Soviet Turkic states.[131] The following raison d'etre for this model of development is offered by a Turkish diplomat: "All this recent history should help to demonstrate that Turkey is a model for those trying to transform from archaic to modern, from reactionary to contemporary. We succeeded, to a great extent, in this irreversible process through a quiet transformation from traditionalism to democratization and from a closed economy to a free-market."[132]

Azerbaijan showed the most enthusiasm among the Turkic republics for forging closer ties with Turkey. As a result of the particularly interlinked ideological and strategic interests of Turkey and Azerbaijan, led by the young nationalist leader Elchibey, Azerbaijan became the fulcrum of this new trend. Turkey aspired to function as the bridge toward natural-resource-rich new members of the community of nations. Turkey naturally was perceived as expansionist (by Russia and Greece) in its policy toward the Black Sea region and the Caspian basin at this stage (1991–4). Turkey advanced its foreign policy of leading integration processes within the Black Sea region, straddling Europe. This Turkish initiative to create the Black Sea Economic Cooperation Region (BSECR) was led by Ambassador Sukru Elekdag. In June 1992, Turkey, Romania, Bulgaria, Greece, Albania, as well as Azerbaijan, Armenia, Georgia, Moldova, the Russian Federation and Ukraine signed the BSECR agreement.[133]

Israel as a like-minded state

David Ben-Gurion, founder of the Jewish State, came to Palestine during the organized immigration known as *Aliyah Bet* (the Second Emigration) (1904–14). This immigration wave's place in Zionist historiography resembles that of the Mayflower generation in American history.[134] Among the Aliyah Bet leadership, Eliezer Ben-Yehuda, pioneer of the Hebrew language revival, Izhak Ben-Zvi, the second president of Israel, and Moshe Sharett, the second prime minister and later foreign minister of Israel, were firm believers in the idea that Zionists should ally themselves with the Young Turks' revolution and the Ottoman cause.[135] This group constituted the first generation of top Israeli leadership and future signatories of Israel's Proclamation of Independence. As a formative element of the Israeli establishment, they affected the general outlook of generations of Israeli policymakers with regards to Turkey.

With the end of the Cold War, Turkish policymakers chose the geo-strategic option of reinvigorating relations with the "unseen or invisible member of the Western alliance," Israel.[136] By doing so, Turkey desired to confirm its Western credentials. Especially important, for Turkey, was to show the United States that it would adhere to a pro-American line in one of the most important regions of American strategic concern: the Middle East. In the long history of the Cold War, Turkey's recognition of the State of Israel on March 28, 1949 played essentially the same role. Two historians of the Cold War period affirm that "in the wake of the Cold War, Turkey by this act desired to express its pro-Western orientation. Turkey wanted to be perceived as a secular and enlightened state by the Western alliance led by the United States."[137] At the dawn of the Cold War, the State of Israel declared its standing in the international community by its policy of "non-identification," somewhat similar to the non-alignment movement. By the end of 1949, however, Israel realized that its security and economic future lay with the Western alliance. Prime Minister David Ben-Gurion, as an ardent anti-Communist, promulgated the policy of "utilitarian non-alignment, not ideological neutrality."[138] Prime Minister David Ben-Gurion soon clarified this policy to Israel's main Western ally, the United States. Ben-Gurion wanted to assure the United States of the Israeli commitment to the Western camp. Already in July of 1950, the leader of the Jewish state summoned the American ambassador and conveyed the Israeli intention "to build with American arms [an] effective Israeli army of 250,000 men, able and anxious [to] aid [the] United States, [the] United Kingdom and *Turkey* [emphasis added] to resist Russian aggression."[139] But the breakthrough in its relations with the United States was made when Israel supported the American-sponsored resolution to intervene in the crisis in Korea at the United Nations in the same year.[140] The first Israeli ambassador to the United Nations, and later foreign minister, Abba Eban left an indelible imprint on the shape of Israeli foreign policy. While serving as ambassador to Washington in 1950, he realized that "the network of our relations with the United States constitutes the most important of all Israel's external relations." According to Uri Bialer, "[h] is assessment remained the cornerstone of Israeli foreign policy even after the end of the Cold War."[141]

Historically, Jewish nationalism, or modern political Zionism, was born out of a distinctly European and secular tradition. According to Shlomo Avineri, Zionism was the most fundamental revolution in Jewish life. It substituted a secular self-identity of the "Jews as a nation" for the traditional and Orthodox self-identity in religious terms. It changed a passive, quietistic, and pious hope of the Return to Zion into an effective social force, moving millions of people to Israel.[142] Western ideas of liberalism, nationalism and socialism were foundational sources of ideology for the founders of the State of Israel. After a period of *etatism* (1950s–1960s) and collectivism, Israeli political culture shifted and the society embraced norms and values of individualism, entrepreneurship and self-reliance in the 1970s. However, many scholars express scepticism about the Western nature of Israeli society. Michael Barnett concludes: "The challenge of classifying and categorizing the Israeli experience leads many to question the suitability of the Israeli case. Neither East nor West, developed nor underdeveloped, capitalist nor socialist. Israel is and is not a Western state; while it exhibits a democratic form of governance, rarely is it situated alongside the historical experiences of other Western states."[143] But the majority of Israeli intellectual and political elites would concur with Yosi Beilin, a former senior Israeli diplomat, who declares that Israel is unquestionably part of the West.[144] Since the 1980s Israeli values and norms have quickly undergone a process of Americanization. An average Israeli experiences the powerful pressure of American culture conveyed not only through cultural products such as movies, advertising and an American-style media, but also through American Jewish tourism, which is a significant stimulus of the support for Israel and of income to the Israeli economy, while also serving as a conduit of American values.

Israel's military and security cooperation with Turkey also should be seen as an extension of its Western vocation. Western European states and the United States funded Turkish activities in the Caucasus and Central Asia directed at stemming Iranian penetration.[145] Their commonality of interests stems from the shared threat perception of "radical Islam." Furthermore, an Israeli security expert stressed that the geographic focus of Israeli–Turkish cooperation "against Iranian subversion" is in countries to the north of Iran, which certainly includes Azerbaijan.[146]

Azerbaijan as a like-minded state

Contemporary Turkey served as the outlet to the West for Azerbaijan in the first years of its independence. As soon as Azerbaijan declared its independence in December of 1991, it adopted the main formal attributes of democracy. Upon joining the OSCE, and again when it applied for membership in the Council of Europe, the Republic of Azerbaijan made international commitments to uphold democratic principles and human rights. But the spread of liberal and democratic ideas among Azerbaijani intelligentsia has historical roots in the period of national renaissance of the late nineteenth century. In fact, many "Western" ideas were transmitted to Azerbaijani discourse by Russian-educated jadidists.[147] Following his election as president in Azerbaijan's first free election, Abulfaz Elchibey, leader of the Azerbaijani National Front, immediately declared a foreign policy course of integration into the Euro–Atlantic structure. During his short rule (1992–3), Abulfaz Elchibey considered Turkey and Israel appropriate models for the development of an independent Azerbaijan.[148] Elchibey called for a decisive departure from the Russian sphere of influence and a rapid upgrade of Azerbaijani–Turkish and Azerbaijani–American relations.[149] During this period, Azerbaijan placed relations with Turkey at the top of its foreign policy agenda. Elchibey thought Turkey, as a NATO member, would serve as an Azerbaijani gateway to the Western alliance. Hostilities with Armenians over Nagorno-Karabagh prompted Elchibey to seek a security treaty with Turkey, but the Turkish authorities declined. President Suleyman Demirel responded: "Our aim is not to broaden the war, but to make it smaller."[150] The Azerbaijani statesman, perceived more as a visionary and romantic than as a pragmatic policymaker, saw in Turkey and Israel successful examples of nation building. At the time, Elchibey's foreign policy advisor Vafa Guluzade, a former *apparatchik* in the Soviet foreign ministry and a Middle East expert, was sent to Israel for an exploratory mission in the summer of 1992. Guluzade met Foreign Minister Shimon Peres and called for Israeli investments in the Azerbaijani economy. In a private meeting with an Israeli ambassador to Moscow, President Elchibey called himself a "Zionist," highlighting the Jews' attachment to their homeland as "natural and understandable."[151] At the same time, Elchibey expressed very negative views about Iran. Abulfaz Elchibey perceived Iran to be a multi-ethnic empire and predicted its demise on the basis of the recent dissolution of the Soviet Union.[152]

The bloodless coup, as a result of which popularly elected President Abulfaz Elchibey was sent into internal exile in Nakhichevan, returned its former Communist leader, Heydar Aliyev, to power. Democratic institutions created in the first years of independence were preserved, but under Heydar Aliyev, Azerbaijan returned to Soviet-style political methods of the "partocracy." Russia and her epigones in Azerbaijan were relieved by the ex-Soviet KGB general's takeover. Pro-Turkish elements in Azerbaijan were in disarray, and Turkish nationalist military and intelligence circles considered the Heydar Aliyev regime illegitimate. A coalition of these forces in Turkish intelligence and the military plotted a coup attempt in March of 1995, but President Demirel personally warned Heydar Aliyev about the impending coup.[153] This personal intervention by the Turkish president re-established the stability of Turkish–Azerbaijani relations.

Despite his Russian ties and sympathies, Heydar Aliyev continued to emphasize the Western liberal model as the goal of Azerbaijan's political development, though his critics would describe the emphasis as purely rhetorical. Like his more outspoken predecessor, President Heydar Aliyev rejected the Iranian Islamic state as a model for Azerbaijan. In 2003, the Azerbaijani president reaffirmed the country's commitment to secularism and Western democracy. During a ceremony to celebrate the 24th Anniversary of the Islamic Revolution in Iran, Aliyev explained the difference between the Iranian political system and the one established in Azerbaijan in 1992. He told the Iranian diplomats: "Our countries are very much alike, but there are many differences in the constitution of our states. The main difference is that since the declaration of Azerbaijani independence, our country is involved in the process of building a *democratic, secular state based on the primacy of law* [emphasis added], and we have accomplished significant progress. This is our main road. We are pursuing this goal."[154]

Shortly after gaining independence, Azerbaijan joined European institutions such as the OSCE and the Council of Europe. A wide consensus among the

Azerbaijani political elites and the mass electorate shares the vision of the state's Western orientation and its secularism—which is the logical outcome of Heydar Aliyev's vision of integration into the Euro–Atlantic alliance.[155] In the context of Azerbaijan's integration into the "West," Eldar Namazov, a former chief aide to President Heydar Aliyev, pointed out that Azerbaijani society saw Turkey and, in a wider perspective, Israel as its main partners in the international arena. He added that "throughout the 1990s the idea of the close partnership with Azerbaijan had a wide resonance in Israeli society and the Jewish lobby in the United States."[156]

Secular states: an overview

In a region where many ongoing conflicts are driven by religious animosities, the secular order of the three states under consideration forms a powerful ideational link between them. A former private advisor to Prime Minister Turgut Ozal, Aydan Kodaoglu stated unequivocally that "secularism is a common element between our three countries . . . it is a great commonality."[157] Azerbaijani officials also stressed secularism as the defining factor in forming strategic ties with Israel. A senior Azerbaijani diplomat pointed out in an interview that Turkey's and Azerbaijan's secularism make them exceptional among Muslim states. He explained that the secular nature of the Azerbaijani state allowed establishing a partnership with Israel.[158] Anar Azimov reiterated that Turkey and Azerbaijan are unique in the Muslim world as two "genuinely" secular states.[159]

Turkey as a secular state

Ataturk promoted a secular doctrine that constituted a threat to the entire religious establishment in Turkey. As an expression of the Western commitment, the principle of secularism represents one of the six arrows of Kemalism. This concept, Laiklik ("secularism") in Turkish, is embedded in the Turkish Constitution.[160] Jenkins observes: "Secularism was not only the driving force behind Ataturk's domestic reforms of the 1920s and 1930s which laid the foundations for the Kemalist state, it was also the most controversial, triggering violent protests and even rebellions.[161] The bloodshed resulted not only in a hardening of attitudes toward anti-secularists in the Kemalist government of the time but also in the creation of a secular martyrology. It also reinforced a perception in the military of secularism as a security issue, with the TGS as its main protector.[162]

Language reform played a dual function in the nation-building project undertaken by Mustafa Kemal. The abrogation of the Arabic alphabet reflected the goals of modernization and secularization of Turkish society. In the Kemalist view, the Arabic language and script were so intimately interwoven with the Quran and the "Islamic past" of the Ottoman Empire that they had to be dislodged from public discourse and education. Second, the introduction of

Latin script indicated the wholehearted embrace of Western concepts, mores and institutions. The Turkish Republic adopted Latin script as a substitute for Arabic in order to bring Turkey closer to the "advanced civilizations." For Ataturk, language reform was one of the central building blocks of his program of modernization.[163]

Israel as a secular state

Like the Turkish nationalists of *Ittihad ve Teraki* ("Unity and Progess"), the early Zionists subscribed to a secular reading of Jewish nationalism in order to join "Western modernity." At the same time, Zionists sought to pre-serve the Jewish ethno-national distinctiveness of their pre-State community (Yishuv) in Palestine. The State of Israel was created on the basis of a com-promise between the Orthodox Jewish authorities in Palestine and secularist nationalist forces, which coalesced around the Socialist Zionists, represented by the leader of *Mifleget Poalei Eretz Israel* (Mapai) ("Party of Eretz Israel Workers"), David Ben-Gurion.[164] For many Marxists among the Zionist political elite, this painful compromise was the price of preserving communal peace, and a counter-measure to prevent a social explosion by the religious Jewish masses in British Mandate Palestine.[165] This historic compromise between secularists and religious authorities gave rise to the notion that the Israeli political system is a form of consociationalism.[166] As a result, society in Israel maintains a balance between a predominantly secular sector and the religious authorities in civil matters such as birth, marriage, divorce and death. The majority of the Israeli Jewish population is secular. About 80 percent of Israeli Jews are not formally religious.[167] The rest are Orthodox Jews. However, state institutions in Israel guard their secular credentials religiously. Kimmerling explains that "the state is administered by universal and secular codes drawn from what is called 'Western culture.' Without these codes, it would be impossible to administer a modern state and to maintain Israel's military might, [sustain] a relatively developed economy and other mechanisms of a strong, highly developed state."[168] Another Israeli scholar describes the status quo in Israel: "One could perhaps observe a separation of religion from the people of Israel . . . the State is not a religious personality. In a point of fact, it is not a religious entity, although it is Jewish in essence. Ours is a state whose laws and justice are secular."[169] Israeli political elites, molded by the ideology of Labour Zionism, are secular. As a result, tradi-tional foreign policy is dominated by the security imperative and "normal-ization" of relations with Muslim countries of the region and beyond.[170]

Azerbaijan as a secular state

President Abulfaz Elchibey emulated the Republican Turkey. As a fervent pan-Turkist nationalist, he emphasized the secular character of the Azerbaijani state. In the early 1990s, Azerbaijan adopted from Turkey many aspects of its

Republican political system. The Azerbaijani National Front government perceived in Shia Islam a reactionary force that would potentially draw Azerbaijan into Iran's sphere of influence. When Heydar Aliyev returned to power, he acknowledged the role of Islam in Azerbaijani society. He explained his position vis-à-vis the issue of religion and state in his country: "This is a part of my strategy—to preserve the national moral values of Azerbaijan. A part of these values is connected to Islam. We do not deny Islam. This is our religion. At the same time, I am trying to synthesize the national moral values of Azerbaijan with European values, the values known to the entire world. I want to see my country as a secular nation, but not separated from its national roots. Every nation has its own peculiarities. And I am very proud of my roots."[171] To reaffirm his public persona as a Muslim, President Aliyev went on a Haj (the religious pilgrimage to Mecca) in May of 1997.

However, in order to safeguard the international legitimacy of his regime and to gain wider acceptance in the West, Aliyev promulgated a new Constitution of Azerbaijan after returning to power in 1993. Azerbaijan's formal Constitution was adopted under Heydar Aliyev's guidance in 1995. The principle that Azerbaijan is a secular republic is enshrined in the Preamble to the Constitution. It is one of the founding principles of the Azerbaijani Republic.[172] Heydar Aliyev clarified to Hojjatoleslam Hasan Rohani, the secretary of the Iranian Supreme Council for National Security, during his visit to Baku in July 2001 that Azerbaijan will never become a religious state like Iran, nor will it sever its relations with the United States or Israel, "despite pressure from Iran."[173] Aliyev said: "We are following the path of secularism and will continue to follow that path of statehood."[174] In 2003, Heydar Aliyev unequivocally stressed Azerbaijan's commitment to secularism in his address to the Iranian ambassador: "Azerbaijan is a secular state, and this is our strategic path. We will not be able to turn from this path neither to this or the other side. We will not be able to turn away, not because we don't want to, but because we consider this way the most appropriate for us."[175] The Azerbaijani government set up a special Ministry to deal with religious affairs based on the prototype of the Turkish Diyanet Bakanligi.[176]

Constitutionally nationalist states

Turkey and Turkishness

Kemalism, a complex political ideology based on Turkish nationalism and positivist philosophical prescriptions for creating social solidarity, served as a unique path to modernization of the Anatolian remnant of the 600-year-old empire. Republican Turkey is considered unique among Muslim states because of its secularism, Western orientation and imperial nationalism that had a precedent in the Ottoman period.[177] In his reforms, Mustafa Kemal adapted the Western ideology of nationalism to the specific Turkish conditions.[178] Mustafa Kemal placed "belonging to the Turkish nation" or

"Turkishness" as a foundation stone of the new state he created.[179] The essential elements of this ideology were declared by the Kemalist party itself as "Six Arrows" (Altı Ok), adopted at the party congress of 1931 and inserted into the Turkish constitution in 1937. They were republicanism, secularism, nationalism, reformism, populism and etatism. Alon Liel argues, "Kemalism is a political philosophy and legacy of Mustafa Kemal, which changed the destiny of Turkey. Ataturk founded a nation-state with clear boundaries on one sixth of the territory of the dying Ottoman Empire. Despite the geographic constraints, he succeeded to enthuse the young republic with a sense of national pride and optimism, which enabled Turkey to embrace modernization and progress unparalleled in her geographic, cultural and religious environment."[180]

The new Turkish nationalism that developed in the 1930s did not recognize any "race" in Turkey other than the Turkish race, and no other language but the Turkish language.

The Constitution of the Turkish Republic, adopted in 1982, reaffirms that "no idea can be upheld against the interests of the Turkish nation, the foundation of the indivisibility of the Turkish existence with its state, its country, its history and moral values, Ataturk's nationalism [Kemalism], principles, revolutions and civilizations." It reiterates that any ideas or activities that do not conform to the principles of the Turkish nation are punishable by law.

The avowed goal was the creation of a "coalescence of nation without classes or privileges."[181] During this period, Mustafa Kemal promoted "the Turkish history thesis," which proclaimed that "the superior Turkish race ... was the mother of all civilizations and races."[182] Turkish authorities sponsored a public campaign to promote the idea of Turkish state nationalism. The government distributed posters to be exhibited in public places. First, enemies and friends of the Turkish people were identified. This division of the world was expressed in the slogan *Turk'un Turk' ten Baska Dostu Yoktur* ("The only friends of Turks are Turks"). Internal enemies included communists, socialists, Muslim fundamentalists, Kurds and other ethnic minorities such as Armenians, Lazs, Greeks and Suryanis (Syriac Christians). During the period of Turkification (1930–40), numerous attacks were organized against these groups. As a result of this assimilation policy toward minorities, legal authorities punished anyone who did not speak Turkish. Two slogans were omnipresent in pre-World War II Turkey: *Bir Turk Dunyaya Bedeldir* ("One Turk is worth all the world") and *Ne Mutlu Turk'um Diyene* ("What happiness to say that I am Turkish").

A major "purification" program of Turkish language was launched after the foundation of the Republic in 1923. A full-fledged reform of the Turkish language was completed in the 1930s. The Turkish language, "the mirror of the national soul," "one of the oldest and most advanced languages in the world" and "the mother of all languages," had come under the influence of Arabic and Persian, diluting its original values. The movement to standardize the Turkish language gained momentum under Kemal Ataturk, who introduced the script reform in 1928. After the death of Ataturk in 1938, his close friend Ismet Inonu succeeded him as leader of the country. As "national chief," Inonu committed himself to adhere to the principles of Kemalism at the People's Republican Party Congress in December of 1936. In 1950, Turkey became a multi-party democracy, but groups identified as internal enemies, including Kurds, other minorities and Islamists, were banned from organizing into political parties. Meanwhile, nationalist parties in many reincarnations, such as Milli Nizam Partisi ("National Order Party"), Milli Selamet Partisi ("National Salvation Party") and Milliyetçi Hareket Partisi ("Nationalist Action Party"), or MHP, regularly participated in national elections.[183] In fact, the contemporary Turkish Constitution, ratified in 1981, states in Paragraph 68: "No party can be created which opposes the state's unity with its nation, its country, and secular republican principles, or which depends on classes." So it has preserved the 1930s categorization of "enemy forces" such as communists, Kurds and Muslim fundamentalists. Within the bounds of the Turkish Constitution, the political spectrum reflects different ideological preferences of Kemalist parties, from the political Right to the political Left.

The breakup of the Soviet Union and the independent status gained by the Turkic ex-Soviet republics gave the pan-Turkist aspirations of nationalists in Turkey a new lease on life. In the 1990s, the National Action Party revived its strength and increased its electoral appeal.[184] MHP played a prominent role in guiding Turkish policy toward the Newly Independent Muslim Republics in the early 1990s. A high-level delegation to Azerbaijan led by Prime Minister Demirel included Alpaslan Turkes, the leader of the Nationalist Movement Party, which was part of the government coalition at the time. Turkes served as key "unofficial" foreign policy advisor to President Elchibey and was also the diplomatic go-between between Demirel and the Azerbaijani National Front government.[185] In 1999, MHP joined the coalition government led by (Ecevit's) Demokratik Sol Party.

Israel and nationalism

Bearing some semblance to the Turkish Republic, Israel was created as the world's only Jewish state. On May 14, 1948, David Ben-Gurion announced "the establishment of a Jewish State in Eretz-Israel, to be known as the State of Israel."[186] This feature of the founding document, in the absence of a constitution, embeds the nationalist (Zionist) ideal as the sine qua non of the State of Israel.[187] Thus, members of non-Jewish minorities are granted citizenship and civil rights, but they are not members of the Israeli nation. The definition of the "Jewishness" of the state, as in the case of the "Turkishness" of the Turkish state, blurs the boundaries between nationalism and religion. Whereas in the Turkish republican definition of nationhood, Islam is defined broadly as a central element of "Turkishness," Judaism serves as an essential part of Jewish nationalism and provides the primary legal basis for belonging to the Israeli nation. As in the case of Turkey, Israeli citizenship is not equivalent to belonging to the nation. Baruch Kimmerling explains, "This situation is expressed in taken-for-granted equivalency between the Jewish religion, on the one hand, and Jewish, as well as Israeli, nationalism and its expressions in the cultural, political, and judicial system, on the other."[188] In that respect, both Israel and Turkey represent a political order defined as "ethnocracy" or "ethnic democracy." Under this arrangement, "the ethnic nation, not the citizenry, shapes the symbols, laws and policies of the state for the benefit of the majority. This ideology makes a crucial distinction between members and non-members of the ethnic nation."[189] Another common characteristic of the two countries is their relationship to members of co-nationals living abroad. Members of the ethnic nation may be divided into persons living in the homeland and persons living in the diaspora.[190] As Diş Turks ("external Turks") are considered members of the Turkish nation and have automatic right to citizenship, so Jews living in the diaspora have a right to Israeli citizenship on the basis of the Law of Return.[191]

The revival and standardization of language also played a prominent role in Israeli nation building. Shlomo Avinery stressed that Zionism *"transformed a language relegated to mere religious usage into a modern, secular mode of intercourse of a nation-state"* [emphasis added].[192] The adoption of Hebrew, the sacred language of Jewish religion, by Zionists as a vernacular was a reflection of the spirit of the enlightenment and modernism. Eliezer Ben-Yehuda, a Zionist cultural leader and scholar who was pre-eminent in the revival of Hebrew in Mandate Palestine, grasped the significance of language in the Jewish national project early on. He realized, during his student years at the Sorbonne, the decisive role of literature in the arousal of French nationalism. Ben-Yehuda wrote in 1880, "I have decided that in order to have our own land and political life it is also necessary to have a language to hold us together. This language is Hebrew, but not the Hebrew of the rabbis and scholars. We must have a Hebrew language in which we conduct the business of life."[193]

The Azerbaijani dilemma: between pan-Turkism and pan-Azerbaijanism

The arousal of a national idea in Azerbaijani society was associated with the emergence of a secular, anti-clericalist and Westernized milieu in the second half of the nineteenth century. The spectacular discovery of large deposits of petroleum in the Western Caspian region by Russian geologists in the late 1860s led to the swift integration of Azerbaijan into the world economy. An Azerbaijani historian concludes that formation of a national bourgeoisie resulted in the growth of an indigenous intelligentsia among Azeri Turks of the Caucasus in the 1870s.[194] In particular, European-educated Azerbaijani publicists and intellectuals expressed their alienation from the conservative and Islamic (Shia) Caucasian Muslim elites, who manifested their attachment to the culture, language and political influence of the Persian Empire. These liberal Azeri intellectuals saw the need for a reform of Islam, and some espoused secularist views.

In the wake the dissolution of the Soviet Union, Azerbaijani pan-Turkists created a flurry of activity, animated by the unexpected opportunity to come closer to realization of their dream.[195] They participated in a number of conferences to appeal to Turkic peoples or Diş Turks ("external Turks") in the Newly Independent Muslim Republics. The most important of these conferences, titled "The Common Alphabet of the Turkic Nations," took place in Ankara in October of 1990. At the conference, the idea of a *lingua franca* for all Turkic-speaking peoples was raised. In order to institutionalize this view, conference organizers formed the Turkish Language History Organization (Türkiye Dil Tarih Kurumu). Around the same time, Turkists called for unification of the alphabet in all Turkic republics on the basis of the Turkish Latin alphabet.

Abulfaz Elchibey espoused an ideology closely linked with the ideology of the Milliyetçi Hareket Party in Turkey. Major political and national reforms were initiated under the Elchibey government in 1992. The Azerbaijani National Front (ANF) professed a nationalist and pan-Turkist ideology from its inception in 1989. This ideology shaped its domestic discourse, and ANF foreign policy priorities focused exclusively on the sole regional player, Turkey. In particular, many innovations in political culture, including the rhetoric of the revival of pan-Turkism and the Greater Azerbaijan project by the Azerbaijani National Front were borrowed directly from Turkey, especially from its more nationalist elements, which coalesced around MHP.[196] The pan-Azerbaijani claims of Abulfaz Elchibey to Iranian Azerbaijan are closely related to pan-Turkism. They can be summarized as follows:

1   Greater Azerbaijan was divided between Russia and Persia.
2   Azerbaijanis have spoken Turkish since the advent of history.
3   Turks have been in the Caucasus for over 5,000 [sic] years.
4   The Safavid Empire was Turkish.
5   Sattar Khan, a leader of the constitutional revolution of Iran (1905–11), was a pan-Turanian separatist.
6   Babak Khorramdin, an Iranian historical icon, who fought to restore Persian independence during the Arabian Abbassid Caliphate in Baghdad (750–1258 CE), was a Turk who fought against Persia.
7   Azerbaijanis and all who speak Turkish are Turkish by race.[197]

Elchibey publicized his irredentist claims to the three Azeri Turk-dominated Iranian provinces in a number of political speeches.[198] On many occasions he attacked Iranian authorities and called for "reunification" with Southern Azerbaijan.[199] The ex-president participated in the Fifth Kurultai ("Congress") of the Azerbaijan Popular Front Party, which took place in Turkey on January 30–1, 1998. In his address to the Congress, Elchibey stated: "The creation of the Democratic Republic of Azerbaijan in some Northern Azerbaijani lands in 1918–21, and its restoration . . . in 1991, do not mean that Azerbaijan's national liberation movement is over . . . The new stage will end with the creation and or restoration of united Azerbaijani statehood . . . Already [in Iran] there are active organizations, whose sole purpose is the national independence of the Azeri Turks."[200] Abulfaz Elchibey used to claim that the whole Azeri population was originally Turkic. Leading members of the Azerbaijani opposition in the 2003 national elections, such as Isa Gumbar, Ali Kerimli and Etibar Mamedov, were all associated, at least in the popular consciousness, with the nationalist policies of the Azerbaijani National Front. Naturally, they were associated with Elchibey's pan-Turkist aspirations, which most non-Turkic minorities perceived as threatening. For example, during the 2003 election campaign, representatives of all major ethnic communities organized a pro-Ilham Aliyev public rally in the Trade Unions' Auditorium in Baku. It included representatives of Russian, Lezgi, Mountain Jews, Talysh, Ukrainian, Kurd, Tartar, European Jews, Greek, Georgian and Avar communities. The main spokesman emphasized the brotherly relations among all ethnic communities in Azerbaijan and that for all this, "we are obliged to the wise nationalities policy of Heydar Aliyev." He concluded, "In Azerbaijan there is no alternative to the political course of her [sic] president. So only Iham Aliyev, who was trained in the school of Heydar Aliyev, who developed himself as an experienced politician and diplomat, is worthy of carrying on his father's cause."

Following the pan-Turkist ideal, Elchibey attempted to enforce the Turkification of many spheres of public life, including employment based on the linguistic principle. These actions triggered a public debate and had negative consequences for retaining the highly trained scientific, technical and government personnel, which was predominantly Russian-speaking. In November of 1992, a law was proposed to change back to the Latin script, a move facilitating Azerbaijani ties with Turkey and the West. A recent change in script reflects the continuity of the Western and specifically pro-Turkish dominant trend of Azerbaijani foreign policy since independence.[201] Azerbaijanis say that this latest alphabet shift restored links with their national past and Western orientation.[202] The Azerbaijani Soviet Republic adopted Latin script in 1926. This was a truly revolutionary change that set Azerbaijan apart from the traditional Muslim societies, which adhered to the Arabic script since their conversion to Islam. It had occurred two years before the script reform took place in Turkey (in 1928). In 1940, under Stalin, the script was changed to Cyrillic in order to integrate Azerbaijani society into the Moscow-centered system of totalitarian control.

With Heydar Aliyev's return to power, the one-dimensional character of Azerbaijani foreign policy toward Turkey was abandoned. Aliyev toned down the acerbic pan-Turkist rhetoric of Abulfaz Elchibey, which seriously aggravated Azerbaijani relations with Iran. President Aliyev introduced a policy of balancing between powerful neighbors, such as Russia and Iran, without rejecting overtures by the United States and European countries. Nevertheless, at every occasion when visiting Turkey, the ex-Soviet Communist Azerbaijani leader asserted the pan-Turkist ideal of a unique bond between Turkey and Azerbaijan. His speeches always emphasized the shared history of the two nations. Addressing the Turkish parliament, he remarked: "I want to tell you that the history of our peoples and the past milestones we shared will serve as the perfect foundation for strengthening our friendly and brotherly relations in the future."[203] Furthermore, Heydar Aliyev, who had come to power through a coup and established an autocratic, personalistic regime albeit with the formal attributes of a presidential democracy, extrapolated the political system of Kemal Ataturk to his own rule. Referring to the experience of the early Republican period in Turkey, he stated: "Looking back on the experience of the Turkish Republic, I noted for myself the following. The Turkish democratic republic was created in 1923, but it took several years to implement the reforms under the guidance of Mustafa Kemal Ataturk and with support of his associates in order to build a genuinely democratic society in Turkey. That is, if the first democratic republic in Turkey was created in 1923, its attributes, or features of a democratic state, were introduced step-by-step. This serves as our example. As a whole, the 70-year history of Turkey constitutes the school of experience. We are using and we will use your experience."[204]

Even during his tenure as a Communist leader of Soviet Azerbaijan, Heydar Aliyev acted as an Azerbaijani nationalist. He always promoted Azerbaijani national interests and culture within the bounds of the Soviet system. He preserved the exclusive status of Azeri Turkish as the titular language of culture and education in Azerbaijan during the Soviet language reform of 1973. An eloquent "convert" to pan-Turkism and an Azeri nationalist, Aliyev's first foreign voyage upon becoming the president of the independent Azerbaijan was to Turkey. In Turkey, he was granted the high honour of addressing the Buyuk Milli Meclis ("the Great National Assembly"), the Turkish parliament, on February 9, 1994. The historic speech was laden with pan-Turkist references reminiscent of the rhetoric of the Azerbaijani Democratic Republic's Musavat government leadership. In his speech, Aliyev stated:

> The Azerbaijani–Turkish ties have a long history. We are *one people, we have common roots*; we have one history, one religion. During many centuries our peoples preserved and developed similar or slightly different traditions, culture and science. We were shoulder-to-shoulder. The relations between Turkey and Azerbaijan were always called friendly and brotherly. These are relations of peoples united by one root. This was our past, and when we have been deprived of the possibility to communicate, we preserved these traditions in our hearts and we have returned to them now.[205]

In a more revealing appeal to the legacy of Mustafa Kemal, Heydar Aliyev was the only leader among the former Soviet Turkic republics to explicitly refer to the pan-Turkist vision of Ataturk, rarely publicized even in Cold War Turkey:

> I want to remind you about one valuable statement by Mustafa Kemal Ataturk because it serves as evidence of the great responsibility Turkey bears and reminds us how far-sighted Mustafa Kemal Ataturk was. At the 10th anniversary of the Turkish Republic, he said: "The Soviet Union today is our friend, neighbor and ally. We need this friendship. However nobody today can predict what will happen tomorrow. States can be dismembered like the Ottomans or divided like the Austro-Hungary. Nations, which are held today by the strong hand, tomorrow can run away. The balance in the world can change, and Turkey needs to know what to do in this case. It is our friend who rules our brothers, with whom a common language and religion unite us, and with whom we are united in our essence. We must be ready to take them under our protection. Not silently waiting for this day, but to be ready for it. How are nations preparing for this eventuality, are they strengthening spiritual bridges? Our faith and history unite us like bridges. We must return to our roots, to our common history divided by events. We must return to our historical roots."[206]

Lonely states

Idris Bal poignantly notes about Turkey: "The belief that Turkey is without support and is '*lonely*' in international relations may be worth emphasizing here as a potentially important factor affecting its reactions and decisions."[207] The State of Israel also perceived itself to be excluded and a pariah state in the international system since its creation in 1948. The Israeli foreign policy elite felt that the end of the Cold War provided it with an opportunity "to build an 'infrastructure of normalcy.' "[208] Eitan Naeh, Israel's ambassador to the former Soviet republic of Azerbaijan, concludes about the psychological factors that tie Azerbaijan to Israel: "those very factors—dangerous neighbors and a history of being oppressed—make Azerbaijan and Israel logical allies. Countries that don't have too many friends find each other."[209]

Turkey as a lonely state

The main sources of Turkish foreign policy are the historical experience of the Ottoman Empire (the tradition of the balance of power); nationalist Kemalist ideology and the creation of the Turkish Republic on the remnant of the Ottoman territory in Anatolia (hence, isolationism); a Western orientation expressed in the policy of Europeanization and modernization (later, NATO membership); and, lastly, a suspicion of foreign powers and interests (the Sevres syndrome). Turkey's geopolitical position on the East and the West, and the North–South axes also greatly contributed to shaping Turkish foreign policy.

In the first half of the 1990s, American calculations about the importance of bilateral relations began to shift. In particular, State Department officials came under strong pressure from Congress. Congressional criticism of Turkey focused on numerous human rights violations by state authorities. The practice of depopulating troublesome Kurdish areas in Southeastern Turkey was recognized as a serious violation of human rights of Turkish Kurdish citizens. Suppression of Kurdish activists and the Islamist press became an issue of concern for American policymakers.[210] The negative response of the European Union to Turkey's application to join the EU strained Turkish relations with European NATO allies in 1989.[211] Turkish foreign policy makers felt a certain sense of isolation from the West. In fact, even the ardent desire of Turks to join the European Union is mixed with the persistent suspicion emanting from the Sevres syndrome and shared by an influential faction in the army and Kemalist elite that this will lead to a dismemberment of Turkey by the Western powers. Following the end of the Cold War in the early 1990s, Turkish policymakers were reminded of the situation that developed after World War I.[212] The Turkish Republic's Western identity was challenged by a confluence of new geopolitical forces. The United States attempted to impose the "Pax Americana," or "New World Order," as George Bush senior called it, in the Middle East following the first Gulf war.

The military significance of Turkey to the Western European countries declined with the end of the Cold War confrontation. Europe claimed that human rights violations and the Turkish approach to solving the Kurdish question presented serious impediments for the accession of Turkey to the EU. West European countries declined numerous Turkish requests for weapons systems in the midst of allegations that Turkey used them against the Kurds or in its occupation of northern Cyprus. Other oft-quoted reasons for the delay in Turkish EU membership include Turkey's lower economic development, the likelihood of mass labor migrations and the burden of Turkish subsidized agriculture. This European attitiude produced anti-European and anti-Western sentiments among a large portion of the Turkish electorate. From the European point of view, Turkey has coped poorly with the rapid normative changes and the European *acquis communautaire* that accompanied the end of the Cold War. On big concept issues, such as the diminution of the state, the emergence of civil society and the centrality of human rights, Turkey has not only failed to change, but even appeared to fail to grasp the dynamics of the new milieu. Robins concludes, "Increasingly Europeans have felt Turkey to be 'not like us,' not for reasons of religion and culture, but because of the growing normative gap on issues of liberal values and institutions."[213] The Turkish population is also aware that the West continues to perceive them as the Other.[214]

The revival of pan-Turkist aspirations among new, assertive leaders of newly independent Azerbaijan found resonance among the Turkish political elite and broader public. Israel, for its part, has sought to establish full diplomatic relations with Turkey since the 1950s. In the early 1990s, Israel was offering military cooperation without interference into the internal affairs of Turkey. For Turkey, this was vitally important since it is the US Congress that approves funding for American foreign aid and arms sales. The pro-Israeli lobby offered the potential to counteract the negative portrayal of Turkey by human rights groups, Armenian, Greek and Kurdish lobbies, and eventually to afford "access" to the highest American political echelons.

Israel as a lonely state

The State of Israel also has perceived itself to be excluded and a pariah state in the international system since its creation in 1948. The Israeli state was established in the traumatic aftermath of World War II as a homeland specifically for Jews. At the time of its creation, Israel adopted a descent-based definition of citizenship, *jus sanguinis*. The particularities that marked the rebirth of the Jewish homeland go a long way toward providing an explanation of why, even after 50 years, its legitimacy continues to be challenged by the states and peoples surrounding it. These birth traumas also assure that the fervent desire for "normality," in effect a desire for full acceptance by other nation-states, will, in all likelihood, not to be fulfilled in the intermediate future. With the end of the Cold War, the Israeli foreign policy elite sensed an opportunity "to build an 'infrastructure of normalcy.' "[215] Eitan Naeh, Israel's ambassador to Azerbaijan, commented on psychological factors that affect the bilateral Azerbaijani–Israeli relations: "Those very factors—dangerous neighbors and a history of being oppressed—make Azerbaijan and Israel logical allies. Countries that don't have too many friends find each other."[216]

Israel also experienced a period of uncertainty about its standing in the American global strategy in the post-Cold War world. This situation was aggravated by the actions and rhetoric of the Bush Administration (especially between 1989 and 1993), which was more responsive to pro-Arab oil lobbyists in the United States. In fact, Israeli–Azerbaijani cooperation from 1992 through 1995 had a low-key and often informal character because both countries co-existed in a "diplomatic vacuum."[217] The alliance with Turkey at this time was crucial for the Israeli political elite, not only symbolizing the ability to create a deep relationship with a Muslim country, but as proof that historical connections and shared values such as parliamentary democracy play a part in foreign policy.

Azerbaijan as a lonely state

Azerbaijan also experienced diplomatic isolation in its first three years of independence. The reason for this state of affairs was a Western perception, which was propagated by the Armenian lobby well connected to the Russian and American political elites, about the religious character of the Nagorno-Karabagh conflict. The conflict was portrayed by some in the international media as a confrontation between peace-loving Christian Armenia and the Muslim "fundamentalist" regime in Azerbaijan.[218] This view was successfully promoted by the Armenian diaspora in Russia and the West.

Once the Baku-Tbilisi-Ceyhan project began to take off in 1999, Azerbaijan experienced a flurry of Western diplomatic activity. This occurred as soon as the European countries realized the importance of the alternative source of Caspian hydrocarbon resources delivered from Azerbaijan through Turkey to its Mediterranean port of Ceyhan.

The perception of Western prejudice against Azerbaijan as a Muslim country persists among the Western political elites. Vafa Guluzade, a former national security advisor to three recent Azerbaijani presidents (1991–9), advanced the thesis that the American fixation on Georgia as a key to its strategy in the South Caucasus was misguided.[219] In his analytical essay, Guluzade asserted that "Americans over-emphasize the significance of Georgia, without considering that the main factor in their victory [in the geopolitical competition for influence in the Caucasus] can only be Azerbaijan, where their political 'stock' is falling precipitously due to the incorrect strategy and tactics to [approach to] the solution of Azerbaijani key problems."[220] In this situation, the value of an Azerbaijani strategic partnership with Israel increases because Azerbaijan can use Israel as a diplomatic back channel in its communication on strategic matters with the United States.

Azerbaijan pursued a role as cusp of the energy routes along the East–West corridor. But completion of the BTC pipeline project changed European calculations, as EU countries realized that they could gain access to competitive sources of oil delivered through Turkey from the Caspian Sea. This might even affect a change of heart in Europe regarding Turkey's military reprisals against the PKK militants.

Conclusion: aspiring states

The state remains the ultimate authority that formulates foreign policy in the international system. The institutional interests of the main state actors contribute to and sometimes determine foreign policy decisions. Security is directly linked to a state's self-perception or identity, and security often serves as a driver of the state's foreign policy. This is especially true in the case of security-deprived countries located in unstable regions. To sum up the regional threat perceptions predicated on the particular state identities that have shaped these strategic partnerships: The immediate neighbors of these countries, Russia, Iran, Armenia and Syria, have generally perceived Israel, Turkey and the newly independent Republic of Azerbaija with suspicion, if not open hostility. Arabs generally consider Turkey a Western country despite its Muslim population. This Arab perception was especially evident during the oil crisis of 1973, when Turkey was also subject to an oil embargo imposed by OPEC.[221] Europeans share a profound ambivalence about their relations with non-Christian nations in the Near East. Greek detractors identify Israel and Turkey as "international outcasts." By the middle of the 1990s, the three states had tenuous relationships, at best, with the two main regional blocs, the EU[222] and CIS,[223] especially when compared with the majority of new independent states of the post-Soviet space that came into being in the post-Cold War period. During the post-World War II period, the division of the international system into two dominant camps defined the primary identity of state actors. The end of the Cold War led to a loss of that ideological marker as an anchor of foreign policy. Nation-states, as members of the emerging international system, experienced crises of identity. In particular, in this period, identity politics and a search for redefinition of state actors' identities became crucial factors in understanding their foreign policy interactions in the international system.

3 The military–security stranglehold

State agents as drivers of the triple entente

Introduction: the role of the military–security apparatus

The current chapter is devoted to analysis of the state institutions that play essential roles in the formation and evolution of this trilateral entente. The following two sections outline the role that the military–industrial complex (in the cases of Turkey and Israel) and security apparatus (that of Azerbaijan) played in forging the strategic relationship between the three countries. As mentioned in the previous chapter, safeguarding national security occupies the primary place in the domestic and foreign domains of the three countries under discussion.

No analysis of the Turkish–Israeli–Azerbaijan axis can be complete without ascertaining the role that military–security institutions played in its formation and evolution in the 1990s and early 2000s. Philip Robins, in his otherwise comprehensive analysis of the formation of Turkish foreign policy in the post-Cold War period, *Suits and Uniforms*, assigns the Turkish military a secondary role in the policy process.[1] Robins concludes, "In the area of foreign policy the military has tended to be less overtly involved."[2] With reference to the Turkish–Israeli entente, two other authors treat the role of the military in this post-Cold War relationship extensively. Gareth Jenkins sees the Turkish military as one of the pillars of foreign policymaking in the same period.[3] Ofra Bengio poins to the connection between the role of the military in Turkey as guardians of the Kemalist state and their particular stance in the direction of Turkish foreign policy, in particular regarding Israel. She insightfully comments: "The most important cause or justification for the military 'soft intervention' in domestic and foreign policy making in the 1990s was the rising power of [Islamist] RP (coinciding with the emergence of the PKK [sic]) and the failure of the center parties to check or counterbalance it"[4] [emphasis added]. I would extend Bengio's analysis to military-to-military relations between Turkey and Azerbaijan.

Pluralist theory provides an explanation for the impact of domestic politics and institutions on foreign policy and the channels through which specific states' institutions and interest groups affect foreign policy.[5] It would be worthwhile in this regard to remind the reader that there were influential detractors of the Turkish–Israeli entente both in Turkey and Israel. In 1998, a number of senior officials of the Israeli Ministry of Foreign Affairs disagreed that it was in the strategic interest of Israel to pursue both intimate and public relationships with Turkey.[6] They were concerned that such close alignment with Turkey would further alienate Israel's neighhbors, especially Egypt, and negatively affect relations with Russia. They blamed the Israeli defense establishment, especially Ambassador David Ivri, for pursuing singlehandedly their parochial interests in military sales to Turkey, without regard to other regional interests of the Jewish state.[7] This tendency in the Israeli political echelons came to be known as the "Egyptian" school.[8] The Egyptian school ascribed critical significance to the relationship with Egypt for the long-term interests of Israel. A former Israeli foreign minister, Shlomo Bem-Ami, who served in office only for one year (1999–2000), led this school of thought. This group, closer to Israel's Ministry of Foreign Affairs, espoused dovish views of the Arab–Israeli conflict and emphasized the importance of a comprehensive solution to the conflict, including peace with both Palestinians and Syrians. According to Leon Hadar, the Egyptian school argued "it would be an irony . . . if the Turkish–Israeli friendship that has been facilitated by the movement toward Israeli détente with the Arabs would end up threatening the Arab–Israeli peace process itself."[9]

The role of the Turkish and Israeli military–security apparatus in the entente

Turkey

This section analyzes the institutional superstructure of the strategic relations between Turkey and Israel and the ascendant impact of the military–industrial complex (MIC) on the mutual relations between these countries. The section highlights the critical role state institutions, in particular the Turkish military and the MIC in Israel, came to play in forming the Turkish–Israeli axis.

In Turkey, in particular, the military traditionally played the role of the ultimate arbiter in the sphere of high politics. This was primarily due to the Sevres syndrome, a deep-seated fear among the Kemalist elite of dismemberment of the Turkish state and the Ottoman tradition. Since the foundation of the Republic, the military were an autonomous power in Turkish politics. In fact, Turkish foreign policymaking was defined as a "tripod" that involved the government, foreign ministry and military (the chief of staff). As three classical military coups (1960, 1971, 1980) and one "post-modernist coup" of 1997 (known as the 28 Şubat Süreci in Turkey) attest, intervention of the military in civilian politics has been a persistent feature of the Turkish polity.[10] The cycle of military interventions and peaceful returns to civilian politics deviates from the classical Western democratic model, though it is more common in the political tradition of the Middle East.[11] After the introduction of the multi-party system with the founding of the Demokrat Party by Adnan Menderes and Celal Bayar in January of 1946, the military saw its main objective as protection of the Republic against ideological threats and the upholding of peace and tranquility in society. The ideological threats to Turkey were identified as Communism, Kurdish nationalism and religious fundamentalism. The Turkish military has retained the prerogative to intervene in the political arena to defend Kemalist principles from encroachment by Islamist ideologues and Kurdish nationalists.[12] In fact, after the 1960 coup, the Turkish military institutionalized its participation in framing the general outlines of domestic and foreign policy by reinvigorating the National Security Council (NSC), first established in 1933.[13] Despite the fact that the NSC was assigned, by the 1961 Constitution, to serve as an advisory body, in reality it served as a forum where a powerful military communicated views on issues of high politics to the elected government. The NSC's functions are outlined in Article 118 of the Turkish Constitution as "the formulation, establishment and implementation of the national security policy of the State."[14] At the same time, the scope of "security," as defined by the Turkish military, is so broad that it includes "almost any policy area, from education and the environment to defense and foreign policy."[15] Until the EU harmonization package was adopted by the Turkish parliament in 2001, the NSC had a voting majority held by members of the military. The NSC was formerly composed of civilian members: the president, prime minister, defense, foreign and interior ministers, as well as military members. The military side dominated NSC decisions because not only did the chief of staff and commanders of land, air, naval and Gendarmerie forces participate in committee meetings, but the seat of the secretary-general was traditionally occupied by a ranking military officer as well.[16] The NSC, known by the abbreviation MGK, produced a confidential document called the Red Book, or the National Security Policy Document, identifying principal security threats and suggesting operational responses to them. As Gareth Jenkins concludes: "In practice, . . . the military's informal authority is such that, when it expresses an opinion, civilian governments rarely try to implement a policy which contradicts it."[17] The Turkish military usually employed persuasion and consensus building rather than issuing ultimatums to the civilian authorities. Turkish generals are also very sensitive to public opinion, especially within the Kemalist elite, due to their desire to frame their policy prescriptions as expressions of the national will.[18] The Turkish general staff is perceived as trying to coordinate foreign policy recommendations and work in unison with rather than against the ideologically harmonious bureaucracy of the Ministry of Foreign Affairs. Gareth Jenkins observes: "While the NSC sets general strategic parameters for foreign policy and usually assumes direct responsibility for its implementation in security-sensitive areas such as Cyprus or the PKK . . ., the MFA has developed considerable de facto autonomy in the day-to-day conduct of foreign policy."[19]

In January–February 1991, President Turgut Ozal adopted an unambiguous pro-American line in Turkish foreign policy and supported the American-led coalition against Saddam Hussein's invasion of Kuwait, despite the wrath of the military. He also took first steps in a diplomatic rapprochement with Israel. In taking this decision, Turgut Ozal was guided not only by international considerations but also by the pragmatic needs of an important sector of the Turkish economy, tourism. After the economic reforms undertaken by Turgut Ozal in the 1980s, the tourism sector has become one of major sources of foreign exchange for the Turkish economy.[20] The first major bilateral agreement between the two governments in the 1990s was an agreement facilitating tourism between Israel and Turkey signed in June of 1992.[21] This reflected a major shift in the Turkish posture toward Israel. As some authors indicate, the dominant mode of Turkish–Israeli relations during most of the 1960s, 1970s and 1980s was one of ambivalence.[22] A Turkish diplomat identified this traditional mode as the "measured equidistance" between Israeli and Palestinian poles.[23] The Turkish military formulated its own conclusions from the outcome of the first Gulf war. They quickly seized on the inadequacy of its military concept and outdated weapons systems.[24] They realized that the allied victory in the war was primarily due to the implementation of a Revolution in Military Affairs (RMA) during the military operations by the American-led coalition forces.[25] Isaac Ben-Israel argues that the RMA, as a new military doctrine, evolved in the period from the Gulf war through the Kosovo and Afghanistan air campaigns and reached its maturity during Operation Shock and Awe in 2003.[26] Israel, because of its advanced military–industrial sector, was capable of offering state-of-the-art weapons systems. Israeli military experts also offered to retrofit and upgrade available air fleet and tanks to enhance Turkey's security and regional standing.[27] Another benefit of this rapprochement, expected by Turkey, was strong support from the United States government, especially Congress.[28]

Turkish military thinking about foreign policy matters is very pragmatic and based on realist assumptions about the balance of power in Turkey's neighborhood. The end of the Cold War has not affected deeply held convictions about threats to the Turkish Republic from outside, including Islamic fundamentalism emanating from Iran and the instability of the independent states of the Caucasus and the Middle East.[29] The more imminent threats of Kurdish ethnic separatism and domestic irtica or Islamic fundamentalism have heightened the security concerns of the military class since 1993.[30] The issue of membership in the European Union was deeply divisive in Turkish society in the 1990s as well. Whereas foreign ministry officials and TUSIAD, a Turkish major business association, were more sanguine about the prospects for EU membership, the military was more cautious, if not reserved.[31] Some powerful, although numerically small, elements in Turkish politics did not share the Turkish interest in EU membership. They include radical Islamist elements, conservative Kemalists and ultra-nationalists, which are well represented in the high echelons of the military establishment.[32] This internal political division was spurred by the controversy over Turkish entry into the Turkey–EU Customs Union in January 1996.

The Turkish military played a decisive role in establishing the Turkish–Israeli entente.[33] Both militaries share a similarity of institutional make-up matched by secular ideology, educational experience and conception of regional threats. In fact, the institutional mechanisms for strategic planning and military procurement in Turkey are very similar to the Israeli system.[34] These common-alities between the militaries of Turkey and Israel only smoothed the way for reaching a strategic understanding or entente between the two nations. Ofra Bengio argues that the Turkish military's drive for deepening relations with their Israeli counterparts was motivated by "three sets of considerations . . . purely military/professional; regional/strategic; and political/ideological domestic concerns."[35] Contrary to the traditional view widely shared by Iran, Greece and the Arab world,[36] the Turkish military first approached the Israelis about concluding the entente.[37] Despite some public dismay, Turkish foreign ministry officials were also staunch proponents of rapid improvement of Turkish–Israeli relations after the beginning of the Peace Process in 1993.[38] The key Turkish figures, who cemented this regional axis, were Çevik Bir, deputy chief of general staff, and Onur Oymen, deputy foreign minister at the time.[39] Çevik Bir was one of the most pro-American members of the general staff.[40] Bir had a track record of long collaboration with the US military, dating back to the UNITAF operation in Somalia.[41] Philip Robins observes that in the case of the UNITAF operation, "For the US, the appointment of Bir was to be a reward for a loyal and valued ally."[42]

The evolution of entente from 1992 to 1999 was a gradual process involv-ing many negotiations and private meetings between Turks and Israelis, and reflecting the relations' complexity and scope. Ofra Bengio concludes that Turkey involved Israel in the most extensive military and intelligence cooperation with a non-NATO country in its history. Likewise, for Israel this cooperation was unprecedented outside of its relationship with the United States.[43] During 1993 and 1994, Prime Minister Yitzhak Rabin negotiated and, in May 1994, concluded the "Agreement on Security and Secrecy," stipulating that security information should not be transferred to third parties. In Novem-ber 1994, a "Memorandum on Mutual Understanding and Cooperation" on fighting terrorism was signed. This memorandum envisioned the creation of "joint committees" to address regional threats. Under the terms of the memor-andum, Turkey and Israel agreed "to cooperate in gathering intelligence on Syria, Iran, and Iraq and to meet regularly to share assessments pertaining to terrorism and these countries' military capabilities."[44] But the most compre-hensive and significant agreement, from a military point of view, was the "Military Training Cooperation Agreement" of February 1996. This secret agreement was signed by General Çevik Bir and Israeli Defense Minister Yitzhak Mordechai in Tel Aviv. It covered an exchange of military informa-tion, experience and personnel; access to airspace of both countries for military flight training and joint training activities; and mutual use of port facilities.[45] Even though the 1996 agreement included no clauses regarding mutual obligations in case of war against either one of the signatories, it included secret provisions. Formalizing the long-term "Defense Industry Cooperation Agreement" in August 1996 marked the same year.[46] The agreement provided the framework for two "upgrading deals," signed in 1997 and 1998, for the modernization of Turkish F-4s and F-5s.[47] In 1997, as a result of this agreement, Israel and Turkey launched a "Strategic Dialogue" involving a biannual process of high-level military consultations by the respective deputy chiefs of staff.[48] Other discussions between the Turkish and Israeli militaries covered large-scale military sales and co-production of various military equipment, including Merkava III tanks.[49] The military-to-military cooperation extended to joint naval exercises with participation of the US Navy, anti-missile defense and even military use of Israeli space satellites.[50] The military benefits of entente have become critical to the national security of both countries. It allows Israel to station fighter planes at Turkish air bases close to the Syrian, Iraqi and Iranian borders. In exchange, Turkish F-16 pilots and crews are learning electronic warfare in Israel.[51] Turkish F-4 Phantom jet squadrons have been reconfigured with Israeli electronics so they can destroy Syrian surface-to-air missiles, while Israeli pilots practice long-range flying over mountainous land in preparation for missions against Iran.[52]

The entente with Israel also served the domestic agenda of the Turkish military. One of these objectives was to maintain the secular order internally and fortify the Kemalist pro-Western (pro-American) orientation of Turkish foreign policy. One Turkish scholar defines the Kemalist identity in the following terms: "The foundational elements of the Kemalist identity are an abandonment of the Ottoman past, the termination of Islamic power in the public sphere—preventing it from functioning as a source of political legitimacy —an understanding of citizenship that excludes non-Muslim minorities [sic], all within an ethno-linguistic and territorial conception of the nation."[53] In effect, as in the case of Azerbaijan, this relationship symbolizes the secular identity of the Turkish state. The phenomenal rise of the Islamist Refah (Welfare) movement to the crest of the Turkish political firmament was unprecedented in the history of the Turkish Republic. An observer of Turkey of the 1990s and *New York Times* correspondent argues: "The most spectacular development was the Islamic revival. The Islamist-led party, which had not been taken seriously in the past, suddenly emerged as the main force in local elections, even winning in the capital, Ankara, and the economic center, Istanbul."[54] Following Ataturk's prescription, the army viewed conservative religious circles with deep suspicion. The coming to power of the Islamist Refah-led government of Necmettin Erbakan in 1996 exposed a deep social cleavage that divided supporters of Kemalism and conservative religious masses. Philip Robins argues: "The critical months between December 1995 and February 1997 proved to be a period when the competing ideological visions of Kemalism and Islamism wrestled and at times battled with each other in the domain of foreign affairs."[55] In his political past, Erbakan called for the creation of an Islamic NATO and an Islamic Common Market and

D-8.[56] As the first foreign policy act after coming to power, the Refah Party leadership accompanied the leader of the Nation of Islam, Louis Farrakhan, as he toured Iran, Iraq, Syria and Sudan, four countries ruled by openly anti-Western regimes, in February of 1996. Necmettin Erbakan and his close associates, among them the current prime minister, Recep Tayyip Erdogan, had long-established relations with radical Islamist international networks.[57] The secularist majority in Turkey was threatened by the civilian government, in which Islamists held the reins of power. Turkish generals felt compelled to take the lead in this popular discontent against the civilian government. In his first six months as prime minister, Erbakan acquiesced to the traditional Kemalist policies in the domestic and international arenas. Despite his election promises, the Islamist prime minister approved conclusion of the 1996 Turkish–Israeli military agreement. However, Erbakan's attempts to resolve the Kurdish problem by using appeals to "Islamic unity" and his foreign policy démarches vis-à-vis Iran and Libya were met with growing apprehension by the Turkish general staff. The attempts by Erbakan to build bridges with moderate elements among Kurdish activists, his amnesty for PKK militants, and his proposal for lifting the ban on the Kurdish language were not welcomed by the military. In fact, these measures were perceived as a direct challenge to the national unity of the Turkish Republic. In order to placate the military, Erbakan gave them carte blanche in handling the budding Turkish–Israeli strategic relationship. Chief of Staff Ismail Karadayi personally assumed oversight of Turkish–Israeli cooperation.[58] The broken promise to his constituents to annul any agreements with Israel and fight against the "Zionist" enemy threatened the viability of Erbakan's government. Concerned about continued Islamist grassroots' support for his government, the Turkish prime minister embarked on two controversial international trips.[59] The first Asian tour, in August of 1996, included visits to Iran, Pakistan, Malaysia, Singapore and Indonesia. After that visit, Erbakan rubber-stamped the Turkish–Israeli defense co-production agreement, which was signed during his Asian tour on August 28, 1996. The second trip, to Africa (September 1996), was also couched by the head of the Refah-led government in the phraseology of the "Third Worldism" and a new anti-Western agenda. After his visit to the "pariah" regime of Nigeria met with considerable domestic criticism, Erbakan cancelled a planned visit to Sudan. In response to these deviations from a pro-Western orientation, the military increased its pressure on Erbakan's government. Meanwhile, there were increasing tensions with Syria over PKK guerrilla bases and the presence of Abdullah Ocalan in his headquarters in Damascus, and Turkey desired assurances that the Israeli government would not sign a separate peace treaty with Syria. In the middle of January 1996, Onur Oymen, foreign ministry under-secretary, came to Israel and received assurances from Prime Minister Shimon Peres that a peace deal between Syria and Israel could not be signed unless the support of Damascus for terrorist organizations, including the outlawed Kurdistan Workers' Party (PKK), was "completely cut."[60] Then Turkish Foreign Minister Ciller publicly expressed gratitude to

Israel, and the ministry officials remarked on the singular importance of the Turkish–Israeli relationship. Onur Oymen stated that talks with the Israeli leadership were "much more important than had been expected."[61]

Nevertheless, conflict between the Turkish military and the Islamist government erupted after the Sincan incident in the spring of 1997. On February 7, 1997, the Iranian ambassador, Muhammed Bagheri, was invited by the Refah mayor Bakir Yildiz to speak on the "Jerusalem Day" in Sincan, near Ankara. During his speech, Bagheri threatened that "those who signed agreements with the United States and Israel would, sooner or later, be penalized by Turkish youths."[62] Several days later, the army demonstrated its position toward the Refah Party by sending a unit of tanks to Sincan "en route to exercises." Shortly after that event, the mayor was arrested and the Iranian ambassador was declared persona non grata and had to leave Turkey.[63] The increasing polarization within Erbakan's cabinet over the direction of foreign policy, especially between the Refah leadership and the Dogru Yol faction led by Foreign Minister Tansu Ciller, allowed the generals to step in and fill the vacuum.[64] The Turkish military submitted a text with eighteen recommendations to be implemented by the Erbakan government during the meeting of the National Security Council on February 28, 1997. In order to remonstrate against the activation of a more radical wing of the ruling party, Turkish Chief of General Staff Ismail Karadayi proceeded on his four-day visit to Israel without notifying the Turkish government. Hakan Yavuz argues that the timing of the General's visit was chosen in order to stem Erbakan's shift toward "Islamic foreign policy."[65] Meanwhile, General Çevik Bir came to the United States and addressed the Jewish Institute for National Strategic Affairs (JINSA). At the briefing, Bir stated that Turkish General Ismail Karadayi's visit to Israel would surely pave the way for greater cooperation between the two democracies, something for which the United States would show support.[66] On February 28, 1997, members of the Turkish general staff convened the National Security Council (NSC) and passed a 20-point plan aimed at combating Islamist movements and preserving Turkey's secular regime.[67] The NSC blueprint called specifically on the government to implement (a) closure of illegal Quranic schools and Imam Hatips; (b) the declaration of "anti-secular" activities illegal; (c) the cessation of recruitment of Islamists into government jobs; (d) close surveillance of religious vakf and Islamist-owned businesses.[68] This series of recommendations included the following: "Acts against Turkey's democratic, secular system based on the supremacy of the law should not be tolerated under any means," and "Koranic [sic] schools in the hands of fundamentalists should be closed and those of such schools that are necessary should be attached to the Ministry for Education."[69] The "February 28 recommendations" also singled out Iran as a state attempting to undermine the secular republican regime in Turkey. One of the recommendations indicated: "Iran's efforts at trying to destabilize Turkey's regime should be followed carefully and where necessary countered."[70] The authority of the army was not to be questioned, as the following stated: "Personal attacks against the integrity of the Turkish Armed Forces are seen to have increased of late. Such attacks should be prevented."[71] And finally, the exclusion of Islamists from the ranks of the army and civil service was indicated in the following directive: "Officers discharged from the armed forces for fundamentalist activities should not be given employment by sympathetic municipalities or in the civil service."[72] As the military and government clashed, the generals engaged in diplomatic posturing. In order to demonstrate their anti-Islamist inclinations and their commitment to the irreversible character of the Turkish–Israeli entente, the military hosted Israeli Foreign Minister David Levy in the midst of these confrontations with the Erbakan government on April 6–9, 1997.[73] The Turkish military asked David Levy for direct Israeli intercession in Washington to release embargoed American weapons systems. To Refah's chagrin, its leader was forced to sign a free trade agreement with Israel.[74] Following this step, the military did not relinquish their public attack on the government. In the end of April, the Turkish general staff released a new Concept of National Military Strategy (CNMS), which branded Islamic movements inside Turkey as "Enemy No. 1," with Kurdish separatism taking second place.[75] Hakan Yavuz concludes about the link between Turkish military relations with Israel and the domestic struggle between the Turkish military and the Islamist government: "What is beyond question is that the military's vigorous pursuit of relations with Israel was in part calculated to embarrass a government whose head had called openly for a break in those ties. By forging ever closer links with Israel, the generals 'turned foreign policy into a domestic political football' and challenged Erbakan to defy them: Erbakan, aware of his powerlessness vis-à-vis the military, reluctantly acquiesced."[76] Rumors of an impending military intervention were circulated in the Turkish media. Eventually, the military prevailed without firing a single shot. At an emergency meeting of the NSC at the end of May, Erbakan's performance implementing the February 28 recommendations was judged a failure, and the first Islamist government in Turkey stepped down.

Meanwhile, at its Copenhagen meeting, the European Commission imposed several preconditions on Turkey for opening EU membership negotiations, which became known as the Copenhagen Criteria. One of the key prerequisites for membership in the European Union was the normalization of civilian–military relations or, in Turkey's case, a reversal of roles in the traditional "unwritten" arrangement between the military and civilian authorities. Specifically, the European Commission expected the Turkish government to enforce diminution of the role of the military in society as well as its subordination to civilian authorities. In order to bring the constitutional arrangement in Turkey closer to European standards, Bullent Ecevit's government adopted a constitutional amendment in October 2001. This amendment provides for a civilian majority in the National Security Council.[77] This was the first constitutional assault on the "shadow" power of the military in Turkish society.

With the Islamist AK Party forming the majority in Turkish parliament following the national elections of November 2002, the issue of the military's stranglehold on foreign policy, in particular regarding the maintenance of the entente with Israel and the blockade of Armenia, re-emerged. In March 2003, Tayip Erdogan, the leader of the AK Party and a former Islamist mayor of Istanbul, was elected head of the Turkish government. Some commentators expressed the view that Erdogan's government used the EU's "harmonization packages" as a ruse to coax control of the "real" reins of power out of the hands of the Kemalist establishment and the army.[78] The seventh harmonization package, adopted by the AKP government in the summer of 2003, dealt directly with civilian–military relations and clearly circumscribed the role of the military in the political process. Barak Salmoni expressed a sentiment shared among American and Israeli policymakers,when he stated: "new limitations on the Turkish Armed Forces' [TSK] interference in civilian politics to protect secularism raise darker questions: Are we witnessing the beginning of the AKP's larger game of hijacking the state through democratic procedures to alter society away from Kemalist secularism and toward socio-political Islam?"[79] If these fears were based on reality, the ensuing limitation of the role of the military in formulation of Turkish foreign policy would have direct negative consequences for the Turkish–Israeli strategic relationship. However, this scenario has not yet materialized. The National Security Council (known as MGK in Turkish) institutional reforms included in the seventh harmonization package prescribed nomination of a civilian head and established civilian majority rule in decision-making, along with the elimination of secrecy in personnel and appointments. The first civilian head of the MGK, Secretary-General Yigit Alpogan, indicated that the National Security Council had turned into a "'think-tank'-like institution, which prepares political papers for council members and state institutions, after the structural reforms."[80] Alpogan stated that MGK had not turned into an executive body but an advisory one.[81] Referring to the updated National Security Strategy Document, which outlines security challenges and foreign policy objectives, Alpogan said, "I do not see anything exciting in the document." As he later stated at a Washington conference, the new MGK preserved the strategic priorities of Turkish foreign policy, namely: (a) integration into the EU; and (b) further development of strategic relationships with the United States and Israel.[82] In fact, in January of 2004, Turkish Foreign Minister Abdullah Gul discussed in Baku a joint project to supply Azerbaijan with military hardware manufactured in Turkey with Israeli electronic components, created for a joint Israeli–Turkish arms effort.[83]

Israel

The Israeli military–industrial complex was the main motivator or driver of Israel's participation in the Turkish–Israeli entente and involvement of Azerbaijan as a junior partner. This section briefly outlines the structure, policy process and concrete contributions of the Israeli defense sector to the strategic axis under investigation. The military–industrial complex (MIC) in the Jewish state has a multifaceted structure. According to Alex Minz, the structure consists of the core (Israeli Defense Forces [IDF], intelligence branches, i.e. Mossad, Shin Bet) and associate members (the civilian Ministry of Defense, and defense industries, both state- and privately-owned).[84] Another Israeli expert, Yoram Peri, subdivides the MIC structure into three components according to their relationship to the Ministry of Defense. The first component includes R&D organizations such as Raphael, the Armaments Development Authority, and Ta'as or the Israel Military Industry (IMI) that comprise a part of the Ministry. This component is responsible to the civilian director general of the Ministry and the chief of staff of the IDF. The second component is made of state military firms, the Israel Aircraft Industries being the largest. Third, there are subcontracting firms, which provide parts to the state military firms.[85] The state, in other words, dominates the military-related industries and has complete control over them. Between 1973 and the 1980s, growth in this industry was so high that it employed a major part of all Israeli skilled labor and was the main source of foreign currency.[86] This was indicative of "the centrality of security" in the economic, political and even social spheres of the State of Israel. Reiser argues that, "Due to these developments, the definition of security has broadened and begun to encompass economic, social, foreign policy, and even psychological factors."[87] The two major military successes of the Israeli Defense Forces in 1956 and 1967 raised the prestige of Israeli arms. Israeli arms exports grew significantly from several million in 1956 to between $12 and $15 million in 1966, and then doubled in one year to $30 million in 1967.[88] During this period, secret military relationships with Ethiopia, Turkey and Iran, known as the Periphery Alliance, were established.[89] Since that engagement, Israel has come to rely on arms sales as an instrument of foreign policy.[90] Israeli authorities tried to make sales in a clandestine manner in order to prevent political crises in relations with some of their more "sensitive" clients.[91] At the time, Israel was gaining many advantages in military R&D from cooperation with and military and nuclear technology transfers from France, but in 1967 this cooperation abruptly ended. Self-reliance, cutting-edge research and innovation in military hardware were the fundamental values propagated by the Jewish state, especially after "the 1967 French embargo."[92] In order to enhance the autonomy of the Israeli Air Force, a project to build an Israeli-made multi-purpose jet fighter known as Lavi ("Young Lion") was undertaken in the 1970s. The development of an air industry project of such scale strained the Israeli treasury. Allocations for the purchase and development of other military hardware had to be shifted to the Lavi project. This fact is relevant to the future of Israeli–Turkish defense cooperation because at that time, Israel Air Industries (IAI) was forced to "reengine" [sic] and retrofit older American F-4 jets for the Turkish Air Force fleet.[93] This experience proved to be valuable when Israel offered to retrofit a significant fleet of Turkish F-4s in the 1990s. The upgrade of 26 F-4 jets by IAI began in 1997, and it was scheduled to be completed in February 2003.[94]

After economic austerity measures were introduced in the 1980s, the Lavi project, previously considered a potential strategic asset and the embodiment of Israeli superiority in avionic technology, folded.[95] A national financial crisis and cuts in military spending compelled the Israeli defense industry to concentrate even more on production of military hardware and aircraft for exports. The technological edge gained by developing the Lavi project translated into the introduction of many technological innovations in such fields as military electronics, advanced communications and command and control systems. This advancement made Israel very competitive in the international arms market.[96] At the same time, Israel developed expertise in another pioneering field—remote-piloted vehicles, known today as Unmanned Aerial Vehicles (UAVs). These high-tech advances in military hardware made the Israeli defense industry an especially desirable partner for the Turkish Defense Forces. This circumstance gained even higher prominence in the mid-1990s, when Turkey experienced a series of arms sales embargoes imposed first by European countries (France, Italy, Germany, Great Britain) and then the United States.[97] From the 1970s, arms exports outpaced most other industrial sectors as a source of foreign currency for the Israeli economy. By 1988 it is estimated this sector of exports brought $2 billion to the Israeli treasury in one year alone.[98] The two largest Israeli companies, IAI and Tadiran, concentrated 50 to 70 percent of their productive capacity on arms exports.[99] In this context, the military entente with Turkey turned out to be a win-win situation for Israel, both politically and economically.

Since its foundation in 1948, the Israeli Defense Forces (IDF), the armed forces of Israel, have played a unique role in the young Jewish state. Ben Meir explains complex civilian–military relations in the Israeli polity using a fusionist theory of administration that emphasizes "military involvement instead of military intervention, and a consideration of sides—civilian and military—of the involvement equation."[100] Constitutional provisions of the Military Jurisdiction Law of 1955 established a precedent that granted significant autonomy to the chief of general staff from the civilian administration.[101] This status contradicted the vision of the founder of Israel, David Ben-Gurion, who stated, "the army is not to determine by itself even its own structure, procedure and its policies."[102] The expanded autonomy of the army had bearing on many aspects of civilian authority, including foreign policy.[103] In particular, this unique character of civilian–military relations had direct implications for such sensitive areas as foreign defense procurement and sales, technology and intelligence transfer, and the training of foreign military and security personnel. As a legislative body in a democracy, the Knesset, the Israeli parliament, possesses the power of the purse and performs political and supervisory functions over matters of defense, security and foreign policy. Due to secrecy considerations, only members of the permanent Foreign Affairs and Defense Committee (FDAC) of the Knesset have authority and access to these areas of decision-making. Even though the effectiveness of parliamentary control over the military and security forces through FDAC improved in the 1990s, the policy dictum of former Israeli President Yitzhak Navon (1978–84) still determines its rather limited role. Navon, who served as chairman of FDAC (1974–7), said: "The IDF draws its own conclusions and continually examines the problems it faces. It improves all the time, and does not need advice from anybody outside."[104] Ben-Gurion envisioned that there would be a clear separation between the military component (IDF) and the civilian component (Ministry of Defense) in the military–security apparatus. In 1953, the first Israeli prime minister introduced cabinet guidelines in which the IDF is assigned the role of fighting and preparing for war, whereas the Ministry of Defense (MOD) deals with the fiscal and support systems, namely procurement and production of weapon systems, construction, etc.[105] But no formal legal structure was devised to provide a legal or normative basis for this division of authority, and it left a wide gray area open to different interpretations and subversion.[106] Ben Meir concludes, "Over the years, mainly as a result of the many wars Israel had to fight, the IDF has slowly but surely encroached on the MOD's domain."[107] Due to its expertise and a large number of staff, the IDF became intrinsically involved in all stages of procurement and export of military airplanes, tanks, weapons and other high-tech systems. Even though MOD has a special directorate tasked with this function, the IDF stands to gain budgetary allocations when Israeli-produced weapons and other security-related systems are exported to third countries. In other words, the IDF derives particular benefits from increases in defense and security-related exports because IDF is directly involved in marketing surplus military equipment. Another aspect of Israel's foreign and security policy needs to be elucidated in order to account for the pervasive role of the military in planning and maintaining the alignment between Turkey, Israel and Azerbaijan. In Israel, it is the military that performs the function of strategic foreign policy planning in the government. More importantly the planning branch of the IDF general staff carries out this traditionally civilian function of strategic planning.[108]

This aspect of IDF responsibilities has particular relevance to the history of the triangular relationship with Turkey and Azerbaijan. One of the key personalities in this strategic involvement on the Israeli side was David Ivri (born in 1934). The ninth commander of the Israeli Air Force and former deputy chief of general staff, Ivri joined the MOD as director general in the late 1980s.[109] He was an intimate of two Israeli defense ministers: Yitzhak Rabin (1984–90) and Moshe Arens (1990–2), both of whom were directly involved in negotiations for American–Israeli military technology transfers, especially sales of advanced F-16 jet fighters.[110] Both Rabin and Arens were staunch proponents of the Turkish–Israeli entente. In his service record, David

Ivri exemplified the fusion of military background with civilian authority as the prerequisite for membership in higher echelons of Israeli government. When he became director general, he firmly imposed his authority and clearly outlined his MOD prerogatives: "There are times when the IDF tries to intervene in matters in which it has no business, such as procurement, or negotiations with foreign firms. I am not willing to accept this. We are dealing with [what should be] a clear-cut division of authority and responsibility with regard to procurement and development of future over military exports."[111] Ivri initiated institutional reforms in the Ministry of Defense to strengthen civilian control over many aspects of foreign policy and defense strategy, restoring MOD's ability to direct and control military procurement and exports.[112] Critically, David Ivri pursued strategic entente with Turkey starting in the early 1990s. He later served as the Israeli ambassador to the United States from 2000 to 2002.[113]

David Ivri, who served under Defense Minister Yitzhak Rabin, extended considerable efforts to enhance military-to-military links with Turkey shortly after the Israeli withdrawal from Beirut in 1985.[114] Later, when Rabin served as prime minister, Ivri worked as a go-between to the Turkish military. Until his death in November 1995, Prime Minister Rabin cherished the vision of a ring of stable states in the Middle East based upon the rapprochement with Turkey.[115] Nevertheless, it is important to realize that there was bi-partisan consensus in the Israeli political and military establishment about the strategic value of close engagement with Turkey. In the 1990s, Likud Prime Minister Yitzhak Shamir (the former leader of militant Stern Gang), Labour Prime Ministers Rabin (former defense minister) and Shimon Peres (former director general of the Ministry of Defense), Benjamin Netanyahu of Likud (former officer of the elite reconnaissance unit),[116] Labour's Ehud Barak (former commander of the elite reconnaissance unit and chief of staff) and Prime Minister Ariel Sharon (former chief of staff, defense minister and foreign minister) were all engaged in efforts to nurture this relationship.[117]

In 1997, after the showdown with Islamist Prime Minister Erbakan, the Turkish side opened talks about procurement and co-production of long-range missiles with Israel. In October of that year, Israeli Chief of Staff Amnon Lipkin-Shahak came to Turkey and conducted sensitive negotiations about the joint production of a military satellite and the long-range missile Delila. This offer provoked great interest in the Turkish military because the Russians declared their intention to deploy Russian S-300 air defense missiles in Cyprus.[118] The Israeli company Raphael expressed readiness to sell Python-2 air-to-air missiles.[119] But more significant was the 1998 Israeli initiative to supply Turkey with a new anti-missile defense system, called Hetz ("Arrow"), co-designed with the United States. Israel offered to receive American authorization for transfer of this technology to Turkey.[120] The system was tested, with the participation of Israel and the United States, during the Anatolian Eagle exercises in Turkey in 2001.[121] Despite the demands of Islamists, the Turkish government renewed its commitment to modernize M-60A1 tanks, contracting an Israeli firm for work worth $688 million.[122] Besides the transfer of military technologies, both countries participate in joint strategic threat-assessment simulations and analyses.[123]

In 2002, annual military exports from Israel to Turkey reached $1 billion. Even after election of the AK Party in November 2002, both countries confirmed their intentions to continue cooperation in the areas of defense and security. This shared commitment to cooperate in the fight against "international terrorism" was reiterated by the Turkish Defense Minister Vekti Gonul and his Israeli counterpart, Shaul Mofaz, during exchange visits in 2003. Robust cooperation between the two countries in anti-terrorist activities was positively evaluated at a joint session of JINSA/Assembly of Turkish American Associations (ATAA), which took place in Washington in October 2003. The joint JINSA/ATAA publication concludes: "In Turkish efforts to combat PKK, the support of Israel has exceptional significance. The Israeli intelligence is active in Northern Iraq for more than 30 years and has close contacts with Kurdish organizations in the region."[124] As this statement indicates, the cooperation between Turkey and Israel goes well beyond the borders of the two countries. Bilateral consultations have been increased with a view to broadening cooperation in an area spanning the Caucasus, Central Asia, the Eastern Mediterranean and the Balkans.[125]

Despite Prime Minister Erdogan's public criticism of Israeli policy toward Palestinians and even branding Israel a "terrorist state," the AKP government military continued business as usual in the area of military cooperation. During his visit to Jerusalem on May 1, 2005, the Turkish leader discussed with Prime Minister Sharon a new deal to upgrade about 30 F-4 Phantoms belonging to the Turkish air force, at a cost of $400–500 million. Two weeks prior, a deal had been signed to sell Israeli-made long-range Heron drones (UAVs) to the Turkish air force. It was planned that Israel Aircraft Industries would supply the planes and Elbit Systems would provide the communications and monitoring systems to the Turkish armed forces in a deal worth $200 million. This was followed by finalizing plans for modernization of 170 Turkish M-60 tanks by Israeli IMI. A one-year agreement was signed with IMI on March 27, 2005.[126]

The role of the Turkish army and Israeli security apparatus in the Turkish–Israeli–Azerbaijani strategic relationship

This section explores the more ambiguous Turkish–Israeli–Azerbaijani "strategic relationship" and the role of the Turkish military and Israeli security forces in it. As far as Turkish–Azerbaijani cooperation, it was the military-to-military relations between Turkey and Azerbaijan that played a paramount role in Turkish strategy toward the South Caucasus in the 1990s. Since the independence of Azerbaijan (1991), Turkey became a strategic ally of this fellow Turkic nation. Turkey assisted Azerbaijan's armed forces in transition from a Soviet colonial holdover to an independent Turkic nation.

Azerbaijan

As a small state still in the throes of nation building, Azerbaijan found itself in a state of war with Armenia over the Nagorno-Karabagh region. As a result, Azerbaijan's foreign policy assigns the highest priority to enhancing the state's security and increasing its defense capabilities. Azerbaijani strategic cooperation with Turkey, and to a lesser degree with Israel, constituted the dominant vector of the country's foreign security policy for the most of 1990s.[127] The importance of the security aspects of Azerbaijani–Turkish relations is signified by the participation of Defense Minister Safar Abiyev in all summit meetings with the Turkish leadership.

Upon gaining independence, Azerbaijan inherited a large cache of Soviet military hardware. Three fully equipped Soviet air force bases were turned over to Azerbaijani authorities. Azerbaijan came into possession of 30 Su-24 bombers in central Azerbaijan, a reconnaissance regiment of 30 Su-24/Fencer and Mig-25/Foxbat airplanes at the Dallar air base, and a ground attack regiment of 30 Su-25/Frogfoot airplanes at Sital-Chay base.[128] According to Elkhan Mekhtiev, the Azerbaijani air force, numbering 8,000 in personnel, has the most educated and professional staff in the Azerbaijani army today.[129] Air defense is based on Soviet surface-to-air missiles of the SA-4/-8/-13 types. The Ganje base preserved a helicopter assault regiment made up of Mi24 and Mi-8 helicopters.[130] Azerbaijan also acquired a fleet of outdated T-55 Soviet tanks, followed later by the purchase of 136 tanks.[131] The Azerbaijani navy primarily is deployed in the Baku harbor. Its 2,000 men operate Soviet-made surface combatants, frigates, patrol and coastal combatants, missile craft, mine countermeasures, amphibious and support and other naval units received from the Caspian flotilla.[132]

Azerbaijan joined NATO's Partnership for Peace framework in May 1994. This act, in the middle of the cease-fire negotiations conducted between the warring parties in the Nagorno-Karabagh conflict, signalled Azerbaijan's intention to leave the Russian sphere of influence and join the Euro–Atlantic alliance. This intention took concrete form when, during the negotiations of the CFE (Conventional Forces in Europe) Flank Document, Azerbaijan insisted on special provisions that debar Russia from stationing its troops on Azerbaijani territory. This international document was signed with American backing in May of 1997.[133] Since the Sintra (Portugal) meeting, on May 30, 1997, Azerbaijan has participated in the 16+1 annual security dialogue with NATO. After joining the GUAM bloc, Azerbaijan was also involved in separate talks between NATO and the GUAM countries.[134] Azerbaijani foreign ministry officials confirmed their commitment to pursue bilateral relations with

NATO and its member countries at the Euro–Atlantic Partnership Council meeting in Brussels in 1998.[135]

Since NATO was noncommittal about restoring Azerbaijani territorial integrity, violated by the Armenian occupation of 20 percent of its territory, Azerbaijan sought to develop bilateral strategic relations. The most vital conduit of NATO's military assistance to Azerbaijan became Turkey. Turkish–Azerbaijani strategic and military cooperation bestows particular depth to the relations between the two countries. Both countries formed the joint Askeri Is Birligi Koordinasyon Kurulu ("Council on Military Cooperation"), with its office in Baku. This institution coordinates the training of Azerbaijani officers in Turkey and in Azerbaijan.[136] The Turkish general staff joined the US Department of Defense in establishing a working group to enhance military cooperation between the NATO countries and the countries of the Caucasus.[137] According to an Armenian expert, "The military ideology and doctrine of Azerbaijan was created by Turkey, which was practically involved in the formation of the armed forces and security forces of Azerbaijan."[138] Azerbaijani military leadership determined in the mid-1990s to adopt the Turkish military doctrine because it allowed them to solve their biggest challenge, i.e. formation of a Western-educated higher echelon in the newly established national army. A large number of Azerbaijani officers have been trained in Turkish military academies since 1992. The Turkish authorities in the period of Suleyman Demirel's presidency made a security commitment to Azerbaijan in May of 1999. In fact, Igor Muradian claims that the "military–political capital of Azerbaijan should be considered as the 'Eastern corps' of the Turkish Armed Forces."[139] According to the same expert, the Aliyev-Demirel agreement has the following provisions:

(a)   Azerbaijan cannot make unilateral decisions about the use of military force without permission of Turkey;
(b)   Turkey guarantees the security of Azerbaijan in the case of aggression and will provide military and political assistance to Azerbaijan in the case of hostilities;
(c)   The strategic cooperation between the two countries designates the three enemies: Russia, Iran and Armenia.[140]

The ideological aspect of this assistance cannot be overestimated. The Turkish military doctrine was revived in the new Azerbaijani army. The historical memory of Turkish military aid during the struggle for establishment of the Democratic Republic of Azerbaijan in 1918 becomes a cornerstone of official military ideology.[141] This was an important aspect of the consciousness raising and the new officer corps training. "Turkism" became the ideological bridge between the two nations. This military aid was critically important for the young nation's armed forces reeling as they were from their defeat by better-trained and organized Armenian forces in the conflict over Nagorno-Karabagh. The Azerbaijani armed forces also received institutional assistance within the framework of NATO's Partnership for Peace Program. The Turkish army was assigned by NATO to mentor and facilitate the transition of the Azerbaijani army to Western standards and military doctrine. The Turkish intelligence services were also unrivalled in shaping the reorientation of Azerbaijani security services from Moscow to Ankara and Washington. For Azerbaijan, the most important outcome of the strategic relationship with Turkey was the security guarantee contained in the Aliyev-Demirel agreement.

In March 2001, President Heydar Aliyev, during his visit to Ankara, requested enhanced military assistance to Azerbaijan. During the same visit, Azerbaijani Defense Minister Safar Abiyev and the president's top foreign policy aide Novruz Mammadov announced that Turkish military officials agreed to back Azerbaijan in case of a new war over Nagorno-Karabagh "with both personnel and equipment."[142] But the Turkish–Azerbaijani military cooperation appears to have stumbled over President Aliyev's decision to grant Russia basing rights at the Gabala strategic radar station. Ankara considered the move to be "against Turkey" and a "deviation from [Azerbaijan's] policies, foreseeing an opening to the West."[143]

The Soviet-era radar installation called Daryal RLS (Radio-Lokatsionnaya Stantsya) was built in the early 1980s in the Gabala district. It has been on combat duty since February 1985. It served as an early warning system for ballistic missile attacks for the southern periphery of the Soviet Union. In particular, Daryal covers the Middle East and the aquatorium of the Indian Ocean. After Azerbaijani independence, the ownership and status of the Gabala radar became a contentious issue between Russia and Azerbaijan. Azerbaijan realizes the global security implications of the station, because it serves as a node of the Russian anti-missile defense system. Heydar Aliyev commented on the future status of the Gabala radar: "In any case, since obtaining state independence Azerbaijan agreed to the existence of the Gabala radar station and we proceed from the view that it is a question of preventing strategic missile attacks." This prevented any speculation that the territory of the strategic installation could be expanded into a Russian military base.[144] Several rounds of talks were conducted about the status and the leasing terms of the facility. As a result of the rapprochement with President Putin in January 2002, the Azerbaijani and Russian sides concluded an agreement for extension of the Gabala radar station's Russian lease for another ten years.[145] Since this action legitimizes the Russian "military presence" on Azerbaijani soil, it caused a strong negative reaction from the Turkish military.[146] The Israeli Russian-language daily *Novosty Nedeli* reported that Israel and Russia had reached an agreement in the wake of the second Gulf war that Russia would provide warning to Israel in case of Iraqi missile attacks, using the Daryal missile defense facility The implication of this Russian–Israeli understanding is that the Azerbaijani government authorized such information sharing.[147] Meanwhile, Israel expressed interest in leasing the Gabala radar station after the Russian lease expires.[148] Despite the contentious issue of the Russian operation of the Gabala radar, in September of 2002 the Azerbaijani defense minister and a representative of the Turkish general staff, Major General Kaya, met to appraise their military cooperation in bringing the Azerbaijani armed forces to the NATO standards and officer training. After signing a protocol about Turkish military aid to Azerbaijan, the Turkish general said: "Turkey will continue to give military support of all kind to the Azerbaijani army in the future."[149]

According to one Armenian author, the Turkish Intelligence Service (Milli Istihbarat Teskilati, or MIT) and Military Intelligence were involved in training and ideological indoctrination of Azerbaijani security services from the time the country gained its independence. MIT's activities are controlled solely by the head of the government. The president, with the approval of the prime minister, nominates the Turkish Intelligence Service's head. Starting in 1992 the agency was headed by Senmez Kensal. This government official participates in the National Security Council and advises the prime minister. The ideals of pan-Turkism and the strong unitary Turkish state formed the ideological foundation of MIT's activities. Muradian observes: "The emphasis in training of intelligence officers is placed on the indoctrination of extreme nationalism and pan-Turkism. During psychological immersion sessions, special attention is paid to the internalization by the trainees of the deep faith in the 'Mission of Pan-Turkism' and ability to disseminate these views among the Turkic-speaking populations."[150] The Turkish security forces coordinate a local Azerbaijani nationalist network, Boz Kurtlar, an affiliate of Milliyetci Hareket Partisi in Turkey. MIT set up training centers to instruct Azerbaijani Special Forces in the village of Pozdek, and the Baku suburbs Nasosny and Shihovo in 1994.[151] During the 1989–93 period, Turkish security services supported the Azerbaijani Popular Front. The Turkish military and security establishment felt that Heydar Aliyev usurped power from the openly pan-Turkist Azerbaijani President Abulfaz Elchibey. But after the failure of the anti-Heydar Aliyev coup in the spring of 1995, the Turkish establishment switched sides for pragmatic reasons and opened channels to the Azerbaijani government. Muradian argues that Turkey developed special relationships with the ruling regional clan of Nakhichevan-Yerivanli as the main protector of its interests.[152] After the conclusion of the military cooperation agreement in 1996, a joint intelligence center was also established in Baku.[153]

Azerbaijan–Israel linkages

Support for the creation of the then triple military–political alliance with Turkey and Israel was widely shared by the Azerbaijani public in the 1990s. This axis was encouraged by the United States following the dissolution of the Soviet Union. This strategic alignment became the topic of high-level discussions with Heydar Aliyev during a visit by Israel's deputy defense minister, Efraim Sneh, to Baku in 1999.[154] The Azerbaijani foreign ministry has also sought to establish an institutional mechanism for strengthening Azerbaijani–Israeli strategic cooperation since the 1990s. The foreign ministry official explained that the Azerbaijani side offered to establish a bilateral strategic dialogue with Israel on the model of the security dialogue with NATO. The Israeli side expressed interest in this initiative in the aftermath of September 11, but the worsening climate in the Middle East and the Second Intifada diminished Azerbaijani willingness to participate in such dialogue in view of its commitments to the Organization of Islamic Conference. This international backdrop, however, did not prevent secret Israeli transfers of military equipment and training of Azerbaijani security forces. According to one source, Israel sent 140 military and security advisors to Azerbaijan.[155] In the meantime, Turkish foreign ministry officials and security personnel have conducted consultations in Israel and briefed appropriate Israeli authorities about Turkish activities in Azerbaijan since 1994. Israeli security services also cooperated with Azerbaijani Ministry State Security in providing general assistance in its anti-terrorist activities.[156]

Strategic relations between Azerbaijan and Israel never reached their full potential for a variety of reasons. Assessing the status of the strategic relationship with Israel in July 2004, an Azerbaijani foreign ministry official commented: "The reasons may be different, but one major reason is a difference in size between Azerbaijan and Turkey. The capacity of Turkish military to pay dealers for a piece of weapon . . . is a major factor. Also an advanced level of development of the American–Turkish, on the one hand, and the American–Israeli relations, on the other hand, is also an important factor. It brings relations between Turkey and Israel to a certain value [sic] where relations between Israel and Azerbaijan are not yet there."[157] However, an infusion of capital into the Azerbaijani treasury from burgeoning oil exports complemented by high oil prices in the world market, after the 2002 American invasion of Iraq, might tip the balance in higher investments into the South Caucasian nation's military capabilities.

4 Foreign policy and its discontents in the age of globalization

Informal networks and transnational levers

Introduction: informal networks in the networked world: state agent drivers and non-state levers

This section will analyze the ascendant impact of transnational factors on mutual relations of the institutional superstructure of the strategic relations between Turkey, Israel and Azerbaijan. This section aims to explain empirically how epistemic communities contributed to the evolving Turkish–Israeli–Azerbaijani entente. Moreover, the epistemic communities to a great extent shaped this framework. The increasing significance of transnational "informal networks," in particular the "American Jewish lobby," will be highlighted as the "fourth pillar" of this trilateral relationship. The role of epistemic communities in the three countries will be elaborated. Lastly, the effect on the trilateral relationship of "transnational levers," such as transnational corporations and transnational diaspora organizations, will be explored.

Every policy process is embedded in a certain conceptual framework. This section aims to explain empirically how epistemic communities contributed to the evolving Turkish–Israeli–Azerbaijani entente. As Antoniades argues, the foreign policy making process is based on a particular understanding of reality. The foreign policy epistemic community circumscribes the broad outlines of this reality.[1] Antoniades states, "As long as 'reality' is mainly knowledge about this 'reality,' those players who possess and control knowledge have a dominant role in the game."[2] Thus, a raison d'etre of epistemic communities is their ability to impose discourse on decision makers and the general public.[3] Epistemic communities are in engaged in what a senior Israeli diplomat calls "political image-making." He argues that: "The stuff of political image-making is political 'news.' Ultimately, this news is about power—the institutions in which power reposes, and the people who control them. It is the real or perceived link with 'power' that makes a 'source' interesting in the press."[4]

However, epistemic communities do not exist outside social reality. Following E.H. Carr's conclusion that "the historian, before he begins to write history, is the product of history,"[5] Antoniades points out that "epistemic communities prior to influencing social reality, are a product of this reality."[6] For instance, one can observe that the role American Jewish organizations have played in determining American foreign policy toward the Middle East since the end of World War II has become embedded in the process. A highly educated and politically active group, American Jewry became an important pillar of American foreign policy making in the Middle East. Throughout the history of the modern State of Israel, American Jewish organizations affected the change from the earlier American orientation toward oil-producing Arab regimes like Saudi Arabia in the 1920s–1930s toward forging an alliance with Israel in the 1960s. But American Jewish support extended beyond US–Israeli relations. The American Jewish lobby also positively impacted US policy toward the states in which Israel's interests were involved.[7]

From tanks to think tanks: the Jewish connection

This section will focus on the role that Israel-oriented foreign policy think tanks and the American Jewish lobby in Washington played and continue to play in the creation and maintenance of the trilateral relationship between Israel, Turkey and Azerbaijan. This section does not claim that the American Jewish lobby single-handedly affected the US strategic interest in promoting the Israel–Turkey–Azerbaijan axis. However, it argues that this amalgam of intellectual and political networks, known as an epistemic community, did not play a merely subservient or functional role but rather served as a fourth pillar of this relationship, as an essential conduit for its promotion, and the back channel for diplomatic efforts between the respective countries. It will explore the ascendancy of foreign policy think tanks as an example of epistemic-community influence in the formulation of American foreign policy in the greater Middle East. This epistemic community aimed to direct discourse to rational need for the creation of the Turkey–Israel–Azerbaijan axis in Washington. Lastly, it will explore the impact of some of the Middle East foreign policy think tanks and the American Jewish lobby in Washington on the maintenance of this relationship.

A point to be made here is that "lobbies"—whether ethnic or otherwise— are much more important in the determination of public policy in the US than in other democracies, such as the UK, where party policy positions are much more firmly established and party leaders normally have control over their back-benchers. Hence, members of European legislatures are much less open to individual persuasion by lobbyists or think tanks than their counterparts in Washington.

According to pluralist theory, polyarchy, i.e. the rule of the many, is a fact of political development in a democratic and pluralist society.[8] Indeed, the major waves of immigration, namely the earlier Irish, Italian and Northern European and the later Eastern European and Jewish emigration, drastically changed the composition of American society. As a result, ethnic American organizations represent one of the vital strands of the American political system. Waxman concluded, "The perception that Israel commands the support of world Jewry has led numerous foreign governments to view good relations with Israel as a means to obtain international aid and investments." Foreign governments never questioned the Jewish identity of the State of Israel. This perception served Israeli foreign policy and provided an indispensable source of "soft power."

Since the 1960s, a number of ethnic organizations in America have demonstrated increasing activism toward American foreign policy. These include Irish, Italian, Greek, Armenian, Hispanic and African American communities, and many others.[9] Turkish and Azerbaijani communities only very recently realized the potential of ethnic lobbying in the American political process. One pertinent illustration can show how an ethnic lobby was able to profoundly affect American foreign policy. It refers to the effect of the Greek American lobby on the situation in Cyprus during the 1974 crisis. For the first time during the Cold War, the Greek lobby was able to change America's even-handed approach toward its NATO allies in the Balkans and the Near East. As a result of the pressure exerted on the US Congress, an arms embargo was imposed on Turkey. This action profoundly affected the geopolitical balance in favor of Greece in the eastern Mediterranean.[10]

The policy communities involved in foreign policy are tasked with defining "what is 'the real' situation" and establishing structural constraints. In this regard the control of discourse in the policy-relevant institutions and media is crucial. Having a strategic role in the construction of social reality, epistemic communities create and reproduce the language that is used to describe and explain this reality.[11] The given epistemic community membership in some cases involves direct participation in the policy process as members of executive or representative branches of the US government. Accordingly, they also perform an important task relevant to the foreign policy area by playing a significant role in the way in which states decipher their environment and define their interest. This section will discuss the role that epistemic communities play in shaping and maintaining this trilateral relationship.

Cross-membership between branches of the government and policy institutes known as think tanks, consultancies and media outlets serves as a second channel for transmission of ideas, information and knowledge. In this way epistemic communities influence foreign and international policy indirectly.[12] When members of epistemic communities gain positions in the government or the bureaucracy, they can determine policy choices directly on the basis of their philosophical or ideological commitments. But the saliency of epistemic communities rises in particular when the international environment is in a state of flux (the end of the Cold War being an obvious instance), because the decision makers are faced with simultaneous challenges of complexity, uncertainty and crisis.[13] Under conditions of complex policymaking, epistemic communities are strategically placed to function as "advisors" and "sources of information."[14] A senior Israeli diplomat cogently advocated this idea in the 1980s. Responding to a proposal for the creation an Israeli information service funded by American Jews, he advised, "What American Jewry can do . . . is translate its political power into an information effort . . . that could be deployed subtly and wisely on Israel's behalf. It would be indirect but a more promising approach."[15]

Another important feature of epistemic communities is that they are not only capable of setting particular agendas in domestic and international politics by mobilizing a variety of political actors, NGOs and media, but they tend to acquire "transnational character."[16] Epistemic communities pursue these objectives by organizing conferences, seminars, press briefings, lectures and publications. Two crucial factors that sustain epistemic communities in a democratic society are access to the press and to state bureaucracies.[17] The final critical function of epistemic communities is their "problem-solving" function.[18] However, as Antoniades argues, the problem-solving process (in foreign policy) can lead to a redefinition of (national) interest.[19]

As early as the 1950s, Turkish policymakers appreciated the fact that alignment with Israel would provide them with the opportunity to gain a prominent ally in Washington, or as Efraim Inbar unequivocally puts it, to "conquer" the US Congress.[20] But the end of the Cold War brought a special poignancy to this aspect of the Turkish–Israeli relationship. With the perceived loss of the strategic value to the United States, Jung and Piccoli claim, "Ankara duly realized that enhanced efforts to gain the support of the pro-Israeli lobby were of increased importance in order to balance the strength of the anti-Turkish lobbies."[21]

Shortly after gaining independence in 1992, Azerbaijan was faced with a military campaign unleashed by its neighbor to gain control of the predominantly ethnic Armenian enclave of Nagorno-Karabagh (or Artsakh). The Armenian diaspora in the United States and Europe, especially France, supported the Armenian nationalist struggle in the Caucasus. The powerful Armenian lobby pressured the US Congress to pass legislation that would penalize Azerbaijan.[22] Experiencing diplomatic isolation, Azerbaijan turned to Israel to break the wall of animosity, especially in the United States. President Heydar Aliyev, in his meeting with Prime Minister Rabin, asked the Israeli leader for diplomatic intervention on Azerbaijan's behalf to win the United States to their side.[23] According to Ha'aretz, Aliyev even asked Rabin for military assistance at their meeting in 1995.[24] This private exchange between Israeli and Azerbaijani leaders subsequently brought pro-Israeli elements of the organized American Jewish community into involvement with the Azerbaijani cause.

The project of creating and later maintaining the trilateral strategic partnership between Israel, Turkey and Azerbaijan was performed through a network of transnational epistemic communities. This task in Washington was performed by a policy community, which coalesced around this objective. A policy community, according to Diane Stone, is a "set of actors bound together by a common interest in a particular policy field."[25] It may include political activists and government officials as well as members of legislative and executive branches of government, consultants, think-tank scholars and representatives of the media. Each community has a commitment to certain policies and a way of doing things. They usually share common beliefs and educational background.[26] In this case, a policy community came into being in the early 1990s. This community has several components. It includes an original nucleus that generates ideas, followed by think tanks that disseminate ideas and establish the discourse of strategic relationship between Turkey and Israel. Soon this agenda came to embrace Azerbaijan as a third pillar of the partnership. The discourse of congruence of geopolitical interests of the three American allies was adopted in the early 1990s and became one of the methods of lobbying and conducting diplomatic activities for a coalition of American Jewish organizations in Washington, Ankara and Baku.

A more concrete strategy of creating a Turkish–Israeli axis, with the possible participation of Jordan, was advanced by an ad hoc group of Jewish American neoconservative scholars who were close to Israeli Prime Minister Benjamin Netanyahu. This group came to be known as the "Study Group on 'A New Israeli Strategy Toward 2000.'" The members of the Study Group convened in Washington. Its membership included: Richard Perle (then of American Enterprise Institute, Study Group Leader); James Colbert (Jewish Institute for National Security Affairs); Charles Fairbanks, Jr. (Johns Hopkins University/SAIS); Douglas Feith (Feith and Zell Associates); Robert Loewenberg (president, Institute for Advanced Strategic and Political Studies); Jonathan Torop (Washington Institute for Near East Policy); David Wurmser (Institute for Advanced Strategic and Political Studies); and Meyrav Wurmser (Johns Hopkins University). An Israel-based Institute for Advanced Strategic and Political Studies published their recommendations in a report in 1996. The Study Group produced a report called "A Clean Break: A New Strategy for Securing the Realm." It was recommended that one of the main foreign policy objectives of Israel was to "work closely with Turkey and Jordan to contain, destabilize, and roll-back some of its most dangerous threats. This implies a clean break from the slogan 'comprehensive peace' to a traditional concept of strategy based on balance of power."[27] Another earlier intellectual champion of the Turkish–Israeli alliance was Daniel Pipes.[28] In 1997 he published an article, "A New Axis: The Emerging Turkish–Israeli Entente," in which he described the strategic rationale for this new regional axis in the conservative National Interest. He wrote, "In the longer term . . . strong Turkish–Israeli ties will enhance the region's stability by serving as a powerful military deterrent against would-be enemies. Aggressive states must watch their step in the face of a formidable combination of the Middle East's largest military force and its most advanced [sic], and this diminishes the likelihood of war." Further, he explained why the United States should support this relationship: "the Turkish–Israeli alignment creates, for the first time, the possibility of developing an alliance of pro-American democracies, such as exists in Europe."[29]

In the case of the post-Cold War alliance between Turkey and Israel, the role of Richard Perle, until recently a chair of the US Defense Policy Board, and Douglas Feith, under-secretary of defense for policy, should not be underestimated. According to Jason Vest, "Not only have the Jewish Institute for National Security Affairs (JINSA) and the Center for Security Policy (CSP) been enthusiastic boosters in the service of assuring a constant flow of US military aid to Turkey, but JINSA/CSP advisors Perle and Feith have spent the past fifteen years—in governmental and private capacities—working quietly and deftly to keep the US arms sluice to Turkey open, as well as drawing both Turkey and Israel and their respective American lobbies closer together."[30] Richard Perle was one of the original proponents of the US–Turkish strategic partnership in the 1980s. During the Reagan administration, in the capacity of the assistant secretary of defense for international security affairs, he was personally deeply involved in the negotiation and adoption of the Defense and Economic Cooperation Agreement with Turkey (DECA) in 1986.[31] Daniel Pipes acknowledges that "to make its case," Turkey "counts on American Jews such as Morton Abramowitz [a former US ambassador], Douglas Feith [defense under-secretary], Alan Makovsky [Senior Fellow at the Washington Institute for Near East Policy], Richard Perle [Defense Policy Board chairman], and Harold Rhode [Office of Net Assessment, Office of the Secretary of Defense], and on institutions such as the American Israel Public Affairs Committee and the Jewish Institute for National Security Affairs."[32] As a former Reagan administration official, Perle has lobbied for Turkish interests since 1989. The same year, Richard Perle and his associate Douglas Feith formed a lobbying and public relations firm, International Advisors, Inc. (IAI). As a head of this company, Perle continued his lobbying efforts against anti-Turkish legislation promoted by the Greek, American and Kurdish lobbies in the US Congress.[33] Other members of the Washington political elite contributed to promoting discourse amenable to the budding Turkish–Israeli relationship. The direct involvement of Paul Wolfowitz, a long-time proponent of the US–Turkey–Israel alliance in the Middle East, seems to have been crucial in its creation.[34] Alan Makovsky, a former Senior Fellow of the Washington Institute for Near East Policy, who currently serves on the staff of the House International Relations Committee in the US Congress, served as a linchpin of the original alliance between Turkey and Israel, which later included Azerbaijan. A senior US diplomat who served in Azerbaijan in the early 1990s commented, "Turks and Israelis agreed that they should pursue a common policy vis-à-vis Azerbaijan. Turkish government stressed ethnic ties. Alan Makovsky was an architect of this political alliance."[35]

The Turkish American Congressional Caucus in the US Congress, which includes 60 members of Congress, also actively supports the strategic axis between Turkey and Israel. In February of 2002, Robert Wexler, co-chairman of the Caucus on US–Turkish Relations, from the predominantly Jewish district of Fort Lauderdale, Florida, led a delegation of six members of Congress to Turkey and Israel, where he praised the two countries for their "critical assistance in the war on terrorism . . . The relationship between Israel and Turkey, which has improved dramatically in recent years, has led to increased stability and security in the region and has improved cooperation on economic, military, cultural, and strategic matters." In July of 2002, the House International Relations Subcommittee on Europe passed a Wexler-sponsored resolution to commend Turkey and Israel. Congressman Wexler hailed it in a press release, in which he called upon the Middle East "to follow the example set by these two nations in promoting democracy, peace, and tolerance."[36] However, Armenian American sources claim that it was the Turkish leadership that insisted on the provision that "the powerful Jewish American lobby—the American Israel Public Affairs Committee, the American Jewish Committee, and several other organizations" would lobby the US government to counteract the influence of the Greek and Armenian lobbies.[37]

Bulent Aras, a critic of the Turkish–Israeli entente, views the activities of the American Jewish community as skewed toward the interests of the Jewish state. He observed, "In short, the pro-Israeli lobbies are making efforts to steer US policies toward the Middle East and Turkey in a way that serves Israeli interests and that maximizes Tel Aviv's regional benefits. They do this by carrying out studies and presenting lectures that Turkish administrators are informed of."[38] However, today Turkey needs Jewish American support on contentious issues such as "the Armenian Genocide" and to deflect criticism by the Department of State and other groups of widely reported human rights abuses, in particular against Turkey's Kurdish citizens. During the mid-1990s, when the Turkish state waged a military campaign against the PKK, the Turkish government needed to counteract the influence on Congress of the coalition of Kurdish, Armenian and Greek lobbies and human rights organizations. Describing the importance for Turkey of the relationship with the American Jewish community, the Turkish ambassador stated, "And our closest relationships in the United States are with Jewish groups."[39] A French expert in geopolitics wrote: "In this highly geopolitical conflict the true interest of Ankara to get allied with Jerusalem is overlaid with other issues, outside of the scope of [military] training and fields of battle. On that side there is a continent and an ocean, which is really in Washington, or even though it may be more than 10,000 km away from the battle field, where the game is played; in its fight against the Kurd separatism—and in particular against the PKK—Ankara needs friends in the House of Representatives as much as it needs armoured vehicles in the South-East of Anatolia. Or in the Department of State and mainly in the [US] Congress, which becomes an active partner of the Jewish State. It gains the support of a more active and powerful pro-Israeli lobby, which is widely embodied by the American Israel Public Affairs Committee (AIPAC)."[40]

The hierarchy of the epistemic communities affecting the relationship

A whole range of epistemic communities is involved in foreign policy. Their impact differs in scope, scale and access to the foreign policy establishment. It can be said there is a hierarchical order in which different components of the epistemic community affect policy outcomes in the present case. I will outline the impact of epistemic communities on the maintenance of the trilateral relationship in the order of importance: (1) pro-Israeli think tanks, followed by (2) AIPAC—an American Israeli official lobby organization; followed by (3) leading national and international Jewish organizations such as the American Jewish Committee, the B'nai Brith International and others; and (4) epistemic communities in Turkey, Azerbaijan and Israel.

The role of think tanks

Even though think tanks exist on the "margins" of the political process, they are an organizational expression "of the blending of ideas, politics and policy."[41] As quasi-governmental organizations they do not replace the power of elected officials and governments to make decisions and set public policy. However, they are capable of providing policy alternatives, building political agendas and propagating their ideas in order to shape public policy. Stone has highlighted their role in the political process by stating that "They attempt to influence the policy process through intellectual argument rather than lobbying." Think tanks occupy a privileged position in policy communities because they serve as incubators of ideas. Generally they claim to possess (1) self-determination of research agendas; (2) policy focus; (3) public purpose; (4) expertise and professionalism; and (5) organizational yield.[42]

The first think tanks emerged in the United States in the beginning of the twentieth century. Since the beginning of the Cold War, think tanks have gained acceptance as epistemic communities that have affected American policymakers. Stone captures the essential functions of think tanks: "They move ideas into politics. By attracting leading scholars, think tanks provide a base from which to market, package and popularize ideas and policy proposals."[43] Think tanks are not involved in policymaking directly but produce policy-relevant research and provide policy options through media and a variety of other forums. In Stone's view, "think tanks are an organizational expression of the blending of ideas, politics and policy outside of the formal political arenas."[44] In other words, these institutions have carved out a niche for themselves in the political sphere, where they generate a strategic discourse on issues of the day, including foreign policy. These quasi-governmental organizations capitalize on their specialist knowledge and have become one of the dominant forces that shape not only the outlines but also the content of the American international outlook.

According to Diane Stone, think tanks, or "independent policy research institutes," started to dominate policymaking as "increasingly visible policy actors" in the last four decades.[45] A senior CNN anchor and a former *Jerusalem Post* Washington correspondent, Wolf Blitzer, has suggested that an insight into the way think tanks affect foreign policy making in the American capital is "absolutely essential" for understanding how the American foreign policy community operates. He provided a "thick" description of the way the think tanks operate in Washington: "Given the traditional power and respect for intellectual [sic] persuasion in America, they occasionally have played significant roles in putting forward ideas for the policymakers to consider. Sometimes, their proposals are officially inspired 'trial balloons,' too sensitive or controversial to come directly from the government. Other times, they represent a new, independent approach to an old problem."[46]

So-called "new partisan" think tanks became prominent on the Washington political stage in the 1970s. They were more specialized and combined several features in comparison with the old-guard think tanks such a the Carnegie Endowment for International Peace (founded in 1910), the Council on Foreign Relations (founded in 1921) and post-World War II organizations such as RAND. They were more ideological and promoted the "New Right" agenda. Noteworthy among them was the Jewish Institute of National Strategic Affairs (JINSA). It was founded as a study group in 1974 in the wake of the 1973 Yom Kippur War, transformed itself into a "defense education group" in 1979, and is now organized as a 501(c)(3) organization under the IRS code.[47]

Since the Reagan administration, the executive and legislative branches of American government have increasingly sought advice from think tanks rather than academicians on issues of foreign policy. This was due to the numerous failures of American foreign policy in the Middle East that was primarily based on the input from American academics. In the 1970s, the Lebanese civil war and then the Iranian revolution shattered this illusion that the modernization theory, promoted as the panacea, would produce political stability and peace in the region. A conservative American academic expressed this consensus: "America's academics have failed to predict or explain the major evolutions of Middle Eastern politics and society over the past two decades." In his book *Ivory Towers on Sand: The Failure of Middle East Studies in America*, Martin Kramer concludes that, "Repeated failures have depleted the credibility of scholarship among the influential public. In Washington, the mere mention of academics in Middle Eastern studies often causes eyes to roll."[48] This new consensus about the diminished value of academic scholarship in the Washington foreign policy establishment can be explained by the ascendancy of the New Right, its emphasis on "small government" and suspicion of so-called liberal institutions, including the media, Hollywood and universities. Martin Kramer expressed this conservative ideological perspective in his book: "A new consensus emerged among Washington policy, defense and intelligence communities that little could be learned from academics—not because they knew nothing, but because they deliberately withheld their knowledge from government, or organized it on the basis of arcane priorities or conflicting loyalties." A partisan critic and academic himself, he made a claim that "academia—poisoned by blind obeisance to the ideas of Edward Said and his left-wing emulators—led many talented people to gravitate to the think tanks, where their work often surpassed university-based research in clarity, style, thoroughness and cogency."[49]

Since the 1970s, American think tanks have become one of the main sources of policy-relevant research and advice for American policymakers in many regions. The greatest impact on American foreign policy toward the expanded Middle East region in general, and Turkey and Israel in particular, was made by Israeli-oriented think tanks. The Washington Institute for Near East Policy (WINEP)[50] and the Jewish Institute for National Strategic Affairs (JINSA) were pre-eminent among them. Diane Stone divides think tanks into two broad categories. According to her typology, WINEP represents a specialist regionally focused institution.[51] JINSA can be described as an ideologically right-wing think tank. Though differences exist, both are generally thought of as pro-Israeli organizations in Washington and internationally.[52]

The Washington Institute for Near East Policy (WINEP) was established in 1985. As its name indicates, this think tank focuses on providing information on and analysis of US interests in the Middle East. WINEP has gained a reputation for timely and policy-relevant research. This dramatically increased its prestige and funding as well as the ability of its senior officers to enter the policymaking echelon of the US government. Ideologically WINEP is closer to the Democratic Party. Generally it opposes the "neoconservative" agenda in Washington. Its founding director, Martin Indyk, was appointed special assistant to President Clinton on the Middle East and later was an ambassador to Israel.[53] As the chief strategist of Middle East policy in the Clinton administration, he identified Turkey as the United States' strategic partner in the region and a cornerstone of American policy toward Iraq and Iran.[54] A Ziegler Distinguished Fellow at WINEP, Dennis Ross served as "a point man on the peace process in both the George H.W. Bush and Bill Clinton administrations."[55] The Washington Institute has acquired a reputation as the leading institution among the think tanks with a regional focus. Specifically it made major contributions to the search for a resolution of the Israeli–Palestinian conflict. In its annual survey of media citations of think tanks, the liberal media watchdog Fairness and Accuracy in Reporting counted WINEP among its top 20 for three years running in 2000, 2001 and 2002. WINEP has focused exclusively on the Middle East for all the years of its existence. It is the most influential think tank in Washington with a bipartisan agenda. Many of its senior scholars, such as Martin Indyk and Dennis Ross, served in the Clinton administrations. Other think tanks involved in research on the Middle East Institute and the Middle East Policy Council have lower prestige and consequently more limited influence on strategic thinking in Washington. Activities of the Washington Institute cover other regional powers besides Israel and its Arab neighbors and provide recommendations for American foreign policy toward them. In particular, the importance of Turkey as a strategic partner in the Middle East found its institutional expression in the creation of the Turkish Studies Program. Due to its privileged position within both Republican and Democratic White House administrations over the last three decades, the Washington Institute was able to go beyond influence; the American government on some occasions adopted WINEP's policy prescriptions.

By the mid-1990s the American government in its public diplomacy had reaffirmed Turkey's strategic significance in the post-Cold War era. Thus Richard Holbrooke, assistant secretary of state for European affairs in the early Clinton administration, reported, "In the earlier part of the Clinton administration, US officials emphasized Turkey's role as a 'front-line state' that is 'at the crossroads of almost every issue of importance to the United States on the Eurasian continent.'"[56] Clinton's political appointee, Deputy Secretary of State Strobe Talbott, asserted that US–Turkish relations have "even more of a hardheaded [sic], geopolitical, strategic rationale in the post-Cold War period than . . . during the Cold War."[57]

In the case of Turkey and its relations with the United States and Israel, the most influential figure in Washington in the 1990s was Alan Makovsky. He organized numerous conferences and was sought out by the US State Department, academic institutions and members of the Turkish foreign policy establishment. As a senior fellow, he contributed to a periodical the Washington Institute publishes called *PolicyWatch*. This publication disseminates policy proposals regarding the Middle East among the Washington foreign policy making elite. He wrote several policy-relevant reports about prospects for the US–Turkish–Israeli strategic relationship and an influential analysis of threats to the strategic interests of the United States in the Middle East posed by the coming-to-power of Erbakan's Refah (Welfare) Party in 1997. In this article, Makovsky outlined some policy prescriptions aimed at preventing a crisis in the Turkish–Israeli strategic partnership, in view of the anti-American and anti-Israeli stance of Turkish Prime Minister Necmettin Erbakan. He also criticized the statements of Nicholas Burns,[58] which allegedly undermined the secular foundations of the Turkish Republic.[59] Throughout the 1990s Makovsky was widely recognized in the Turkish press as one of the most important agents of influence in Washington and Ankara.[60] As a significant member of the policy community he was able to not only contribute to the discourse of the relationship, but also to clarify the positions of the parties and resolve misconceptions. He was often referred to as the "famous American expert on Turkey."[61] In March 2000 he participated in the Institute's Policy Forum panel, which included Cengiz Candar, one of the most influential Turkish journalists, and Efraim Inbar, an Israeli academic and a former member of the Israeli Political Strategic Committee of the National Planning Council. At this forum, Alan Makovsky stated, "The emergence of close Israeli–Turkish relations is one of the significant strategic developments in the post-Cold War Middle East."[62]

The influence of the Washington Institute in shaping Turkish foreign policy toward Israel was viewed with suspicion by Turkish domestic critics and journalists. But even they acknowledge that "most of respected Turkey experts in Washington are either Jewish Americans or Israel-concentrated."[63] General Çevik Bir, a former Turkish deputy chief of staff and an architect of Turkish–Israeli strategic relationship, addressing a Washington Institute conference, presented the following rationale for this relationship, "Turkey became a 'front country' in the region when new threats emerged after the Cold War. This new situation led Turkey to become a 'strategy-producing' country. The initiation of Turkish–Israeli relations should be seen in this light. Contrary to the beliefs of some, neither the United States nor any other third party initiated Turkish–Israeli cooperation or the 1996 military training and cooperation agreement. These were the initiatives of the Turkish leadership."[64]

The JINSA effect

The Jewish Institute for National Strategic Affairs (JINSA) was founded in the aftermath of the Yom Kippur War. Its primary objective is to promote strategic and military ties between the United States and Israel.[65] According to the organization's website, JINSA has a two-fold mandate:

1   To educate the American public about the importance of an effective US defense capability so that our vital interests as Americans can be safeguarded; and
2   To inform the American defense and foreign affairs community about the important role Israel can and does play in bolstering democratic interests in the Mediterranean and the Middle East.[66]

In the mid-1990s, JINSA's agenda expanded and embraced support for the budding Israeli–Turkish axis. In its current public statement of objectives, the organization says, "JINSA plays a leading role in fostering expanding relations between the United States and Israel with Turkey."[67] JINSA organized numerous briefings and symposia with the top echelons of the Turkish military regarding Turkish–Israeli cooperation in the strategic sphere. Among them was a key meeting on February 1, 1996 when General Çevik Bir informed his audience of a series of protocols between Israel and Turkey.[68] The Washington Institute for Near East Policy and the Jewish Institute for National Security Affairs have also organized various meetings for Turkish political and military leaders with their American counterparts.[69] JINSA, in coalition with AIPAC, also lobbied against anti-Turkish legislation on Capitol Hill.[70]

American pro-Israeli think tanks affect the internal debate about American strategic policy in Turkey as well. In particular, the outreach of JINSA was noted and raised concerns for some pro-Islamist intellectuals in Turkey. Bulent Aras claimed that the American Jewish lobby manipulates internal debates in Turkish foreign policy circles. In his words, "[American Jewish] lobbying institutions may play important roles in the manipulation process [of Turkish foreign policy]." He drew particular attention to the interaction between Çevik Bir and JINSA, claiming that, "It was the several Jewish lobbies and think tanks that the Turkish deputy chief of the general staff— the acting leader of the 28 February Period—visited regularly."[71] For example, in his speech at JINSA, Çevik Bir blamed Iran for assisting terrorism against Turkey."[72]

JINSA not only monitors progress in military and political aspects of the Turkish–Israeli relationship, it works to enhance communications between the military–political elites of the two countries. In order to do that, the Institute organized meetings with Turkish diplomats and the Turkish American community. JINSA and the Assembly of Turkish American Associations sponsored meetings with the Turkish ambassador in the United States, and JINSA holds meetings with Turkish diplomats at the embassy.[73]

A Jewish advocacy coalition

If promotion of the discourse of Turkish–Israeli relations fell within the purview of pro-Israeli think tanks, the engagement of Israel with Azerbaijan was encouraged by a coalition of American Jewish organizations. Its main opponent in the US Congress is a powerful coalition of Armenian, Greek and Kurdish lobbies. According to Daniel Mariaschin, "The relationship with Azerbaijan was a subset of the Turkey–Israeli axis."[74] This division of responsibilities between think tanks is also due to their limited capacity to lobby directly on behalf of Israel, Turkey or Azerbaijan. This has to do with the nature and legal status of institutions like WINEP or JINSA under American law.[75] The lobbying function is performed by a broad advocacy coalition, which is composed of advocacy groups. The leadership role in this coalition is played by AIPAC, an established Israeli lobbying organization, and activist organizations, namely B'nai Brith and the American Jewish Committee. Jewish American organizations serve two functions, which are vital for strengthening and further developing the trilateral relationship between Israel, Turkey and Azerbaijan. These organizations lobby for the interests of both Turkey and Azerbaijan, and they provide a diplomatic "back channel" for communication between the Israeli, Turkish and Azerbaijani governments. A senior officer of B'nai Brith has emphasized that support for Israeli involvement with Azerbaijan was an independent initiative of a coalition of Jewish American organizations. He said: "Israeli–Turkish relations took off around the same time. The deepening of the Israeli relationship with Azerbaijan occurred around the same time [1997–9]. Our organization came to realize how important the relationship with Azerbaijan is. We came to this conclusion independently [of the Israeli government] prompted by the consensus of eight Jewish organizations."[76] In fact, former President Heydar Aliyev also attached great importance to his direct contacts with American

Jewish leadership. In the May 2000 he expressed his appreciation for their help in promoting the Azerbaijani cause in the United States.[77] One of the major achievements of the Jewish coalition was the approval of the presidential waiver of Section 907, a piece of American legislation that prohibits US bilateral aid to Azerbaijan, in January of 2002. Since 1997 a coalition of ten Jewish organizations lobbied Congress for a waiver of Section 907 of the Freedom Support Act of 1992. Section 907 restricts American governmental aid, including military aid, to Azerbaijan as a result of the Nagorno-Karabagh conflict. After September 11, when the US began its "war against international terrorism," the role of Azerbaijan became critical for the US and their allies' operations in the region. Azerbaijan guaranteed overflight rights to coalition forces for their campaign against the Taliban regime in Afghanistan. The American Jewish coalition advocated for presidential support for the waiver, and it finally passed in Congress in January of 2002. The Armenian lobby, especially the Armenian National Committee of America, reacted strongly to the passage of this waiver. It specifically mentioned the American Jewish coalition led by B'nai Brith as one of the main actors that promoted the opening of American military aid to Azerbaijan.[78] The Armenian lobby, in coalition with the Greek lobby, coordinate their efforts and wage campaigns against issues of concern both to Turkey and Azerbaijan. Pro-Armenian members of Congress singled out Jewish organizations for criticism for their efforts on behalf of Azerbaijan and Turkey. After the presidential waiver of Section 907 in 2002, a Congressman from California, where the Armenian lobby is influential, expressed his concern "over reports of Jewish American organizations' stance on issues of concern to the Armenian American community, including Section 907 and the Armenian Genocide Resolution."[79]

The role of AIPAC

As noted above, the American Jewish community is a powerful force that has affected US foreign policy since World War II. The American Israel Public Affairs Committee, or AIPAC, occupies a unique position among American Jewish communal organizations. It was founded in 1959. Its current budget is $45 million, while its current membership is estimated at almost 100,000 persons. It is the only Jewish organization in America that has registered under the Federal Registration Lobbying Act. The organization has publicized several clear objectives: (1) to secure continuing aid to Israel on the most favorable possible terms; (2) to obtain the most advanced US weapons possible; (3) to move the US embassy from Tel Aviv to Jerusalem; (4) to preserve tax-exempt status for Jewish fundraising in the US; and (5) to oppose strongly any US measures or proposals seen as a threat to the security of Israel, including arms for Arab countries and peace proposals that might require Israeli concessions. To reach the American public, AIPAC promotes certain themes, notably that Israel is the only democracy in the Middle East and that it is a strategic partner of the United States as well as a reliable ally.

However, the main focus of AIPAC's activities is the US Congress. Influence derives from encouraging contributions both to candidates favorably disposed to AIPAC's goals and to the opponents of those who have voted against the positions of the lobby. Although AIPAC itself does not contribute to candidates, it prepares information for voters on the records and positions of members of Congress and has been credited with the defeat of more than one member considered to be anti-Israel. The organization enjoys broad grass-root support in the American Jewish community. The organization promotes its goals by carefully orchestrated visits to Israel for elected officials and political candidates. AIPAC organizes mass mailings and telephone calls by American Jewish community members and Israel sympathizers, in particular evangelical Christians.[80]

More recently AIPAC officers became more involved in strengthening Turkish–Israeli cooperation and conducting a public relations campaign for Turkish interests. In the period between 1987 and 1989, Israel re-engaged with diplomatic activity on behalf of Turkey in Washington to create conditions for substantial improvement of Turkish–Israeli relations. Israel advised American Jewish groups to counteract the anti-Turkish lobby in the US Congress. A special role in this campaign was assigned to AIPAC, already involved in a lobbying effort, which led to the narrow defeat of an Armenian-backed Senate resolution that denounced World War I massacres of Turkish Armenians as "genocide" in 1989.[81]

The American legislature controls all foreign appropriations and wields great power over America foreign policy. Both Greek American and Armenian lobbies coordinate their lobbying efforts with pro-Kurdish and human rights lobbies to block legislation that has a positive impact on US–Turkish/ US–Azerbaijani relations. Many Turkish and Azerbaijani foreign policy experts concluded that forging deeper strategic and security-related relations with Israel would provide both countries with powerful leverage in Washington. Keith Weissman, formerly of AIPAC, indicated that the Azerbaijani leadership came to the realization in the mid-1990s that they would "have quicker (sic) opportunities in Washington through the Israeli card."[82] The timing of this decision was especially important because both Turkey and Azerbaijan needed to find close allies to counteract the strong influence of American Greek and Armenian lobbies in the US Congress. This period coincided with the Turkish military campaign to suppress PKK activities in the early and the mid-1990s. Thus between 1992 and 1996, the US Congress cut American foreign aid to Turkey and demanded that the administration prepare reports on the use of American equipment in situations of human rights violations. The powerful lobbying capacity of human rights and arms control groups together with anti-Turkish ethnic lobbies on the Cyprus and Armenian issues significantly reduced the executive branch's ability to shield Turkey. Indeed, the State Department's Office of Humanitarian Affairs and Human Rights found itself preparing reports undermining the administration's ability to pursue its close links with Turkey. As a result of these factors, there were substantial cuts in US foreign assistance to Turkey during the mid-1990s, and the transfer of remaining aid was made conditional on Turkey improving its human rights performance. Despite active lobbying by AIPAC and other American Jewish organizations, during the same period several pieces of legislation were passed that had a negative effect on American aid to Turkey and Azerbaijan in the early and mid-1990s.

AIPAC and other Jewish organizations possess a formidable diplomatic expertise. This diplomatic strength derives from a historical effort to explain and represent the American position to official Jerusalem and significant cross-membership between the American foreign policy establishment and Jewish organizations.[83] AIPAC has used this "soft power" to mediate political crises and resolve misunderstandings in Turkish–American and Turkish–Israeli relations since the mid-1990s.[84] Gradually these efforts expanded in the direction of Azerbaijan and other countries in the Caucasus and Central Asia. In their capacity as the "back channel," representatives of AIPAC have conducted behind-the-scenes missions to explain the American Jewish, Israeli and occasionally US government's positions to the leadership of Turkey and Azerbaijan since the early 1990s.[85] On occasion, when serious tensions in bilateral relations arise to threaten the Turkish–Israeli entente, AIPAC, the American Jewish Committee and other Jewish organizations deliver their concerns to the Turkish government. On April 4, 2002, Prime Minister Bulent Ecevit accused Israel of "genocide" against the Palestinians. The AJC and other American Jewish groups responded quickly and forcefully to these accusations. The next day a coalition of American Jewish organizations wrote the Turkish prime minister a letter stating that his "use of the term 'genocide' to describe Israel's military operations in the West Bank is 'absolutely wrong as fact and offensive as comment.'"[86] This communication was followed by a meeting of the leaders of this coalition, led by AIPAC, with Turkish Ambassador Faruk Logoglu on April 9 to convey their protest. Barry Jacobs, of the American Jewish Committee, expressed his surprise and indignation: "We have put a lot of effort in on behalf of Turkey." He added the AJC and other American Jewish groups were "stung and angered" by Ecevit's words.[87] At the meeting on April 9, Ambassador Logoglu reiterated the Turkish commitment to friendship with Jews and the State of Israel.[88] Turkish Foreign Minister Ismail Cem confirmed that, "the Jewish lobby has always supported Turkey against any injustices that have been made or that were going to be made."[89] He specifically pointed to the importance of the Jewish lobby's support in connection with the Armenian genocide allegations. By April 6, Prime Minister Ecevit had been compelled to issue two separate apologies, and a public campaign of apologies from Turkish Americans brought this diplomatic crisis to a closure.[90]

AIPAC officials also shared organizational know-how with opinion leaders in Turkey and Azerbaijan. They disseminated information about effective methods of lobbying in the United States and trained their Turkish and Azerbaijani colleagues.[91] They were also involved in explaining Israeli positions on many sensitive issues to Turkish government officials.[92]

Since 1997 AIPAC has been involved in a public campaign on issues related to the energy security of Turkey and delivery routes for Caspian oil and gas to the West. AIPAC favored creation of the East–West energy corridor, which includes the Baku-Tbilisi-Ceyhan oil pipeline (BTC) and the South Caucasus gas pipeline.[93] Keith Weissman, a former senior AIPAC official, promoted a plan for the Turkish import of Azerbaijani gas from the Shah Deniz field. He canvassed the Turkish government against the Blue Stream project, a recently completed underwater pipeline under the Black Sea that delivers Russian gas to Turkey. Some energy and geopolitics experts expressed concern that implementation of the Blue Stream project would make Turkey extremely dependent on Russia for its supply of natural gas in the long term.[94] Weissman stressed in his public appearances and private meetings with Turkish officials that the Blue Stream project has delayed many projects associated with the "East–West corridor." During his visit to Istanbul in June of 2000, vice-president of the American–Israel Public Affairs Committee Keith Weissman stated on Turkish television, "No matter which way you look at this issue it is the Russians' success. Even if the project would not be realized, Mavi Akim (Blue Stream) blocked and caused serious delays on other projects."[95] He also indicated that the discovery of gas in the Shakh Deniz field in the Azerbaijani Caspian shelf was as critical for both Turkey and Azerbaijan as the BTC project.[96]

The East–West corridor, or the Main Export Pipeline (MEP), for transportation of the Caspian hydrocarbon resources remains the preferable option for American and Israeli governments. MEP includes the Baku-Tbilisi-Ceyhan (BTC) oil pipeline and the South Caucasus gas pipeline.[97] Since the completion of the Blue Stream project, Israeli leadership has changed its priorities and looks to transport Russian gas through Turkey, which coincides with the vision of the Prime Minister Recep Tayyip Erdogan.[98]

B'nai Brith—"The Children of the Covenant"

B'nai Brith (BB) is the oldest secular Jewish organization in the United States. B'nai Brith was founded as a fraternal order in New York in 1843. The B'nai Brith organization covers several areas of Jewish concern such as the welfare of the State of Israel, Jewish education and protection of civil rights, and international welfare, as well as the fight against anti-Semitism and racism. B'nai Brith has been registered as an NGO with the United Nations for 50 years. According its mission statement: "With members in more than 50 countries, B'nai B'rith maintains an active interest in issues affecting Jewish communities worldwide . . . we are able to be effective advocates for Jewish issues and the broader human rights agenda on a global scale."[99]

B'nai Brith monitors human rights and supports Jewish community institutions in many countries of the former Soviet Union. During their international visits, the B'nai Brith leadership meets heads of states, government officials and legislators. As one of world's largest Jewish organizations, its functions are not limited to the advancement of interests of local Jewish communities and communication with the Jewish diaspora. The American Jewish organizations perform diplomatic functions for the State of Israel.[100]

B'nai Brith has conducted diplomatic activity vis-à-vis Turkey since the early 1990s. The B'nai Brith representatives met President Turgut Ozal in 1992. This meeting served as an impetus for B'nai Brith's involvement in lobbying the International Monetary Fund (IMF) for easier terms for Turkish-related international loans. Since that time, B'nai Brith's leadership has established a pattern of regular meetings with Turkish prime ministers and other government officials. B'nai Brith also forcefully lobbies European Union institutions for the admission of Turkey into the organization.[101]

Since 1997 Azerbaijan has been a country of great interest and strategic concern for Jewish American organizations. Diplomatic and community care visits by Jewish American representatives of B'nai Brith to Azerbaijan have been numerous in recent years. American diplomat Carol McLelland observed that "there is a constant stream of representatives of American Jewish organizations visiting Azerbaijan."[102] B'nai Brith officials met with President Heydar Aliyev when he came to visit Washington in 1997 and in Baku in 1998.[103] The organization also was very active in promoting the Baku-Tbilisi-Ceyhan pipeline project in American foreign policy circles. B'nai Brith officials explicitly stated in an influential American Jewish weekly editorial: "Azerbaijan, a country with a population of less than eight million and an area the size of Maine, has been eager to establish strong ties with Western countries and the United States in particular ... American Jewish organizations, including B'nai B'rith [sic] International, have been supportive of these efforts." The editorial further continued, "these republic[s], like Turkey to the west, serve as models to the Islamic world that moderate Muslim countries can establish warm relationships with Israel."[104]

The American Jewish Committee

The American Jewish Committee (AJC) was founded in 1906. From its foundation, the declared mission has been "to promote pluralistic and democratic societies where all minorities are protected." The organization advances the following objectives: "To safeguard the welfare and security of Jews in the United States, in Israel, and throughout the world; to strengthen the basic principles of pluralism around the world, as the best defense against anti-Semitism and other forms of bigotry; and to enhance the quality of American Jewish life by helping to ensure Jewish continuity and deepen ties between American and Israeli Jews."[105]

The end of the Cold War and the establishment of strategic relations between Turkey and Israel brought the focus of the American Jewish Committee's activities to Turkey.[106] During his visit to Turkey in July 1999, Barry Jacobs, then AJC director of strategic studies, said to the Turkish press: "Over the last two to three years, the Jewish American community, under the leadership of a few organizations, has decided that the relationship between Israel and Turkey and Turkey's importance on a host of other issues requires that we take an active and vigorous role in being friends of Turkey in the United States."[107]

Azerbaijan, as a Muslim, Western-oriented state that established diplomatic relations with Israel, also attracted the attention of the American Jewish Committee as a potential strategic partner in view of its proximity to Iran, the most dangerous enemy of Israel. The American Jewish Committee took the lead in the fight against Section 907 in its lobbying efforts in the US Congress. Barry Jacobs explained the strategic importance of American support for Azerbaijan. He said, "The US should do what it can to encourage Azerbaijan, especially in light of Israel's relationship with Azerbaijan and Azerbaijan's general relationship with the West."[108]

The critical role of the AJC's diplomatic efforts gained a special relevance in view of the recent "cooling-off" of Turkish–Israeli relations since Recep Tayyip Erdogan criticized Israel as "a terrorist state" because of heavy-handed treatment of Palestinians during the al-Aqsa Intifada. The president of the American Jewish Committee, David Harris, and his delegation paid a visit to the Turkish prime minister to discuss the rise of anti-Semitism in the world, and prospects for the Israeli–Palestinian Peace Process, on October 13, 2004. During this visit, Prime Minister Erdogan said to the Jewish delegation, "Our friendship is not for bargaining. We attach a great importance to it."[109] Erdogan pointed out at the meeting that Turkish friendship with Israel has a firm foundation and cannot be affected by current events.[110]

The journey to passage of the Silk Road Bill

Since 1997 the Jewish advocacy coalition has made a consistent lobbying effort for an important piece of legislation that directly affects the future of the newly independent republics of the Caucasus and Central Asia. This legislation is called the Silk Road Strategy Act or Silk Road Bill. As its name indicates, it refers to the revival of an ancient trade route between China and the Mediterranean. In particular, this act of the US Congress deals with the geopolitical situation of countries of the Caspian basin, in particular Armenia and Azerbaijan. Senator Sam Brownback (R-KS) introduced this bill on the Senate floor in 1997. The following is a summary of its objectives presented by the staff of Senator Brownback:

> The Silk Road Strategy legislation provides an overarching policy for the US with regards to the countries of the South Caucasus and Central Asia.

It authorizes assistance in a gamut of areas and is intended to safeguard US national interests in the region: (1) to promote sovereignty, independence with democratic government; (2) to promote tolerance, pluralism, and understanding and counter-racism and anti-Semitism; (3) to assist actively in the resolution of regional conflicts; (4) to promote friendly relations and economic cooperation; (5) to help promote market-oriented principles and practices; (6) to assist in the development of infrastructure necessary for communications, transportation, and energy and trade on an East–West axis; (7) to support US business interests and investments in the region.[111]

This legislative bill attempted to waive Section 907 of the Freedom Support Act of 1992, a provision that is very important for Azerbaijan.[112] A coalition of Jewish organizations wrote a letter of support to Senator Sam Brownback. This coalition included Agudath Israel of America, the American Jewish Committee, the American Jewish Congress, the Anti-Defamation League, B'nai Brith International, the Conference of Presidents of Major American Organizations, Hadassah, the Jewish Council for Public Affairs, the National Conference on Soviet Jewry, the Jewish Institute for National Security Affairs, and the Union of Orthodox Jewish Congregations of America. In this letter the American Jewish organizations provided three reasons for their support for the Silk Road Bill legislation:

> Much of the region enjoys significant petroleum and natural gas reserves. Accordingly, both the US and Israel stand to reap enormous dividends through investing in pipelines through these lands to Turkey. Reducing the dependence on Persian Gulf oil would benefit both countries' national security interests and help their consumers. Furthermore, Israel, which enjoys a burgeoning strategic and economic relationship with Turkey, is interested in solidifying additional relationships with moderate Muslim governments that are wary of Iranian and Russian ambitions . . .
>   As noted above, Iran continues to work hard to bring the nations in the region into its sphere of influence. Similarly, Russia still seeks to exert control over the region it once controlled when it was the Soviet Union. The reactionary Taliban forces in Afghanistan threaten the stability of the nations of Central Asia.[113]

This bill was passed as an amendment to the Foreign Operations Appropriations Bill, but the presidential waiver authority was removed by a close vote on June 30, 1999.[114] Senator Brownback argued strenuously to retain the waiver authority, but Senators McConnell, Sarbanes and others prevailed. The Azerbaijani government was disappointed with the outcome. However, American Jewish organizations continued their lobbying efforts. In the aftermath of September 11, President Bush waived Section 907 in January of 2002.

The meeting place for new concepts: epistemic communities in Turkey, Azerbaijan and Israel

In contrast to the United States, where epistemic communities have established their position in the policy process since the beginning of the twentieth century, think tanks and other independent research centers are still a novelty in all three countries under consideration.[115] But in the twenty-first century, some epistemic communities, especially in Turkey and Israel, have gained public recognition and traction in the political sphere. Meanwhile, Azerbaijan is making some first steps in this direction. With reference to the influence of epistemic communities among the three countries, Azerbaijan occupies the least privileged position, while Israel has the largest advantage in this area, and Turkey occupies the middle rank.

Turkey

Until the liberalization reforms of Turgut Ozal of the 1980s, due to its long statist tradition Turkey had not engendered any significant non-governmental sector.[116] As Suat Kiniklioglu, himself a senior member of one of the leading think tanks in Turkey, the Ankara Center for Turkish Policy Studies, concludes: "The think tank sector is a rather new phenomenon in Turkey."[117] All other institutions concerned with foreign policy traditionally operated under the purview of the foreign ministry. The only influential research center that existed in Turkey before 2000 was the Foreign Policy Institute in Ankara.[118] In 2000 the Center for Eurasian Strategic Studies (Avrasya Stratejik Arastirmalar Merkezi, or ASAM) was founded by Dr. Umit Ozdag. Strategically situated in a prestigious suburb of Ankara, ASAM has the close access to the main centers of power in Turkey: the military, the president's palace in Cankaya and the Ministry of Foreign Affairs. This think tank was uniquely positioned to respond to the pressing needs for policy-relevant research experienced by the foreign policy making community. ASAM built capacity for plotting future strategic directions of Turkey's foreign policy after the Cold War. The continued uncertainty about the process of European integration compelled the Turkish leadership to consider other options (Russia, Eurasia, the neo-Ottoman foreign policy). ASAM assumed an even more important role in Turkey after 2002, when AKP formed the government. Other smaller think tanks, Stratejik Arastirmalar Merkezi in Turkish, or SAMs, proliferated in Turkey after 2000. But the ability of these new think tanks to affect decision-making in Ankara has been insignificant.[119] Many of the Turkish think tanks were formed primarily with a view toward creating an institutional framework for influence peddling. Suat Kiniklioglu concludes about Turkish think tanks in general: "More often than not, think tanks are seen as vehicles that provide access to decision-making rather than institutions that produce original thinking."[120]

ASAM has made a unique contribution to Turkish foreign policy since its foundation in 2000. Not only has the center championed ground-breaking research on the new states in the Southern Caucasus and Central Asia, particularly relevant is its research on the foreign policy, history, geopolitics and economy of Azerbaijan.[121] The leading figures in ASAM, Dr. Umit Ozdag, the founder and co-chairman, and Necdet Pamir, the Director for Energy Policy, spearheaded the vision of deepening the Turkish–Israeli axis based on Turkish strategic interests. Both Necdet Pamir and Umit Ozdag actively participated in numerous colloquiums in Israel and contributed to the publications of Israeli think tanks.[122] Currently, ASAM continues to serve as a stalwart Turkish think tank that produces quality analysis of foreign policy. One proof of the continued influence of this think tank on Turkey's foreign policy is the fact that the recent ambassador to the United States and senior diplomat Ambassador Faruk Loguoglu took over as its head in 2007.

Israel

If Israeli think tanks have been in existence for a longer period, they still represent a novelty in the foreign policy making sphere. The Israeli statist political regime also prevented the emergence of non-governmental institutions such as think tanks for a long period.[123] In their influence and structure, Israeli think tanks are much closer to the original American model. They are also recognized for their innovative thinking.[124] The current Israeli prime minister, Ehud Olmert, provided the following assessment of the impact of epistemic communities in Israel: "The value [of these centers] is very important."[125] The most influential think tank in Israel is the Inter-Disciplinary Center (IDC). The IDC attracts the highest echelons of Israeli government, including prime ministers, foreign ministers, presidents and foreign dignitaries, to the annual conferences in Herzliya. The Inter-Disciplinary Center serves also as a base for GLORIA (The Global Research in International Affairs Center). The head of GLORIA, Professor Barry Rubin, is a prolific writer and Israeli opinion-maker. He combines his public persona as an editorial writer in the *Jerusalem Post* with co-editorship of the *Middle East Review of International Affairs* (MERIA).[126] In his editorial pieces Barry Rubin devotes significant attention to domestic politics in Turkey and Iran as well as Turkish–Israeli relations.[127] GLORIA's rival for influence in regional security and Israeli foreign policy related to Turkey and Azerbaijan is the Begin-Sadat Center for Strategic Studies (BESA). BESA is led by one the most vocal Israeli proponents of Turkish–Israeli entente and a member of the Israeli National Security Council, Efraim Inbar.[128] Efraim Inbar was personally involved in several rounds of negotiations of Israeli arms sales and military technology transfer agreements with the Turkish side between 1998 and 2000, when General Huseyin Kivrikoglu was the Turkish chief of staff.[129] Efraim Inbar also visited Azerbaijan on security-related issues on several occasions.[130] BESA has gained the recognition of leading American newspapers such as the *New York Times* as a bona fide source of expert advice on strategic issues concerning the Middle East.[131] Turkish- and Israeli-oriented think tanks and institutes such as the Center for Eurasia Strategic Studies (ASAM) and the Begin-Sadat Center for Strategic Studies (BESA) exchange scholars and regional threat analyses.[132]

Azerbaijan

In Azerbaijan intellectual and professional networks dedicated to foreign policy research were very weak until recently. First, Azerbaijan, as a newly independent state, did not even have its own foreign policy independent from Moscow. Moscow also executed centralized control over the Republic's diplomatic staff.[133] Vafa Guluzade concludes: "Our foreign ministry has neither experience nor traditions of exercising a full-scale foreign policy. It does not have a proper structure of a foreign political agency."[134] The Azerbaijan Diplomatic Academy, the fist academic institution to train professional staff for the Azerbaijani diplomatic service, just opened in March 2007.[135] Naturally, Azerbaijan could hardly be expected to become a breeding ground for economic and foreign policy think tanks, as has been the case in the United States for the most of the twentieth century. Another significant factor is authoritarian control by the ruling Aliyev clan over economic activity and the lack of resources for funding non-state sponsored centers for economic and policy research.[136] Due to state control of all main non-Western sectors of the economy through informal and political networks connected to the Aliyev clan, independent press and research centers were deprived of sources of funding. A few centers, which do exist, have a pronounced corporatist character due to the hierarchical structure of the political order in Azerbaijan. But there are some exceptions to this rule. After the fallout with President Heydar Aliyev over the Azerbaijani concessions in the negotiations over the settlement of Nagorno-Karabagh, two key foreign policy advisors left the government in 1999.[137] They formed the first independent Azerbaijani think tanks, namely the Caspian Policy Foundation created by Vafa Guluzade and the Public Forum for Azerbaijan created and led by Eldar Namazov in 2000. The Caspian Policy Foundation includes powerful international figures on its board of trustees, including Henry Kissinger, Zbigniew Brzezinsky and James Baker. Another Azerbaijani think tank, the Peace and Conflict Resolution Center led by Elhan Mehtiyev, also earned recognition as one of the centers of independent thinking about international issues and geopolitics in Azerbaijan.[138] Arif Yunusov, the leading expert on regional security and armed forces, from the Peace and Conflict Resolution Center, regularly contributes to Azerbaijani and Russian publications such as *Zerkalo*, *Exo*, *Den* and academic journals.[139] Eldar Namazov and Arif Yunusov contributed to the enhancement of the Turkish–Israeli–Azerbaijani cooperation by promoting public awareness of its importance to the geopolitical interests of Azerbaijan. But the most influential Azerbaijani foreign policy expert, Vafa Guluzade, took an active role in promoting this trilateral entente in the 1990s.[140] In particular, as the pre-eminent Middle East expert in Azerbaijan and a Turkist who has broad experience of diplomatic service in Moscow since 1969, Vafa Guluzade advanced the concept of deepening the Azerbaijani–Turkish relationship throughout the last decade of the twentieth century. The Azerbaijani diplomat called on Turkey to defend Azerbaijan militarily, in case the Nagorno-Karabagh ceasefire would be broken. On the same occasion, Guluzade stated: "Turkey stayed indifferent when Azerbaijani territories were occupied during 1992–3. But the times have changed and Azerbaijani–Turkish relations now grew to a grand new level."[141] He added that if Turkey fails to fight on the side of Azerbaijan, "Turkey will lose the respect of its own nation because we are not Azerbaijanis, but we are Turks residing in Azerbaijan."[142] In the late 1990s, Guluzade canvassed the idea of forming a federal union or unified state with Turkey at many forums.[143] Possessing intimate knowledge of the Arab–Israeli conflict, Guluzade initiated a special diplomatic channel with Israeli leadership, while preserving the personal friendship of Chairman Arafat.[144] When President Ilham Aliyev made a commitment in principle to open a diplomatic mission in Tel Aviv in May of 2006, Vafa Guluzade topped the list of candidates for the position of Azerbaijani ambassador to Israel.[145]

Impact of transnational corporations: BP, Merhav, Magal and Bateman Litwin

Under conditions of globalization, transnational corporations increasingly came to play a major role as non-state actors in international politics. In fact, because of their economic power, transnational corporations act as quasi-political entities, especially in underdeveloped regions of the world. As Azerbaijan and Central Asian countries were opening their sovereign territories for exploitation of natural resources, they became embroiled in geopolitical competition for the control of the hydrocarbon resources of the Caspian. In particular, the BTC project operated by British Petroleum (BP) and a consortium of transnational oil corporations became a fulcrum of the American strategy, starting in 1995, to redirect the flow of Caspian-region petrochemicals away from the Russian energy network. Due to the scale of its investments in the Azerbaijani oil shelf, BP acquired the power to affect the geopolitical landscape in the Caspian region and beyond. Even the government of the sole superpower, the United States, was unable to realize its geopolitical project in the Caspian without the active involvement of transnational corporations such as BP. In other words, without commercial interests and the capital of transnational oil corporations such as British Petroleum, this project would have remained unrealized.[146] This section will analyze how transnational corporations, in particular British Petroleum (BP), Israeli Merhav, Bateman Litwin, and Magal, affected the trilateral relationship from the geo-economic perspective.

The US policy to encourage diversification of world oil supplies in order to reduce future dependence on Persian Gulf oil provided critical impetus to the promotion of this alliance. Turkey, as a long-standing American ally, possessed a competitive advantage in pipeline and industrial construction, and looked to America for support of the Baku-Tbilisi-Ceyhan project. In this endeavor, Turkey and Azerbaijan also solicited the help of the American Jewish lobby, which coincided with an improvement in Turkish–Israeli relations. Turkey, the United States government and the American Jewish lobby promoted the BTC project as means of building a geopolitical bridge to the West for Azerbaijan and other Turkic countries of the Caspian basin.[147] The Caspian has no outlet to international trade sea routes. Thus one of the main problems for the Caspian region is that three oil and gas producing countries (Kazakhstan, Turkmenistan and Azerbaijan) are landlocked. This creates a set of conditions that these countries must overcome in order to export their resources to the world market. These circumstances provide numerous opportunities for manipulation by the regional powers (Russia, Iran and China) and necessitate the cooperation of regional as well as international and transnational actors. A case in point is the implementation of the Baku-Tbilisi-Ceyhan (BTC) project in 2006 and the failure to complete the Transcaspian Gas Pipeline project in 2003. The realization (or lack thereof) of these projects certainly affects the geo-economic balance in the region.[148] The construction of the BTC pipeline also accomplishes other geopolitical goals of the United States, Turkey and Israel, i.e. isolation of Iran and decoupling of the Azerbaijani economy from dependence on Russia and its energy pipeline network.[149]

The impact of globalization

Since the adoption of neoliberal economic policies by the Anglo-Saxon countries, such as the United States, the United Kingdom, New Zealand and Australia, in the 1980s, the key international financial institutions (the World Bank and the International Monetary Fund) have embraced neoliberal principles. These international institutions, which are traditionally guided by American policymakers, imposed the strictures of free market and privatization on the global economy; these policies especially affected economically poor/resource-rich Third-World countries. This process of global economic restructuring came to be known as globalization. The major outcome of globalization is the internationalization of the domain of the state in the form of intergovernmental organizations (World Trade Organization, GATT, IMF) and international NGOs (Greenpeace, Human Rights Watch, Amnesty International). Another outcome is de-territorization of economic activity, i.e. the process of state sovereignty losing its prerogative over economic activity. As a result, the scope of economic activity becomes global. The state and political power are affected by globalization, and political activity increasingly focuses on cross-border (transnational) issues.[150]

Transnational corporations (TNCs), as powerhouses of global capital, serve as levers in this restructuring process. In other words, globalization serves the interests of TNCs, which seek new areas for higher yield investment and new markets for their products.[151] TNCs compete with nation-states and sometimes form coalitions with local private capital sources for control of power and control of resources.[152] As the process of de-territorization advances, transnational corporations affect political developments at intrastate and interstate levels. The main function of TNCs in the global economy is their engagement in foreign direct investment (FDI) and the organization of the production of goods and services. The FDI by transnational corporations reached $80 billion in the developing world, including newly industrializing countries.[153] In the petrochemical sector, the "Seven Sisters"—notably Exxon (then Standard Oil of New Jersey), Royal Dutch/Shell, British Petroleum (previously Anglo-Iranian), Texaco, Mobil, Chevron (then Socal) and Gulf—continued to maintain their pre-eminence in the post-Cold War period.[154] With an estimated world energy demand projected to reach 97 million barrels a day in 2010, due to its "huge oil reserves," Mehdi Amineh concludes that "this [Caspian] region plays an important geopolitical role in the global political economy of the twenty-first century."[155]

All three countries are a part of the globalized economy. Since the 1980s, Turkey and Israel have followed the Export Oriented Industrialization (EOI) policy, and their economies are profoundly affected by the international financial institutions.[156] For the political elites of Turkey and, to a lesser degree, of Israel, Azerbaijan appeared to be a dependable source of petrochemical resources. Azerbaijan possesses in proven and possible reserves nearly 40 billon barrels of oil. More importantly, Azerbaijan was seen as the key transit country for Caspian oil. Azerbaijan's own hydrocarbon resource estimates pale in comparison with Kazakhstan. Kazakhstan is the largest oil producer in the Caspian region with estimated oil wealth of 100 billion barrels.[157] Even higher priority for Turkey was President Turgut Ozal's strategic vision of a pipeline constructed in the East–West direction (from the Caspian toward Turkey), which was capable of making Turkey a global energy hub on the Mediterranean and increase its strategic value for the West, in particular the United States.[158] The Republic of Georgia was involved in this project from the initial stages, and a segment of the Baku-Tbilisi-Cyhan runs through its territory.[159] Even before access to Caspian oil was made available through the BTC, which was completed in July of 2006, Turkey served as a main conduit for Iraqi oil to the Western markets beginning in 1977.[160]

Azerbaijan, as a newly independent state, sought a unique niche in the globalized economy as a hydrocarbon producer for the West and a transit country for other Caspian oil and gas reserves.[161] In order to accomplish this goal, the Azerbaijani government signed major oil exploration and production agreements with 30 corporations from 15 countries.[162] Successive Azerbaijani governments (under Elchibey, Heydar Aliyev and Ilham Aliyev) attached geopolitical importance to offshore oil and gas contracts with the international consortium of TNCs, representing major Western powers such as the United States, Great Britain, France and Japan. As one observer stated: "In the case of Azerbaijan, an appropriate vehicle was found in the form of foreign energy companies, in particular Western oil companies, whose long-term, capital-intensive presence in Azerbaijan would, it was thought, bend their home governments toward more sympathetic relations with Azerbaijan."[163] After the post-independence decline, since 1997 Azerbaijan has been capable of increasing its oil production due to the massive investments by the Azerbaijani International Oil Consortium (AIOC).[164] Israel also hoped to reap energy benefits from strategic ties with Azerbaijan.

The Clinton administration, after 1995, sought to establish a zone of geopolitical influence in the South Caucasus, and in the Caspian region generally. Over the ensuing decade, the United States became the most active and influential non-regional power in the Caucasus of the post-Soviet era.[165] This reflected a major shift in the American global strategy from acquiescence to Russian reassertion of its power in the "near abroad," to a policy of active engagement in Eurasian affairs, a broad geographic area including Central Asia, the Caucasus and particularly the Caspian region. Before September 11, the fundamental reason for this realignment of American policy was the pursuit of alternative sources for petrochemical resources.[166] The main policy objectives of the United States in the region are summarized in the following remark of United States Senator Sam Brownback: "Investment in the region could ultimately reduce United States dependence on oil imports from the volatile Persian Gulf and provide regional supplies as an alternative to Iranian sources."[167]

BP and the BTC paradox

British Petroleum, a major transnational petrochemical corporation with annual capital expenditure of over $200 billion and the largest investor in the Azerbaijani petrochemical industry, was the key actor in the realization of the Baku-Tbilisi-Ceyhan pipeline. Igor Muradian argues: "The musical director of this game [the geo-economic competition for access to the Caspian hydrocarbons—ABM] was British Petroleum, and its merger with AMOCO determined the unification of American and British interests. The goal of this Anglo-American 'petroleum pivot' was the creation of strategic oil reserves that could be used as an agent provocateur on the oil market. This project was directed against the leading oil-exporting countries in order to reach geo-economic objectives."[168] Transnational corporations as profit-seeking entities are naturally less concerned with geopolitical stratagems of host governments and external powers, but are primarily preoccupied with political and financial risks involved in international projects of such scale. As the commercial director of BP clarified the role of his corporation: "We are not an aid agency or charity. Our purpose is to create wealth on behalf of our shareholders. Our interests will thrive if the societies in which we invest also thrive."[169]

As the American diplomat rejoined: "The crunch [for the BTC realization—ABM] was that it was a problem of 'dollars and cents.'"[170] Through 1998 the position of two key AOIC shareholders, BP and Amoco, was that the BTC project was untenable.[171] In fact, in November of 1998, BP CEO Sir John Browne made the statement that the BTC project would only be viable with the assistance of "free public money." Eventually BP took a lead role in the international pipeline construction project, while other members of the Azerbaijani International Oil Consortium took lesser roles.

Even though the multi-state and host government agreements were signed at the Istanbul OSCE meeting in November of 1999 and the project received the official endorsement of the United States government, only when transnational corporations found it profitable to invest in this project did it become feasible.[172] In this regard, the role of British Petroleum in the realization of the BTC was crucial. An American diplomat stated: "Only when BP took a leadership role (after BP took over Amoco in 1999), other companies followed."[173] But even a powerful corporation such as BP was not capable of assuring the profitability of the BTC. In fact, the composition and distribution of financial shares among the consortium members were not finalized until June 2002.[174] The financial and feasibility issues remained mostly unresolved until implementation of the project started in January of 2003.

In order to minimize the risks of political upheavals and domestic instability affecting their investments, British Petroleum and the other TNCs involved in exploiting Azerbaijani oil and gas resources signed a series of production-sharing agreements (PSAs). PSA contracts, once signed by the consortium members and the Azerbaijani government, are ratified by the Milli Majlis and assume the force of state law. The PSA frameworks specify that foreign consortium members recover all costs (capital expenses and investments) upfront, in the early stages of production. Only then is "profit oil" slated to begin, split unevenly between the Azerbaijani government (controlling the major share) and consortium members. AIOC is a $13 million project to produce crude oil from the Azeri, Chirag and the Deepwater Guneshli fields, which are located in the waters of the Caspian Sea, about 100 kilometers offshore from the Absheron Peninsula (usually referred to as the ACG project). These combined fields contain proven reserves of 5.4 billion barrels of oil.[175] Before realization of the BTC project, most Azerbaijani oil was exported to Western markets through the Baku-Novorossisk pipeline ("northern route"). When the "early oil" from ACG became available, reaching the output of 125,000 barrels a day in 2002, it was pumped through the Baku-Supsa ("western route") pipeline.

The critical year for Turkish, Georgian and Azerbaijani strategy to become major transit countries for Caspian resources was 1999. Failure of the BP-led consortium to discover new oil fields in the Azerbaijani shelf since the initial stage of the ACG project put the viability of the BTC project at risk.[176] Despite promotion of the East–West "Main Export Pipeline" by the US and Turkish governments, BP remained non-committal. Several factors tipped the balance.

BP began seriously considering this alternative pipeline project part of its Caspian venture only after the corporation acquired and merged with the American company AMOCO in 1999. The merger with Amoco, a major partner in AIOC, also significantly expanded BP's financial and capital resource base.[177] The realization by the BP corporate leadership of the immense environmental threats posed by continued shipping of Caspian oil through the Bosporus also positively affected BP's decision to pursue the risky project.[178] In February of 1999, BP started drilling for oil, gas and gas condensate at Shakh-Deniz oil field.[179] Shakh-Deniz turned out to be one of the largest gas discoveries in the world in the last 25 years. According to the field's operator, BP, the Shakh-Deniz field contains "potential recoverable resources" of approximately 14 tcf (400 billion cubic meters).[180] This revived corporate interest in building a pipeline critical to the Turkish strategic vision. It also offered alternative gas supplies for Turkish markets. At the time, Azerbaijan did not possess routes for export of natural gas. Eventually, the Shakh-Deniz discovery proved critical for BP's decision to go ahead with the BTC project.[181] BP and SOCAR determined that by 2008 combined oil production from ACG and the Shakh-Deniz gas condensate would be sufficient to fill the pipeline to the 1-million-barrels-per-day capacity.[182] In order to bring the Shakh-Deniz gas to export markets, an infrastructure needed to be created. The prospect of building a gas pipeline parallel to the Main Export Pipeline became feasible. BP envisioned that the "South Caucasus Pipeline," also as known as the Baku-Tbilisi-Erzrum pipeline, capable of transporting gas to Turkey and beyond, would serve this purpose. The infrastructural projects of such scale involve great capital investment. By building two parallel pipelines, the operators intended to save many costs (route determination, land compensations, environmental assessment, transition fees, etc.).

Nonetheless, BP still took more precautions to extricate itself from any potential business failures. BP was extremely conscious of geopolitical rivalries among Russia, Turkey, Iran and the United States surrounding the BTC project.[183] In order to avoid liability and to have a free hand in future investment decisions in the Caspian region, BP crafted an intergovernmental agreement (IGA) between Azerbaijan, Georgia and Turkey, as well as an individual host government agreement (HGA) between each of the three governments.[184] These agreements allow the TNCs to abandon and or/ re-route the oil deliveries at any time.[185] A journalist who followed the negotiation process of the relevant BTC agreements concludes: "These agreements have largely exempted BP and its partners from any laws in the three countries—present or future—which conflict with the company's project plans. The agreements allow BP to demand compensation from the governments should any law (including environmental, social or human rights law) make the pipeline less profitable."[186]

BP holds the largest share in the BTC consortium (30.1 percent) and serves as its operator. Since the initial stage of the project, BP made participation in the BTC project conditional on obtaining loans from international financial institutions (IFIs) in order to spread financial risk, especially after the failure to obtain loans from commercial banks such as British Barclays Bank and American Citibank Group.[187] In fact, BP and Unocal, two shareholders in the BTC consortium, intended to finance 70 percent ($2.5 billion) of the construction costs through loans. The International Financial Corporation (IFC), an arm of the World Bank, approved the BTC pipeline lending scheme. BP sought loans and guarantees for the BTC from the European Bank for Reconstruction and Development, the American government-backed Export-Import Bank and British governmental loans.[188] The combined loans for the BTC project from the IFC and European Bank for Reconstruction and Development reached 250 million USD.[189]

The case of Israeli transnationals: Merhav Group and Bateman Litwin

Israeli transnational corporations made significant inroads in strategic areas of the Turkish market such as military and high technology exports, water development (GAP) and tourism.[190] Israeli TNCs were less successful in penetrating the Azerbaijani market. This section will highlight attempts by two medium-size transnational corporations, Merhav and Bateman Litwin, to expand their activities in the energy and infrastructure markets in Azerbaijan. Magal Group was more successful in obtaining a substantial contract to provide security for Bina, the main international airport in Azerbaijan.[191]

Israeli-based Merhav Group, as a leading foreign investor in Turkmenistan's gas and oil sector and irrigation, desired to expand its business in the Caspian region.[192] In 2001 Merhav owned 58 percent of Ampal America, a holding and investment company traded on NASDAQ with activities in energy, industry, communications, high-tech and real estate. Portfolio companies include Granite Hacarmel (20 percent), Mirs Communications (25 percent), Coral World International (50 percent), Epsilon Investment House (20 percent), Carmel Container Systems (20 percent) and over 40 start-ups.[193] By 2000, Merhav had won more than $1.5 billion in government contracts in Turkmenistan.[194] At the time, Merhav's president, Yoseph Maiman, served as a special ambassador to President Saparmurat "Turkmenbashi" Niyazov. Since the mid-1990s, Merhav had been exploring the idea of bringing Turkmen gas to export markets through Iran, but under pressure from the United States, Yoseph Maiman switched to supporting the East–West route for gas exports.[195] Since Merhav chose the strategy of bringing Turkmen gas to Turkish and Israeli markets, its president was lobbying US Congress, through a public relations firm, for realization of the "East–West energy corridor" vision.[196] A gas pipeline carrying Turkmen gas to Turkey was promoted as a part of the American grand vision, which found its political expression in the Silk Road Bill.[197] In order to accomplish that, Maiman needed the cooperation of Turkmenistan's neighbor, Azerbaijan. In November of 1998, Merhav brokered a $3 billion deal to construct a gas pipeline, later known as the TransCaspian Pipeline Project (TCP).[198] In fact, Turkey's President Suleiman Demirel and his Turkmeni counterpart, Saparmurat Niyazov, signed a long-term agreement for the supply of Turkmeni gas to Turkey via the TransCaspian Pipeline Project in the same month. In order to accomplish specified objectives, the TCP needed to connect with the Main Export Pipeline on Azerbaijani territory. Merhav sought to negotiate the right-of-way with Azerbaijan and Georgia and to construct a 2,000-kilometer pipeline capable of transporting a yearly 30 billion cubic meters of gas.[199] Yoseph Maiman paid a visit to Heydar Aliyev in February of 1999; Merhav's president told the Azerbaijani president: "Azerbaijan's participation was crucial not just because of the transit value of the country for the pipeline but also because Azerbaijan could be a large exporter of gas in the future along the pipeline."[200] Aliyev responded that he welcomed the Israeli company's participation in the Transcaspian project and he would consider the company's proposals. After the Shakh-Deniz gas discovery, however, Azerbaijani authorities felt that Turkmen gas delivered through the TCP would be in direct competition with Azerbaijani gas exports. Azerbaijan made unrealistic demands for transition fees for the Turkmen gas to be delivered through TCP and negotiations stalled. In March of 2003, the project was terminated.[201]

A major Israeli energy engineering company with branches in France and Kazakhstan, Bateman Litwin entered into negotiations with Azerbaijani authorities to modernize energy pipelines and transportation infrastructure in the Nakhichevan region. Due to the exorbitant license fees demanded by the Azerbaijani state "regulators" and inability to gain state guarantees, the Israeli company withdrew from the negotiations in the early 2000s.[202]

5 The heart of entente
The security dimension of the relationship

Introduction: common threat perceptions

By the mid-1990s, the strategic trilateral relationship of Azerbaijan, Turkey and Israel deepened in response to the crystallization of the Armenia–Russia–Iran–Syria axis. These alignments came into being as the result of a complex dynamic shaped by transnational and subnational agents/institutions and their interactions. They were also shaped by the regional realities. The forging of strategic ties by Turkey and Israel with Azerbaijan reflected the convergence of interests of both countries in the emerging Caspian region.[1] In general, regions themselves defy clear-cut definitions and some experts introduce instead the concept of the "security complex."[2] The impact of a new East–West energy corridor on energy security, the Western orientation of Israel and Turkey as their strategic choice and transnationalism were dealt with in other chapters. This chapter will explore the range of security threats and the regional realities that brought this axis into existence. In order to adequately reflect this complexity in the post-Cold War period, the concept of security is extended beyond military security and intelligence or "hard security" to include "soft security" such as diplomatic support, lobbying influential governments and public diplomacy.

In the aftermath of the ideological competition between Western liberal democracies and the Communist bloc, the United States perceived new global threats, such as Islamic fundamentalism and the proliferation of weapons of mass destruction (WMDs). The United States needed strategic allies in the expanded Middle East region for the construction of what US President George H.W. Bush called the "New World Order" based on American hegemony.[3] This New World Order was based on a strategy of "dual containment" of Iraq and Iran. After the demise of the Soviet threat, Turkey and Israel felt the need to reinvent themselves as "pillars" of this American strategy in the expanded Middle East.

The emergence of an alliance between Israel, Turkey and Azerbaijan not only reflected the new geopolitical realities of the post-Cold War era, but also consummated the logical historical evolution of relations among these three secular and Western-oriented states in a region where most states are characterized by endemic anti-Western (particularly anti-American) hostility. Both Turkish foreign policy elites and the military realized that new approaches were required to thwart new strategic threats that emerged after the Cold War. Deputy Foreign Minister Onur Oymen and Deputy Chief of Staff Çevik Bir promoted military–political cooperation with Israel as the key component of this new foreign policy approach.[4] This new reality became even more evident after the first Gulf war of 1991, when Turkey proved its relevance as a strategic American ally in the Middle East.[5] Turkey provided strategic basing facilities at Incirlik Air Base, logistical support and over-flight rights for the coalition forces in their military campaign against Iraq in January 1991. This conflict challenged the myth of inter-Arab solidarity since Saudi Arabia, Kuwait, the Gulf States, Egypt and even Syria participated in the anti-Iraq coalition. This provided Turkey with an opportunity to upgrade diplomatic relations with Israel and enhance strategic cooperation with Israel based on previous Turkish–Israeli interactions.[6] Araz Azimov, the Azerbaijani deputy foreign minister, sums up this congruency of interests: "These three are close to each other in this piece of the world in terms of their geopolitical and geo-economic interests, closer approach to the United States, realistic approach to the problems between Arabs and Israelis. More or less Turkey and Azerbaijan, being moderate Islamic countries and Israel having been in a long search for partners among the Islamic states."[7]

At the height of cooperation between Turkey, Israel and Azerbaijan in the mid-1990s, regional powers such as Russia, Iran, Egypt and Syria expressed concern about this change in the strategic balance in the Greater Middle East region, which, after the break-up of the Soviet Union, included the Caucasus and Central Asia.[8] Turkey also grew in importance for the United States as a conduit for American global policy in the Transcaucasus and Central Asia.

The protagonists

The Israel–Turkey–Azerbaijan axis came into being because many strategic threats and interests of the three states overlap. As Meliha Altusink described it: "[The] alignment with Israel constitutes one of the most important aspects of post Cold War Turkish foreign policy. Close relations with Israel largely resulted from a redefinition of Turkish regional security concerns, as Turkey's political and military elite came to view its Middle East policy as directly tied to Turkish regime maintenance, secularism, and territorial integrity."[9] The Turkish–Israeli entente rapidly gained momentum and became one of the most important aspects of post-Cold War Turkish foreign policy. One author maintained "that many Turks felt relations with Israel were tied to issues at the very core of Turkish national survival."[10] Azerbaijan is the junior partner in this tripartite relationship. However, Azerbaijani, Iranian and Armenian experts all agree about the role the Caucasian nation plays in the shared geopolitical vision of all three countries.[11] A strategic bilateral relationship between Turkey and Azerbaijan manifested in strong Turkish support for

Azerbaijan during the Nagorno-Karabagh conflict, 1992–3. The Azerbaijani strategic choice of the Baku-Tbilisi-Ceyhan pipeline to deliver its oil to the West via Turkish territory solidified this relationship further.[12] Azerbaijani leadership perceives Turkey as a brotherly Turkic nation epitomized in Heydar Aliyev's slogan "Bir Millet, Iki Devlet" ("one nation, two states"). Israel also backed Azerbaijan in this Azerbaijani–Armenian conflict. Israel provided diplomatic recognition and military assistance to Azerbaijan.[13] Furthermore, Azerbaijani–Israeli bilateral relations are based on a mutual fear of Iran and access to the influential Jewish lobby in the United States.[14] Azerbaijan also sees Israel as an important secular, Western power that possesses great technical and military potential. Turkey and Israel envisioned Azerbaijan as a key ally in the Caucasus in geopolitical competition with regional powers Russia and Iran (also China, although China is outside the scope of this book) for control over the development of the great fossil energy resources of the Caspian basin and their transport to the West.[15] This complex of novel threats compelled Turkey to forge an alignment with Israel that later has extended to include Azerbaijan.

Strategic objectives of the Israel–Turkey–Azerbaijan axis:

A   In the wake of the Cold War, the Turkish Republic and the newly re-established Republic of Azerbaijan wanted to boost their credentials as members of the Euro–Atlantic alliance. Since Israel has been an "invisible" member of the Western alliance since the 1950s, the two countries decided to forge strategic relations with Israel.[16]

B   Under the new unipolar reality, both countries wanted to gain the favor of the United States and sought American strategic support. One way to achieve this goal was to align with Israel since the United States has a special relationship with Israel.

C   Israel needed an expanded circle of friends in the Muslim world and to forge a bloc against Iran.

D   Both Israel and Turkey needed to enhance their energy security through access to reliable sources of petrochemicals in the Caspian and Central Asia. Azerbaijan had a double function as a supplier and a transit country.

E   All three countries wanted to establish themselves as "frontline states" in the global war against radical Islam, which, after September 11, 2001, morphed into the "war on terror."[17]

F   The regional goals of the three countries are Turkey's fight against the PKK, Hizballah and ASALA (the Armenian Secret Army for Liberation of Armenia); Israel's fight against the Lebanese Hizballah, Islamic Jihad and Hamas; and Azerbaijan's fight against Armenian separatists in Nagorno-Karabagh and Armenian links with international terrorism.

Thus these countries served as conduits of Western policy designed to combat WMD proliferation and other transnational threats. From the Euro–Atlantic perspective, both Israel and Turkey wanted to change their status from being "consumers of security" to the status of "security producers."[18]

Structural change and new challenges

In order to understand the genesis of this alignment we need to elucidate the security challenges in response to which this axis arose. There is a plurality of security challenges that brought these three countries together to form an entente. Some of these challenges pre-date the end of the Cold War. Turkey and Israel had a common foe in the Cold War years. It was represented by the threat of domestic penetration by the Soviet Union and the threat of regional instability stirred by the Soviet Arab satellites in the Middle East. The end of the Cold War removed some challenges such a frontal confrontation with Russia and the threat of Soviet-sponsored Marxist domestic militancy in Turkey. But, as two democratic and Westernized countries with secular political elites, Turkey and Israel faced new challenges to their security. Both sought allies in the post-Soviet space, in particular in the Caucasus and Central Asia, in order to prevent the spread of radical Islam in their "neighborhood." Azerbaijan became the focus of intensive diplomacy and security cooperation by Turkey and Israel for both historical and pragmatic reasons. All three countries faced a shared threat of Islamic radicalism emanating from Iran. Ethno-national separatism threatened the territorial integrity of these states. As relatively new states, both Turkey and Israel were involved in low-intensity conflicts in the frontier areas from the time of their creation.[19] Azerbaijan was embroiled in armed conflict with Armenia over Nagorno-Karabagh even before gaining independence in 1991.[20]

The political geography of the Turkish frontiers also underwent a dramatic change with the end of the Cold War. Instead of the Soviet threat embedded, in the bipolar division of the globe, from the north, Turkey has been faced with a new reality containing seeds of unrest and opportunity. The territory of the Transcaucasus and Central Asia came to be divided into territorial units of the eight newly independent states, five being Turkic speaking (Azerbaijan, Kazakhstan, Kyrgyzstan, Turkmenistan and Uzbekistan). However, the Transcaucasus is of particular strategic concern for Turkey. On the positive side, Caspian energy reserves of Turkic-speaking Azerbaijan could serve Turkish future interests. On the negative side, Russian involvement in the unresolved ethnic and regional conflicts with the secessionist regimes in Nagorno-Karabagh, Abkhazia and the South Ossetia potentially threatened Turkish security.

The disappearance of Communist ideology, which kept in check many historical rivalries, re-ignited ethno-national conflicts in the underbelly of the former Soviet bloc. This affected Azerbaijan directly in the conflict with Armenians over the Nagorno-Karabagh region. Turkey was affected by the inter-ethnic wars in the Caucasus and former Yugoslavia.[21] Ethnic conflagrations in the ex-Communist bloc served as models for increased militancy of

Kurdish and Palestinian nationalists and Islamist groups such as Lebanese Hizballah, Hamas and the Palestinian Islamic Jihad that threatened both Turkey and Israel.[22] Iran and Syria actively supported anti-Turkish and anti-Azerbaijani insurgency by minority groups, in particulars the Kurds (Turkey) and the Talyshs (Azerbaijan). Turkey, wanting to extend its sphere of influence among the Turkic ex-Soviet republics, signalled to Azerbaijan that it would support its struggle against the secessionist Armenian enclave of Nagorno-Karabagh. Israel, in turn, wanted to solidify its influence over Azerbaijan as a geopolitical bridgehead to Central Asia between Russia and Iran. As Prime Minister Benjamin Netanyahu emphasized in his speech in Baku in August of 1997, Israel attaches critical importance to cooperation between Israel, Turkey and Azerbaijan against Iranian Islamism.[23]

History of the post-Cold War entente

The recent alignment of Israel and Turkey is the culmination of the long history of amity between Jewish and Turkish people based on the tradition of Turkish tolerance and Ottoman hospitality toward Jewish refugees from Europe, in particular the victims of the Jewish expulsion from the Iberian peninsula in the fifteenth century. The Republican regime, led by Kemal Ataturk, applied thoroughgoing measures to eradicate the influence of Islam as part of modernizing Turkish society. In its foreign policy, Turkey attempted to shed the Ottoman imperial legacy and to align with Western-minded regimes in Asia such as Afghanistan, the Pehlevi Iran and Pakistan. Following World War II, a number of Arab states gained independence; Turkey had strained relations with most of them, except for the Kingdom of (Trans) Jordan. The Turkish secular elite held in disdain the elites and populations of the Arab East. The attitude of hostility was reciprocated by Arab leaders who perceived Turkey as a Westernized version of the Ottoman Empire. Many Arabs even today consider Turks to be "thinly disguised colonial imperialists."[24] Turkey was the first Muslim country to recognize and establish diplomatic relations with the State of Israel in 1949. Against the background of Arab intransigence, Turkey recognized the State of Israel on March 28, 1949. The traditional belief in far-reaching Jewish influence strengthened the determination of the Turkish government to pursue pro-Israeli policies.[25] Thus, establishing diplomatic ties with Israel was a clear signal that Turkey was firmly allied with the Western camp in the Cold War confrontation. Turkey wanted to be perceived as a secular and enlightened state by a Western alliance led by the United States.[26]

Surrounded by Arab enmity, the Jewish state sought alliances with non-Arab populations in the Middle East and the Horn of Africa. David Ben-Gurion, the first Israeli leader, envisioned Israel as "an island in the hostile Muslim Arab sea."[27] As a strategic counter-measure, Ben-Gurion formulated the strategy of the "alliance of the periphery" that guided Israeli Middle Eastern policy from the first years of Israeli independence.[28] In order to safeguard its future, Israel needed to form alliances further away from the "Arab sea," i.e.

on its periphery. Implementing this strategy, Israel sought alliances with both state and non-state actors. In the 1950s, Israel established secret alliances with Iran, Ethiopia and Turkey.[29] This strategy included the creation of links with non-Arab segments of Arab states such as the Maronite Christians in Lebanon, the Kurds in Northern Iraq, and the Copts in Egypt.[30] The first major step in the creation of the strategic cooperation between Turkey and Israel took place after the break-up of the Baghdad Pact.[31] Turkey's attempt to enter into the British-supported Baghdad Pact floundered because of the takeover of power in Baghdad by Colonel Kassem in 1958. As part of the pro-Western camp in the Middle East, Turkey and Israel shared a fear of Soviet penetration and radicalization of Arab regimes. The success of the Israeli military against the Arab foe, Egypt, during the Sinai campaign provided another argument for the Turkish security establishment to pursue strategic cooperation with Israel. The United States government prompted both countries to cooperate under the American umbrella. The same year, Israeli Foreign Minister Golda Meir unofficially visited Turkey and prepared the way for a secret summit meeting. In the summer of 1958, Turkey and Israel concluded agreements for cooperation in diplomatic, military and intelligence spheres, as well as in commerce and scientific exchanges. On August 29, 1958, the leaders of the two countries, Adnan Menderes and David Ben-Gurion, signed an agreement of cooperation against Middle Eastern radicalism and "Soviet influence."[32] Despite views expressed by some scholars, this secret alliance, which later included Iran, endured until the Islamic Revolution in Iran of 1979.[33] According Harun Yahya, the Mossad had maintained a Turkish base for intelligence-gathering operations against the Soviet Union since the 1950s. In the same period, Israeli security services started to provide training for the Turkish security apparatus in tandem with Savak, the Iranian security service, under a trilateral agreement code-named "Trident."[34] This agreement covered the cooperation of the Turkish, Iranian and Israeli secret services with the aim of exchanging secret information. It also included a schedule for two annual meetings each year between the chiefs of the three secret services. This agreement gave rise to critical and long-term cooperation. A former head of the Mossad, Isser Harel explained, "We strove for creation of an effective security and intelligence system with these countries (Iran and Turkey). Especially we worked to train special forces and police forces to enable them to stamp out every manifestation of revolutionary overthrow and foreign occupation . . . As a result these two countries formed shared persistent security perceptions with us and we took pains in order to reward this established trust."[35] The Paris meeting between Ismet Inonu and Levi Eshkol in June of 1964 confirmed that the 1960 coup did not affect this secret collaboration. In the 1970s, when Turkey was on the verge of the civil war, Israel was involved in security operations against radical left-wing and right-wing organizations.[36] Since the 1980s Israel has pursued a policy of "normalization" and establishing diplomatic relations with countries of the Muslim Middle East and Africa. In order to raise diplomatic and political relations to the public level, a meeting was arranged between Turkish Foreign Minister Vahit Halefoglu and Israeli Ambassador Meir Rosen on April 4, 1985. According to Israeli sources, at this meeting Israel offered the aid of the Israeli lobby to safeguard Turkish interests in Washington. After this meeting, Turkey began to receive large-scale assistance from the United States.[37] The Madrid Conference of 1991 and the beginning of the Arab–Israeli Peace process provided Turkey with a diplomatic excuse to upgrade diplomatic relations with Israel. In order to be seen by her Arab neighbors as even-handed, Turkey also opened an embassy of the PLO in Ankara in 1991.

The realities of the Azerbaijani–Turkish strategic relationship also reflect a history of ideological and strategic cooperation. In 1992 Turkey was the first state to confer diplomatic recognition on the Republic of Azerbaijan. This diplomatic move was calculated to provide international legitimacy to the re-established Azerbaijani state in the Caucasus. Turkey played a critical role in the establishment of the first short-lived Azerbaijani republic of 1918–20. The Ottoman troops, in accordance with the agreement of peace and friendship of 1918, signed in Batumi, intervened on behalf of an independent Azerbaijan in June of 1918.[38] Linguistic, ethnic and cultural ties added emotional resonance to the union of the two geographically proximate Turkic states. Turkey perceived Azerbaijan as a new strategic ally in its close neighborhood. Azerbaijan, especially under leadership of its first president, Abulfaz Elchibey (Aliyev) (1992–3), sought to establish a close political union with Turkey. As a Turkist, Elchibey viewed a secular Western-oriented Turkey as the principal model for Azerbaijani political development.[39] During the hostilities in Nagorno-Karabagh, all sectors of Azerbaijani society expected that Turkey would openly side with Azerbaijan in the conflict. In fact, the Azerbaijani parliament passed legislation that extended special Turkish protection of the Azeri enclave of Nakhichevan to the whole territory of Azerbaijan.[40] By this legislative act, the Azerbaijani government intended to oblige Turkey to intervene militarily in the hostilities. Indeed, from the formation of modern Azerbaijan, Turkey actively participated in the forming and training of the Azerbaijani armed forces. During the Elchibey administration, Turkey was involved in funding and assisting political movements and paramilitary organizations in Azerbaijan. However, beyond some covert operations, Turkey disappointed public expectations in Azerbaijan by not contributing openly in the Nagorno-Karabagh conflict.

The Israeli connection to Azerbaijan was shaped by a history of positive treatment of the Jews, exceptional for many Islamic societies in the twentieth century. The first post-Independence leadership of Azerbaijan saw Israel as another pro-Western strategic ally. This posture raised the ire of the Islamic Republic of Iran. Through its agents of influence and the pro-Iranian press in Azerbaijan, Iran condemned the Azerbaijani Popular Front leaders as "the Zionist agents."[41] Israel in turn supported Azerbaijan during its conflict with the Armenians over Nagorno-Karabagh. According to a report in Al-Wassat, Israel and Turkey provided Stinger missiles to the Azerbaijani government during the hostilities.[42] Israeli security forces also played a critical role in the training of security and intelligence services of Azerbaijan.[43]

The shared threats of the 1990s

The Kurdish question

Regional powers in the Middle East have traditionally used discontented minorities to undermine their rivals. The Kurdish peoples are a case in point. Estimates of the Kurdish population range from 13 to 25 million people. Kurdish sources claim that there are 40 million Kurds worldwide, including 20 million in Turkey, 8 million in Iran, 6 million in Iraq, 2 million in Syria and 150,000 in the NIS. The Kurds were a common factor in regional rivalries that predated the creation of nation-states in the region during the post-World War II period. Southern Kurdistan is one of the richest oil regions in the world. The land of the Kurds is situated at the nexus between Turkey, Iraq, Iran, Syria and Armenia. Control over Kurdish-populated regions allows governments to influence the geopolitical situation in the whole Middle Eastern region.[44] The Kurdish question impacts Turkish foreign policy toward Iraq, Iran, Syria, Russia, Armenia, Azerbaijan and Greece. Iran uses the Kurds in its struggle with Iraq, while the Hussein regime in Iraq attempted to use the Kurds against Turkey. Syria, which has border disputes with Turkey, has provided bases for the PKK since the creation of that Kurdish militant organization.[45] For purchase of weapons and ammunition in the early and mid-1990s, the PKK relied heavily on countries that are considered "friendly," namely, Iraq, Syria, Iran and Armenia.[46] The Russian government historically used the Kurdish issue to promote its imperial interests in Persia and Turkey, while Armenia and Greece used their political and covert alliances with the Kurds to undermine their erstwhile nemesis, Turkey.[47] In January 1995, Russia agreed to cut back on PKK activities in the Federation, although the PKK still maintains an office in Moscow.[48] During the Soviet era, Azerbaijan served as a forward base for anti-Turkish activities by the PKK.[49]

The PKK (the Kurdish Workers Party) was formed in the Turkish village of Fise (Vilayet Dyarbakir) in November 1978. Abdullah Ocalan assumed leadership from the party's founding. He determined the objectives and defined the program of the party. The PKK espoused Marxist revolutionary ideology and chose military struggle as the primary means for achieving its goals. The maximum objective was the creation of an independent state on the whole territory of Kurdish settlement. More recently the Kurdish Workers Party has moderated its demands and seeks autonomy status for a Kurdish region within the Turkish state.[50] PKK has broad support among Kurdish citizens of Turkey and Kurdish refugees in Western Europe, Russia and North America. According to former Turkish Chief of Staff Dogan Gures, roughly one-tenth of ethnic Kurds support the militant movement. This amounts to approximately four hundred thousand persons.[51] The movement has adopted "revolutionary violence" tactics against the Turkish state as a means of Kurdish national liberation since 1984. After the 1980 military coup, the PKK cadres left Turkey and moved to Palestinian guerrilla bases in Lebanon. Earlier, positive, Turkish perceptions of the PLO declined after the Palestinians provided these bases and military training to PKK operatives and ASALA in Lebanon.[52] ASALA, an Armenian terrorist group, had initiated its terrorist operations with attacks that cost the lives of over 30 Turkish diplomats in 1975. The ideology and methods of the organization were similar to those of the PKK. ASALA also found support from PLO factions based in Lebanon. In 1980, the two organizations signed an agreement in Sidon, Lebanon, to coordinate their activities against Turkish targets.[53] During the 1982 Israeli campaign against Palestinians in Lebanon, Israeli forces overran many guerrilla bases, including Armenian ones. Israel passed captured intelligence regarding the Armenians to Turkey, which the latter utilized accordingly. With the realization that the anti-Turkish guerrilla groups trained their members with the cooperation of the PLO at Palestinian bases came new caution toward all-embracing support of the Palestinian cause by the moderate Left and nationalist political elites in Turkey.[54] In 1982, PKK militants gained military experience through participation in the hostilities between Israeli troops and Palestinian factions during the Israeli invasion of Lebanon. In 1985, a cluster of Kurdish organizations coalesced around the PKK core. This formation was called the Front for National Liberation of Kurdistan (FNLK), which claimed the authority to represent all national organizations of Kurds on international arena. The military wing of the FNLK, called the Army for National Liberation of Peoples of Kurdistan (AFNLPK), was formed in 1986. It had 15,000 under arms. Ultimately, this led to a series of violent protests against the Turkish government in the cities of Cizre and Nusaybin between 1990 and 1992 that were called the Kurdish Intifada, or serhildan.[55]

In response to the Turkish military incursion into Iraqi Kurdistan, the PKK undertook a major raid in Turkey in August of 1984. The Kurdish guerrillas occupied the Turkish cities of Eruh and Shamdiv. Turkey moved its troops into the southeastern region where a guerrilla war has been waged since. Thousands of Turkish troops have been killed in operations against Kurds, and the Kurds have inflicted devastating damage on the Turkish civilian population. As a result of the Turkish military reprisals against the Kurds, between 25,000 and 30,000 civilians have been killed and 3,000 Kurdish villages have been burned to the ground.[56]

The Turkish losses account for 10,000 troops and 5,000 Kurdish collaborators (among the Democratic Party of Kurdistan supporters). Turkey has lost two or three helicopters and probably ten tanks. By different estimates the military operations against the Kurds have cost between $11 billion and $25 billion annually. Nearly 2.5 million Kurds have been deported to western Turkey. According to Kurdish sources, 3.5 million became refugees as a result of the Turkish military actions. Under the guise of addressing the Kurdish problem, 16 cities were placed under martial law legislation. Many Kurdish intellectuals—scientists, journalists, lawyers and teachers—were imprisoned in Turkey. According to Kurdish sources, 2,000 Kurdish intellectuals were killed. Extra-legal Turkish groups such as the Kontrgerilla were allegedly involved in many violent activities.[57]

In the winter of 1994, a contingent of 350,000 Turkish troops in the southeast was increased to 500,000, fully half of the Turkish army on active duty. On the eve of the 1994 elections, members of the Kurdish Democratic Party in local government were arrested and the Party banned. Six Kurdish members of the Turkish parliament were arrested in the summer of 1994. In 1995, the Turkish troops undertook a military operation code-named Dawn in northern Iraq. The operation was undertaken unilaterally, while 350,000 Turkish troops were placed in Turkish Kurdistan to safeguard the rear. As two major Kurdish factions, the Patriotic Union of Kurdistan (PUK) Unity party and the Kurdish Democratic Party (PDK), clashed in a struggle to control the Kurdish "safe haven" area in northern Kurdistan, Turkey attempted to promote its interests in Iraq. As a result of this operation, the KDP, supported by the Turkish military, took control of Iraqi Kurdistan. This led to the creation of a buffer zone between the Turkey-backed KDP militia and the PUK, closely aligned with Iran. Robert Olson concludes, "Ironically, the areas proclaimed as safe havens for the Kurds in 1991 would fall almost completely under the control of the KDP and, thus, indirectly under the influence of Turkey. The area of northern Iraq under KDP control could come to resemble the security that Israel established in southern Lebanon in 1978."[58] The PKK, however, emerged strengthened and took advantage of the internecine fighting between the two other Kurdish factions. The Turkish military publicly stated that they saw the PKK as the most important threat to Turkish security.[59] Anti-Turkish PKK militancy peaked when Abdullah Ocalan was arrested in Kenya in 1999.

Iran: Islamic radicalism and the spread of weapons of mass destruction

All three members of the entente are concerned about the issue of the ideological penetration of radical Islam and the potential for increased militancy among their domestic populations. The military in Turkey is an institution that single-mindedly maintained the principles of secularism and modernization as fundamental to the preservation of republican order. They saw the Islamist domestic opposition to these principles, sponsored by Iran, as a state security threat.[60] The National Security Policy Document (MGSB), or the "Red Book," a document updated every five years that summarizes the strategic threats to Turkey, has listed Iran as a threat since the 1979 Revolution.[61] Iran was also implicated in the support of the Kurdish incursions into Turkey.[62] Turkey perceives Iran as a rival in the competition for influence among Muslim Newly Independent States, in particular Azerbaijan.

Since seizing power in 1979, the Islamic government in Teheran has been providing ideological and material aid to radical Palestinian factions that conduct terrorist operations against Israel. The Iranian regime supports anti-Israeli groups such as the Abu Nidal, Lebanese Hizballah, the Islamic Jihad, Hamas and others.

Meanwhile, many Azeris badly resent the open political, financial and military backing the Islamic Republic provides for the Christian Orthodox Armenians that have occupied large portions of Azeri territories in Nagorno-Karabagh, dealing a severe blow to the pride and morale of the Azeris.[63] Azerbaijan is also connected through its history, culture and the Shiite branch of Islam, with Iran. However, the Azerbaijani authorities perceive the export of Islamic revolution from its southern neighbor as an existential threat. Iran's Azeri population (by some estimates as high as 30 million) serves as a source of tension between the two countries because of the threat of irredentism. The Republic of Azerbaijan possesses significant hydrocarbon resources in the Caspian shelf, but it also faces Iranian claims on some of its oil fields as a result of Iranian refusal to acknowledge the 20 percent division of the territorial waters of the Caspian Sea among coastal states. Over the last 12 years, Iranian gunboats have made several incursions into Azerbaijani territorial waters. The last major conflagration occurred on July 23, 2001. Azeri officials say that in order to oppose the Tehran–Moscow–Yerevan axis they have no other choice but to get support from powers like Washington, Tel-Aviv or Ankara, now Baku's main ally and backer.[64] In the 1990s, Israel, Turkey and Azerbaijan shared a fear of the growing range of Iranian missiles and the potential threat of development of military nuclear capability.

The Syrian knot

In the 1990s, both Turkey and Israel shared the high threat perception of Syria. Israel continues to face substantial regional threat from Syria. The Syrian government has supported anti-Israeli terrorist groups such as the Abu Nidal, Lebanese Hizballah, Islamic Jihad and others since the end of the military campaign "Peace for Galilee." Israel had to contend with incursions by Syrian- and Iran-supported Hizballah from Lebanon. The Syrian regime claims in its official rhetoric that "historical Palestine" belongs to Syria.[65] Syria possesses a dangerous stockpile of chemical weapons that threaten Israel and Turkey.[66] However, Turkey was most concerned about the Syrian threat at the time. Syria actively supported Kurdish guerrilla warfare against Turkey. The issue of the province of Hatay (Iskanderun), which formerly was a part of French-mandate Syria, continued to be a source of Syrian territorial claims against Turkey. Conflict over the distribution of water from the Euphrates River between Turkey and Syria aggravated Syrian–Turkish relations in the 1990s. Syria internationalized the water issue by drawing in the Arab world (Egypt and the Gulf States) to accuse Turkey of depriving her neighbors of a fair share of the water from the rivers. This Arab position was formalized in the Damascus Declaration.[67] Even more threatening, from the Turkish perspective, was an understanding reached between Syria and Greece that envisaged the use of Syrian air bases and air space in a military conflict between Greece and Turkey in 1995.[68]

In the late 1980s, the Syrians allowed PKK militants to train in the Bekaa valley in Lebanon and to pass through Syrian territory to strike at targets inside Turkey. After a series of diplomatic threats indicating that Turkey would attack PKK bases in Syrian territory, a conflagration on the Syrian border erupted that threatened to transform into open military conflict in the fall of 1998. Turkish authorities announced that Syria was waging an "undeclared war" on Turkey and that Turkey would respond in kind. The Turkish military sent army reinforcements ready to be deployed to the border with Syria. Syria perceived itself under pincer pressure from two neighbors, Turkey and Israel. The Syrian regime backed down and Syria signed the Adana agreement of October 1998. This agreement obligated Syria to expel Abdullah Ocalan and cease supporting the PKK.[69] Despite improvement of bilateral Turkish–Syrian relations, the outstanding issues of Syrian irredentism, unresolved water conflict and proliferation of WMDs remain.

The peace process with Arab nations created a suitable atmosphere for improving Turkish–Israeli relations. The Oslo Agreement of 1993 between Israel and the PLO was followed shortly after by the first official visit to Israel by Turkish Foreign Minister Hikmet Cetin. At that time, Israel pursued three-track diplomacy with the Palestinians, Jordanians and Syrians.[70] Not all aspects of the Arab–Israeli peace process, which was lauded by Turkish politicians, were completely embraced by the Turkish foreign policy establishment. In particular, the attempt at Syrian–Israeli rapprochement was negatively perceived in Turkey, because Turkey was concerned that a peace treaty between Syria and Israel would change the power balance in Syria's favor. The elimination of Israel from the power equation would allow Syria to apply substantial pressure on Turkey on the Hatay issue and the division of water resources. The expectation that peace with Israel would contribute to the cross-border operations of the PKK also contributed to the high threat perception of Syria.

Greece and the Cyprus question

The territory and population of the modern Greek republic was carved out of a large part of the Ottoman Empire as a result of bloody conflicts and population exchanges. This historical ill feeling has dominated the dynamic of the Greek–Turkish relationship. The mutual suspicions persist even into the present, despite the rapprochement in Greek–Turkish relations after 1999. After the division of Cyprus into Greek and Turkish zones in 1974, the Greek state maintained attempts to manipulate the Cyprus issue in order to stymie Turkish efforts to enter the European Union. Tensions flared up in the Aegean over counter-territorial claims over the continental shelf, airspace, management of military and civil air-traffic control zones.[71] In the last quarter of the twentieth century, both states came to the brink of war over territorial incursions in the Aegean on three occasions, the most recent instance in 1996. In Cyprus, the confrontation between the two nations was heightened by the proposed sale of Russian S-300 surface-to-air missiles to be deployed in the Greek zone of the island in 1998.[72] Greek support of the PKK was also a serious irritant in Turkish–Greek relations. In Greece, there is prevalent public sympathy with the Kurdish cause. Turkish authorities suspect that Greece provides facilities and training to PKK guerrillas, despite Greek denials.[73]

The Nagorno-Karabagh issue

As a result of the Nagorno-Karabagh conflict, the Armenian enclave and the adjacent regions (constituting 20 percent of Azerbaijan's territory) came under occupation by the secessionist regime of the self-proclaimed Republic of Nagorno-Karabagh. As a result of Russian involvement in the Nagorno-Karabagh conflict on the Armenian side and persistent Russian efforts to enhance Armenian military capabilities, Azerbaijan drifted away from the position of Russia's footstool in the Caucasus. Over the 1990s it became a potential NATO member and a new player in the international oil markets in its own right.[74] Since President Abulfaz Elchibey established the first post-Soviet regime in June of 1992, Azerbaijan has sought to form a pro-Western alliance with Georgia in the Caucasus. After the return of Heydar Aliyev, Azerbaijan gradually eased out of the Russian sphere of influence. There are three main indicators of this development in Russo–Azerbaijani relations. The first one is redeployment of Russian troops from Azerbaijani territory. President Aliyev was categorically opposed to allowing Russian bases in the country and handing over control of the borders to Russia. The second factor was Azerbaijani opposition to the hegemonic position of Russia within the CIS, and, third, Azerbaijan was suspected of aiding Chechen rebels in the Russo–Chechen war of 1993–4.[75] Not unnoticed by such regional powers as Russia, Iran, Armenia and Greece, Turkey and Israel have tacitly extended security and military cooperation to Azerbaijan.[76] Indeed, Turkey made the commitment to provide long-term aid and training to Azerbaijani military forces.[77]

The hour of dire need: the impact of the revolution in military technology on the formation of entente

Already in the 1980s, a program was drawn up for full-scale military modernization and rearmament of the Turkish military. Faced with both traditional and new post-Cold War challenges, Turkish military leadership recognized that the need to modernize the Turkish Armed Forces (TAF) had become even more pressing. General Çevik Bir commented, "The Turkish military came to the conclusion that Turkey had to revolutionize and strengthen its armed forces because of its unique geography. Turkey borders fourteen nations, including the Black Sea littoral countries . . . In order to face new threats we need to increase combat effectiveness of our armed forces."[78] TAF urgently needed to overhaul its weapon systems and catch up with the revolution in military technology in order to meet these challenges. After the first Gulf war, the task of completely upgrading military hardware, technology and electronic warfare was considered critical.[79] Turkey approached its NATO allies and individual Western European governments in search of sophisticated weapons systems and technological know-how. But, as a result of real or fictitious concerns over the Turkish military campaign against Kurdish separatists (which included "scorched earth" tactics), Turkey was denied access by the West to the most up-to-date military technology and hardware. This made Israel an ideal ally, one able to satisfy military and intelligence needs. Ofra Bengio argues that, "military technological know-how was the main motivation for the Turkish military establishment's approach to Israel [as far back as the] 1980s."[80] Strategic partnership with Israel was based to a large degree on access to Israeli advanced weapons systems and cooperation with Israeli technology-oriented industry in upgrading Turkish military hardware. Turkey pursued upgrades of older generation, American-made tanks and F-4 military airplanes as well joint military technology projects (anti-missile-oriented, electronic warfare and intelligence).[81] Hen-Tov concludes that "It is no coincidence that the military modernization program was announced at the same time that the cooperation agreements with Israel were signed in 1996."[82]

Azerbaijan also desired to benefit from acquisition of "new generation" weapons systems from Israel. However, as the Azerbaijani deputy foreign minister, Araz Azimov, emphasized, the small size of the armed forces (compared with Turkey's) and a lack of financial resources prevented Azerbaijan from becoming a vital consumer for Israeli-oriented manufacturers.[83] At the same time, Azerbaijan benefited from some transfers of electronic intelligence equipment, airport security equipment and state security personnel training methods from Israel.[84]

Pieces of the puzzle: the making of entente

As noted earlier, the timing of forging this entente was not coincidental. Since the late 1980s, Turkey had experienced increased Kurdish insurgency in the frontier area where Turkey borders Iran, Iraq and Syria. Guerrilla operations by the PKK launched from Syria became a critical factor in Turkish–Syrian relations. The increase in electoral support for Islamist parties in Turkey, in particular that for the Refah (Welfare) Party, during the 1988 elections worried the Kemalist establishment. As anti-PKK operations expanded, the military sought to increase public support and assume greater control over foreign policy. By the mid-1990s, the political echelons of Turkey were in disarray; the Turkish military again assumed control over foreign policy. As part of an overall strategy to reassert their status as guardians of the secular Republic, the military decided to elevate diplomatic relations with Israel, a sworn enemy of traditional Islamists. The military explained it as a strategic decision enhancing the security of the Turkish Republic.[85]

The siginificance of the Syrian–Israeli track as part of the comprehensive peace negotiations of 1995–6 was not lost on the Turkish security establishment. Progress in Syrian–Israeli negotiations caused great concern for the military in Turkey because the security of Southeast Turkey could have been compromised. Turkey felt that the timing was right to broker a bilateral agreement with Israel in order to counterbalance any Syrian–Israeli agreement.[86] In fact, Turkey expected assurances that Israel would not sign any agreement with Syria that failed to stipulate that Syria would cease support of anti-Turkish terrorism. Israel provided this guarantee to Turkey in January of 1996.[87]

Israel's security establishment noted with concern the spread of radical Islam in Central Asia and the Caucasus coterminous with Iranian penetration of the region. As an additional benefit of strategic relations with Turkey, Israel realized that Turkey was capable of enhancing state security in two ways. First, Turkey offered an alternative, Western-oriented model of development for the newly independent Muslim states.[88] Second, Israel would benefit from Turkish influence over the Turkic republics (particularly Azerbaijan) both as a "good will" messenger and as a conduit for Israeli economic and strategic cooperation.[89] Vafa Guluzade laid the groundwork for strategic relations with Azerbaijan during his visits to Israel in 1992–4. Vafa Guluzade, the chief foreign policy advisor to three Azerbaijani presidents, took the initiative in establishing an Azerbaijani–Israeli strategic understanding. In an interview, Guluzade said that in meeting with Foreign Minister Shimon Peres in Israel in 1992, he suggested opening an unofficial channel for consultations on security between the two countries.[90] From a separate vantage point, Iran was also very concerned about growing strategic ties between Israel and Azerbaijan. The Iranian regime threatened Azerbaijan with negative consequences if Azerbaijan persisted in furthering relations with Israel.[91] During his visit to Kazakhstan for the 1995 summit meeting of Caspian states, the Iranian foreign minister, Ali Akbar Velayati, warned Azerbaijan to stay away from Israel or risk instability in the Caucasus region.[92]

During his landmark visit to Baku in August of 1997, Israeli Prime Minister Benjamin Netanyahu cemented the relationship between Israeli and Azerbaijani leadership. At their meeting, Netanyahu and the president of Azerbaijan, Heydar Aliyev, discussed the possibility of extending the Baku-Tbilisi-Ceyhan oil pipeline into the Mediterranean, thus permitting the delivery of Azerbaijani oil directly to Israel. Another subject that drew the attention of both leaders, was intelligence cooperation between Azerbaijan, Turkey and Israel against the Islamic regime in Teheran.[93] The most substantive meeting was that between Prime Minister Ehud Barak and Heydar Aliyev in Istanbul in March 1999.[94]

The greatest success of Turkish diplomacy in the early 1990s was in Azerbaijan when the pro-Turkish Azerbaijan Popular Front (APF) and its leader, Abul Fazl Elchibey, came to power in June 1992. Elchibey idolized Ataturk and had previously expressed the wish that Turkey and Azerbaijan would someday form a confederation. During the short-lived Elchibey presidency, Turkey also established security relations with Azerbaijan, including the training of Azerbaijani military personnel; this relationship would survive the collapse of the Azerbaijani Popular Front (APF) government. A new stage of strategic cooperation between the two countries evolved in 1997–9. The improved relations, including close foreign policy coordination, arose from the excellent personal relationship of President Suleyman Demirel and President Heydar Aliyev. In April of 1999, a formal understanding on full-fledged strategic cooperation was concluded. According to Igor Muradian, the most crucial element of this understanding was the coordination of Azerbaijan's foreign and domestic policy with Turkey. Azerbaijan's leadership committed itself to several principles such as (a) not opening military actions without the consent of Turkey; (b) the irreversibility of the break with Moscow; (c) integration into NATO and Euro–Atlantic institutions; (d) American involvement in the strategic cooperation; (e) cessation of persecution of radical pan-Turkist opposition; and (f) cooperation against Iran and other states hostile to the United States and Turkey.[95] In March 2001, Azerbaijan and Turkey concluded a state-to-state agreement to swap gas at below market prices in exchange for weapons transfers. But Turkish–Azeri military cooperation appears to have withered following Aliyev's decision to grant Russia basing rights at Gabala strategic radar station. Ankara considered the move to be "against Turkey" and a "deviation from [Azerbaijan's] policies, foreseeing an opening to the West."[96] However, Turkish–Azerbaijani cooperation was deeply tested in August of 2001. Over the years, a series of Iranian air force overflights had occurred, and incursions into Azerbaijani territorial waters of the Caspian were frequent. Finally, a major violation occurred on July 23, 2001, when an Iranian warship ordered an Azerbaijani exploration ship contracted by British Petroleum to withdraw from exploration operations in a disputed zone. The Iranians asserted that Soviet–Iranian treaties of 1921 and 1941 determined the status of the Caspian. The Iranian ambassador to Baku, Ahad Qazaie, said in a BBC interview: "Any exploitation of the Alborz oil field by Azerbaijan was illegal and contrary to international conventions."[97] The crisis further escalated when Iranian authorities warned Azerbaijan against permitting foreign companies to explore the disputed waters: "Iran will hold Azerbaijan responsible for any such acts."[98] One month later Turkey sent an air force squadron on a "friendly" visit to Baku, highlighting the Turkish commitment to the security of Azerbaijani territorial waters. In 2002 Heydar Aliyev signed a declaration with Ankara cementing "deeper strategic cooperation." This document envisaged long-term Turkish military assistance to Azerbaijan, as Azerbaijani armed forces undertook a "restructuring process."[99]

Meanwhile, Turkey embarked on an aggressive program of military modernization. Turkey officially announced this multi-billion dollar program in 1996. This program anticipated the purchase of high-technology equipment and upgrading of older systems. The program, central to Turkey's long-term political–military strategy, was allocated for $25–$30 billion for the first eight to ten years and is expected to total $150 billion over 30 years.[100]

The Turkish military guided the process of building strategic relations with Israel. Since 1991, more than 23 agreements in political, economic/commercial, cultural and military spheres have been concluded between Turkey and Israel. In May 1994, an "Agreement on Security and Secrecy" was signed. It stipulated that security information should not be transferred to third parties. Later that same year, the two sides signed the "Memorandum on Mutual Understanding and Cooperation" to fight terrorism.[101] The key agreement that defines the strategic and practical parameters of the Turkish–Israeli entente is the "Military Training Cooperation Agreement," signed in February 1996. This agreement included, among other things, an exchange of military information, experience and personnel. This agreement caused a strong negative reaction in Islamist circles at home.[102] The Turkish military provided scripted explanations and ardently defended this pact. In fact, as noted earlier, domestic critics have accused the military of entering into military commitments with Israel above the government and the heads of civilian ministers. Thus, however long the Islamists might be at the helm of Turkey's coalition politics, they will not venture any measures that undermine the accords previously negotiated by the Turkish military, unless the latter assents to the changes.

The most vigorous proponent of a Turkish–Israeli military alignment was General Çevik Bir. The military, through media leaks and friendly journalists, made this accord the subject of public knowledge to the disappointment of Israelis who wanted to keep it secret. On the Israeli side, the key figure in forging this axis was David Ivri, an ex-air force general, who at the time served as director general in the Israeli Ministry of Defense headed by Yitzhak Rabin.[103]

Çevik Bir indicates that by signing a bilateral military cooperation agreement in 1996, both Turkey and Israel sent a political message to "the region and beyond."[104] The overarching purpose of this agreement was to increase the deterrence capabilities of both countries against present and future regional threats. These threats included Islamist militancy, proliferation of WMDs and spreading ethno-national conflict. The target audience of this message was primarily anti-Western regimes in the region (Syria, Iran and Iraq). The goal was, as General Bir put it, to "deter those who have a different idea about security and regional stability" in the greater Middle East.[105]

The second objective was to combine efforts at increasing the military capabilities of both countries. In particular, the training of Turkish pilots in Israeli Kfirs is advantageous in that the Israeli planes contain the same advanced avionics systems, including radar, electronic warfare and navigation systems, that were to be installed into 54 Turkish F-4 fighter bombers as part of a $600–$650 million, five-year deal between Turkey and Israel. The agreement for upgrading the Turkish jets was initiated in April 1996.[106]

The Israeli combat experience against Soviet-made weapons systems, with which Turkey's potential enemies, in particular Syria, were equipped, made this training of critical importance for Turkey's military. Beyond the joint training exercises, the high-level military, political and non-governmental exchanges, as well as the spectacular rise in commercial and trade relations between the two states, invigorated the strategic relationship.

In the shadow: intelligence and covert cooperation

By midsummer 1996, multiple examples of cooperation could be cited, all indicative of a secret agenda for Israeli–Turkish accords. A case in point was the super-sensitive issue of the Kurdish rebellion. In this context, the Turks had received intelligence data on Kurdish guerrilla operations within Turkey from those Western countries involved in Operation Provide Comfort as well as from Israel. On the basis of this intelligence, Turkish troops, supported by American-supplied Super Cobra helicopters, engaged the Kurds in a fierce one-week fight at Saqqoze, near the unofficial Kurdish capital, Diyarbakir. The clashes, which ended a four-month PKK ceasefire, reportedly foiled plans for a surprise spring offensive, already finalized by the PKK.

Another example of the depth of Turkish–Israeli cooperation in assessing regional threats was the capture of Mossad agents in the Republic of Cyprus. Israel provided Turkey with intelligence on military developments on Cyprus at this critical juncture.[107] The capture of the Israeli agents followed shortly after the shipment of the Russian S-300 missiles to Greek Cyprus in 1997. According to Alon Liel, a former Israeli ambassador to Turkey and later director general of the Israeli Ministry of Foreign Affairs, it was expected that the intelligence "pipeline" contained a lot of information on shared strategic threats for exchange between Turkey and Israel.[108] Israeli security services participated in a raid on the Turkish Hizballah cell in 1997.[109] Israeli intelligence also assisted Turkey in the capture of Abdullah Ocalan, the leader of the PKK. Even though Prime Minister Netanyahu flatly denied Israeli involvement in this operation, Prime Minister Bulent Ecevit confirmed this report.[110] In an act of retaliation, PKK supporters in Germany attempted to assault the Israeli mission in Berlin.[111]

The majority of Turkish secret service inductees have been recruited from nationalist and pan-Turkist elites. Turkish security services actively forged connections among the Turkist-oriented politicians and intellectuals in Azerbaijan. Turkish External Intelligence (MIT) actively supported political parties with a pan-Turkist orientation even before the independence of Azerbaijan. According to one Armenian analyst, Turkish security services train Azerbaijani Special Forces at the Nasosnaya and Shihovo training camps.[112]

Israel also has contributed to the training of Azerbaijani security forces, airport security and protection of high political officials.[113] In fact, Israel has one of the largest intelligence operations in the CIS states in Azerbaijan. As one measure of Azerbaijain's diplomatic importance to Israel, the Israeli embassy in Baku employs 200 diplomats.[114]

Limitations of the triangle

Turkey's entente with Israel and Azerbaijan was useful for the three countries, but it had natural limitations. Turkish public sympathy with the Palestinian cause affected political decisions in the foreign policy sphere.[115] Ofra Bengio points to this as a "special case, which, on the one hand, attracted Turkey's genuine domestic affinity, solidarity and identification with their cause, but on the other, provided the most effective tool for applying pressure on Turkey to disengage from Israel."[116] Since the 1970s, the trajectory of the Turkish–Israeli relations followed the ups and downs of the Palestinian–Israeli conflict. As an expression of historical connection with Palestinian aspirations for statehood, Turkey recognized the Palestinian Liberation Organization as the sole legitimate representative organization in January of 1975. When Eastern Jerusalem was proclaimed a part of the "eternal capital" of Israel, the Turkish government "vigorously protested" and reduced diplomatic representation between the two countries to second secretary level in December 1980.[117] After the beginning of the Madrid Peace Process and under the Oslo Accords, the Turkish foreign policy establishment developed a "balanced approach" to the Israeli–Palestinian conflict.[118] Ankara attempted to use its regional influence as a means for mediation of the conflict. Turkey participated as a mentor in Arms Control and Regional Security talks as a part of the Madrid Peace Process. The strategic relationship with Israel, backed by military and security apparatus contacts, is likely to survive the stress of deterioration on the Palestinian track.[119] However, in the unlikely scenario of complete Islamization of political life in Turkey, the weight of Arab opinion will precipitate a termination of the Turkish–Israeli entente. Another source of increasing tension is the Turkish perception that Israel covertly supports Kurdish political autonomy in Northern Iraq.

The question arises whether alignment with Israel affects detrimentally Turkey's bid for EU membership.[120] Some experts believe that increased Turkish involvement in Middle Eastern affairs may delay Turkey in fulfilling the long-cherished dream of becoming a full-fledged member of the European Union, while others express concern regarding the impact of Turkish entente with Israel on the Turkish bid for EU membership.[121] However, Feridun Sinirlioglu, a veteran Turkish diplomat and Turkish ambassador to Israel, was convinced that the prospective entry of Turkey into the European Union would serve both Turkish and Israeli interests. He said, "Turkish membership in the EU will ensure the universalization of secularism in

Europe that is not only important for Israel but also for the Jews in general."[122] Despite this optimistic view, the controversy surrounding Turkish entry into the European Union might have unpredictable and possibly negative conse- quences for the future of Turkish–Israeli entente. Finally, entente with Israel has not been cost-free for Turkey in its domestic politics, thanks to strong domestic criticism of the Sharon (and subsequent) government's actions in the occupied territories. If the peace process picks up again, this may improve.

The close links Turkey has established with Azerbaijan do not extend to involvement in concrete military commitments—for example, over Nagorno- Karabagh—that would lead to potential conflicts with Russia. Turkey treads lightly in what Moscow considers its sphere of influence because Turkey needs good relations with Russia for economic and strategic reasons. With regards to the Nagorno-Karabagh conflict, Azerbaijani President Abulfaz Elchibey summarized the Turkish geopolitical posture. After Turkey declined military support to the Azerbaijani campaign to regain Nagorno-Karabagh in 1992, Elchibey concluded, "it became clear that Moscow, not Ankara, was the external determining factor in the Transcaucasus."[123] According to Idris Bal, many leaders of the Turkic NIS realized that Turkey was not an alternative to Russia.[124]

Overall, the Kurdish issue negatively affects the Turkish–Israeli–Azerbaijani axis. As noted above, Israel provided active assistance to Turkey in its struggle against PKK terrorist activities. But an established historical link between Israel and Kurdish guerrilla forces, particular in Iraq, dates back to the height of the "Periphery Alliance" strategy of the 1960s. This Israeli–Kurdish con- nection breeds a deep suspicion among the Turkish military and public.[125] Islamist intellectuals like Haron Yahya, publishing widely, circulate "con- spiracy theory" books and articles on the subject in Turkey.[126] When an NGO in Israel invited a (Kurdish) leader of the banned Kurdish Democratic Party (DEP), the Turkish government put Israel on notice and the invitation was withdrawn. This incident underscored Turkish sensitivities to the Kurdish issue as well as Israeli responsiveness, even though Turkey denies any parallels with the Palestinian issue.[127] In the case of Azerbaijan, the Kurdish issue has international relevance. Kurds have a compact residence in the Azerbaijani border area of Lachin and Kelbajar. There are some Kurdish villages in the enclave of Nakhichevan that borders on Turkey. There were numerous allegations that Heydar Aliyev's regime provided patronage to the Kurdish clan of Eyubovs. On many occasions, the Azerbaijani opposition accused the government of turning a blind eye to the proliferation of NGOs that might serve as recruitment and fundraising centers for the PKK.[128] In particular, Turkish ire was raised by the statements of Abdullah Ocalan during his trial in 2000 in which he publicly announced that the PKK had a most extensive support network in Azerbaijan.[129] During his visit to Baku, Prime Minister Erdogan complained that Kurdish militants continued to be based in Azerbaijan under the guise of various cultural organizations.[130]

Conclusions

The Turkish–Israeli military accords fall short of a conventional military alliance. But what has been revealed about them, so far in Turkey, Israel and the United States, suggests that the two states intend to establish a comprehensive military collaboration. Consequently, this alignment, with US support, will lead to a realignment of the power matrix in the greater Middle East region. Israel has a long-standing policy of nurturing relations with non-Arab Muslim countries. As one British intelligence expert concludes, "For Israel, a close working relationship with Turkey is an important element in its strategic and diplomatic survival in the region."[131] In the case of Azerbaijan, Israel sought not only to expand its diplomatic presence in post-Soviet space, but Israel and Azerbaijan shared perceived threats of Iranian intrusion and the proliferation of ballistic missiles. The Baku-Tbilisi-Ceyhan pipeline and the South Caucasus gas pipeline were viewed as jointly creating an "energy corridor" to deliver Caspian oil and gas to the West. The Jewish state saw in the construction of this Transcaspian energy corridor a strategic opportunity to enhance the diversity of its energy resources. Meanwhile, both projects were opposed by Russia, Iran and Armenia. Azerbaijan, a state still in the formative stages of shaping foreign policy and state building, intermittently undergoes abrupt shifts in its foreign policy behaviour. This certainly affects the stability of Azerbaijani interactions with each of its foreign partners. In this regard, the Israeli relationship with the third partner of the strategic axis, Azerbaijan, is also open to wide fluctuations. Even Turkey has unresolved issues with Azerbaijan.

If in the early 1990s the United States had conceived of Turkey and Israel as primary promoters of its interests in the Caspian region, particularly with reference to Azerbaijan, in 1994 the United States government decided to deal directly with Baku without any mediators. This obviously seemed like an attractive option for the Azerbaijani leadership itself. Azerbaijan, as a bordering state, had been facing direct pressure from Iran and Russia, both of which have significant levers of influence in the Caucasus. This factor alone made the leadership extremely cautious in exposing strategic relationships with Turkey and Israel.[132] Even Turkey toned down its "Turkish World" rhetoric and tried to conduct more balanced policy vis-à-vis Azerbaijan's erstwhile enemy, Armenia. The Turkish strategic relationship with Israel also has had important limitations. Since the entente was conceived as primarily a military-to-military affair, it suffers from public and media exposure. This reflected the growing impact of negative views held by a wide segment of the Turkish public regarding an Israeli role in the Middle East.[133] Following resolution of the Ocalan crisis, Turkey warmed to the idea of improving relations with Syria. The continued pattern of Turkish dependence on exported petrochemicals, especially natural gas, compelled it to show flexibility in its relationship with the staunchly anti-Zionist regime in Teheran.[134]

At the same time, given the pervasive role of the military in Turkish politics and in matters of national security—i.e. Turkey's military and geo-strategic needs, apprehensions and regional ambitions—the relationship will persist. It will continue to play a decisive role in the domestic and foreign policy of the Turkish state. In conclusion, any future decision as to whether to further expand, freeze or cancel the Turkish–Israeli entente will be taken by the Turkish military and not by any civilian authority. The implications of co-operation between Turkey and Israel go well beyond the territories of the two countries. Bilateral consultations have been increased with a view to broadening cooperation in a geography spanning the Caucasus, Central Asia, the Eastern Mediterranean and the Balkans.

An intense engagement with Europe in search of the eventual membership in the European Union reflects Turkey's Western "vocation." Since this search is unpredictable and its outcome unknown, the question remains whether this pursuit of multi-vector policy is compatible with or serves as an alternative to eventual Turkish membership in the EU. However, according to Sinirlioglu, after entry into the EU, Turkey will change the internal balance of the EU decision-making process as one of the "great" five most populous members. He added that, "As much as we can put our stamp on the decision-making process [of the European Union], it will be to the interest of Israel, because we look to certain threats from the same angle."[135]

6 Fluctuating zones of influence

Involution of the alignment, 2000–5

Introduction: identities and counter-identities

Like any alliance or strategic relationship, the triangular relationship between Turkey, Israel and Azerbaijan is subject to varying security requirements, threat perceptions and limitations of domestic origin. This chapter will focus on those factors that have limited further development of the axis under discussion. These factors, which will be addressed in detail, gained particular prominence in the period between 1999 and 2005 and negatively affected the strategic relationship(s). Particular attention will be paid to the developments in Azerbaijan since the shifts in the dynamics of Turkish–Israeli relations in the late 1990s have been explored to a greater extent in the existing literature.[1]

As a result of profound changes in the domestic and international arenas in the period between 1999 and 2005, an involution of the trilateral axis occurred. In other words, the axis became increasingly exposed to perturbations and fluctuations in the domestic politics of the three countries. This chapter postulates that state corporate identity is subject to competition by sub-national actors such as foreign policy elites, the military, and ethnic, religious and business professionals. State identities can also be challenged by popular identities. Whether states succeed in reproducing the actor identity favored by their political elite depends on the congruence, or non-congruence, of the elite identity with popular (mass) identities. Generally, elites are severely constrained in reproducing pro-Western secular identities, while mass identities favor more religious/nationalist agenda. This trend in the last two decades manifested itself in the Turkish case as mass electoral support for "Islamic politics," i.e. the Islamist Refah (Welfare) (1996–7) Party and its later reincarnation as the more pragmatic or "moderate" Islamist AK ("Justice and Development") Party (2002–present). The increased role of public opinion and the rising prominence of Islamic solidarity has shaped foreign policy since the late-1990s—in particular, empathy with the Palestinian cause, opposition to American support for Israeli policies toward Palestinians, and last, but not least, strong public antipathy toward the American-led campaign against Saddam Hussein's regime in Iraq supported by Israel. The AK Party's drive to reorient its foreign policy toward Middle East neighbors (Iran, Syria) and attempts to form an anti-Kurdish coalition with these Israeli foes have dampened expectations for an invigoration of the Turkish–Israeli military alliance in the short term.[2] The return to power of the right-wing Likud in Israel following the failure of Camp David summit talks between Ehud Barak and Yassir Arafat in 2000 also negatively affected the atmospherics of Israeli–Turkish relations.

In Azerbaijan, the particularistic interests of the Aliyev clan began to dominate domestic and foreign policy in 1999–2005.[3] The exclusive goal of retaining the reins of power in the hands of the Aliyev family drove foreign policy. From the Constructivist perspective, authoritarian rule by the Aliyev clan, massive illegal capital flight and labor migration to Russia, rampant tax evasion and pervasive corruption are social practices that undermine and constrain efforts by the Azerbaijani elite to form an international identity that is Western, liberal and democratic. In general, state identity can be understood as a product of these competing forces; under conditions of globalization, supranational actors also participate in the reproduction of state.

Islamism in Turkey

After victory against the Greek army and Western allies, Kemal Ataturk began to re-create Turkey as a secular republic with clearly defined borders. His reforms were directed not only at the constitution of a new Turkish nation-state, but also at profound transformation of Turkish society in the spheres of religion, culture and public conduct. The conventional wisdom about the top-down modernization in Turkey asserts that the Turkish population accepted the ideological precepts of Kemalism and the secular republic became the focus of popular allegiance.[4] But the conservative, primarily rural, masses of Anatolia failed to fully absorb the Kemalist ideology.[5] According to one author in the 1970s, "Thousands of peasants are not aware that they live in a secular republic; for them the War of Independence was a religious war, which was crowned by the victory of Islam over the infidels."[6] The Anatolian peasantry viewed Kemal Ataturk as a Ghazi, a religious warrior who brought glory to Islam after centuries of slow and dispiriting imperial decline.[7] They worshipped him as a hero who was able to reverse the Ottoman decline and was building a new state as a base for the new Ghazavat.[8]

According to Hakan Yavuz, Ataturk's nation-building project was profoundly misunderstood by the traditional masses of Turkey. In fact, drastic attempts at secularization and nationalization of diverse ethnic groups in the predominantly Muslim population engendered resistance and disassociation from the modernizing elites.[9] Yavuz claims that Kemalist policies actually politicized the Kurdish ethnicity.[10] Since the majority of Kurds lived in the political and geographical periphery of the Turkish Republic, their marginal status produced a spirit of militant rejection of Kemalist centralizing policies.

Kurdish aspiration for recognition as a separate ethnic component (if not full-fledged independence promulgated by the Sevres Treaty of 1918) in the Turkish Republic led to a fusion of ethnic resurgence with more radical opposition to suppression of Sufi orders and other institutions of traditional Islam.

Despite the strides that Kemalist education made in socializing the young of the Turkish Republic over 70 years, Islam continued to be the source of primary allegiance for millions of Turkish citizens, especially in rural areas and central Anatolia. Bernard Lewis claimed in 1961 that: "To this day the Western notions of patriotism and nationality have never superseded the older pattern—indeed, though dynastic loyalties have faded, religious loyalty is in our own day showing renascent vigour."[11] The Western concept of nation as a homogeneous linguistic and territorial entity remained alien to the less educated rural population. This population served as the main political base for the politicized Islam that emerged in Turkey in the 1980s.[12] Islamists appealed to the more historically familiar and egalitarian concept of the Umma, the transnational religious community or the community of the believers.

The revival of Islam in Turkey dates back to a post-coup attempt to marry the ideology of Turkism to moderate state-sponsored Islam, known as the "Turkish–Islamic Synthesis," of the 1980s.[13] The military sought to translate the allegiance of the conservative Turkish masses to traditional Islam into a new ideological platform that provided a new generation of Turks, exposed to the agitation of Maoist and other extreme Leftist movements of the 1970s, with a conservative value system. The military needed to create a new national consensus that would justify their intervention in the political sphere and re-establish the legitimacy of the state institutions. This concept was designed to reflect a new emphasis on the traditional values of Islam and counteract the attraction of an increasingly young population toward radical ideologies. In 1983, the Turkish military ceded power to the Anavatan ("Motherland") Party, or ANAP, led by Turgut Ozal. ANAP saw itself as a bridge between traditional secular Kemalism and conservative religious circles. President Ozal himself belonged to the officially banned Nakshibendi tariqat, or brotherhood, and espoused moderate Islamic views.[14] The Anavatan Party actively advocated (Turkish–Islamic) Synthesis policies and the army supported them. Economic liberalization, accompanied by privatization of state enterprises and a decrease in state subsidies, brought millions of destitute traditional farmers into major Turkish urban centers, especially Istanbul. Turgut Ozal attempted also to provide grounds for reconciliation with the alienated and impoverished Kurdish population of the Turkish Southeast. In pursuit of this goal, Ozal alleviated the ban on Kurdish language and culture. During Ozal's era (1989–93) Turkish foreign policy underwent a brief but radical transition in two ways. In these years, the foreign policy of Turkey shifted from preservation of the status quo and inaction toward dynamism and broad initiatives that bordered on temerity. President Ozal also changed the traditional pattern of policy formation and assumed broader control over the strategic directions of Turkish foreign policy.

While General Kenan Evren, the leader of the military coup, stayed as president until 1990, Turgut Ozal, elected prime minister in 1983, had liberalized many social and legal controls over religious education and other civic activities. As a member of the officially banned Naqshibendi brotherhood, he obviously was receptive to the new ideology promoted by the military.[15] Turgut Ozal's party Anavatan (The Motherland) in many respects served as an ideological precursor of the Adalet ve Kalkinma (AK) Party.[16] According to the party manifesto, the Anavatan was a "nationalist and conservative party," "devoted to national and moral values," and had "a political platform . . . very similar to the avowed conservative democracy" espoused by the AK Party.[17]

Despite its Islamist credentials and fiery rhetoric, in a pragmatic attempt to appease the Turkish military, the Necmettin Erbakan government signed a five-year military cooperation agreement with Israel in 1996. This action provoked very strong negative reactions from governments in the Arab world and Iran. A significant part of the Refah Party electorate felt betrayed by this unexpected foreign policy démarche of the Islamist party. However, Turkish Islamists were brought back into popular favor by a natural disaster. The earthquake of 1999 was devastating, and state rescue efforts and those of the Turkish Armed Forces met with lukewarm success. In contrast, Turkish–Islamist grassroot associations organized an effective nation-wide campaign of assistance and promoted their political aspirations on a massive scale.[18] This human misfortune provided the Islamist Refah and its successor Fazilet (Virtue) Party with opportunities to conduct broad-based outreach.[19]

The Adelet ve Kalkinma (Justice and Development) Party was formed by a liberal faction of Erbakan's Refah (Welfare) Party. AKP also gained significant support from more conservative elements that coalesced around Milli Gorus (The National Outlook) after the military "post-modern" coup of February 28, 1997. The symbolism of this new Islamist party had obvious Ottoman references. The Turkish word *adalet* has its historical precursor in the Arabic concept of *adala*, the central function of the sultan in guaranteeing justice for his subjects. This political ideal provided legitimacy for the Sultans in the Ottoman Empire. This conception was widely embraced in Islamic political theory and has roots in Arabic and Persian traditions. So the AK Party offered to Turkish voters the vision of Adil Duzen ("the Just Order") and promoted slogans of the "fight against corruption" and "social justice" in its election campaign of 2002. This message was embraced by the majority of Turkish voters. The AK Party replicated the electoral success of the Refah Party, which became the largest single party in parliament in 1996, in 2002. This repeated victory in the national elections of a party with Islamist roots engendered surprise and apprehension among the Turkish military. The leadership of the Turkish Armed Forces exerted great efforts to prevent the AK Party from running in the 2002 elections and attempted to close down the new party as they had done with Erbakan's party five years before.[20]

A "moderate" Islamic turn in Turkish foreign policy under the AK Party

Turkish foreign policy discourse toward the Middle East since the end of World War II is guided by traditional concerns and positions. These include a balanced approach to the Arab–Israeli conflict, flexibility and independence from other prominent actors in the Middle East. However, the legacy of the Ottoman Empire continues to affect particular sensitivities to regions like the Middle East, the Balkans and the Caucasus. In particular, the Palestinian cause evokes intense sympathy from the Turkish people. Both left-leaning intellectuals and conservative masses in the country emotionally support Palestinian demands and view the Israeli stance as an "aggression" against the Muslim world.[21] One of the constant concerns of the Turkish foreign policy establishment was the special status of Jerusalem.[22] The relationship with Israel flourished in the immediate post-Cold War period (1991–9) because Turkey needed to reassert its Western "security identity" and demonstrate to its Western allies a continued commitment to remaining a secular parliamentary democracy in the Middle East. Turkish policymakers perceived Israel as the key Western (primarily American) ally in the region and inferred that strong ties with the Jewish state would serve as a guarantee of Turkish member-ship or "an entry pass to the Western club." Bulent Aras noted: "Turkish foreign policy makers' cooperation with Israel served to maintain an image of 'political correctness' and 'cultural' correctness—in Western terms—during and after the Cold War."[23] As an intellectual polemicist of the Islamist persuasion, Bulent Aras provides further critical assessments of Turkish engagement with Israel. He concludes: "As a result of its military cooperation agreements with Israel, Turkey has lost touch with the psychological mode of the Arabic world, and has declined to an unfavorable position with the OIC."[24] Such criticisms provide intellectual ammunition to the AK Party ideo-logues, at least on the rhetorical level. On a practical level, Turkish foreign policy under the AK Party (2002–present) completed several U-turns in its relations with Israel. Even though, responding to the ideological expectations of a core Islamist electorate, Prime Minister Erdogan publicly accused Israel of "state terrorism" on several occasions in 2004, it would be premature to speak of the demise of the strategic axis with Israel.[25]

Since the end of the Cold War, Turkish foreign policy, which had been based firmly on the verities of Kemalism for 70 years, has undergone a trans-formation. This transformation hinges on the emergence of neo-Ottomanism as a doctrine of Turkish foreign policy.[26] Turgut Ozal, the first president of Turkey in the post-Cold War era, laid the foundations of this new foreign policy concept. However, the new doctrine took its more mature and com-prehensive shape under the Justice and Development government lead by Recep Tayip Erdogan. This doctrine, known as the Strategic Depth doctrine, found particular resonance among the AK Party leadership and its core electorate.[27] The acceptance of such a dramatic shift in foreign policy vision is also due to changed perceptions, by the foreign policy establishment and the military of external circumstances (Syria and Iran ceased to be viewed as enemies after the resolution of the Turkish–Syrian crisis in 1999), and heightened domestic empathy with Muslim causes, such as the Palestinian cause and rejection of the American occupation of Iraq. According to Graham Fuller, "[S] trategically, Turkey has become part of the Middle East."[28] The doctrine's originator is Ahmet Davutoglu, who occupies a position of chief foreign policy advisor to Prime Minister Erdogan and has become the architect of the new Turkish foreign policy. Under Prime Minister Erdogan, Turkish foreign policy chose as its motto "problem-free relations with our neighbors."[29] Among the new initiatives of Turkish foreign policy in the early twenty-first century was an active search for reconciliation with Armenia. Turkey continued to advocate peaceful resolution of the Nagorno-Karabagh conflict, but it deviated from the earlier held position of strict adherence to Azerbaijani demands.[30] During a bilateral meeting of Turkish and Armenian officials in 2002–3, the Turkish side came with more pragmatic demands from the Armenian side. The following were proposed as conditions for opening the Turkish–Armenian border and normalization of relations between the two countries:

1   at minimum, a partial withdrawal of Armenian military forces from the territory of Azerbaijan;[31]
2   a formula satisfactory to both sides that would deal with the historical claims of the Armenian genocide;
3   a commitment to stop territorial claims on the territory of Turkey;
4   acceptance that Turkey will not damage its relations with Azerbaijan.[32]

In the spring of 2003, Turkey dropped the first condition and limited relations continued. Turkey maintains trade with Armenia through Georgia. Turkey has a charter flight with Yerevan. According to Foreign Minister Abdullah Gul, there are 40,000 Armenians who conduct trade or have employment in Istanbul. The current negotiations focused on one symbolic point: opening a border crossing at Leninakan (formerly Gumru).[33] The active interactions between Turkey and Armenia caused increasing protests from the Azerbaijani side, but to no avail.[34] William Hale comments on these developments: "Obviously, this is not to Azerbaijani liking. This controversial policy toward Armenia weakens traditional bonds with Azerbaijan."[35] Azerbaijani officials expressed misgivings about Erdogan's shift from the previous policy of unquestioning support of the Azerbaijani position vis-à-vis the Nagorno-Karabagh conflict. The Azerbaijani deputy foreign minister stated: "In our relations, we started feeling the negative side of this pragmatism of Erdogan's government . . . In the Azerbaijani–Armenian NK conflict, the Turks started not speaking loudly, but more and more talking about opening [the] border between Turkey and Yerevan, which is pushed by EU and the United States seriously for a different number of reasons."[36]

Prime Minister Erdogan's political inclinations and his Islamist past obviously had a chilling effect on the atmosphere of Turkish–Israeli relations. As Michael Rubin noted: "The first victim of Turkey's shifting diplomacy has been Israel."[37] Turkish authorities used the neo-Ottoman discourse in projecting an image of a "just and impartial arbiter" in policy toward the Middle East. In particular, Turkey extended new diplomatic efforts in bringing peaceful resolution to the Syrian–Israeli and Israeli–Palestinian conflicts. Turkish leadership has undertaken bold steps to mediate regional conflicts in the Middle East. The new Turkish government demonstrated its willingness to reconcile with the Muslim world. In particular, the Erdogan government took an activist approach in its relations with neighbors to the east (Iran) and south (Iraq, Syria), while bilateral relations with Israel entered a cooler period. Nevertheless, Arab opinion continued to view Turkish intentions vis-à-vis Arab neighbors, in particular Iraq, with great suspicion. The Saudi news agency Arab News editorialized about Turkish foreign policy goals in Iraq: "As the region's former colonial master, Turkey is claiming a historic duty to intervene in Iraq ahead of a debate today on sending troops there, while Kurdish leaders in the north of the occupied nation are vehemently against the deployment."[38]

New activism in foreign policy toward Iran

The Erdogan administration also attempted to open a new era in Turkish–Iranian relations with the AK Party government, leading this relationship in a turnaround. In May 2001, the former Turkish Prime Minister Tansu Ciller described relations as "neither black nor white, but a shade of gray."[39] In particular she cited Iranian support for PKK terrorist activities inside Turkey and pursuit of WMDs as persistent causes for tension in Turkish–Iranian relations. She said that "Turks are approaching these latest developments [with Iran] very cautiously," and reiterated the necessity of the US-imposed policy of "double containment."[40] Over the ensuing three years, the rhetoric of Turkish leadership changed significantly. In July 2004, Prime Minister Erdogan visited Teheran and signed agreements for delivery of Iranian gas to Europe through Turkish territory.[41] In response to American diplomatic warnings, the Turkish prime minister said, "Just as all other countries in the world develop relations with their neighbors, so too will Turkey develop its relations with its neighbors. And it is determined about this."[42] In broad reference to the Strategic Depth doctrine, he added at a press conference in Teheran, "Before we came to power, we promised that we would develop relations with our neighbors and included this in our action plan. We did not make any discrimination among our neighbors. The regional peace will be set up in this way."[43]

Mediation of regional conflicts

Israeli–Syrian track

The AK Party government also gave new impetus to Turkish efforts to mediate conflict between Syria and Israel. The current conflict dates back to the Six Day War of 1967, when Israel occupied the Golan Heights. Syrian government intends to exchange peace for the return of the Golan Heights.[44] The Erdogan administration made several attempts to mediate between the warring parties. During the first summit in January 2004 between Erdogan and Bashar Assad, Israel used the good offices of Prime Minister Erdogan to pass a message to the Syrian leader.[45] Prime Minister Erdogan personally got involved in the diplomatic effort. After Bashar Assad's visit, he met Israeli Ambassador Pinhas Avivi and relayed that "Syrian President Bashar Assad said he is serious in his intention to renew peace talks with Israel, and intends taking all the necessary steps to reach a peace agreement in the Middle East."[46] Furthermore, Israel itself might be very interested in Turkey's intercession with Syria.[47] With reference to an emerging reality in the post-Saddam Middle East, former Israeli Prime Minister Benjamin Netanyahu commented on the prospects of the Syrian track: "I think there is the opportunity today to explore possible contacts with Syria."[48] However, Turkey very soon exhausted its diplomatic efforts over the divergence of Syrian and Israeli positions. The Turkish foreign minister commented in February of 2004: "Turkey will not play the role of mediator between Syria and Israel, though it is a state with excellent relations with both parties."[49]

Israeli–Palestinian track

From the beginning of the Peace Process at the Madrid Conference in 1991, and especially following the Oslo Accords of 1993, Turkey advocated an even-handed approach to resolution of the Israeli–Palestinian conflict. However, the strategic axis with Israel that evolved after 1996 derogated the Palestinian cause to a secondary consideration. In 2000, when the al-Aqsa Intifada started, the Turkish government was forced by domestic pressures to distance itself from Israel.[50] When the AK Party came to power in Ankara, the attitude toward the plight of Palestinians in the West Bank and Gaza became a prominent factor in Turkish foreign policy, and this inevitably affected Turkish–Israeli ties. Initially Prime Minister Erdogan delayed his visit to Israel for an indefinite period in the spring of 2003. Foreign Minister Abdullah Gul suggested upgrading diplomatic relations with the Palestinian Authority to an ambassadorial level. But the most drastic deterioration of relations with Israel occurred in May of 2004 as a result of Israeli military actions in Gaza with numerous civilian deaths. Erdogan expressed open criticism of Israeli policies and he called Israel a "terrorist" state. He also temporarily recalled Turkey's ambassador in Israel in protest.

Nonetheless, both economic and military cooperation between Turkey and Israel continue. Turkey and Israel signed a multi-million dollar water deal for 20 years in January of 2004.[51] Turkey has bought $3 billion worth of Israeli weapons since 1996. In May of 2004, a contract to build three gas plants by Turkish companies worth $800 million was signed by Prime Minister Erdogan.

Azerbaijan: the frail democracy

After declaring independence in December of 1991, Azerbaijan gradually adopted the main formal attributes of democracy. The Republic of Azerbaijan made international commitments upholding democratic principles and human rights when it joined the OSCE and later applied for membership in the Council of Europe. Democratic institutions were created in the first years of independence, but under Heydar Aliyev, Azerbaijan returned to Soviet-style political methods of "partocracy." In the case of Azerbaijan and other Caucasian and Central Asian republics, partocracy thrived upon a complex hierarchy of traditional and Soviet-era political and economic clans.

As typical for the Muslim NISs, Heydar Aliyev (1993–2003) was a powerful president who, an ex-first secretary of Soviet Azerbaijan and a former KGB general, imposed authoritarian rule in the country. A charismatic leader, Heydar Aliyev created a personality cult in Azerbaijan to the extent that many Azerbaijani citizens called him "Baba" or "Dedushka" ("grandfather" in Russian).[52] In 1995 parliamentary elections, Yeni Azerbaijan ("New Azerbaijan") Party, as the official party of the government, won 90 percent of the vote, a result that made Western observers call it a "farce." Given that Azerbaijan has a presidential system, the 1998 presidential election naturally became a focus of international attention. Initially, the regime issued an electoral law that was rejected by both the OSCE and the opposition, leading to a boycott of the elections. In response to OSCE's criticism and after dialogue with the opposition, the Azerbaijani government reformed the flawed electoral law and abolished press censorship. These changes, despite the problems that remained, won the OSCE's approval, and several opposition parties, including the large Azerbaijan National Independence Party (AMIP) led by Etibar Mamedov, decided to participate in the parliamentary elections. The other major opposition parties regarded the reforms as insufficient and boycotted the elections.

Heydar Aliyev did not effectively share power with the Milli Mejlis, local authorities or the judiciary. As an experienced politician of the Soviet era, he realized the potential of Azerbaijani oil wealth for his family and his clan.[53] In fact, all aspects of the "Contract of the Century" were negotiated and finalized personally by Heydar Aliyev in September 1994. The oil/gas exploration and exploitation contracts were based on production-sharing agreements, known as PSAs, with multinational corporations. After the contracts were signed, without ratification of the parliament, they acquired the power of state law.[54] In reality, only the president and his close advisors made important policy decisions, bypassing parliament. The state apparatus tightly controlled the court system and the electronic media, as was evident during the last elections. The ex-president and his team directly managed the national economy of Azerbaijan. Profits of the oil sector, the main source of foreign revenue in Azerbaijan, were controlled by the ex-president himself with the aid of top management at the State Oil Corporation of Azerbaijan (SOCAR). The three top executives of SOCAR either were linked to President Heydar Aliyev as blood relatives or were directly supervised by him. The newly elected president, Ilham Aliyev, formerly served as the SOCAR vice-president, while other activities of SOCAR were delegated to SOCAR President Natik Aliyev and Valekh Alekperov, who, as head of the Foreign Investments Department of SOCAR, conducted negotiations with foreign oil companies. In fact, one prominent case of bribery, which involved a senior SOCAR official and a representative of the international Investment Consortium, was prosecuted by the United States Department of Justice.[55] In the meantime, foreign investment in the non-petrochemical sector experienced several setbacks. The major disincentive for foreign investment in small and medium business was exorbitant bribes demanded by Azerbaijani state officials and the lack of state guarantees.[56] Proposed bilateral projects in agriculture and attempts by Israeli infrastructure and water treatment companies to enter the Azerbaijani market were rebuffed; the share of Israeli investment in Azerbaijan was not significant.[57] In particular, a major Israeli energy engineering company, Bateman Litwin, entered negotiations with Azerbaijani authorities to modernize infrastructure in the Nakhichevan region. But due to the exorbitant license fees demanded by the Azerbaijani state "regulators" and an inability to gain state guarantees, the Israeli company withdrew from negotiations in the early 2000s.[58]

Clan-based society and the Aliyevs

Historically, Azerbaijani identity experiences a tension between its predominantly Turkish ethnic identity, which has tied it to the Ottoman Empire and its twentieth-century successor, the Turkish Republic, and its majority religious affiliation, Shi'ism, which is the dominant branch of Islam in Iran. Cultural influences of Iran and Russia are also quite strong in Azerbaijan due to the colonial legacy of the Persian Empire and, later, the Tsarist (Soviet) Empire. Furman describes Azerbaijan as a country with the "original" political life. He points out that "the 'Western' and 'Eastern' features are interwoven in contemporary Azerbaijan. Incredible laudatory speeches about [Heydar] Aliyev by state officials, the clan-family nature of the regime, systematic and grandiose national elections frame-ups, large-scale and wide corruption (higher than in Russia) coexist with the presence of a massive and robust opposition capable of seizing power."[59] Azerbaijani political hierarchy continues to be based on family and clan ties.[60] This pre-modern nature of the state handicaps Azerbaijani national integration. In the past, the clan-type family structure was common among the Azeri Turks. The clan, or *hoj*, was usually named after a common ancestor. Clan members shared pastureland and were bound to provide mutual aid to each other. They frequently acted as a unified entity in business dealings. It was also common for up to 40 members of an extended family to live together in large dwellings called *gazma*. In the pre-Soviet past, landless peasants, called *tavyrga*, made up the lowest class of Azeri Turkish society. Marriage within the family was encouraged in order to protect traditional institutions.[61] As a result, sub-national structures, such as territorial clans, persist and delay the social transition of Azerbaijan to a solidified, liberal, "Western-type" nation. Furman contends that extreme difficulties that prevent the consolidation of democracy in Azerbaijan have to do with the "habits and deep traditional values of Azerbaijani society (such as clannishness, family orientation) and an absence of the habit of submission to the law rather than personalities, and the weak identification with the state."[62]

In Azerbaijan, clan also delineates a group of people from a vatan, or a local "little homeland." From a historical perspective, the clan factor also determined the shape of modern Azerbaijani identity. Azerbaijani identity is molded by the dialectic of an attachment to a particular territory and the idea of a state.[63] In particular, Azerbaijan has preserved the clan structure of its society because the country's population is made up of 115 ethnic and sub-ethnic groups. The most important of these is ethnic Azeri Turks who make up roughly 78 percent of the population. The second largest is Talyshs. Lezgins, Avars, Kurds, Russians and Udins represent other significant minorities of Azerbaijan. All of these groups have preserved their languages and traditions. About 20,000 Jews live in Azerbaijan. The minorities of Azerbaijan typically intermarry within their clans and raise families according to local customs and laws. This ethnic and clan diversity was always appreciated and was considered, according to Heydar Aliyev, "a part of the Azeri way of life."[64] In the case of the deceased Azerbaijani leader Heydar Aliyev (1923–2003), his family originates from Nakhichevan region.[65] The Aliyev clan is identified by an ethnic marker "Nahcivanli," which includes Azeris who migrated from Erevan, the capital of Soviet Armenia. The Nakhichevan clan continues to play an important, if not the dominant, role in the political life of Azerbaijan today.[66] In order to maintain the Aliyevs' rule, the Nakhichevan clan deploys its members in strategic positions in security, military and foreign policy apparatus.[67] Furman and Abbasov described the system that Heydar Aliyev established during his tenure as the Soviet leader of Azerbaijan. First, he purged the corrupt party apparatchiks who had served under his predecessor. Then "in accordance with the Azerbaijani 'value system,' he [Aliyev] filled all vacated positions with his relatives, relatives of his relatives and his Nakhichevan fellow-villagers, the Nakhichevan clan."[68]

In the case of Azerbaijan, the Aliyev clan represents the power elite with its roots in the mountain exclave of Nakhichevan perched along the Iranian border.[69] Continuity in the possession of power is very important for the Aliyev clan, which has controlled Azerbaijan with only short remission since the 1960s. As a result, the foreign policies of Azerbaijan as well other political domains are exploited to serve the interests of this clan. The top four richest people in Azerbaijan are Kemaleddin Heydarov, the chairman of the Customs Committee; Jalal Aliyev, the brother of Heydar Aliyev and a deputy of the parliament; Ramil Usubov, the minister of internal affairs; and Ali Insanov, minister of health.[70] The members of their clan realize that if power slips from the hands of Ilham Aliyev, they would lose their position of power and cede control over economic and political resources and illegal networks, in particular opium and human trafficking.[71] Many Turkish politicians, including Prime Minister Tansu Ciller, saw the usurpation of power by Heydar Aliyev in Azerbaijan in 1993 as a negative development for Turkish–Azerbaijani relations.[72] The attempted coup of April–May 1995 against Heydar Aliyev engineered by a coalition of Turkish ultra-nationalists, members of Boz Kurtlar organization, and Azerbaijani opposition leaders, seriously damaged Azerbaijani–Turkish relations. Only the intervention of President Suleyman Demirel, who established personal rapport with President Aliyev, prevented this overthrow.[73]

In the period since 1999, there were several important reversals in the foreign policy of Azerbaijan. The clan-based nature of the Aliyev regime, which makes preservation of clan's dominance the determinant of domestic and foreign policy, brings an element of irrationality and fluidity into the foreign policy domain. This factor had inevitable debilitating effects on Azerbaijani–Turkish and Azerbaijani–Israeli relations in the first half-decade of the twenty-first century.

The Aliyev clan had historically close relations with the ethnic Kurdish population.[74] The majority of Kurds migrated to Azerbaijan in the 1920s from Iran and Turkey. Joseph Stalin granted autonomy to the Kurdish-populated districts of Lachin and Khelbadjar, known as "Red Kurdistan," until this autonomy was revoked in 1929. In the 1990s, the Kurdish population of Azerbaijan decreased to 50,000. Other wide-ranging population estimates claim numbers between 12,000 and 200,000 for 2001.[75] As a result of the Armenian occupation of Lachin in 1992 and Kelbadjar in 1993, most Kurds became refugees in various parts of Azerbaijan. Thus the Kurds fill an important niche in the ethnic hierarchy maintained by the Aliyev regime. According to some circumstantial evidence, they serve as the "eyes and ears" of Heydar Aliyev.[76] Some leaders of the Azerbaijani opposition charged that Aliyev's regime have colluded with radical Kurdish organizations that support the PKK. In particular, these allegations focused on the link between Heydar Aliyev and Beyler Eyubov, Aliyev's relative and his chief bodyguard, who has overseen the presidential guard division, Azerbaijan's best-trained armed unit of several thousand men. The ethnically Kurdish Eyubov family is reportedly one of the most influential clans in Azerbaijan.[77] Under Heydar Aliyev's rule, ethnic Kurds owned most Turkish small and medium-size businesses, which heavily invested in the Azerbaijani economy.[78] The influx of Kurds and the proliferation of Kurdish cultural centers and NGOs gradually have grown to such proportions as to cause serious complications in Turkish–Azerbaijani relations. Most Turkish political elites were alienated by multiple reports about the "Kurdish connection" within the power structure of the Aliyev clan. According to Yeni Musavat and Hurriyet newspaper editors Rauf Arifoglu and Aydin Guliev, a secret network of the Kurdistan Workers' Party (PKK) was operating in Azerbaijan, running at least four training camps and controlling several companies and one bank.[79] When the AK Party leader and current Prime Minister Erdogan visited Baku in January of 2003, he complained about the fact that Kurdish separatists located their base in Azerbaijan.[80] Another factor that led to signs of alienation in Turkish–Azerbaijani relations was the personal chemistry and close cooperation between the two leaders, Heydar Aliyev and Suleyman Demirel. This came to an end with the departure of the latter from the political arena in 2000.[81] All Turkish governments from 1992 through 2002 had business dealings with the Heydar Aliyev family. But with the ascension to power in Turkey of the AK Party (*ak* in Turkish has connotations of the "clean and pure") in November of 2002, Azerbaijani–Turkish relations had to start from a clean slate. The AK Party, which won the elections on the platform of fighting corruption, was less open to the "traditional" Azerbaijani way of doing business. According to Rauf Mirkadirov, the new political elite that came to power with the election of the AK Party had no history with or particular loyalty to the Aliyev regime.[82] The Erdogan administration desired re-establishing balanced relations with all South Caucasian nations, including Armenia. As a result, the Azerbaijani leadership felt a sense of alienation from the new, Islamist, Turkish administration.

Since the establishment of diplomatic relations between Israel and Azerbaijan in 1992, the absence of an Azerbaijani embassy in Israel and the lack of reciprocity in exchanges at the ministerial level on the Azerbaijani part served as a constant irritant in bilateral relations. The personalistic and unpredictable style of Heydar Aliyev's rule affected this relationship too. The issue of a visit by an Azerbaijani foreign minister to Israel came to a head in 1999. After numerous promises and delays, Tofik Zulfugarov, then a foreign minister of Azerbaijan, was scheduled to embark on a state visit to Israel in the spring of 1999. The Israeli side was informed about the agenda and scope of the visit in advance. When Tofik Zulfugarov was leaving his office to board the plane to Israel, Vafa Guluzade, then chief foreign policy advisor, received a personal phone call from Heydar Aliyev to immediately inform the foreign minister that the trip was cancelled.[83] This incident caused surprise even among the closest advisors of the Azerbaijani leader and consternation on the Israeli side.[84]

The official explanation of the cancellation of the Azerbaijani foreign minister's visit was the pressure applied by the Islamic Republic of Iran, a senior member of the Organization of Islamic Conference (OIC). The Azerbaijani government needs the support from OIC and is sensitive to its demands not to upgrade diplomatic relations with Israel. Azerbaijan, as a Muslim state, cannot disregard the opinion of the Islamic conference because OIC is the only international organization that has recognized Armenia as the aggressor in the Nagorno-Karabagh conflict.[85] Rauf Mirkadyrov challenges the official explanation of the Azerbaijani government's sensitivity to the demands to suspend diplomatic relations with Israel. According to this leading Azerbaijani journalist, illicit activities of the regime created an imbalance in Azerbaijani–Israeli relations. Mirkadyrov claims that a large amount of oil extracted from the territory of Azerbaijan, approximately 1 million tons a year, was under-reported by the state authorities. It could have been easily shipped in the form of raw oil and refined oil products through the pipelines, which are not monitored by any international authority, to the northern provinces of Iran and swapped for Iranian oil in the Persian Gulf.[86] Mirkadyrov indicated that "This 'normal' economic exchange [between the Azerbaijani Aliyev clan and the Iranian regime] will continue to exist for some time until a strict international oversight control will be established [over Azerbaijani oil flows] . . . This occurred because at a particular stage the direction of global energy corridors for the regional petrochemical resources was traded for implementation of particular [American geopolitical] policy."[87] Given the personalistic and corrupt regime under Aliyev, Iran could have served as a conduit for illegal (undocumented) oil sales. Consequently, the Iranian regime expected a quid pro quo from the Azerbaijani leadership, i.e. concessions in the areas of domestic and, especially, foreign policy, in exchange for illegal sales of oil by the Azerbaijani ruling family. The sudden reversals and fluctuations in Azerbaijani–Israeli relations over time can be traced to this "intimate" link between the private interests of the Aliyev clan and the Islamic regime in Iran.

Clan politics re-emerged in the run-up to the seminal October 2003 elections, which were marked by the issue of Heydar Aliyev's succession. The Nakhichevan clan demonstrated its hold on the reins of power by controlling the nomination of Heydar Aliyev's son.[88] The Nakhichevan clan supported the single candidate, Ilham Aliyev, as successor to his father. According to a BBC report, it was not the Yeni Azerbaijan Party leadership who nominated Ilham Aliyev as a candidate for the presidency, but a group of voters from the Nakhichevan exclave. A BBC report identified Nakhichevan as "the Aliyevs' power base." It was Ilham Aliyev who, by all accounts, not only inherited his father's leadership of the country but retained significant influence over Azerbaijan's most important economic resources—oil and natural gas—as a former vice-president of the State Oil Corporation of Azerbaijani Republic (SOCAR). The transition of power from father to son on the basis of heredity is more akin to authoritarian rule as in Syria, North Korea and

Iraq before the toppling of Saddam Hussein, rather than a representative democracy.[89] The Aliyev regime in Azerbaijan manifests features of (semi) authoritarianism or sultanism.[90] In other words, the regime possesses formal institutions of democracy with one party dominant in the legislature, but it is tightly bound by informal networks of control and influence.[91]

In the international arena, the Aliyev regime reassessed the value of a strategic relationship with Israel in 1999. As mentioned elsewhere, the relationship with Israel was to a considerable degree predicated on the ability of the Jewish lobby to overturn anti-Azerbaijani legislation, particularly Section 907 of the Freedom Act. When, after several attempts to pass the Silk Road Act, which included a provision to suspend Section 907, legislation failed to materialize, the unreserved faith in the power of the Jewish lobby subsided. This also put further into question the necessity of maintaining a special relationship with Israel.

Islam in Azerbaijan

Despite the fact that traditional Islam among Azerbaijanis is a reflection of their historical ties to Iran, after gaining independence in 1991, the Muslim population of Azerbaijan (officially 93 percent) in their majority has rejected the teachings of political Islam propagated by Iran. Until the twentieth century, most Azerbaijanis had identified themselves as Muslims rather than Azerbaijanis or Turks. They believed that being a "spiritual community of Islam" was much more important that being a nation. Recently the Sunni influence has increased under the impact of the madrasas funded by "Wahhabi" Saudi Arabia foundations and a system of elite Turkish lyceums (preparatory colleges) funded by the Fettullah Gullen ("Nurcu") movement.[92] In general, in the twentieth century, under the influence of Turkism and a 70-year exposure to Sovietization, Islam became an expression of cultural identity rather a comprehensive belief system.[93] Despite attempts to export the Islamic revolution from Iran, a majority of the population preserved secular lifestyles and attitudes inherited from the Soviet period.[94] Among Azerbaijani Muslims, religious practices are less restrictive of women's activities than in most other Muslim countries. Among members of the political elite, there is no active pro-Iranian faction, although there is a strong pro-Russian faction.[95] Nevertheless, Iranian intelligence services were able to create an underground grassroot network of activists who espouse the Iranian "revolutionary" form of Shi'ism in Azerbaijan.[96] In fact, in 1995 the Iranian authorities openly threatened Azerbaijan with the possibility to fomenting religious strife in the country. Iran warned Azerbaijan to distance itself from Israel or risk instability in the Caucasus region. Iranian Foreign Minister Ali Akbar Velayati warned Heydar Aliyev that "any further rapprochement between Azerbaijan and Israel will harm Islamic unity and 'those governments themselves'" at the summit in Alma Aty on August 8, 1995.[97] In 1996 the leading members of the Islamic Party of Azerbaijan were arrested and charged with espionage in favor of Iran and planning a coup d'etat.[98] The Azerbaijani leadership was concerned about the possible negative effect these Iranian-sponsored networks could have on the stability of the political regime.[99] In fact, Azerbaijani officials expressed openly their discontent in talks with Iranian representatives.[100]

Alongside the involvement of Iranian security services in the Republic of Azerbaijan, the more extremist Shia clerics were engaged in anti-American and anti-Israeli agitation and recruitment in secret cells. The pro-Iranian communal agitation had political repercussions, especially in the first decade of the twenty-first century. Anti-government communal protests, which became known as the Nardaran events, were a case in point.[101] The secular and pro-Turkish policies of the post-independence authorities were a cause of irritation for the population of Nardaran, which is predominantly made up of zealous followers of the main Shia Imam Hussein. The conservative religious practices of Nardaran clashed with the Western cultural and political values advocated by the state-run media from Baku. The imposition of a state policy against hijab wearing by schoolgirls fomented protests against the government in 2001. Allegations of Iranian influence on the Nardaran movement leadership by Azerbaijani officials abounded, fuelled by the discovery of Iranian leaflets and religious literature during police reprisals.[102] According to a relevant media report, "Azerbaijani security officials contend that the village of Nardaran is a 'hotbed' of Islamic extremism and serves as a base for Islamic terrorists with strong ties to Iran."[103] The first riots took place in June 2002 over what protestors deemed inadequate living standards, and later riots in January 2006 resulted in the deaths of three people.[104] Even though this series of protests was initially driven by genuine social grievances and enduring unemployment in this suburb of Baku, evidence of Iranian influence surfaced during the investigation.[105] Political circles in Azerbaijan interpreted these social eruptions as a warning to Azerbaijani authorities against upgrading relations with Israel.[106] These events caused more deliberations in the Azerbaijani corridors of power about the opening of an embassy in Israel. In the meantime, the government decided to proceed cautiously and delay any embassy opening for the time being.

The Iranian factor

President Heydar Aliyev and Azerbaijani foreign policy officials always stressed the importance of the Iranian factor for the foreign policy of Azerbaijan. There were three main practical considerations that compelled Azerbaijan to maintain a modicum of good relations with Iran. First, Iran as a powerful neighbor was capable of stirring irredentist agitation, particularly among Persian-speaking Talyshs. Second, land access to the Azerbaijani exclave of Nakhichevan from mainland Azerbaijan, bypassing a hostile Armenia, depends on the goodwill of Iran. And third, Iran feeds the energy grid of Nakhichevan. Beyond this, Azerbaijan is linked to Iran through its history, culture and the Shiite branch of Islam. In the long term, this religious affinity will be a significant feature of Azerbaijani–Iranian relations. Shia religious holidays, especially Magerram, which immortalizes the death of Imam Huseyn in Karbala in 680 CE, play an important symbolic part in Azerbaijani nationalism. Even the national celebrations of the Azerbaijani martyrs in struggle for the national liberation and independence of Azerbaijani Democratic Republic, who fell in a major battle with Armenian Dashnak paramilitaries in March of 1918, are timed to coincide with Magerram.[107] As a result, Azerbaijani authorities perceive the export of Islamic revolution from its southern neighbor as an existential threat. Under Heydar Aliyev, all references to Karbala and the death of Husseyn were dropped from political speeches and rituals that mark tragic events in the history of Azerbaijan.[108]

Iran continues to view Azerbaijan as a major threat to its integrity. Azer Rashidoglu concludes: "Iran wants to see Azerbaijan weakened both politically and economically. The strong Azerbaijan presents threat to Iran."[109] Iran's 20 million Azeri Turk population (by some estimates as high as 30 million) serves a source of tension between the two countries because of the threat of irredentism. Azerbaijan is concerned about Iranian territorial claims on the oil-rich Caspian Sea.[110] The Republic of Azerbaijan possesses significant hydrocarbon resources in the Caspian shelf, but it also faces Iranian claims on some of its oil fields as a result of Iranian refusal to acknowledge the 20 percent division of territorial waters of the Caspian Sea among coastal states. In particular, the unresolved sea boundaries division of the Caspian Sea strains Iranian–Azerbaijani relations. The Islamic Republic of Iran, despite its verbal declaration of support for Azerbaijan's just demands of territorial integrity, maintains friendly relations with Armenia. The Organization of Islamic Conference (OIC) is the only intergovernmental organization that declared its public support for the Azerbaijani position on Nagorno-Karabagh. Iran as an OIC member officially shares this position, despite its burgeoning trade with Armenia and a new gas pipeline that Iran intends to build to supply gas to this party to conflict in the South Caucasus. The support for and widening economic ties with Armenia serves as an extra irritant in Azerbaijani–Iranian relations. This issue surfaced during the crisis in Iranian–Azerbaijani relations after Azerbaijan initiated oil exploration in the disputed Alborz oil field (identified as the Alov field) in the Caspian shelf. In response to Iranian threats, the Azerbaijani state-run ANS agency stated: "As Mr. Rohani was objecting to Azerbaijan's friendly relations with Israel, a Middle East nation Iran wants to eradicate from the map of the world, Baku cited Teheran's support for Armenia."[111] Iran and Armenia believe that Azerbaijan is a member of a geo-strategic axis that includes Turkey, Israel and Georgia (and possibly Jordan and Ethiopia).[112]

Since Ilham Aliyev came to power in 2003, Iranian high officials again started a campaign of intimidation of Azerbaijani authorities. During his visit to Azerbaijan in July 2004, President Mohammed Khatami raised the issue of disputed exploitation rights of Caspian resources. This visit was followed by an Iranian military mission, led by the chief of staff, to Baku in August of 2004. This group of Iranian high military officials urged Ilham Aliyev to stop intelligence and military cooperation with Israel in exchange for improved relations with Iran.[113]

The Russian factor

The preservation of power in the hands of the Nakhichevan clan became an important factor that caused Azerbaijan's reorientation from an almost exclusive orientation toward Turkey to rapprochement with Moscow in 2002. Heydar Aliyev needed to guarantee the succession of power in Azerbaijan to his son. Since Heydar Aliyev showed a greater willingness to be more flexible and responsive to Russian concerns in the Caucasus than his nationalist predecessor, Abulfaz Elchibey, Russia decided to reciprocate. The improvement of relations with its oil-rich South Caucasian neighbor also reflected Moscow's interests. Russian leadership under President Putin supported the succession of power to Ilham Aliyev. Obviously, a peaceful transfer of power in Azerbaijan to the Moscow-educated scion of Aliyev's clan matched Russian projections in the "near abroad." Putin's administration took a pro-active role in assuring that power was passed to Heydar Aliyev's son as a guarantee of its continued influence over developments in the domestic and foreign policy of Azerbaijan. According to the Russian print media, Russian presidential campaign experts were directly involved in advising Heydar Aliyev how to secure transition of power to his son through parliamentary mechanisms, i.e. conducting a national referendum in order to pass a Constitutional amendment that would guarantee that in the absence of the president, a prime minister should assume his responsibilities. This schema incidentally followed the transition of power from Boris Yelstsin to Vladimir Putin in Russia.[114]

When Vladimir Putin became Russian president, bilateral relations between Azerbaijan and Russia dramatically improved. The Azerbaijani daily *Zerkalo* commented that Lukoil, a major Russian oil multinational corporation that sold its share in the Azerbaijan International Operating Company (AIOC)'s "contract of the century" in December of 2002, used to serve as a "bridge" between the political elites of the countries, but it lost its significance in the relations between Azerbaijan and Russia because, "in juxtaposition with Yeltsin, today Heydar Aliyev does not have any problems with the current Russian leadership."[115] Aliyev and Putin had 15 official and unofficial meetings: "the first meeting between me and Putin was expected to last 30 minutes, but lasted four hours." The article commented, "We suppose that the fact that Aliyev, who is cautious, and Putin, who is enthusiastic, understand each other well, was conditioned by certain parallels in their lives."[116] Putin, having been elected Russian president, in the CIS framework paid his first official visit to Azerbaijan and gave an important gift to his Baku colleague. Putin gave Aliyev a graduation diploma from the Leningrad academy of the

State Security Committee (KGB), where Aliyev studied but did not receive a diploma, according to Russian Nezavisimaya Gazeta in an article entitled "The Russian–Azerbaijani Love Affair Has Entered the Honeymoon Stage." This article unequivocally highlights the role of the shared past in the ranks of the KGB of the two leaders in the relations between two countries.[117] The sixteenth visit by Heydar Aliyev to Russia within three years (2000–3) focused on the critical issue of political succession in Azerbaijan. It was his last foreign visit due to a rapid deterioration in health for the Azerbaijani president in the spring of that year. The Azerbaijani–Russian informal understanding manifested itself in the form of concrete bilateral agreements and declarations. During the last two of Heydar Aliyev's visits to Moscow, the parties concluded several important agreements in political, strategic and military fields.

The unexpected rapprochement with Moscow had a cooling effect on Turkish–Azerbaijani relations. This reorientation away from the Turkish vector in foreign policy further strengthened under Ilham Aliyev (2003). Elhan Mehdi, who advises the chairman of the main opposition Musavat Party on foreign affairs, believes that Aliyev junior's inexperience will lead to major changes in the republic's foreign policy. "Azerbaijan's foreign policy will take a pro-Russian slant, drifting away from Turkey, especially in the military field," he predicted.[118]

Right-wing Messianism in Israel and the United States

Three key factors negatively affected the Turkish–Israeli relationship in the period from 1999 to 2005. They were the derailment of the Israeli–Palestinian peace process after the failure of the Camp David summit in 1999 and the Second Palestinian Intifada (the Al-Aqsa Intifada); the coming to power in Israel of the hard-line politician Ariel Sharon in 2001 and the conduct of targeted assassinations of the radical Palestinian figures and field commanders of Hamas, the Palestinian Jihad and Tanzim; and the intervention in Iraq by the "Coalition of the Willing," spearheaded by the United States in March of 2003. The cumulative effect of these three major events resulted in marked deterioration in the quality of the Turkish–Israeli relationship. Some uncertainty arose whether the term "strategic partnership" was still justified in describing this relationship once the AK Party came to power. But the relationship has survived, although in a less intense and cooler fashion. This section will briefly explore these events and the effect produced by them on the Turkish–Israeli entente.

The unfulfilled promise of Camp David

For historical and religious reasons, Turkey always supported the Palestinian right for self-determination. On many occasions Turkey backed the PLO positions at the United Nations and other forums. At the same time, Turkey always had a special relationship with Israel, a sister democracy in the Middle East and an influential Western ally. The signing of the Oslo accords in 1993 provided a diplomatic opportunity to open a new era in Turkish–Israeli relations. These relations quickly thrived, and by the end of the decade Turkey and Israel became allies in a region ripped by chronic instability and religious intolerance.[119]

The summit meeting between Israeli Prime Minister Ehud Barak and Chairman Yassir Arafat at Camp David, the summer retreat of American presidents, in July of 2000 held great hope. Both parties were expected by the international community to make historical breakthroughs and put an end to the Israeli–Palestinian conflict that undermined stability in the Middle East for decades from the beginning of the twentieth century. The unresolved issue of Palestine served as a major grievance shared by all Muslims, and it served as the rallying cry of Islamists world over. After a series of all-night sessions, the negotiations stalled over control of Jerusalem and the "right of return" for Palestinian refugees. If Barak was willing to reach a compromise over the issue of Jerusalem, the demand for "the return" of potentially millions of Arab refugees to the state of Israel was a non-negotiable issue for Israel.[120] Barak offered 84–90 percent of the West Bank and all of Gaza, but Arafat demanded all of the West Bank and all of Gaza.[121] As the result of the intransigence of both and their unbridgeable positions, the Camp David negotiations collapsed. The hopes for peace in the Middle East and a new international era of understanding promoted by the Clinton administration were thwarted.

The previous year was marked by another major international event that had broad implications for the strategic relationship between the three countries. The OSCE summit meeting took place in Istanbul in November of 1999. During this meeting the Baku-Tbilisi-Ceyhan pipeline project was officially endorsed by President Clinton. The three countries directly involved in the BTC (Azerbaijan, Georgia and Turkey) signed all the necessary documentation.[122] Among the Middle Eastern Cooperation partners, Ehud Barak participated in this international forum. Ehud Barak met the three key leaders who were involved in this relationship. The Israeli leader discussed the developments in the Middle East with President Bill Clinton, as well as other global issues.[123] Ehud Barak also met Bulent Ecevit, the Turkish prime minister, on November 16, and, most importantly, Barak held an unofficial meeting with President Heydar Aliyev. Araz Azimov, Azerbaijani deputy foreign minister and the main strategist of Azerbaijani foreign policy, described this meeting as the most substantial exchange between Israeli and Azerbaijani leaders to date.[124] They discussed a wide array of issues including security, anti-terrorism cooperation and energy flows from Azerbaijan potentially to Israel.[125]

However, the worsening situation in the Middle East (2000–4), particularly the renewed cycle of violence between Israelis and Palestinians known as the Al-Aqsa Intifada, and the major military campaign of the United States against Iraq tested the resilience of the trilateral relationship. The Israeli military actions against Palestinian militants negatively affected bilateral relations when the Islamist AK Party came to power in Turkey, despite the security and intelligence ties remaining strong. But even military relations suffered, especially in the area of Turkish military procurement from Israel. Several important contracts for the Israeli defense industry were cancelled or delayed. So in July 2001, Turkey rejected the Russo–Israeli bid to sell the co-produced Israeli Air Industry/Kamov Ka-50/52 helicopters. Instead, Turkey purchased American helicopters manufactured by Bell Textron for $4.5 billion. A deal, worth $1 billion, for an upgrade of old American-made M-6 tanks by the Israeli Military Industries Company was suspended in the same year.[126] During this period Azerbaijan also distanced itself from Israel. Since Azerbaijani–Israeli relations always follow the trajectory of Turkish–Israeli relations, there was no tangible progress in this plank of the relationship.

After the failure of the Camp David II (2000) to produce any tangible results, and after the national elections in Israel and the United States, the Middle East region eerily returned to its status of the 1980s. The tenor of international politics swung back to the right-wing conservative agenda, where military power, not negotiations became de rigueur. The fall of 2000 witnessed an event that served, some experts claim, as a pretext for the bloody overture of the new Intifada.[127] On September 28, 2000, on the eve of Rosh haShana (the Jewish New Year), Ariel Sharon paid a visit to the Temple Mount, known to Muslims as al-Haram al-Sharif, guarded by an escort of a thousand Israeli policemen.[128] Reflecting the perception held by influential circles in the Turkish establishment, this is how a senior Turkish diplomat described this visit: "Was it not a fateful Thursday, September 28, 2000, that the prime minister decided to pay a provocative visit to Al Aqsa Mosque, the holiest of the holy places in Jerusalem, as a deliberate show of force, accompanied by thousands of policemen—the straw that broke the camel's back."[129]

General Ariel Sharon, during his military career in the Israeli Defense Forces, earned the universal reputation as a ruthless and audacious soldier, known for his tactical maneuvers that reversed the course of the 1973 War (known as the Yom Kippur War). Early in his service he developed the tactic of the "hot pursuit" and sought retribution for every raid by Palestinian fedayuun ("Martyrdom Seekers") who penetrated Israeli territory from the Egypt-controlled Gaza and Jordan. Even though Western tourists and some Israelis regularly visited the Dome of the Rock, Ariel Sharon's visit was considered an outrage by Palestinians, given the Israeli general's involvement in many bloody operations against Palestinian fedayuun and allegations that he ordered the massacre of Sabra and Shatila.[130] The next day, during Friday prayers, the Imam of the al-Aqsa mosque called Muslims to resist the occupation and defend the mosque. Immediately the Arab residents of Jerusalem started rioting. As a result of the clashes with Israeli police on that day, five Palestinians were killed and 200 wounded.[131] Yassir Arafat described Sharon's visit as "a serious step against the Islamic holy places."

The Palestinian leader urged "the Arab and Islamic world to move immediately to stop these aggressions and Israeli practices against the Islamic holy Jerusalem." These proclamations only further exacerbated the explosive situation, and massive rioting took place in many Arab population centers both in Israel and the West Bank. Shaykh Hassan Nasrallah, the Hizballah leader in Lebanon, called for "Jihad" against Israel and the second Intifada began, with thousands rallying against Israel across the Muslim world.[132] A campaign of terror unleashed by Palestinian militants against Israeli civilians brought forceful Israeli military retaliation. The Turkish government viewed this as an asymmetric response of the Israeli Armed Forces, who fought against militant cells spread among the civilian population in the Palestinian-controlled territories in Israel, with increasing concern.[133] In October 2000, Turkey voted in favor of a UN resolution condemning Israel for using excessive force against the Palestinians, and later that month, President Ahmet Sezer harshly denounced Israel at an Islamic economic conference in Istanbul.[134] In February of 2001, Arafat visited Turkey and complained that it was Israeli closures of the West Bank that led to the escalation of violence.[135] The Turkish diplomat quoted earlier compared the Israeli military action to Nazi atrocities during World War II. In fact, he stated: "It was like traveling back in time to the World War II years of the Nazi concentration camps, where millions of innocent captives were branded with an unmistakable Jewish identity. It was an incredible sight to witness that the same obnoxious practise [sic] being repeated, but this time, unbelievably, by Israeli forces against their own [sic] Palestinian people. This was a terrible irony of history."[136]

The election of the "born-again" President George W. Bush in the United States provided Ariel Sharon with a unique opportunity to shape American policy in the Middle East on the basis of the eschatological evangelical Christian beliefs of the American president. President Bush channelled his religious zeal into reshaping the region according to the neoconservative mantra of "democratization." The newly elected Israeli prime minister, Ariel Sharon, touched a sensitive chord in President Bush because he confirmed a more apocalyptic vision of the Arab–Israeli conflict in his American counterpart. In fact, in October of 2000, Prime Minister Ariel Sharon addressed a delegation of 4,000 evangelical Christians in Jerusalem. At this occasion Sharon proclaimed that though "the land of Israel" was sacred to Jews, Christians and Muslims, "it was promised by God only to the Jews"—and he added that Jerusalem is "the undivided capital of Israel" as the Bible said.[137] When Ariel Sharon won the Israeli elections in February of 2001, he reminded his audience about his close personal friendship with President Bush. He referred back to their private helicopter tour of the West Bank in 1988 when Bush was governor of Texas and they established a unique personal rapport.[138] The Turkish public met the news of Sharon's electoral victory with trepidation and anger.[139] Sharon was viewed as an extremely unpopular Middle East leader by the majority of Turks.[140]

At the same time, powerful representatives of the neoconservative move-ment took key positions in the first Bush administration (Vice-President Richard Cheney, Secretary of Defense Donald Rumsfield, Deputy Secretary of Defense Paul Wolfowitz, Douglas Feith and others).[141] These American high civil servants expressed affinity for Samuel Huntington's "clash of civiliza-tion" thesis and advanced a doctrine of pre-emptive military strikes against radical Islamist foes and new ideological divisions between the Judeo–Christian West and the Muslim East. Since 2001 Prime Minister Sharon had initiated a series of military actions against Palestinian militants in the West Bank and the Gaza Strip, a policy tacitly supported by the White House.[142] The intense cycle of violence unleashed by the al-Aqsa Intifada (2002–4) made Israeli policymakers focus primarily on internal security and the fight against Palestinian militants. Israeli authorities disengaged from active foreign policy and were preoccupied with shoring up international support for their actions. In particular, the Israeli policy of targeted assassinations of Palestinian radical leaders (e.g. the spiritual leader of Hamas Sheykh Yassin's assassination in March of 2004) gave rise to international condemnation. The Israeli actions had a palpable negative effect on the tenor of diplomatic relations with Turkey. Turkish Prime Minister Erdogan accused Israel of "state terrorism" in March of 2004.[143] Azerbaijani senior diplomat Araz Azimov, who planned an unofficial visit to Israel to initiate security dialogue in May of 2004, cancelled his visit.[144] In June of 2004 Prime Minister Erdogan blamed the Israeli government for rising anti-Semitism in the world.[145] "We agree [with Israel] on most issues, but we think differently on one or two matters," Erdogan told members of his Justice and Development Party in parliament. "We don't have a problem with the Israeli people, but unfortunately, the Israeli administration's current actions are increasing anti-Semitism in the world."[146] Turkish ambassador to Israel, Feridun Sinirlioglu, was called to return to Turkey for consultations.[147] However, the harsh tone of Erdogan's accusation was mostly used for Turkish domestic consumption.[148] Soli Ozel concludes that there was no fundamental change in Turkish–Israeli relations despite Erdogan's public posturing.[149] Two weeks after the crisis in Turkish–Israeli relations, Prime Minister Erdogan softened his rhetoric and Feridun Sinirlioglu returned to Israel.

However, an ideological shift in thinking about the leadership of the world's sole superpower had more profound effects on the regional realities of the Middle East. The neoconservative ideology of the first George W. Bush administration shared by the Israeli leadership during this period most negatively affected the Turkish–Israeli relationship. Neoconservative thinking in foreign policy was based on three main propositions, in particular, the adoption of pre-emptive military strikes against potential threats, more ideologically driven foreign policy affected by the fundamentalist Christian fervor and the conception of America as the "City on the Hill," and the Wilsonian principle of the American mission to spread democracy in the Third World, particularly among the Islamic nations of the Middle East. The war in

Iraq of 2003, which originally had been intended to destroy the Iraqi nuclear program, in correspondence with the pre-emption doctrine, later morphed into a component of the democratization program after the nuclear weapons and their production facilities were not discovered. So the rationale for the second Gulf war was changed post hoc and became regime change in Iraq. The support offered by Kurdish military factions (primarily represented by members of the Party of United Kurdistan [PUK] and the Party of Democratic Kurdistan [PDK]) to the United States military forces in their campaign against the Baathist regime aroused the suspicions of the Turkish government toward the United States. Rumors were circulating in Turkey that the United States intended to divide Iraq into several US-controlled mini-states. Turkey did not share American threat perceptions and viewed American intervention as an imposition of American hegemony upon Turkey's neighbors. The Kurds' activities during the post-Saddam period in the Allied "protected zone" of northern Iraq further raised Turkish suspicions. The Turkish military concluded that American troops would not intervene to prevent the creation of an independent Kurdish entity in Northern Iraq, where a Kurdish population predominates.[150] Here especially, Turkish and Israeli public perceptions of American intervention diverged widely. While the majority of Turks opposed the war, Israelis overwhelmingly supported the American military campaign in Iraq in the spring of 2003.[151]

The most divisive issue in the Turkish–Israeli strategic relationship in the aftermath of the second Gulf war (2003), however, was not Turkish support for the Palestinian cause. The issue that nearly precipitated a Turkish split with Jerusalem was a series of allegations that Israeli Special Forces were providing training to a Kurdish semi-official army known as the Peshmerga.[152] This issue came to the top of the Turkish–Israeli agenda because Turkey is extremely sensitive to the Kurdish separatist movement, PKK, which found bases in Northern Iraq, while Israel had historical ties with Kurds in Iraq.[153] When Netanyahu became Israeli prime minister in 1997, in order to consolidate the Turkish–Israel entente, he declared that Israel would support the Turkish struggle against the Syria-based Kurdish terrorists. He specifically announced that the separatist PKK organization was considered by Israel to be a terrorist organization.[154] Soner Cagaptay stated: "Turkish–Israeli relations face a potential crisis. On the Turkish side, the readiness of the public to accept tight military, security, and political relations with Israel—the bedrock of the bilateral links—is being eroded by the ripple effects of the Iraq War."[155] The Kemalist establishment (the army, foreign ministry and secular intellectuals), representing the core base of support for the strategic relationship with Israel, was wary of a growing series of allegations that Israel is pursuing a clandestine alliance with the two main Kurdish factions in Iraq.[156] *Le Figaro* described the (Turkish) concern that, "The leadership in Jerusalem may have decided that its alliance with Ankara was a lesser priority than seeing a divided, weak Iraq with a decentralized government. Such an entity would naturally constitute less of a threat to Israel. Turkey, on the other hand, would of course prefer a strong central government to keep a tight rein on Kurdish irredentism."[157] In particular, an article entitled "Plan B" by Seymour Hersh published in *The New Yorker* provided the most damning allegations that raised the ire of the Turkish leadership.[158] Hersh claimed in the article that Israel was involved in enhancing the military capabilities of Kurds in Iraq to fight against the growing Shiite militias in Iraq and create a base to spy on Iran, specifically its nuclear program. The Israeli government immediately denied these allegations. The Israeli ambassador, Pinhas Avivi, vouched to the Turkish foreign ministry officials that "Israel had decided long ago not to meddle in Iraqi affairs."[159] The Turkish foreign minister accepted these assurances, despite lingering suspicions. According to Anatolia News, Abdullah Gul said, "The Israelis tell us those allegations are not true. But everybody understands both regional and Turkish sensitivity to this issue, so we have to believe what we are told." He added, "I hope our trust [of Israel] won't prove misplaced."[160] In February of 2005, Gul came to Israel for a first official visit. His mission was to resolve these concerns and re-establish a positive atmosphere in the relations between the two countries.

Conclusion: change(s) in foreign policy identities or fluid security perceptions

Formulation of foreign policy in democratic states is a complex process that involves reaching consensus among different institutions, centers of power and personalities. After the 1970s, the decade punctuated by violent clashes between left-wing guerrillas and right-wing paramilitaries in Turkey, the military adopted the ideological concept of the "Turkish–Islamic Synthesis" in the 1980s.[161] This doctrine fused the nationalist Turkist ideals with traditional Islam. The Turkish military saw this doctrine as an antidote to left-wing radicalism affecting large numbers of young people in Turkey. The emergence of an Islamic-centered elite in the 1980s prepared the ground for the AK Party's electoral victory in 2002. As the party of government, AKP manifested a Conservative/Islamist identity. This political orientation of the government obviously had a dampening effect on Turkish–Israeli relations, because of the natural inclination to attune its policies with other Muslim nations of the Middle East. However, it would be premature to conclude, as French *Le Figaro* did: "Ankara's visible shift away from Israel has the potential to meaningfully alter the region's dynamics. If Turkey continues to drift from its traditional moorings toward a more European orientation, the US may no longer be able to consider Turkey the staunch ally it was when facing down the Soviet Union."[162] Some Turkish experts concluded that in the post-Iraq war world, Turkish and Israeli regional interests had widely diverged and this would precipitate the demise of the axis.[163] Others point to Turkey's adopting the "European perspective" on the Middle Eastern and South Caucasus regional issues, as the process of Turkish integration into the European Union accelerates.[164] Gregory Burris concludes: "Ankara is also under pressure to align its foreign policy with that of Europe and decouple it from the United States. Were these pressures from inside and outside to combine, they could raise the political cost of the Turkish–Israeli relationship within Turkey to prohibitive levels."[165] The state visit by Prime Minister Erdogan to Israel on May 1, 2005 undermined these pessimistic prognoses. Erdogan brought a delegation to Israel that included 100 businessmen, and new military technology agreements were signed.[166] Israeli leadership perceived this visit to Israel as a return to "business as usual" between the two countries.[167] Thus the demonstrated resilience of the axis and expanded cooperation between the two countries in areas of military anti-missile technology, intelligence, anti-terrorism, and, more recently, energy security indicate viable prospects for the future.

As this chapter indicates, the Israeli–Azerbaijani relationship suffered due to the vicissitudes of the clan-based regime. The general poverty of the population (at least 60 percent of the population lives below the poverty line), economic and social dislocation, the usurpation of power by the president and his close associates, widespread corruption and nepotism remained an important dimension of the political situation in Azerbaijan.[168] Clannishness and nepotism affect all Azerbaijani state institutions. Clans divide state institutions into spheres of influence, and their members occupy leading positions in these institutions.[169] In general, the transition to democracy in Azerbaijan under Aliyev's personalistic rule experienced a number of setbacks.[170]

Under his personalistic regime, Heydar Aliyev (and, by extension, Ilhan Aliyev) was the apex of decision-making in foreign and domestic policy in Azerbaijan. The Azerbaijani leader himself shaped foreign policy according to his preferences. Heydar Aliyev as a "pure" realist in international relations conducted very pragmatic policy toward Turkey and Israel.[171] When Heydar Aliyev regained power in 1993, he re-established good relations with Russia and Iran. Realizing the importance of the Jewish lobby in the United States for improvement of bilateral relations, he made numerous promises to open an embassy in Israel and have an exchange of foreign ministers between Azerbaijan and Israel. Following the Turkish example, he realized another dimension of a close relationship with the Jewish lobby in Washington, namely the ability to counteract anti-Azerbaijani public perceptions and the legislation in US Congress generated by Armenian and Greek lobbies. As mentioned in Chapter 5, Azerbaijan needed the support of the Jewish lobby in its struggle to combat Section 907. However, when the pro-Azerbaijani coalition failed to strike down Section 907 in 1998, the value of the Jewish lobby for Azerbaijani foreign policy came under critical reassessment. Azerbaijan continued to balance between Iranian pressure to increase distance from Israel and an intention to improve bilateral relations with the United States.[172] After the Istanbul OSCE summit of November of 1999, where the Baku-Tbilisi-Ceyhan pipeline received official backing from American President Bill Clinton, the primacy of this relationship has declined. In other words, after the successful signing of the Baku-Tbilisi-Ceyhan pipeline project, Azerbaijan became the subject of greater interest to American policy-makers. Overall, the Azerbaijani–Israeli strategic partnership suffered from benign neglect due to the foreign policy calculations of Heydar Aliyev. Thus, in the period from 1993 to 1999, the relationship with Turkey was the sine qua non of the strategic vision of Heydar Aliyev. When bilateral relations with the United States improved due to the September 11-induced changes in the American vision of its role in the South Caucasus, the entente with Israel and Turkey became a less favorable option.

On their part, Israeli foreign policy makers realized that the strategic relationship with Azerbaijan suffers from chronic instability under the authoritarian and personalistic Aliyev regime. Israel is currently more cautious in pursuing this alignment and did not make any further specific policy commitments. Efraim Inbar, a member of the Israeli National Security Committee, who was deeply involved in all stages of the relationship with Azerbaijan, commented in the spring of 2005: "When the Azerbaijani side will get serious [about their diplomatic commitments vis-à-vis Israel], we shall be ready to re-engage with them."[173]

In 2006, the prospect of a Turkish–Azerbaijani–Israel strategic triangle was revived by the shared threat of a nuclear Iran, cooperation in the combined production of military hardware, and especially energy.[174] Despite the Israeli military campaign against the fellow-Shiite militant organization in Lebanon, Azerbaijan avoided a diplomatic confrontation with the Jewish state. As one Azerbaijani journalist pointed out, "the more pragmatic analysts in Azerbaijan believe that Israel is more important to secular Azerbaijan than is Lebanon."[175]

7   Conclusion

The primacy of identity/security in the relationship

The neorealist school has held sway over international relations (IR) thinking since World War II. According to neorealist theory, foreign policy is the practice of states, which possess fixed and stable identities, in their external relations with other states. The foreign policy of a particular state is formulated to defend the clearly definable "rational" interests and security of that state. Therefore, conventional foreign policy analysis has been extremely state-centric, since it is based on the assumption that states are homogeneous actors representing and perfectly coinciding with unproblematic, undifferentiated, unitary entities. However, this book asserts the importance of state identity in determining foreign policy and the specific understanding of security that framed this trilateral entente.

A multi-causal model was advanced in this book for explaining causes of the formation of a new type of post-Cold War alliance. My main argument is that it was, primarily, the commonality of state identities that brought these three countries together to form an entente after the collapse of the Soviet Union. But several other conditions were necessary for the emergence of this axis, including (a) a systemic change that played a definitive role, namely, the end of the Cold War itself; (b) state institutions, which became the drivers of this relationship; and (c) transnational forces and agents that emerged under conditions of globalization after the 1980s. As any model, it specifies factors that potentially limit one-directional development of the process of alliance formation.

Among aspects of the structural change, I would enumerate America's emergence as the sole superpower in the region, and the weakening of Arab power and the political vacuum in the Russian southern periphery combined with the rising challenge from Iran. The underlying cause of the creation of the strategic partnership between Turkey, Israel and Azerbaijan was a logical extension of the American geopolitical expansion into Eurasia.

The United States communicated to both countries that it was reassessing its relations with Turkey and Israel after the end of the Cold War, symbolically marked by the destruction of the Berlin Wall in 1989. In the mid-1990s,

Turkish relations with the United States deteriorated as a result of numerous criticisms of human rights violations by Turkish authorities. The negative response of the European Union to the Turkish application for membership in December 1989 only exacerbated strains on Turkish relations with European NATO allies. Turkish foreign policy makers felt a certain sense of isolation from the West. In the early 1990s, the Turkish predicament reminded Turkish policymakers of the situation that had developed after the First World War.[1] The Western identity of the Turkish Republic was challenged by a confluence of new geopolitical forces, e.g. expansion of the European Union and NATO into Eastern Europe. Turkish foreign policy makers' cooperation with Israel served to maintain an image of "political correctness" and "cultural correctness"—in Western terms—during and after the Cold War era. In a sense, improving relations with Israel has been a holdover from the radically pro-American attitudes of the Cold War era and of a deepening identity crisis thereafter; these relations served, in the eyes of official Turkey, as "reinforcements for Turkey's modern Western identity."[2] Israel, at this critical juncture, was able to offer to Turkey military cooperation without undue attention to human rights observance and also served as a conduit for the American political echelons, i.e. the US Congress, which approves funding for American foreign aid and arms sales. The revival of Turkist aspirations among significant elites in Turkey in the early 1990s found resonance among Azerbaijani leadership. At this time, Azerbaijan, as a newly independent state, was searching to establish itself on the world stage as a pro-Western and secular Muslim state.

In the case of Turkey, Israel and Azerbaijan, this book argues that these states share several features of state identity. These characteristics made them "like-minded" states and formed the basis of their strategic commitment to each other. Indeed, this "like-mindedness" created natural allies who shared common enemies. This confluence of interests brought the triple entente into existence. In essence, it was preservation of state identity that was at the core of the genesis of the triple entente that Turkey formed with Israel and Azerbaijan in the post-Cold War period. The domain of security is intimately linked with state identity because threat perceptions of external and domestic actors as well as ethno-national militant movements emanate from it.[3] There is a consensus among scholars that Turkey and Israel formed an entente because they were an exception in their neighborhood as democratic and pro-Western countries. As a result, these countries had identical regional threat perceptions and strategic interests. As such, both countries sought an extension of their relationship in the geopolitically important Caspian region in building a strategic relationship with newly independent Azerbaijan. I advance a proposition that the core identities of these states can be characterized by the following features: the garrison-states; like-minded or "Westernistic" states; secular states; constitutionally nationalist states; and lonely states. These descriptive constructs allow us to explain why these countries sought to form an axis in the first place in the early 1990s.

This book also examined institutional drivers of this trilateral entente. In the case examined here, the role of the "shadow state" and its institutions was the sine qua non of the relationship.[4] The roles of three institutions— the military, the military–industrial complex and the security apparatus—are quintessential for understanding the forging of this alignment or entente between Turkey, Israel and Azerbaijan. In this context, the entente with Israel (and Azerbaijan) was indicative of the Turkish general staff's mission as the bulwark of the Kemalist establishment in formulating foreign policy. It also ensured the military's position as the guardian of Ataturk's vision of a secular and Western-oriented state. With the demise of Turgut Ozal, the institutional interests and views on the foreign policy priorities of Turkish general staff diverged so widely from the civilian government that one can speak of two separate foreign policies in Turkey.[5] This was evident in the fact that a series of military-to-military secret agreements were signed, but not vetted, by the Turkish parliament in the period 1994–6.[6] When the Erbakan government radically reoriented foreign policy from the traditional pro-Western position to a foreign policy based on Islamic solidarity, the military perceived that the "Islamic shift" was an open challenge. The signing of military cooperation agreements indicated that the army leadership would not allow deviation from the Kemalist foundations of the Republican foreign policy. The highly publicized conclusion of the Military Training Cooperation Agreement led to a rapid expansion in bilateral links covering a whole gamut of military and security realms. The signing of additional agreements later that year, while the prime minister was away, reasserted the dominant position of the military in Turkish foreign affairs. The public opening with Israel provided the military not only with the political benefits of expanded control of foreign policy, but also an elevated status in the body politic. In order to respond to new regional challenges—e.g. the Iranian and Syrian threats, the Kurdish insurgency—the Turkish military embarked on a program of military modernization that required access to the new generation of weapons systems.[7] Since the Turkish military sought up-to-date Western military hardware, Israel became the unique Turkish arms supplier because it was not bound by any arms embargo due to humanitarian concerns.[8] Israel was capable of solving predicaments of the Turkish military by upgrading military capabilities to match the higher requirements in the age of the revolution in military affairs. The entente with Israel served another strategic objective of Turkey, i.e. maintenance of the balance of power in the Eastern Mediterranean by strengthening an anti-Armenian–Greek–Syrian coalition.[9]

There is also a consensus about the primacy of military–strategic cooperation in this relationship. But most scholars did not provide actual analysis of the features of this commonality that formed the basis of the entente. Turkey's ties with Israel and Azerbaijan may be described as central to the strategic triangle, whereas each leg represents a significant set of bilateral interactions. However, the relationship as a whole has a larger importance, and is indicative of the new strategic role Turkey seeks to assume in the post-Cold War era.

Turkey perceives itself as the potential leader of an evolving community of Turkic-speaking states and regional power in the Middle East. Turkey desires to utilize its relatively advanced economic and technological development based on Western standards and the pre-eminence of the Turkish language among Turkic languages as a means for communication among newly independent Turkic states.[10] At the same time, by aligning with Israel, Turkey intended to change the power balance in the greater Middle East in its favor vis-à-vis Iran and Syria. Turkey and Israel hoped that Jordan and Egypt would join their informal alliance or entente. In particular, the strategic commitments covered intelligence sharing, security dialogues and military training. In the Israel–Turkey axis, this commitment included transfers of advanced military hardware. The role of military–security institutions in the three countries cannot be overestimated in the analysis of this triple entente. The army and security establishment played the dominant key in the forging and maintaining of these relationships until the present. The security cooperation will likely dominate the relationships in the foreseeable future.

Poorly explored in the general literature were the actual transnational linkages, infrastructure and domestic/institutional mechanisms that made up the core of this relationship. Many scholars mention the importance of the American Jewish lobby as a factor in this relationship, but few, with the exception of Ofra Bengio, pay attention to it. The significance of the Jewish lobby in American and epistemic communities both as a desirable asset for Turkish foreign policy vis-à-vis Washington and an active instrument or an external pillar that brought Azerbaijan into the orbit of the Turkish–Israeli entente was underestimated. In general, transnational interactions are generally excluded from the discussion of relations between Turkey–Israel and Turkey–Azerbaijan, but these interactions increasingly affect the state of these relations. This book explores as significant factors not only the importance of the American Jewish lobby, but also transnational corporations and religious and diasporic networks when analyzing this complex trilateral relationship.

The pluralistic and open system of the American government allows access for special interest groups to the domains of high politics such as security and foreign policy. An analysis of the interventions of major American Jewish organizations on behalf of Turkey and Azerbaijan reveals there is an indispensable association of identity and interest between these three countries. The Jewish advocacy coalition actually serves as an essential pillar in this relationship. This role is appreciated and reciprocated by the ruling elites both in Turkey and Azerbaijan. Hence, it appears that access to the formidable Jewish lobby in the United States was one of the essential reasons for creating an axis with Israel. However, one should not conclude that the political activism of the American Jewish community in the area of American foreign policy is an aberration or an exclusive area of Jewish dominance. This trend for American ethnic communities (the so-called "diasporas") to engage in lobbying campaigns in support of foreign policy positions favoring home countries has been increasingly recognized as an accepted part of political life in America. Foreign governments realized that they could influence those foreign policy outcomes that in turn affect their own countries. To quote one former American diplomat, "Every nation in conflict saw its future in Washington. Leaders in office and in opposition in other countries realized that understanding and influencing the processes of government and opinion in the US capital could lead to substantial military and economic aid, the opportunity to buy weapons, support in the United Nations and in multilateral lending agencies."[11] Thus, since the end of the Cold War, Jewish organizations have been active in promoting the strategic partnership between Israel, Turkey and Azerbaijan. Systemic shifts occurring at the end of the Cold War prompted the formation of a policy community in the United States, which supported the creation of the trilateral entente between Turkey, Israel and Azerbaijan. This advocacy coalition ultimately tried to institutionalize the discourse of this relationship and convince the American government of its strategic importance.[12]

American Jewish organizations also perform another important function, essential for the trilateral relationship, by serving as a conduit for "back channel diplomacy" between Israel and the two other members of this informal alliance. While AIPAC and the American Jewish Committee are more active on the Turkish track, B'nai Brith and the National Council for Soviet Jewry assign higher priority to the Azerbaijani track. Nonetheless, diplomatic activity of the major American Jewish organizations often overlaps in both countries. The significance of this contribution is attested by the fact that after the election of the Justice and Development (AK) Party in November of 2002, the leader of this party, a former Islamist mayor of Istanbul, Recep Tayyip Erdogan, met American Jewish leaders before he went to a meeting with President George W. Bush in the White House. At that meeting with American Jews, Recep Erdogan said that he favored this relationship without any preconditions and was interested in expanding it.[13] In January of 2004, the American Jewish Congress presented Prime Minister Erdogan with the Profiles in Courage award.

Another sphere where transnational actors play a decisive role is energy security. In this case, the viability of the American-sponsored geo-strategic project (BTC) intended to connect the energy networks of Azerbaijan and Turkey (and, potentially, Israel) hinged on support by leading transnational oil corporations. As it was shown, BP eventually committed both capital and technical resources to the realization of this project. At the same time, Turkish and Israeli corporations have had a much lower success rate in penetration of the Azerbaijani market.

Last but not least, the fluidity and unpredictability in the psychological atmosphere in the immediate aftermath of the Cold War contributed to the formation of the tripartite entente, and it was the confluence of these conditions that brought about recourse to the instrumental use of historical memory to guide Turkish foreign policy of the early 1990s. The revived collective memories of Turkish–Jewish, Turkish–Azerbaijani, Azerbaijani–Jewish amity was crucial to introducing public and diplomatic discourse about the legitimacy and continuity of Turkish–Israeli, Turkish–Azerbaijani, Israeli–Azerbaijani relations. This certainly reflected the profound inclination among Turkish elites to view history as a body of critically important stories that says who the Turks are, where they come from, what their formative experiences have been, and even what their mission is in the modern world.

Summary: findings and implications

All of the three states have special relations with the world hegemon, the United States.[14] The expanded cooperation with Israel and extension of the strategic relationship with Azerbaijan by Turkey reaffirmed its Euro–Atlantic identity. Consequently, these foreign policy steps enhanced the value of Turkey for the United States as a component of America's greater strategy in the broader Middle East and Eurasia.[15] In this context, the support of the United States is a sine qua non for this relationship.

In the end of the 1990s, the United States decided to become directly involved in the affairs of the Caspian region, rather than acting through intermediaries (Turkey, Israel). During the 1999 OSCE summit, the United States administration clearly indicated that it intended to pursue its policy in a more forceful and direct manner toward the South Caucasus, in particular Azerbaijan. The priority of the energy resources of the Caspian and their reliable delivery to the Western markets became a new cornerstone of American policy in the region. In particular, the United States hoped to resolve the regional ethno-national conflicts (the Nagorno-Karabagh and Abkhazia) in the South Caucasus and thus to acquire the role of regional arbiter.

State identity proved to be the central factor underlying the tripartite entente of these nations. After a period of convergence in Turkish–Israeli strategic relations, which lasted up to 1999, fissures appeared as result of a transformation of state identity for Turkey. Revived enthusiasm about entry into the European Union, concurrent with a slowdown in the Peace Process between Israel and the Palestinians, shifted Turkish foreign policy priorities. Turkey started to stress its European vocation. When the moderate Islamist government of Erdogan came to power, Turkish state identity began to reflect an increasing Islamization of state institutions, even the army (officers corps). This trend called the shared threat perceptions in question. The emphasis of Turkish foreign policy shifted from its earlier preferential linkages to the Turkish world (i.e. the Turkic republics) toward its Turkish Middle Eastern neighbors (Iran, Syria, Saudi Arabia and the Gulf States). As one Azerbaijani diplomat observed: "Under Erdogan, Turkey, instead of stressing their Turkishness, the government started to claim that they are Muslims first. They turned to Islam or what they call under the label of Euro–Islam. This obviously puts in question the entente based on the similarity of internal order or 'political model' and common perceptions of external actors such as Iran and Syria."[16] At the same time, the military-to-military and intelligence cooperation among the three countries develops unabated, even during the moderately Islamist Erdogan administration.[17] During Erdogan's May 2005 visit to Israel, a contract was finalized to upgrade Turkish M60 tanks. The first 250 tanks are to be produced between 2004 and 2008.[18] An Israeli expert comments on the status of security cooperation between the two countries under the AKP government: "In practice, Israel can expect security cooperation with Turkey to continue, since this aspect of its relations with Ankara is governed by the Turkish military."[19] The prospects of the Turkish–Israeli defense cooperation improved recently because Yasar Buyukanit, the new chief of general staff, appointed in August 2006, is a strong advocate of continued strategic relations with Israel.[20]

Meanwhile, the reinvigorated bilateral relationship with the United States decreased the diplomatic value of engagement with Israel for Azerbaijani leadership.[21] Hence, the intended exchange at the prime ministerial level between Azerbaijan and Israel was assigned a secondary priority. In the beginning of the twenty-first century, the idea of a greater Turkic world (especially the fraternal relationship with Azerbaijan) lost some of its lustre and Turkey shifted course in the direction of rapid integration with Europe. Success of the Turkish journey to its European integration is not guaranteed. Even in the best-case scenario, the process of European integration is a long and complicated one. The vehemence of this pursuit was judged not to be warranted by subsequent events.[22]

The Turkic–Israeli alliance in the twenty-first century

In the post-Cold War period, the Turkish political elite realized that a deepening of its relationship with Israel would have a positive effect on its relations with the United States. Not only would it prove Turkey's commitment to American foreign policy objectives in the Middle East as a strategic partner of Israel, but it would also gain access for Turkey to a powerful Jewish lobby in Washington as an antidote to Greek, Armenian and Kurdish lobbies. Even though the relationship peaked in 1999–2000, it consolidated into a more mature and less "emotional" form under the Islamist AKP government. Despite the commitment of Turkish elites to a European future, the primacy of the strategic partnership with the United States remains a cornerstone of Turkish foreign policy. In this connection, invigoration of Turkish–Israeli relations will remain a guarantee of future American good favor. At the same time, the prospect of long-term improvement in Arab–Israeli relations seems dubious. Demographic and geographic factors will force Israel to maintain alliances with the "like-minded" regional powers.

Turkey, as a rising Eurasian power, has several options. The most favorable option for Israel is Turkey embedded in the European Union and part of the Euro–transatlantic structures. If the Europeans reject a common future with Turkey in the EU, Turkey can emerge as a leader of the Turkic world, which stretches from the Wall of China to the Mediterranean. Another option for Turkey is to realign itself with the Russo–Chinese axis in the East. In all these scenarios, Israel should deepen its relationship with Turkey and Azerbaijan as a guarantee of its existence and well-being with tested regional allies. According to one Turkish Air Force General, Israel should seek a further deepening of the Turkish–Israeli alignment. Especially, he emphasized the need for going beyond the scope of military and strategic relationship. He called for developing vital people-to-people contacts. He stressed the historical common destiny of Turkic and Jewish people. In particular, such broadening and deepening of the relationship is essential for a small state such as Israel in the hostile and unpredictable environment of the Middle East. Specifically, Israel confronts aspirations of Palestinian nationalism. As Baruch Kimmerling and Joel Migdal in their *History of Palestinian People* concluded, "the basic tenet of Palestinism" is the "the right of return" for an estimated 5 million descendants of 700,000 Arabs of Palestine. As the late Faisal Husseini said, "I worry about today. But the Israelis should worry about the future."[23] "Even if Israel cedes territories in the West Bank as it did in the Gaza Strip in August of 2005, Israel still will continue to face a Palestinian state with an exploding rate of population growth."[24]

Since 2000, Azerbaijan has made strides in re-enforcing its relationship with the United States. In particular this relationship focuses on the security of the East–West corridor pipelines (BTC and the South Caucasus gas pipeline). In recent years, the strategic importance of Azerbaijan drastically increased because it is a neighbor of Iran. Given international concerns about the pro-liferation of nuclear weapons, Iran became a focus of international attention in the last decade. The United States and Israel perceive Iran as the main threat to international peace because the Islamic Republic accelerated its covert nuclear program. Most international experts concur that Iran is pursuing the creation of nuclear weapons. This development is particularly pernicious because Iran developed and tested medium-range ballistic missiles. If the international sanctions adopted by the UN Security Council will fail to convince Iran to cease uncontrolled pursuit of nuclear technology, or unless regime change will occur in Iran, the possibility of a military confrontation undertaken by the United States or Israel is almost warranted. Azerbaijan as a pro-Western border state would be drawn into this conflict with Iran. It would be naïve to think that Israel is not gathering intelligence on Iran from Azerbaijani territory. Turkey is also likely to be involved in this effort.[25] This intelligence-gathering operation most likely will depend on the use of unmanned aerial vehicles, a technology in which Israel is a world leader.[26] Therefore, security cooperation with Israel is likely to expand unless the tensions surrounding the Iranian nuclear program subside.

Directions for future research

The concept of "fluctuating zones of influence," i.e. a fluid pattern of relation-ship between states, which has not been examined in any theoretical depth in the existing literature, has great research potential. The concept can serve as a new model of state interactions relevant to the twenty-first century, when a dynamic international environment is seized by globalization. In order to realize this potential, the model needs further elaboration, clarification and investigation.

In Chapter 6, I focused on those factors that have limited further development of the axis under discussion. The axis became increasingly exposed to perturbations and fluctuations in domestic politics of the three countries. As a result, the commonality of foreign policy goals and interests among the countries has been undermined, if not dissipated. In general, state identity is commonly believed to be stable and consistent, but it also undergoes critical changes due to external (systemic) factors and internal (domestic) agents. As a result of the assumed static nature of the factors described in the method of difference argument, analysis needs to be extended to reflect the fluidity of state identity. In order to describe a dynamic situation, Mill offers an alternative method. It is called the method of concomitant variations. It states that when one of the factors increases or decreases, the phenomenon varies in the same direction.

Primarily, the consolidation of a moderate Islamist AKP Party, which came to office in Turkey in November 2002, led to weakening of the secularist or Kemalist identity of the Turkish state. The trilateral axis began to unravel. The so-called "zero problem" foreign policy advocated by Abdullah Gul and Erdogan led to rapid improvement of relations with Turkey's neighbors, Iran and Syria.[27] An attempt was made by Erdogan's government to engage Armenia in substantive negotions, especially in 2003, and to open the mutual border for trade and other exchanges. These AK Party foreign policy intitiaves impinged upon the interests of Israel (in the cases of Syria and Iran) and Azerbaijan (in the case of Armenia). Erdogan's government consistently pursued a policy of weakening the grip of the military on reins of power, which is the main pillar of the Turkish entente with Israel and Azerbaijan. Using European demands for civilian control over the military as a precondition for entry into the European Union, part of the EU "Harmonization" program, Erdogan's administration shifted to civilian leadership in the National Security Committee and transferred to parliament the authority to oversee and determine the military budget that had been a prerogative of the general staff. I concur with an opinion expressed by Yoav Karny that "under the European umbrella, he [Erdogan] does not have to worry about generals who could dislodge him from power. Europe (in his eyes) is the only road to gradual elimination of secularism without resorting to violent revolution and spilling of blood. Those who want to be a part of Europe cannot limit the right of women to wear veil. Under the European umbrella, the party of government will be empowered to dismiss generals, carry out reorganization in the army and sack members of the National Security Council in order to squeeze out the Kemalist glue of secularism from the body of Turkey."[28] This political change in Turkey highlights the problematic co-existence of democracy and liberalism in the Middle East.[29]

The strategic Turkish–Israel–Azerbaijani axis is bound to dissolve as the AKP government realigns Turkish foreign policy in the direction of greater cohesion with its Middle Eastern neighbors. As Karny observes: "The close strategic partnership which developed between Turkey and Israel came into being because generals took this subject out of jurisdiction of government. There is no chance that Erdogan and Gul will destroy this alliance in one day, but they have begun the process of destruction."[30] The axis came into being under circumstances of a crisis of identity caused by the end of the Cold War. As new geo-economic and geopolitical concerns assume greater weight (the emergence of China and India, for example) in the international system, the survival of this US-backed axis is hardly assured.

Notes

1 The entente of Turkey, Israel and Azerbaijan

1 Turkey was one of the original members of Central Treaty Organization or the Pact of Mutual Cooperation concluded by Iraq, the United Kingdom, Pakistan and Iran on February 24, 1955. *American Foreign Policy, 1950–5, Basic Documents*, Vol. 1, Department of State Publication 6446, *General Foreign Policy Series* 117, Government Printing Office, Washington, DC, 1957.

2 Duygu Sezer, "Turkey's Political and Security Interests," in *The New Geostrategic Environment of the Expanded Middle East*, Stimson Center Occasional Papers, No. 19, Washington, DC, July, 1994, p. 25.

3 Entente, in *Webster's Encyclopedic Unabridged Dictionary of the English Language*, New York: Portland House, 1989, p. 476.

4 See Philip Robins, *Turkish–Israeli Relations: From the Periphery to the Center*, The Emirates Occasional Papers, Abu Dhabi: The Emirates Center for Strategic Studies and Research, 2001, p. 6.

5 This was an intiative of Prime Minister Erdogan's chief foreign policy advisor, Ahmet Davutoglu. Khaled Mashal met with Abdullah Gul, then foreign minister in Ankara. Barçın Yinanc, "AKP Not in Love but Certainly More Understanding of Israel," *Zaman*, August 30, 2007.

6 See Efraim Inbar, *The Israeli–Turkish Strategic Partnership*, Ramat Gan, Israel: The Begin-Sadat Center for Strategic Studies, 2002.

7 See Philip Robins, *Turkish–Israeli Relations: From the Periphery to the Center*, op. cit., p. 4.

8 Dietrich Jung and Wolfgang Piccoli, "The Turkish–Israeli Alignment: Paranoia or Pragmatism?" *Security Dialogue*, Vol. 31, No. 1, 2000.

9 M.C. Geokas and A.T. Papathanasis, "The Turkish–Israeli Alliance Is a New Destabilizing Factor in the Middle East and Southern Europe," available at www.thirdworldtraveler.com/New_World_Order/PowerBloc_TurkeyIsrael.html.

10 Ariel Colonomos, "Transnational Networks: Old Game, New Rules," in Marie-Claude Smouts (Ed.), *The New International Relations: Theory and Practice*, London: C. Hurst & Co., 2001, p. 116.

11 Alexander Wendt, "Identities and Structural Change," in Yosef Lapid, Friedrich Kratochwil (Eds.), *Return of Culture and Identity in IR Theory*, Boulder, CO: Lynne Rienner Publishers, 1996.

12 Susan Strange, *States and Markets*, London: Pinter, 1988; also Ariel Colonomos, op. cit., p. 116. In particular, such transnational corporations as British Petroleum, the Western corporations involved in the Baku-Tbilisi-Ceyhan project, as well as Israeli Merhav Corporation, are actively involved in maintenance of this relationship.

13 Ariel Colomonos, op. cit., p. 120.

14 Bulent Aras, *The New Geopolitics of Eurasia and Turkey's Position*, London: Frank Cass, 2002, p. 34; Svante Cornell, "The Conflict in Nagorno-Karabagh," in Dmitry Furman (Ed.), *Azerbaijan and Russia*, Moscow: Letny Sad, 2001, p. 471; Zeyno Baran, "The Caucasus: Ten Years after Independence," *The Washington Quarterly*, Winter Section: Eurasia after Ten Years, 2002, Vol. 25, No. 1, p. 223; Hrair Dekmejan and Hovann Simonian, *The Troubled Waters: The Geopolitics of the Caspian Region*, London: Tauris Publishers, 2001, p. 89.

15 See Jacob Abadi, "Israel's Quest for Normalization with Azerbaijan and the Muslim States of Central Asia," *Journal of Third World Studies*, Vol. 19, No. 2, Fall 2002, pp. 63–88.

16 See Alexander Murinson, "Israeli Foreign Relations with the Islamic Newly Independent States: General Overview," in *The Cyber-Caravan*, Central Asia-Caucasus Institute publication, SAIS, August, 1999.

17 As quoted in Neill Lochery, "Israel and Turkey: Deepening Ties, 1995–8," *Israel Affairs*, Vol. 5, No. 1, August, 1998.

18 Qadir Nasri Meshkini, "Challenges of Iranian Policy in Central Asia and the Caucasus," *Amu Darya: The Iranian Journal of Central Asian Studies*, Spring/ Summer 2000, Vol. 4, No. 5, pp. 85–99; Mohammad Noruzi, "Contention of Iran and Turkey in Central Asia and the Caucasus," in *Amu Darya: The Iranian Journal of Central Asian Studies*, Vol. 4, No. 5, Spring/ Summer 2000, pp. 113–33.

19 This vision was reiterated at the meetings of Heydar Aliyev with representatives of leading Jewish organizations in the United States in 1994, 1995, 1996 and 1997. Personal interview with Eldar Namazov, July 29, 2004.

20 The legend of the Blind Men and the Elephant originated in the Pali Buddhist Udana, which was apparently compiled in the second century BCE. It spread to Islam through the work *Theology Revived* of the orthodox Sufi theologian Muhammad al-Ghazzali (1058–1128 CE). Ghazzali refers to the tale in a discussion on the problem of human action, a problem in which the inadequacy of natural reason becomes most evident. Available at: www.kheper.net/topics/blind_men_and_elephant/Sufi.html.

21 See Chapter 4 in Ian Lesser, "Western Interests in a Changing Turkey," a Rand Monograph. Available at: www.rand.org/publications/MR/MR1241/MR1241.chap4.pdf.

22 There is an array of Russian-language in-depth studies of the Israel–Turkey–Azerbaijan nexus, which are unfamiliar to the general readership. See Igor Muradian, *Politika SSHA I Problemy Bezopasnosty Regiona Yuzhnogo Kavakaza*, Yerevan: Antares, 2000, pp. 61–87; Igor Muradian, *Geoekonomicheskye Problemy Kasvakazsko-Kaspiskogo Regiona*, Yerevan: Caucasian Center for Iranian Studies, 1999; N. Kireev, "Turtsia i Israel-Strategichiskye Soyuzniki na Blizhnem Vostoke," in V. Isayev and A. Filonik (Eds.), *Blizhny Vostok I Sovrremennost*, Moscow: Institut Izucheniya Izraeilya I Blizhnevogo Vistoka (IIIBV), 1998, #5; I. Ivanova, "Turetsko-Israelskiye Otnoshenya I Problemy Regionalsnoy Bezopasnosty," in M. Aruniova (Ed.), *Blizhny Vostok: Problemy Regionalnoy Bezopasnosty*, Moscow: IIIBV, 2000; F. Konovich, "Turetsko-Israelskie Otnosheniya v 90e gody," in A. Fedorchenko and A. Filonik (Eds.), *Vostkovedny Sbornik*, Moscow: IIIBV, 2002, #4; Sergey Minasyan, "Israel–Turtsiya: Voenno-Politicheskye I Voenno-Technocerskoye Sotrudnochestvo v Aspekte Problem Regionalnoy Bezopsasnosty," *Centralnya Asia I Kavkaz*, No. 1, 2004. Most English-language studies focus on the Turkish–Israeli alignment. See the most important works: Philip Robins, *Turkish–Israeli Relations: From the Periphery to the Center*, The Emirates Occasional Papers, Abu Dhabi: The Emirates Center for Strategic Studies and Research, 2001; Efraim Inbar, *The Israeli–Turkish Partnership*, Ramat Gan, Israel: The Begin-Sadat Center for Strategic Studies, 2003; and the most recent account by Ofra Bengio, *Changing Ties of Middle Eastern Outsiders*, New York: Palgrave Macmillan, 2004.

23 Efraim Inbar, "Turkey's New Strategic Partner: Israel," in Michael Radu (Ed.), *Dangerous Neighborhood*, New Brunswick, NJ: Transaction Publishers, 2002, p. 175.
24 John Gerard Ruggie, "Continuity and Transformation in the *World Polity*: Toward a Neorealist Synthesis," *World Politics*, Vol. 35, 1992, pp. 261–85.
25 Since 1991, more than 23 agreements in the political, economic/commercial, cultural and military fields have been concluded between Turkey and Israel. The Turkish government agreed to back Azerbaijan in the case of a new war over Nagorno-Karabagh "with both personnel and equipment" in March, 2001. Meanwhile, Azerbaijan purchased artillery, anti-tank and infantry weapons mostly from Turkey, Israel and Ukraine totaling $300 million annually. See Ali Murat Koknar, "Turkey and the Caucasus: Security and Military Challenges," in Michael Radu (Ed.), *Dangerous Neighborhood*, New Brunswick, NJ: Transaction Publishers, 2003, p. 221.
26 The concept of the "like-minded states" was introduced by Turkish academics in 1998. See Ali Carkoglu, Eder Mine and Kemal Kirisci, *The Political Economy of Regional Cooperation in the Middle East*, London: Routledge, 1998, pp. 1–2.
27 According to some sources, 50,000 Jews from Azerbaijan live in Israel.
28 Israel is currently the second largest importer of Azeri oil, according to official statistics, and it also imports Caspian Sea fish from Azerbaijan according to www.ncsj.org/AuxPages/081102JTA.shtml.
29 Turkey is a pivotal state in international politics because of its critical geographical location astride the Balkans, the Black Sea, the Mediterranean, the Middle East and the Transcaucasus. See Gareth M. Winrow, *The Turkish Policy Toward Central Asia and the Transcaucasus*, Washington, DC: The Washington Institute for Near East Policy, 2000, p. 116.
30 Even though Turkey is a member of NATO, while Israel has a special strategic relationship with the United States, both would like to reap significant economic benefits of membership in or close association with the European Union. Azerbaijan has already become a member of the Organization for Security and Cooperation in Europe, but the Azerbaijani leadership continues to consider the option of attaining full NATO membership.

2   State identities as building blocks of the relationship, 1992–9

1 Maja Zehfuss, a post-modernist critic of the Constructivist school, concludes: "a phenomenon became inescapable." Maja Zehfuss, *Constructivism in International Relations: The Politics of Reality*, Cambridge: Cambridge University Press, 2002, p. 2.
2 Kimmerling further concludes: "As powerful and strong as it may be, the state cannot detach itself from the identities and self-perceptions of its society's population." Baruch Kimmerling, *The Invention and Decline of Israeliness: State, Society and the Military*, Berkeley: University of California Press, 2001, p. 58. More recent contributions include the conclusion, "On the Road toward a More Adequate Understanding of the State," by Peter Evans, Dietrich Rueschemeyer and Theda Skocpol in Peter Evans, Dietrich Rueschemeyer and Theda Skocpol (Eds.), *Bringing the State Back In*, Cambridge: Cambridge University Press, 1985, pp. 347–66; Stephen Krasner, "Approaches to the State: Alternative Conceptions and Historical Dynamism," *Comparative Politics*, Vol. 16, 1984, pp. 223–46.
3 Introduction to Shmuel Harely, *Turkiya, mivne arza, toldoteyha, mishtara ha medini, hevrati ve kalkali* ("Turkey: Its Geography, History, Political, Social and Economic System"), Jerusalem: Reuven Mas, 1941, p. 4.
4 Ibid.
5 See also Stephen Kinzer on the impact of Ataturk's reforms on Turkey in Stephen Kinzer, *Crescent and Star*, New York: Farrar, Straus & Giroux, 2002, p. 10.

6 Duygu Sezer explains that shortly after the collapse of the Berlin Wall, Turkey's elites were preoccupied with maintaining the stability of the political regime and domestic order based on the principles of Kemalism. As a result, strategic foreign policy decisions were made on the basis of their conformity to this "philosophical–ideological world view." Duygu Sezer, *Turkey in the New Security Environment in the Balkan and Black Sea Region*, Oxford: Westview Press, 1998, p. 79.

7 Duygu Sezer highlights that the post-Soviet Azerbaijan occupies a unique position for Turkey among Turkic states due to their special historical, linguistic and cultural ties and, most importantly, their proximity. Duygu Sezer, ibid., p. 89.

8 Personal interview with Araz Azimov, deputy foreign minister of Azerbaijan, August 3, 2004.

9 Personal interview with Eldar Namazov, July 29, 2004.

10 Ibid.

11 See Ali Carkoglu, Eder Mine and Kemal Kirisci, op. cit., pp. 1–2, passim; Philip Robins, *Suits and Uniforms*, Seattle, WA: University of Washington Press, 2003, p. 215. Daniel Ayalon, a former ambassador of Israel to the United States, used the same words recently when describing the position of Turkey and Israel today. In the predicament in the Middle East that followed the second Gulf war, he added: "Today, Turkey remains one of Israel's best friends in a hostile region." Daniel Ayalon, "The Israel–Turkey Friendship: Common Values, Common Interests," *A Quarterly Review of Cooperation: US, Turkey and Israel*, publication of The Jewish Institute for National Security Affairs (JINSA) and The Assembly of Turkish American Associations, November 13, 2003.

12 The adherence to democratic norms by the last ruler of the post-Soviet republic, Heydar Aliyev, and his son Ilhan Aliyev, the current president, is highly question-able, but Azerbaijan possesses the institutional and constitutional framework of a democracy. Yuksel Soylemez, a former Turkish ambassador to the United States, characterized the Aliyevs' rule in the following way: "[Heydar Aliyev], a remarkable man and very tough politician, he did not share his powers with his ministers or his people. There was very little opposition in the Azeri parliament [sic] which acted mostly as his rubberstamp. He was described by a diplomat serving in Baku, who knew him, as a very smooth operator . . . He himself made all the decisions with no power sharing. He groomed his son to succeed him against criticism that he was creating a dynasty, which has become true." *Turkish Daily News*, October 31, 2003. Compare with Mustafa Kemal's regime under the one-party rule, which was essentially a "one-party dictatorship."

13 Barry Buzan and Thomas Dietz, "The European Union and Turkey," *Survival*, Spring 1999, p. 49.

14 Stephen Walt states that "the more similar two or more states are, the more likely they are to ally." Stephen M. Walt, "Alliance Formation and the Balance of Power," *International Security*, Vol. 9, No. 4, Spring, 1985, cited in Michael E. Brown, Sean M. Lynn-Jones and Steven E. Miller (Eds.), *The Perils of Anarchy: Contem-porary Realism and International Security*, London: MIT Press, 1995, p. 209.

15 "Turkey and Israel to Cooperate on Security: Common Threats to be Met with Complementary Capabilities," Briefing by General Çevik Bir, deputy chief of the Turkish general staff, JINSA, Washington, DC, February–March, 1996. Available at: www.jinsa.org/articles/articles.html/function/view/categoryid/102/documentid/281/history/3,2360,102,281.

16 In fact, during the Pehlevi rule, Iran was an Israeli strategic ally as a pro-Western, albeit authoritarian, state until the Islamic Revolution of Khomeini in 1979. See M. Heller, "Continuity and Change in Israeli Security Policy," *Adelphi Papers* 335,

London: Institute for International Security Studies, 2000, p. 15. Turkey and Azerbaijan also perceive the threat of an "export" of the Islamic revolution as a threat to national security.

17 Çevik Bir, JINSA Newsletter, op. cit.
18 See Rouhholah Ramazani, *The Northern Tier: Afghanistan, Iran and Turkey*, Princeton, NJ: Van Nostrand Company, 1966, p. 117. For a broader definition that includes states from Pakistan in the east to Libya in the west, see George Haddad, *Revolutions and Military Rule in the Middle East: The Northern Tier*, New York: Robert Speller & Sons, 1965, p. 7.
19 The text of the report is in J.C. Hurewitz, *Diplomacy in the Middle East and the Near East: A Documentary Record, 1914–1956*, Princeton, NJ: Van Nostrand Company, 1956, pp. 337–42.
20 Çevik Bir, op. cit. See also: Igor Muradian, *Politika SSHA I Problemy Bezopasnosti Regiona Yuzhnogo Kavakaza*, Yerevan: Antares, 2000, p. 63; Ian Lesser, *NATO Looks South: New Challenges and New Strategies*, Santa Monica, CA: Rand Corporation, 2000, p. 17.
21 General Çevik Bir stressed that "contrary to the beliefs of some, neither the United States nor any other third party initiated Turkish–Israeli cooperation or the 1996 military training and cooperation agreement. These were the initiatives of the Turkish leadership" (op. cit.).
22 "Turks and Jews Enjoy Solid Friendship," The Assembly of Turkish American Associations and the Jewish Institute for National Security Affairs, Newsletter No. 1, May, 2002.
23 Personal interview with Tahir Taghi-zade, a former deputy chief of mission of the Azerbaijani embassy to the United States and spokesman of the Azerbaijani Ministry of Foreign Affairs (2005–8), June 15, 2004.
24 The collapse of the Soviet Union and the dissolution of the Warsaw Pact eliminated the threats of Soviet military intervention and Soviet nuclear attack on Western Europe.
25 The Iran–Iraq war, two recent Gulf wars, the Israeli–Palestinian conflict, the Kurdish separatist militancy in Turkey and the frozen Nagorno-Karabagh conflict directly affect the relevant countries.
26 Philip Robins concludes about Turkey: "Though the Turkish state and its boundaries were born of indigenous agency, unlike so many other 'imposed' states in the Middle East, the sense of existential insecurity, epitomized by the Sevres blueprint, resonates for Turkey's decision-making elites." See "The Foreign Policy of Turkey," in Raymond Hinnebusch and Anoushiravan Ehseshami (Eds.), *The Foreign Policy of Middle East States*, Boulder, CO: Lynne Rienner, 2002, p. 321.
27 Andrew Mango, "Turkey and Arabs," in Sylvia Haim (Ed.), *Arab Nationalism and a Wider World*, New York: American Academic Association for Peace in the Middle East, 1971, p. 42.
28 Personal interviews with Çevik Bir and retired Turkish generals, May 26, 2004; personal interview with Aydan Kodaloglu, May 26, 2004.
29 Personal interview with Andrew Mango.
30 Rouhoallah Ramazani, op. cit., p. 39.
31 Since 1984, the PKK, or Kurdistan Workers Party, has fought the Turkish state in an attempt to carve out an independent zone for Kurds in Turkey's southeast, although there have been recent indications the PKK might settle for autonomy. The Turkish government, however, has opposed concessions to the PKK, claiming that the organization's real goal remains the dissolution of Turkey. The Turkish government regards the PKK as a terrorist organization. See "Weapons Transfers and Violations of the Laws of War in Turkey," *Human Rights Watch*, November, 1995.

32 Duygu Sezer, "Turkey in the New Security Environment in the Balkan and Black Sea Region," op. cit., p. 72. According to the former Turkish foreign minister, Hikmet Cetin, with the dissolution of the Soviet Union and the vacuum of influence of extra-regional "power centers" in the Middle East, Turkey was transformed from a "flank" state into a "frontline" state facing multiple fronts on its borders. Quoted in Duygu Sezer, "Turkey's Political and Security Interests in the New Geostrategic Environment of the Expanded Middle East," *Stimson Center Occasional Papers*, Washington, DC, No. 19, July, 1994, p. 25.

33 Interview with Araz Azimov, op. cit.

34 Lasswell hypothesizes that in the future, the world of the garrison-states will prevail—and power will be transferred to the specialists of violence. See Harold Lasswell, "The Garrison State," *The American Journal of Sociology*, Vol. 46, 1941, pp. 455–68.

35 George Haddad, op. cit., p. 13.

36 Ibid.

37 Ibid.

38 Securitization, according to Barry Buzan, means "the move that takes politics beyond the established rules of the game and frames the issue either as a special kind of politics or as above politics." B. Buzan, O. Waever and J. De Wilde, *Security: A New Framework for Analysis*, Boulder, CO: Lynne Rienner Press, 1998, p. 23.

39 See a detailed account of the role of the military–security apparatus in the post-1980 coup in Turkey in Philip Robins, *Suits and Uniforms*, Seattle, WA: University of Washington Press, 2003, pp. 75–9.

40 William Hale, *Turkish Politics and the Military*, London: Routledge, 1993, pp. 2–3; Gareth Jenkins, "Context and Circumstance: The Turkish Military and Politics," unpublished paper, February, 2001.

41 Ibid.

42 Dunkworth Rustow, "The Army and the Founding of the Turkish Republic," *World Politics*, July, 1959; Sidney Fisher (Ed.), *The Military in the Middle East*, Columbus, OH: Ohio State University, 1963, pp. 21–40.

43 George Haddad, op. cit., pp. 106–7.

44 Stephen Kinzer, *Crescent and Star*, New York: Farrar, Straus & Giroux, 2002, p. 14.

45 Shlomo Ben-Ami emphasizes "the special role of the military" in Turkey as "guardians of the Constitution." Personal interview with Shlomo Ben-Ami, a former foreign minister of Israel and a scholar of fascism in Spain and Italy, February 6, 2003.

46 Gareth Jenkins, *Context and Circumstance: The Turkish Military and Politics*, Oxford: Oxford University Press, 2001, Adelphi Paper 337, p. 23. Accordingly, the National Security Council (NSC) was composed of five generals (the chief of staff and the commanders of the army, navy, air force and gendarmerie) and five civilian officials (the president, prime minister and ministers of defense, interior and foreign affairs). The chief of staff held the post of secretary-general of the council. Gareth Jenkins, "Symbols and Shadow-Play: Military–JDP Relations 2002–4," unpublished report, 2005, p. 7. In November of 2004, the structure, appointments and official secrecy status were changed in conformity with the European Union-required reforms of the civilian–military relations in Turkey. "Civil Secretary, Civil MGK," *Zaman*, December 2, 2004.

47 Stephen Kinzer, op. cit., p. 164.

48 As quoted in Gareth Jenkins, "Symbols and Shadow-Play: Military–JDP Relations 2002–4," unpublished report, 2005, p. 3. Further, the Turkish Armed Forces Internal Service Directive is more explicit. Article 85/1 of the directive states: "It is the duty

of the Turkish Armed Forces to protect the Turkish homeland and the republic, by arms when necessary, against internal and external threats." Ibid.

49 George Haddad, op. cit.

50 The deposed prime minister, Menderes, has built more mosques than schools and restored Arabic Ezan (the Muslim call to prayers) earlier translated into Turkish under the Kemalist program of Turkification of the 1930s. George Haddad, op. cit., p. 118.

51 See Stehen Kinzer, op. cit., p. 14. Chief of Staff Necip Torumtay resigned in protest against Ozal's commitment to support the Allies' military action against the Saddam regime in 1991. For details, see Nicole Pope and Hugh Pope, *Turkey Unveiled*, Woodstock, NY: Overlook Press, 1997, pp. 219–24.

52 Chapter 3 of this volume will explore institutional mechanisms through which the Turkish–Israeli–Azerbaijani entente came into being and continues to be maintained today.

53 Personal interview with William Hale, August, 2005.

54 Suha Bulukbasi, "Baku-Centered Policy: Has it Failed?" *Middle East Journal*, Vol. 51, No. 1, 1997, pp. 80–94.

55 As quoted in Jolyon Naegele, "Turkey: Foreign Relations Good with Two of Eight Neighbors," *Radio Free Europe/Radio Liberty*, August 13, 1998.

56 See details in Philip Robins, *Suits and Uniforms*, op. cit., pp. 145–55.

57 Philip Robins, "The Foreign Policy of Turkey," in Raymond Hinnebusch and Anoushiravan Ehseshami (Eds.), *The Foreign Policy of Middle East States*, Boulder, CO: Lynne Rienner, 2002, p. 321. For a detailed account of the military as the main institutional actor in formation of the Turkish–Israeli axis, see Chapter 3 of this volume.

58 Jenkins concludes that "this ideological dimension to the military's perception of its role has meant that its definition of security extends beyond public order and Turkey's political or economic interests to include threats to the country's Kemalist legacy" (op. cit., p. 1).

59 Yael Navaro-Yashin, *Faces of the State: Secularism and Public Life in Turkey*, Princeton, NJ: Princeton University Press, 2002, p. 119.

60 Ibid.

61 Personal interviews with Turkish citizens in Istanbul, Ankara and Washington, DC, 2004–5.

62 Stephen Kinzer, op. cit., p. 144.

63 Eliezer Livneh, who wrote extensively on the norms and values that characterize Israeli society, remarks: "The Israeli makes far-reaching identification between the fate of the state of Israel and his personal destiny". See Eliezer Livneh, "Values and Society in Israel," in Israel Naamani, David Rudavsky and Abraham Katsh (Eds.), *Israel: Its Politics and Philosophy*, New York: Behrman House, revised in 1974, p. 108.

64 Stephen Kinzer characterizes the sense of anxiety and lack of trust among Turkish leaders toward the neighboring countries: "Here, Turkish leaders like to say, is Turkey's difference. Their argument goes something like this. Of course, Norway and Portugal can afford to allow their citizens virtually unlimited freedoms. They are surrounded by friends and allies, all of whom understand that the rise of one nation helps all its neighbors. But where we live, the rules are different. We are surrounded by vipers waiting to strike, enemies who plot against us day and night" (Stephen Kinzer, ibid., p. 145). Israelis frequently employ similar imagery and rhetoric to describe their neighbors. An Israeli named Koby eloquently summarizes Israeli views of Israeli public: "No one knows where the first big attack will come from. Lebanon, Syria, Iran. Maybe al-Qaeda." He notes that the name Israel means "he who wrestles with God." "Our struggle is as old as Jewish history. Will it ever end? Israelis are the only people who always have lived in fear of unconventional attacks. Israelis

always have lived with air raid sirens and bomb shelters. Israelis are the only people who have been in a state of war or semi-war with at least half of their neighbors. Israel is in the bull's eye of a region some call the 'New Missile Middle East.' " Donna Rosenthal, *The Israelis*, New York: Free Press, 2005, p. 22. See also Eliezer Livneh, op. cit., p. 109.

65 Donna Rosenthal, op. cit., p. 48.

66 See Howard Sachar, *A History of Israel from the Rise of Zionism to Our Time*, New York: Alfred Knopf, 1998, pp. 213–15.

67 Especially see Howard Sachar, ibid., p. 300.

68 The first attack on Jewish civilians occurred on November 30, 1947. See Eli Barnavi (Ed.), *A Historical Atlas of the Jewish People*, London: Kuperard, 1998, p. 243.

69 Howard Sachar, op. cit.

70 Gareth Jenkins, op. cit., p. 5. See also Albert Howe Lybyer, *The Government of the Ottoman Empire in the Age of Suleiman the Magnificent*, Cambridge, MA: Harvard University Press, 1913, pp. 90, passim; William Hale, op. cit., p. 2.

71 See the detailed accounts of the role of the military in the Israeli education system in Ester Yogev and Eyal Naveh, *Histories: Towards Dialog with the Past* (in Hebrew), Tel Aviv: Bavel, 2002; and of state rituals in Azaryahu Maoz, *State Cults: Celebrating Independence and Commemorating the Fallen in Israel* (in Hebrew), Sde-Boker, Israel: Ben-Gurion Center, 1995.

72 Michael Feige, "Peace Now and the Legitimation Crisis of Civil Militarism," *Israeli Studies*, March, 1998, p. 89.

73 See also Uri Ben-Eliezer, *The Making of Israeli Militarism*, Bloomington: Indiana University Press, 1998, p. 147.

74 Livneh notes: "the Israel Army, its regular personnel and scientific associations, constitute a sort of Western island of efficiency and competition in Israel society" (Eliezer Livneh, op. cit., p. 109).

75 Baruch Kimmerling, *The Invention and Decline of Israeliness: State, Society and the Military*, Berkeley: University of California Press, 2001, p. 209.

76 David Rudge, "Optimism Rises among Jewish Israelis, Except in the Territories," *Jerusalem Post*, December 10, 2004.

77 Yitzhak Laor, "Before Rafah: On Israeli Militarism," *The London Review of Books*, June 3, 2004.

78 See also Uri Ben-Eliezer, *The Making of Israeli Militarism*, Bloomington: Indiana University Press, 1998, pp. 148–9.

79 Eva Etzioni-Halevi, "Civil–Military Relations and Democracy: The Case of the Military–Political Elites' Connection in Israel," *Armed Forces and Society*, Vol. 22, No. 3, 1996, p. 401.

80 Compare with the more direct involvement of the military in the Northern Tier and Latin American countries, in Dan Horwitz, "The Israel Defense Forces: A Civilianized Military in a Partial Militarized Society," in R. Kolkowitz and A. Korbonski (Eds.), *Soldiers, Peasants and Bureaucrats*, London: Allen & Unwin, 1982, pp. 79–80.

81 Personal interview with Araz Azimov, August 3, 2004. Personal interview with Vafa Guluzade, August 5, 2004.

82 Personal interview with Vafa Guluzade, August 5, 2004.

83 Igor Muradian, op. cit., p. 78.

84 Heydar Aliyev, "Heydar Aliyev's Address to the Buyuk Milli Meclis," Turkish parliament, Ankara, February 9, 1994.

85 The precepts of this ideology include the Turkish national version of Islam and the national virtues of Central Asian ancestors and membership in the Western civilization. See, for example, Janet R. Jakobsen and Ann Pellegrini, *Secularisms*, Durham, NC: Duke University Press, 2008, p. 67.

86 Personal interviews with Azerbaijani students, Baku, August, 2004. Also a personal communication from Orxan Jafarov, August 3, 2004.
87 Igor Muradian, op. cit., p. 79.
88 Heydar Aliyev, "Address to the Buyuk Milli Meclis," Turkish parliament, Ankara, February 9, 1994.
89 At the end of October 2002, a special conference entitled "National Security Concept" was convened jointly by the European Marshall Center and the Ministry of Foreign Affairs of Azerbaijan. Its avowed goal was to formulate foundations for the Azerbaijani national security framework in cooperation with Azerbaijani government officials and members of parliament. It was attended by only one member of the Azerbaijani parliament, retired Major General Vladimir Timoshenko, who implied that the state's priorities in protecting the country's security and harmonizing civilian military relations had been previously ignored. Teymur Huseyinov, "Towards Crafting a National Security Doctrine in Azerbaijan," *Central Asia-Caucasus Analyst*, March 26, 2003.
90 Ibid.
91 A detailed account of counter-identities in Turkey, Azerbaijan and Israel will be covered in Chapter 6.
92 Andreas Gross and Guillermo Martinez Casan, "Functioning of Democratic Institutions in Azerbaijan," Report of Committee on the Honouring of Obligations and Commitments by Member States of the Council of Europe (Monitoring Committee), Doc. 10030, January 12, 2004.
93 A terrorist attack was carried out by the Lezgin nationalist movement Sadval on the Baku subway system on March 19, 1994. In the attack, 14 people were killed and 52 wounded.
94 Suzanne Goldenberg, *Pride of Small Nations: The Caucasus and Post-Soviet Disorder*, London: Zed Books, 1993, p. 128.
95 Personal interview with Anna Zelkina, February 10, 2002. Personal interviews with staff members of *Azadliq* newspaper, August 2, 2004.
96 Navaro-Yashin, op. cit., p. 133. Personal interview with Boris Trepetin, a former Soviet Azerbaijani academic and a high Communist Party official, February 12, 2005.
97 Ramin Nagibov, a former security officer claims: "Before I was fired from my work, I knew that there was a tariff system for every promotion in rank, averaging five thousand dollars." Available at: Agentura.ru.
98 Igor Muradian, op. cit., p. 98. Also see *The Security Services of Azerbaijan* at www.agentura.ru. There is a more detailed treatment of this cooperation in Chapter 3 of this volume.
99 Personal interview with Eynat Shlein-Michael, a policy officer of the Israeli embassy in Washington, DC, February 5, 2005. See also Agentura.ru website.
100 Eynat Shlein-Michael, op. cit. In particular, Israeli Magal Corporation is involved in security contracts with Azerbaijan. See "Israel, Turkey Plan Joint Weapons Deals for Azerbaijan," *World Tribune On-line*, February 2, 2004. Available at: www.World Tribune.com.
101 Personal interview with Qanimat Zahidov, July 30, 2004.
102 Qanimat Zahidov, editor-in-chief of the independent *Azadliq* daily, reported that about 50 percent of Azerbaijani citizens who travel to Iran are exposed to intimidation by Iranian authorities in order to co-opt them to serve for *Ettelaat*, the Iranian security service. Personal interview with Ganimat Zahidov, July 30, 2004.
103 For information on political prisoners in Azerbaijan, see http://mitglied.lycos.de/politzek/reports.htm.
104 This group was led by generals Vahid Musayev and Rafik Agayev. See Agentura.ru, op. cit.

105 There were reported multiple attempts on the lives of Heydar Aliyev and his son Ilham. See Agentura, ibid. On popular perceptions of repression in Azerbaijan, see also Daniel Heradstveit, "Local Elites Meet Foreign Corporations: The Examples of Iran and Azerbaijan," *Global Society*, Vol. 15, No. 1, 2001; on the "police state" in Azerbaijan, see also Mark Almond, "Aliev in Britain," *The Daily Mail*, July 20, 1998.

106 Personal interviews with Anar Azimov and Tahir Taghi-zade, February 23, 2004.

107 See, for example, Jacob Abadi, "Israel and Turkey: From Covert to Overt Relations," *The Journal of Conflict Studies*, Publication of Center for Conflict Studies, University of New Brunswick, Vol. XV, No. 2, Fall, 1995.

108 Personal interview with Shlomo Ben-Ami, op. cit. Gökhan Bacik reiterates that "from the very beginning secularism has been the essence of the alliance." Gökhan Bacik, "The Limits of an Alliance: Turkish–Israeli Relations Revisited," *Arab Studies Quarterly*, Vol. 23, Issue 3, Summer, 2001.

109 Tahir Taghi-zade, op. cit. Another Azerbaijani diplomat pointing to Azerbaijan's neighbor to the north (Russia) and its southern neighbor (Iran), called the geopolitical position of Azerbaijan "a spicy South Caucasian sandwich."

110 European nations, especially France, Germany and Austria, are less than sanguine about the prospect of Turkish membership in the EU. After reported failures to implement reforms in the area of human rights and the opening of the Turkish sea and airports to Greek Cypriots, a new EU member, the European Union has recently decelerated the process of negotiations about Turkey's full-fledged membership of the Union. Philip Robins commented, "For those located closer by, such as the Western Europeans, Turkey's importance is also palpable, but not necessarily palatable." Philip Robins, *Turkish Foreign Policy*, available at www.biu.ac.il/SOC/besa/publications/mfa3.html.

111 Israel is not a member of NATO, even though it has bilateral military and economic relations with many NATO countries, in particular the United States. Israel and the United States signed a formal strategic alliance during the Reagan administration in the 1980s.

112 Stephen Kinzer, op. cit., p. 133.

113 "Gharbzadeghi" in Farsi is translated in various ways, for example "West-struck" and "Westoxicated." Iranian Islamist ideologues such as Jalal Al-e Ahmad coined the synonym "Occidentosis." See Hamid Algar (Ed.), *Occidentosis: A Plague from the West*, translated by R. Campbell, Berkeley, CA: Mizan Press, 1984, passim.

114 Mahmood Sariolghalam, "Israeli–Turkish Military Cooperation: Iranian Perceptions and Responses," *Journal of Political and Military Sociology*, Vol. 29, Winter, 2001, pp. 293–304.

115 *Veliky Oktyabr and Turtsiya* ("The Great October and Turkey"), Tbilisi: Metsnireba, 1982, p. 42.

116 Yuksel Soylemez, *Issues and Opinions on Foreign Policy*, SAM Papers No. 3/2002, Center for Strategic Research, Ankara, December, 2002, p. 12.

117 See Navaro-Yashin discussion. She explained that "[W]hat was conceptualized in Turkish occidentalism as Europe in early Republican years—with special reference to France, Italy, Germany and England—would be later transformed into a notion of the West with the United States as a central reference, after Turkey joined NATO following the Second World War." Yael Navaro-Yashin, op. cit., p. 210.

118 "In a very few years after 1923," writes Stephen Kinzer, "Mustafa Kemal Ataturk transformed a shattered and bewildered nation into one obsessed with progress. His was one-man revolution, imposed and steered from above. Ataturk knew that Turks were ready to break violently with their past, embrace modernity and turn decisively to the West." Stepen Kinzer, op. cit., p. 10.

119 Yael Navaro-Yashin, op. cit., pp. 65–6.
120 Yuksel Soylemez, op. cit., p. 12.
121 Alexey Rodionov, a former Soviet ambassador in Turkey, notes that in the 1980s the state ideology affected only a small portion of population, while 75 percent of the population lived in the rural areas, in "conditions like centuries ago, according to the traditions and customs of the Ottoman Empire." Alexey Rodionov, *Turtsya: Perekrestok Sudeb*, Moscow: Mezdunarodnye Otnoshenya, 2006, pp. 237–8.
122 See Ferenc Vali, *Bridge across the Bosporu: The Foreign Policy of Turkey*, Baltimore, MD: Johns Hopkins Press, 1971; Nicole Pope and Hugh Pope, *Turkey Unveiled*, 1997, op. cit., especially pp. 186–7.
123 Yuksel Soylemez, op. cit., p. 57.
124 Yael Navaro-Yashin, op. cit., p. 210.
125 Andrew Mango, *Ataturk*, Woodstock, NY: The Overlook Press, 1999, p. 527.
126 Andre Mango, *The Turks Today*, Woodstock, NY: The Overlook Press, 2004, p. 233.
127 Jacob Landau, *Pan-Turkism: From Irredentism to Cooperation*, Bloomington: Indiana University Press, 2004, pp. 202 and passim.
128 Heinz Kramer, *A Changing Turkey*, Washington, DC: Brookings Institution, 2000, p. 93.
129 Bulent Aras, "Turkish Foreign Policy and Jerusalem: Toward a Societal Construction of Foreign Policy," *Arab Studies Quarterly*, Fall 2000, p. 14.
130 Jacob Landau, op. cit., p. 202.
131 Idris Bal quotes President George Herbert Walker Bush in the meeting with Prime Minister Suleiman Demirel in Washington, DC, on February 13, 1992. Bush proposed to the prime minister that Turkey should serve "[a]s the model of a *democracy, a secular state, which could be emulated by Central Asian republics.*" See Introduction to Idris Bal, op. cit.
132 Yuksel Soleymez, op. cit., p. 18.
133 Israel obtained an observer status in BSECR.
134 Donna Rosenthal, *Israelis*, p. 100.
135 Moshe Pearlman, *Ben-Gurion Looks Back*, New York: Simon and Schuster, 1965, p. 47.
136 Shirin Akiner suggested that since its foundation Israel was seen as an unofficial member of the Western alliance. She used the term "invisible" ally of the West. Personal interview with Shirin Akiner, September 12, 2006.
137 In fact, Turkey recognized Israel just a few days before the Turkish foreign minister met with American President Truman. See Bruce Kuniholm and Ian Lesser, "Turkish–Israeli Relations during the Cold War," Lecture at the Conference The History of Turkish–American Relations, Bogazici University, Harran University and Public Affairs, June 4–10, 2006; Jacob Abadi, "Israel and Turkey: From Covert to Overt Relations," Fall 1995, op. cit.
138 S. Sandler, "Ben-Gurion's Attitude towards the Soviet Union," *Jewish Journal of Sociology*, Vol. 21, No. 2, 1979, pp. 145–60.
139 Ben-Gurion reiterated that a "pre-equipped and enlarged Israeli army would guarantee Israeli unity in support of [the] West." In response, the American ambassador pointed out: "The prime minister could not have been more explicit in [his] willingness [to] commit Israel unreservedly to [the] West." See M. Gazit, "Ben-Gurion's Efforts to Create Military Ties with the United States," *Gesher*, 32, 1986/7, pp. 57–63.
140 Israel voted for the "Uniting for Peace" resolution, passed to stop North Korean aggression on June 27, 1950. Lester Brune, *Korean War, 1950–1953*, Westport, CT: Greenwood Publishing Group, 1996, pp. 87–8.

141 Uri Bialer, *Between East and West: Israel's Foreign Policy Orientations, 1948–1956*, Cambridge: Cambridge University Press, 1990, p. 224.
142 Shlomo Avineri, *The Making of Modern Zionism: The Intellectual Origins of the Jewish State*, New York: Basic Books, 1981, p. 13.
143 Michael Barnett, "Israel in Comparative Perspective: Challenging the Conventional Wisdom" in Michael Barnett (Ed.), *The Politics of Uniqueness: The Status of the Israeli Case*, Albany: State University of New York, 1996, p. 5; see also Samuel Koenig, "East Meets West in Israel," *Phylon*, Vol. 17, No. 2, 2nd Qtr., 1956, pp. 167–71.
144 Yosi Beilin, *A Concise Political History of Israel*, New York: St. Martin's Press, 1992, p. 1. See also Samuel Koenig, "Israeli Culture and Society," *The American Journal of Sociology*, Vol. 58, No. 2, September, 1952, pp. 160–6.
145 "The West Europeans contribute to the US efforts to help finance the implementation of Turkish aims in Central Asia. According to a senior Israeli officials, Israel has been helping Turkey promote those aims in its own ways." Yosi Melman, *Haaretz*, March 12, 1993.
146 Ibid.
147 Westernism penetrated Azerbaijani society as a result of Russian influence. Azerbaijanis were exposed to Russian colonialism longer than other Muslim populations, and the Russian imperial state had trained and acculturated the Azerbaijani bureaucracy since the 1820s. See Introduction to Dmitry Furman, op. cit.; see also Tadeusz Swietochowski, "Russian Rule, Modernizing Elites and Formation of National State Identity," in Dmitry Furman, op. cit.
148 Personal interview with Yoav Karny, July 20, 2006; personal interview with Nariman Gasimoglu, August 6, 2004.
149 Personal interview with Eldar Namazov, July 29, 2004.
150 See Jacob Landau, op. cit., 2004.
151 Aryeh Levin, *Envoy to Moscow: Memoirs of an Israeli Ambassador, 1988–1992*, London: Frank Cass, 1996, p. 363. Narim Gasimoglu stated in an interview that in Iranian media and pro-Iranian newspapers in Azerbaijan, both he and Abulfaz Elchibey were branded "Zionists." Interview with Nariman Gasimoglu, August 6, 2004.
152 Yoav Karny interview, op. cit.
153 Nuh Gomultas, "Bakü'de yarım kalan hesap," *Sonsaniye*, October 17, 2003, available at www.sonsaniye.net/yazioku.aspx?id=373.
154 President Heydar Aliyev, "Aliyev's Address on the Occasion of the 24th Anniversary of the Islamic Revolution in Iran," Iranian embassy, Baku, February 12, 2003.
155 Personal interviews with Eldar Namazov and Tahir Taghi-zade. There are detractors from this view in the political elite of Azerbaijan. Vafa Guluzade indicates that there is a rapid process of Islamization in Azerbaijan. He predicted that in 10–15 years there would be an Islamic regime in Azerbaijan. Personal interview with Ambassador Vafa Guluzade, August 5, 2004. Ambassador Nasib Nasibli, Azerbaijani ambassador to Iran under President Elchibey, predicted that because of economic deprivation and political repression there would be a Khomeini-style revolution in Azerbaijan. Personal interview with Nasib Nasibli, August 6, 2004.
156 Eldar Namazov, ibid.
157 Personal interview with Aydan Kodaloglu, May 26, 2004.
158 Personal interview with Tahir Taghi-zade, February 23, 2004.
159 Personal interview with Araz Azimov, August 3, 2004.
160 It is more analogous to the French Republican concept of *laïcité*, or laicism.
161 The most serious occurred in the southeast of the country in 1925. It was triggered by Ataturk's abolition of the caliphate, religious schools and Islamic *sharia* law courts

in 1924, which was the precursor to the redefinition of Turkey as a secular state in 1928. The revolt was led by and subsequently named after Sheikh Said, a Kurdish tribal chieftain, and combined elements of Islamism and incipient Kurdish nationalism. The rebellion was eventually crushed, and Sheikh Said and several hundred of his supportes were tried and executed by special itinerant courts known as the "independence tribunals."

162 Gareth Jenkins, *Symbols and Shadow-Play: Military–JDP Relations*, 2004.

163 G.L. Lewis, "Ataturk's Language Reform and Modernization," in Jacob Landau (Ed.), *Ataturk and the Modernization of Turkey*, Boulder, CO: Westview, 1984, pp. 195–213. According to G.L. Lewis, the language reform played a positive role in the rise of literacy in Turkey from 9 percent in 1924 to 60 percent in 1975. Ibid., p. 195.

164 Asher Cohen and Bernard Susser, *Israel and the Politics of Jewish Identity*, Baltimore: Johns Hopkins University Press, 2000, p. xi; see also Nathan Rotenstreich, "Secularism and Religion in Israel," in *Israel: Its Politics and Philosophy*, op. cit., pp. 135–53.

165 Lijphart explained that consociational arrangements depend on the elite governing cartel's "commitment to the maintenance of the system and to the improvement of its cohesion and stability." See Arend Lijphart, "Consociational Democracy," *World Politics* 21 (2), 1969, p. 216; see also Nathan Rothenstreich, "Secularism and Religion in Israel," op. cit.

166 Arend Lijphart, ibid., p. 212.

167 Only Jews who espouse Orthodox Judaism are considered "religious" in Israel. See Donna Rosenthal, op. cit., p. 222.

168 Baruch Kimmerling, op. cit., p. 174.

169 Yisrael Yeshayahu, "The Status of Religion in the State of Israel and among the Jews of Israel," in *Israel: Its Politcs and Philosophy*, op. cit., p. 174.

170 Personal interviews with Shlomo Ben-Ami, Alon Liel and Efraim Inbar in April 12, 2005; Eynat Shlein-Michael, February, 2004.

171 Interview with Heydar Aliyev, *The Washington Times*, February 26, 2002. Available at: www.internationalspecialreports/ciscentralasia/01/azerbaijan/despiteaidban.html.

172 Personal interview with Anar Azimov, op. cit.

173 "Iran Protest to Baku over Oil Activities in the Aborz Area," *Iranian Press Service*, July 23, 2001.

174 Ibid.

175 Heydar Aliyev's Address in the Iranian embassy, op. cit.

176 Israel also has a *Misrad Datot* ("Ministry of Religions") that performs a similar function.

177 Obviously the process of Westernization of Turkish society has roots in the Ottoman *Tanzimat* period. As Robert Jackson observes, "The Ottoman Empire . . . gained admission as sovereign states to Western-dominated international society in the nineteenth century. Recognition was required to be reciprocal: . . . the Turks were obliged to adopt as a condition of membership, what then were still European norms and practices concerning international law, diplomacy, commerce and so forth." Robert Jackson, "The Weight of Ideas in Decolonization," in Judith Goldstein and Robert Keohane (Eds.), *Ideas and Foreign Policy*, Ithaca: Cornell University Press, 1993, p. 116.

178 United States policymakers in the early 1990s, however, perceived Kemalism more broadly as a successful path to nation building and modernization for Muslim countries. See Idris Bal, *The Rise and Fall of the Turkish Model*, Aldershot, UK: Ashgate, 2001.

179 Kemal's predecessors, who formed the Ittihad ve Taraki ("Unity and Progess") Party, based belonging to the Turkish nation on adherence to the ideal of Turan, i.e. the "Great Turkish Empire."

180 Alon Liel, *Demo-Islam: Mishtar Hadash b'Turkiya* ("Demo-Islam: The New Regime in Turkey") (Hebrew), Tel Aviv: Am Oved, 2003, pp. 10–24.

181 *Kadro* (magazine), January, 1932 (1st ed.), and November, 1932 (11th ed.), pp. 17–18.

182 Ismail Besikci as quoted in Yucel Yerilgoz, "The Practice of a Century—Kemalism," in Tore Bjorgo and Rob Witte (Eds.), *Racist Violence in Europe*, New York: St. Martins's Press, 1990, p. 326.

183 The Milliyetçi Hareket Partisi ("Nationalist Movement Party"), also known as Milli Hareket Partisi, was formed by Arpaslan Turkesh in 1969. Jacob Landau, "The Nationalist Action Party in Turkey," *Journal of Contemporary History*, Vol. 17, No. 4, October, 1982, pp. 587–606.

184 The electoral bloc of the Islamist Refah ("Welfare") Party and MHP won 17 percent of votes in the parliamentary elections in October 1991; MHP won 8 percent in the March 1994 elections.

185 Philip Robins, *Suits and Uniforms*, op. cit., pp. 277–8.

186 *Declaration of Establishment of the State of Israel*. Available at the Israel Ministry of Foreign Affairs website: www.mfa.gov.il/mfa/go.asp?MFAH00hb0.

187 Arab non-citizens suffer from discrimination in Israel. At the same time, the civil rights of Arab Israeli citizens are protected by law. Israel is the only state where Jews constitute the majority, whereas Arabs have 20 nation-states with Arab majorities. Still some left-wing advocates and pan-Arabist critics claim that Israel is a xenophobic, even racist state.

188 Baruch Kimmerling, op. cit., p. 173.

189 Sammy Smooha, "The Model of Ethnic Democracy: Israel as a Jewish and Democratic State," *Nations and Nationalism*, Vol. 8, No. 4, October, 2002, pp. 475–503.

190 In the Turkish case, these people are known as Diş ("external") Turks.

191 Compare to the status of "ethnic" Germans in the Federal Republic of Germany.

192 Shlomo Avineri, *The Making of Modern Zionism: The Intellectual Origins of the Jewish State*, New York: Basic Books, 1981, p. 13.

193 Quoted in Howard Sachar, *A History of Israel: From the Rise of Zionism to Our Time*, New York: Knopf, 1998, p. 82.

194 Igrar Aliyev, *Istorya Azerbaijan: Ot Drevneyshih Vremen do Nachala XX veka*, Baku: Elm, 1995, pp. 304–5.

195 See details in Jacob Landau, op. cit., 2004, pp. 205–15.

196 Ibid., p. 197.

197 Kaveh Farrokh, *Pan-Turanism Takes Aim at Azerbaijan*, unpublished paper, p. 14.

198 See a detailed account of ethno-religious cleavages in Iran in "Religious, Ethnic Discrimination Threaten Iranian Unity," 2002 at www.globalsecurity.org/wmd/library/news/iran/2002/32-260802.htm.

199 See also Svetlana Lurye, "Shiitskiy Faktor," *Speznaz Rossii*, No. 6 (81), June, 2003.

200 See Abulfaz Elchibey, "The Current Socio-Political Situation and the Tasks of the Azerbaijani Popular Front Party," Address to the II (V) Congress (Kurultai) of the Azerbaijan Popular Front Party (APFP), January 30–1, 1998, available at www.geocities.com/Vienna/7124/elchibey.html. See also Kaveh Farrokh, op. cit., p. 22.

201 Since August 1, 2001, the official alphabet of Azerbaijan is Latin, although the parliament approved the Latin alphabet back in 1993.

202 Personal interviews with Azerbaijani journalists and students, 2004–5.

203 Heydar Aliyev's Address to the Buyuk Milli Meclis, the Turkish parliament, Ankara, February 9, 1994.
204 Ibid.
205 Ibid.
206 Ibid.
207 Idris Bal, *The Rise and Fall of the Turkish Model*, Aldershot, UK: Ashgate, 2001, p. 56.
208 See Philip Robins, *Turkish–Israeli Relations*, op. cit., p. 8.
209 Richard Allen Greene, "Greater Ties for Israel, Azerbaijan?" *Cleveland Jewish News*, April 30, 2002, www.azembassy.com/archive/2002/media/cjn29apr02.htm.
210 Philip Robins, *Suits and Uniforms*, op. cit., pp. 32–8; see also pp. 197–8.
211 See the discussion about the role of Turkey in the post-Cold War European security architecture in Colin McInnes (Ed.), *Security and Strategy in the New Europe*, London: Routledge, 1992, pp. 42–9.
212 Personal interviews with Aydan Kodaloglu and General Çevik Bir, May, 2004.
213 Philip Robins, 'Turkish Foreign Policy," Lecture, Begin-Sadat Center for Strategic Studies, Ramat Gan, August 1999, available at www.biu.ac.il/soc/besa/publications/mfa3.html.
214 For a notable discussion of this perception, see A. Isyaev, "Orientiry Sovremennoy Gosudartsvennoy Ideologii I Politiki (PostKemalizm)," in N. Kirreev (Ed.), *Turtsya mezhdu Evropoy i Aziey*, Mosva: Institut Vostokovedenya RAN, 2001, pp. 254–5.
215 Philip Robins, *Turkish–Israeli Relations*, op. cit., p. 8. See also the strategic vision of Israeli foreign policy presented by former Foreign Minister Shimon Peres, *The New Middle East*, Shaftesbury, Dorset: Element, 1993, passim.
216 Richard Allen Greene, "Greater Ties for Israel, Azerbaijan?" *Cleveland Jewish News*, April 30, 2002, www.azembassy.com/archive/2002/media/cjn29apr02.htm.
217 Anar Veliev, "Treugolnik Izrail–Turtsya–Azerbaijan: Realnost y Perespektivy," in *Zerkalo*, September 3, 2004.
218 Dmitry Furman, Introduction to *Azerbaijan i Rossia*, op. cit., p. 3.
219 Personal interview with Vafa Guluzade, August 5, 2004.
220 Vafa Guluzade, "V Bitve za Kavkaz SSHA Seryozno Proygryvayet 'Tantsuya pod Dudku Moskvy," *Regnum*, July 27, 2004. Guluzade highlights the Russian one-sided approach to the Nagorno-Karabagh conflict, which favors Armenia. Specifically, Guluzade refers to the secret Russian arms deliveries to Armenia (estimated value $1 billion) in 1992 and the official military alliance between Russia and Armenia concluded in September 1997.
221 The leader of Egyptian pan-Arabism, Gamal Abdel Nasser, even declared that Turkey was *persona non grata* in the Arab world. Nicole Pope and Hugh Pope, op. cit., p. 223.
222 Turkey is a candidate for EU membership pending the implementation of the Copenhagen Criteria in December 2004. Turkey has had a Customs Union with the EU since 1995. Both Turkey and Israel have associate status with the EU. In 1975, Israel reached a Free Trade Area Agreement with the European Community (today known as the EU). In 1996 Israel concluded a Free Trade Area Agreement with Turkey, which had a Custom Union Agreement with the EU since the end of 1995. Azerbaijan was admitted to membership of the Council of Europe on January 25, 2001 (along with Armenia and Georgia). Azerbaijan has had representation in the European parliament since 1996.
223 The Aliyev administration made an official statement that "Azerbaijan will not participate in any attempt to achieve greater integration within the CIS until a 'just solution' of the Karabakh conflict is reached." *Interfax*, reported on October 27, 1997. *Radio Free Europe/Radio Liberty Newsline*, Vol. 1, No. 148, October 29, 1997.

3 The military–security stranglehold

1 Barak Salmoni, "Review of 'Suits and Uniforms: Turkish Foreign Policy Since the Cold War,' by Philip Robins," *Strategic Insights*, Vol. III, Issue 4, April, 2004.
2 Philip Robins, *Suits and Uniforms*, op. cit., p. 77.
3 Gareth Jenkins, "Context and Circumstance: The Turkish Military and Politics," *Adelphi Papers*, 337, International Institute for Strategic Studies, London, 2001.
4 Ofra Bengio, op. cit., p. 83.
5 Patrick Dunleavy and Brendan O'Leary, *Theories of the State: The Politics of Liberal Democracy*, London: Macmillan Education, 1987, p. 19.
6 In fact, a former senior Israeli UN correspondent maintains that "there is an inter-elite clash over the nation's geopolitical orientation, involving of members of foreign policy establishment, that centers on Israeli relations with Turkey." Leon Hadar, "Orienting Jerusalem toward Ankara or Cairo? Israel's New Geostrategic Debate," *Mediterranean Quarterly*, Summer, 2001, p. 12.
7 Ofra Bengio, *Turkish–Israeli Relationship: Changing Ties of Middle East Outsiders*, New York: Palgrave Macmillan, 2004, p. 90. See also Gökhan Bacik, "The Limits of Alliance: The Turkish Israeli Relations Revisited," *Arab Studies Quarterly*, Vol. 23, No. 3, Summer, 2001.
8 Ofra Bengio, op. cit.
9 Leon Hadar, op. cit., p. 24.
10 The dismissal from power of the Islamist Prime Minister Erbakan was consummated by means of the public campaign for his resignation by trade unions, universities and Kemalist intellectuals in 1997. This campaign was orchestrated by the military after the Sincan incident and became known the first post-modernist coup. See also Marvine Howe, *Turkey Today: A Nation Divided over Islam's Revival*, Boulder, CO: Westview, 2000, p. 134.
11 Cf. George Haddad, *Revolutions and the Military Rule in the Middle East*, New York: Robert Speller & Sons, 1965, p. 13.
12 Gareth Jenkins, "Context and Circumstance: The Turkish Military and Politics," *Adelphi Papers*, 337, International Institute for Strategic Studies, London, 2001, p. 4.
13 Philip Robins, *Suits and Uniforms*, op. cit., p. 76.
14 For the text of the Constitution of the Turkish Republic, see http://en.wikipedia.org/wiki/Constitution_of_Turkey. For a detailed account of the Turkish legislative reforms, see Barak Salmoni, "Turkey's Summer 2003 Legislative Reforms: EU Avalanche, Civil–Military Revolution, or Islamist Assertion?" *Strategic Insights*, Vol. II, Issue 9, September, 2003.
15 Gareth Jenkins, op. cit., p. 25.
16 Philip Robins, *Suits and Uniforms*, op. cit., p. 76.
17 Gareth Jenkins, op. cit., p. 26.
18 Ibid., p. 25.
19 Ibid., p. 30.
20 "The Impact of Globalization on the Turkish Economy," May, 2002, Report of the Central Bank of the Republic of Turkey, p. 21. In fact, during the period 1990–9, the tourism sector comprised 21.4 percent of Turkish revenues from export. Ibid., p. 23.
21 See Hakan Yavuz, op. cit., p. 28; also personal interview with Aydan Kodaloglu, May 26, 2004.
22 Ofra Bengio, op. cit., p. 72.
23 Yuksel Soylemez, *Issues and Opinions on Foreign Policy*, Ankara: Center for Strategic Research, December, 2002, p. 343.

24 In their account of the Turkish military participation in the first Gulf war (1991), Nicole and Hugh Pope describe the state of "preparedness" of Turkish ground forces: "The age of trench warfare certainly came to mind during the first press view of exercises on the Turkish army front lines before the Gulf war. With bayonets fixed and blood-curdling yells of 'Allah, Allah, Allah,' Turkish paratroopers charged at each others' lines. The soldiers were disciplined and tough, but although they loosed off a few anti-armour rockets, their machinery of war seemed dated." Nicole Pope and Hugh Pope, op. cit., p. 227.

25 The concept of the Revolution in Military Affairs (RMA) was developed in the aftermath of the 1991 Gulf war. RMA was essentially the paradigmatic shift in the American military doctrine in response to the "information revolution" that brought new capabilities in computation, satellite communication and computer imaging. See Isaac Ben-Israel, "The Revolution in Military Affairs and the Operation in Iraq," in Shai Feldman (Ed.), *After the War in Iraq: Defining the New Strategic Balance*, Brighton: Sussex Academic Press, 2003, p. 62.

26 The key to understanding RMA was use of (conventional) precision stand-off fire to eliminate the enemy's main forces. Ibid., p. 55.

27 Sergey Minasyan, "Israel–Turkey Strategic Co-operation in the Context of Regional Security Problems," *21 Century*, Vol. 2, No. 4, 2004, p. 96.

28 Alain Gresh, "Turkish–Israeli–Syrian Relations and Their Impact on the Middle East," *Middle East Journal*, Vol. 52, Spring, 1998, p. 191.

29 Gareth Jenkins, op. cit., p. 29.

30 See Efraim Inbar, *The Israeli–Turkish Strategic Partnership*, Ramat Gan: BESA, 2002, pp. 167–8.

31 Personal interview with Çevik Bir, May 26, 2004.

32 As Lenore Martin and Dimitris Keridis conclude, "They are reluctant to give up the state's mechanisms of social control and the army's prerogatives in favor of an elusive and distant European future." Dimitris Keridis, "Conclusions," in Lenore Martin and Dimitris Keridis (Eds.), *The Future of Turkish Foreign Policy*, Cambridge, MA: MIT Press, 2004, p. 336. On the conception of the "military-guided democracy" in Turkey, see also Dimitris Keridis, "Political Culture and Foreign Policy: Greek–Turkish Relations in the Era of European Integration and Globalization," NATO Fellowship Final Report, Cambridge, June, 1999, p. 51.

33 See Ofra Bengio, op. cit., pp. 80–2.

34 The Defense Industry Executive Committee (DIEC), which is chaired by the prime minister and includes also the defense minister, the civilian Undersecretariat for Defense Industries under-secretary and the chief of staff. In practice, the DIEC is dominated by the military. Gareth Jenkins, op. cit. See details of the Israeli institutional structure later in Chapter 3.

35 Ofra Bengio, op. cit., p. 86; see also Hakan Yavuz, "Turkish–Israeli Relations through the Lens of the Turkish Identity Debate," *Journal of Palestine Studies*, Vol. XXVII, No. 1, Autumn, 1997, p. 27.

36 See also Philip Robins, *Turkish–Israeli Relations*, op. cit., pp. 12–16.

37 Alain Gresh, "Turkish–Israeli–Syrian Relations and their Impact on the Middle East," *Middle East Journal*, Vol. 52, Summer, 1998, p. 191.

38 See Hakan Yavuz, op. cit., p. 28.

39 See M. Hickok, "Hegemon Rising: The Gap between Turkish Strategy and Military Modernization," *Parameters*, US Army College Quarterly, Summer 2000, pp. 106–11.

40 Hakan Yavuz, op. cit., p. 31.

41 As a Lieutenant General, Çevik Bir was the commander of the US-sponsored operation in Somali (UNITAF) under the aegis of the United Nations in December of 1992.

42 Philip Robins, *Suits and Uniforms*, op. cit., p. 46.

43 Ofra Bengio, op. cit., p. 104.

44 Michel Chossudovsky, "Triple Alliance: The US, Turkey and Israel and the War on Lebanon," *Global Research*, August 6, 2006, available at www.globalresearch.ca/index.php?context=viewArticle&code=CHO20060806&articleId=2906.

45 See Sergey Minosyan, "Turkish–Israeli Military and Political Cooperation and Regional Security Issues," *Iran and Caucasus*, Vol. VII, Leiden-Boston: Brill, 2004, p. 96.

46 For a chronology of Turkish–Israeli strategic cooperation, see "Timeline of Turkish–Israeli Relations, 1949–2006," available at www.washingtoninstitute.org/documents/44edf1a5d337f.pdf.

47 The two largest contracts included a joint upgrade with Israel Air Industries of 54 F-4 Phantoms, worth $650 million, and a joint production with Israel of Popeye II air-to-ground missiles, worth $100 million, in 1997. Keith Parkins, "Stop Arms Sales to Turkey," *Campaign against Arms Trade*, January, 1999, rev. 6, available at http://home.clara.net/heureka/sunrise/tr-arms2.htm.

48 *Milliyet*, July 14, 2006.

49 See I. Ivanova, "Turetsko–Izrailskiye Otnoshenya I Problemy Regionalnoy Bezopasnosti," in M. Arunova (Ed.), *Blizhny Vostok: Problemy Natzionalnoy Bezopasnosti*, Moscow: IIIBV, 2000.

50 See details in Sergey Minosyan, op. cit.

51 Personal interview with a Turkish military attaché, Washington, DC, May, 2006.

52 Daniel Pipes, "A New Axis: The Emerging Turkish–Israeli Entente," *The National Interest*, Winter, 1997/98, p. 31.

53 Bulent Aras, "Turkish Foreign Policy and Jerusalem: Toward a Societal Construction of Foreign Policy," *Arab Studies Quarterly*, Fall, 2000, p. 3.

54 Marvine Howe, op. cit., p. xii.

55 Philip Robins, *Suits and Uniforms*, op. cit., p. 160.

56 Gregory Burris, "Turkey–Israel: Speed Bumps," *Middle East Quarterly*, Fall, 2003, pp. 2–3, available at www.meforum.org/article/569.

57 In the opposition, Erbakan developed links with the Muslim Brotherhood in Egypt and Syria and the Palestinian radical Hamas (the Islamic Resistance Movement). In 1996, under the auspices of the Islamic Communities Association, Erdogan, then mayor of Istanbul, invited as guests of honour Syrian and Egyptian leaders of the Muslim Brotherhood and the leadership of Hamas. See Philip Robins, *Suits and Uniforms*, op. cit., p. 151.

58 See Marvine Howe, op. cit., p. 136.

59 During his visit to Libya, Prime Minister Erbakan was lectured about the rights of the Kurdish people in Turkey. In fact, Colonel Qadhafi called for the creation of an independent Kurdish homeland. See Philip Robins, *Suits and Uniforms*, op. cit., p. 158.

60 "Turkey: Israel Sets Terrorism Condition to Syria. Ciller Assures Israel that Good Relations Will Continue and Flourish," *Turkish Daily News*, January 16, 1996.

61 Turkish officials noted that these talks produced "a convergence of views on almost all the topics discussed from security and the need for more democracy in the Middle East for the sake of ultimate stability in the region." Semih D. Idiz, "Full Assurance from Israel on All Points of Concern Prime Minister Shimon Peres Says Syria Will Not Be Let Off the Hook as Long as It Supports Terrorism," *Turkish Daily News*, January 15, 1996.

62 Quoted in Ozden Oktav, "Changing Security Perceptions in Turkish–Iranian Relations," *Perceptions*, Vol. IX, No. 2, Summer, 2004, p. 104. This is how the Sincan incident is depicted by a Turkish eyewitness: "The Iranian ambassador to Turkey,

Mohammad-Reza Baqeri, addressed a group of people in a district of Ankara in February [sic] 1997, including a mayor and politicians from the Turkish Welfare Party, amidst chants God is Great ('Allah Akbar'), marking the anniversary of Jerusalem Day. Speaking under a poster of Palestinian Islamic Jihad and Hizbullah leaders, Baqeri conveyed the message that those who sign agreements with the United States and Israel will, sooner or later, be penalized." Yavuz Hakan, "Turkish–Israeli Relations through the Lens of the Turkish Identity Debate," *Journal of Palestine Studies*, Vol. 27, No. 1, 1997.

63 Marvine Howe, op. cit., pp. 138–9.
64 As Marvine Howe concludes: "In fact, Erbakan and Foreign Minister Ciller, themselves at odds over foreign policy, appeared to step aside and let the military handle key issues. Army chief of staff, General Ismail Hakki Karadayi, personally took over the warming relations with Israel and was received there like a head of state by the president and prime minister as well as top military personnel." Marvine Howe, op. cit., p. 136.
65 "Gen. Karadayi Meets with Israeli Counterpart and Defense Minister," *Milliyet-Cumhuriyet*, February 7.
66 The summary of the JINSA Briefing concludes, "Bir was outspoken in the Turkish military's commitment to its blossoming relationship with Israel and expressed hope that delays in receiving excess American military equipment pledged to Turkey by the Clinton administration would be resolved." See "Pro-American Turkish Leaders Work for Closer Ties with Washington," *JINSA Briefings*, February–March, 1997, available at www.jinsa.org. For details about JINSA's role in the entente, see later in Chapter 3.
67 For a detailed account of the February 28 Process, see Niyazi Günay, "Implementing the 'February 28' Recommendations: A Scorecard," *Research Note*, Washington, DC: The Washington Institute for Near East Policy, May 10, 2001.
68 Hakan Yavuz, op. cit., p. 30.
69 See "The Bulk of NSC Recommendations to the Government Today Concern the Preservation and Protection of Turkey's Secular Regime," *Turkish Daily News*, March 3, 1997.
70 Ibid.
71 Ibid.
72 Ibid.
73 Gil Sedan, "Tensions Thaw as Israel, Turkey Build New Relations," *Jewish Telegraphic Agency*, April 18, 1997.
74 Hakan Yavuz, op. cit., p. 30.
75 Ibid.
76 Ibid., p. 31.
77 Philip Robins, *Suit and Uniforms*, op. cit., p. 76.
78 Personal interview with Aydan Kodaloglu and Yola Habif, February, 2004. See also "Erdogan's Ascent Has Been Closely Watched in Turkey and Abroad," *Time Magazine*, November 4, 2002, available at www.time.com/time/europe/magazine/2002/1104/turkey/story_2.html.
79 Barak Salmoni, "Turkey's Summer 2003 Legislative Reforms: EU Avalanche, Civil–Military Revolution, or Islamist Assertion?" *Strategic Insights*, Vol. II, Issue 9, September, 2003, available at www.ccc.nps.navy.mil/si/sept03/europe.asp.
80 "Civil Secretary, Civil MGK," *Zaman*, November 30, 2004.
81 Ibid.
82 Secretary-General Yigit Alpogan, Briefing, The Washington Institute for Near East Policy, Washington, DC, January 24, 2006.
83 "Israel, Turkey Plan Joint Weapons Deals for Azerbaijan," *World Tribune*, February 2, 2004.

84 Stuart Reiser, *The Israeli Arms Industry: Foreign Policy, Arms Transfers and Military Doctrine of a Small State*, New York: Holmes & Meir, 1989, p. ix.
85 Ibid.
86 Ibid., p. x.
87 Ibid.
88 Ibid., p. 67.
89 See Chapter 5 of this volume.
90 See details of Israeli arms exports to the developing world and West European countries in Stuart Reiser, op. cit., pp. 67–72, especially p. 72.
91 Ibid.
92 France refused to support Israel in the 1967 crisis and banned deliveries of jets to Israel. For details, see Howard Sachar, *A History of Israel: From the Rise of Zionism to Our Time*, New York: Knopf, 1996, pp. 625–62.
93 Stuart Reiser, op. cit., p. 167.
94 "Turkish Air Force Modernized," *Hurriyet*, January 28, 2000.
95 Ibid., p. 170.
96 See details in Stuart Reiser, pp. 186–95.
97 See Philip Robins, *Suits and Uniforms*, op. cit., pp. 200–1.
98 Stuart Reiser, op. cit., p. 204.
99 Ibid.
100 Yehuda Ben Meir, *Civil–Military Relations in Israel*, New York: Columbia University Press, 1993, p. 3. See also John Sweetman (Ed.), *Sword and Mace*, London: Brassey, 1986, pp. ix, xv.
101 Ibid., p. 34.
102 Ibid., p. 35.
103 Until the 1991 Basic Law, Army was enacted, the prime minister was not even mentioned in any legislation dealing with defense matters. Ibid., p. 38.
104 Quoted in Yoram Peri, *Battles and Ballots: Israeli Military in Politics*, Cambridge: Cambridge University Press, 1983, pp. 188–9.
105 Ibid., p. 88.
106 Ibid., pp. 88–9. There was a series of indictments on graft and bribery charges in the highest echelons of the Israeli Air Force in the early 1990s. See: "Israel Investigates Air Force Graft Assertions," *New York Times*, December 20, 1990, p. 3; Richard Stevenson, "US Accuses G.E. of Fraud in Israeli Deal," *New York Times*, August 15, 1991, p. 1; Joel Brinkley, "Israeli General Pleads Guilty in Bribery Case," *New York Times*, March 19, 1991, p. 7; Richard Stevenson, "Pentagon Disciplines G.E. for Role in Bribe Scandal," *New York Times*, June 3, 1992, p. 1.
107 Ben Meir, op. cit.
108 During his tenure as director general of the Israeli Ministry of Defense, David Ivri criticized this well-established practice. He concluded that the planning branch does not represent "an overall comprehensive national view and has neither the requisite level of accessibility nor of responsibility." Ibid., p. 144.
109 David Ivri was in command in the early stages of operation, Peace of the Galilee (the War in Lebanon of 1982–3), when the biggest dogfight in the jet-plane era took place, involving more than 150 planes and concluding with 47 downed Syrian jets without even one Israeli loss. He was also one of the people in charge of the Israeli air strike against the Iraqi Osiraq nuclear reactor in June 1981.
110 Jonathan Nitzan, *The Global Political Economy of Israel*, London: Pluto Press, 2002, pp. 281–3.
111 Ben Meir, op. cit., p. 191.
112 Ibid.

113 See http://en.wikipedia.org/wiki/David_Ivry [sic].
114 Ofra Bengio, op. cit., p. 96.
115 Ibid., p. 97.
116 See below for details on the *Clean Break*.
117 See Ofra Bengio, op. cit., p. 97.
118 Under international pressure, the Russians changed their plans and deployed them in Crete.
119 N. Kireev, "Turtsiya I Izrail—strategicheskie souyzniki na Bliznem Vistoke (hronika venno-politicheskogo sotrudnicestva v 1994–7," in V. Isayev and A. Filonik (Eds.), *Bllizny Vostok I Sovremennost*, Vol. 5, 1998.
120 V. Kozyulin, "BTC: Rossisko–Izrailskoy Protivostotanie," *Yaderny Kontrol*, Vol. 9, No. 1, Spring, 2003, pp. 33–4.
121 "The Arrow Missile Interceptor Deployed in Israeli–Turkish–US Air Exercise," *Middle East NewsLine*, July 22, 2001.
122 *Jane's Defense Weekly*, April 10, 2002, p. 4.
123 Personal interviews with Efraim Inbar; see also Ofra Bengio, op. cit., p. 92.
124 *The Observer, A Quarterly Review of Cooperation: US, Turkey and Israel*, JINSA/ ATAA, Washington, DC, No. 4, October, 2003, pp. 3–4.
125 Alexander Murinson, "Foreign Relations between Israel and the Islamic Newly Independent States," *The Cyber-Caravan*, Publication of the Central Asia-Caucasus Institute School of Advanced International Studies, Johns Hopkins University, Vol. 1, August, 1999, Part 1. See www.eurasianet.org/resource/regional/cyber.html.
126 Tolga Akiner, "Erdoganin ziareti ilerdi,"*Radikal*, May 1, 2005.
127 The strategic relationship with the United States developed after the 1999 Istanbul Meeting of the OSCE.
128 For a comprehensive account of Azerbaijani armed forces after the Independence Elkhan Mekhtiev Project, see "Security Policy in Azerbaijan," unpublished report, NATO-EAPC Research Fellowship 1999–2001, p. 33.
129 Ibid.
130 Ibid.
131 Ibid.
132 Ibid.
133 Ibid., p. 25.
134 GUAM is a regional security and cooperation organization of former Soviet republics (Georgia, Ukraine, Azerbaijan and Moldova). It was formed in 1997. Originally the organization included Uzbekistan, which withdrew in 2005.
135 Ibid., p. 44.
136 Ibid.
137 "Turkish and US Military Set Up Working Group for Transcaucasia," *Turkish Daily News*, January 25, 2000.
138 Igor Muradian, *Politika SSHA I Problemy Bezopasnosti Regiona Yuzhnogo Kavakaza*, Yerevan: Antares, 2000, p. 79.
139 Ibid., p. 78.
140 Ibid. For more details, see ibid., pp. 82–6.
141 By one of the first government's acts, a memorial to the Turkish soldiers who fell in the struggle for the first Azerbaijani independence was erected. It is located in the Azerbaijani war memorial complex called Shahitler Caddesi ("Avenue of Martyrs") in Baku.
142 See "Azerbaijan and Turkey Said to Be Planning 'Weapons for Gas' Deal." Available at: *Ekho*, March 14, 2001; *Turan*, March 15, 2001; *Azerbaijan News Service*, January 10, 2001; *Turkish Daily News*, March 13, 2001; *Zerkalo*, April 4, 2001.
143 Ibid.

144 *Newsline Transcaucasia and Central Asia, Radio Free Europe/Radio Liberty,* October 13, 1998.
145 Alexander Murinson, "The Impact of American Foreign Policy after 9.11 on the October 2003 Presidential Elections in Azerbaijan," *Insight Turkey,* April/June, 2004.
146 R. Gabigoglu, "Osnovnye Batalii Sostoytsya v Budushem Godu," *Zerkalo,* January 2, 2003.
147 R. Ahmedov, "RLS 'Daryal' Pereshla na Usilenniy Rejim," *Exo,* February 21, 2003.
148 Elkhan Mekhtiev, op. cit., p. 38.
149 "Turkey to Maintain Military Aid to Azerbaijan," *Turkish Daily News,* September 25, 2002.
150 Igor Muradian, op. cit., p. 96.
151 Ibid., p. 98. For a detailed account, see pp. 98–112.
152 Ibid.
153 Ibid., p. 94.
154 Sergey Minosyan, op. cit., p. 107.
155 Ibid., p. 109.
156 See Chapter 5 of this volume.
157 Meeting with an Azerbaijani foreign ministry official, August 3, 2004.

4 Foreign policy and its discontents in the age of globalization

1 Albert Yee, "The Causal Effects of Ideas on Policies," *International Organizations,* Vol. 50, No. 1, 1996, pp. 95–9; see also Eva Etzioni-Halevy, *The Knowledge Elite and the Failure of Prophecy,* London: George Allen & Unwin, 1985, pp. 26–7.
2 Andreas Antoniades, op. cit., p. 29.
3 Antoniades describes this as the "ability to influence people's and collectivities' self-understanding (identity formation) and therefore their understandings about their wants and interests. This includes the ability to influence the knowledge and ideas comprised within social structures." Andreas Antoniades, op. cit., p. 29. See a further discussion in Albert Yee, op. cit., p. 99.
4 Wolf Blitzer, *Between Washington and Jerusalem,* New York: Oxford University Press, 1985, p. 39.
5 E.H. Carr, *What Is History?* London: Penguin, 1964, p. 40.
6 Andreas Antoniades, op. cit., p. 29.
7 Dov Waxman, "Defending the Nation/Defining the Nation: Foreign Policy and the Politics of National Identity in Israel," Ph.D., Johns Hopkins University, 2002, p. 132.
8 Poliarchy is a well-recognized fact of the American political system that is accepted by the American public. In this regard, the noteworthy reference is a classical work of Robert Dahl, *Who Governs?,* New Haven, CT: Yale University Press, 1963. See also the discussion of "polyarchy" in Patrick Dunleavy and Brendan O'Leary (Eds.), *The Theories of the State,* London: Macmillan Education, 1987, pp. 18–19.
9 See, for further reading, Thomas Ambrosio (Ed.), *Ethnic Identity Groups and US Foreign Policy,* New York: Praeger Publishers, 2002; Mohammed E. Ahrari (Ed.), *Ethnic Groups and US Foreign Policy,* Westport, CT: Greenwood Press, 1987.
10 Paul Y. Watanabe, *Ethnic Groups, Congress, and American Foreign Policy: The Politics of the Turkish Arms Embargo,* Westport, CT: Greenwood Press, 1984, p. 60.
11 "Language not only enables knowledge [of world politics], but is knowledge of world politics." Roger Tooze, "Ideology, Knowledge, and Power in International Relations and International Economy," in T. Lawson, J. Rosenau and A. Vedun (Eds.), *Strange Power: Shaping the Parameters of International Relations and International Economy,* Ashgate: Aldershot, 2000, p. 189.
12 Peter Haas, "Introduction," op. cit., p. 4.

13 Andreas Antoniades, op. cit., p. 32; Peter Haas, "Introduction," op. cit., pp. 13–14; Diane Stone, op. cit., pp. 89–90; Yee, op. cit., p. 86; Anthony Giddens, "Risk, Trust and Reflexivity," in *Reflexive Modernization: Politics, Tradition and Aesthetics in the Modern Social Order*, in U. Beck, Anthony Giddens and S. Lash (Eds.), Cambridge: Polity Press, 1995, pp. 183–5.

14 Andreas Antoniades, op. cit., p. 32.

15 Blitzer, op. cit., p. 39.

16 Andreas Antoniades, op. cit., p. 33.

17 Peter Haas, "Introduction," op. cit., pp. 31–2; Diane Stone, op. cit., pp. 92–9.

18 Robert Cox, "Social Forces, States and World Orders: Beyond International Relations Theory," in Robert. Keohane (Ed.), *Neorealism and Its Critics*, New York: Columbia University Press, 1987, pp. 207–10.

19 Andreas Antoniades, op. cit., p. 33.

20 Efraim Inbar, "The Turkish–Israeli Strategic Partnership," Lecture at the Woodrow Wilson Center, Washington, DC, September 16, 1998.

21 Dietrich Jung and Wolfgang Piccoli, "The Turkish–Israeli Alignment: Paranoia or Pragmatism?" *Security Dialogue*, 31, 2000, pp. 91–104.

22 Thus the Section 907 legislation, which will be discussed later in this chapter, was born.

23 The two leaders met in New York on October 23, 1995. See Jacob Abadi, 2002, op. cit.

24 *Haaretz*, October 24, 1995.

25 Diane Stone, op. cit., p. 91.

26 Paul Sebatier, "Political Science and Public Policy," *PS: Political Science and Politics*, Vol. 24, No. 2, 1991, pp. 144–56.

27 Study Group on "A New Israeli Strategy Toward 2000," *A Clean Break: A New Strategy for Securing the Realm*. Available at: www.israeleconomy.org/strat1.htm.

28 Daniel Pipes is the founder and director of the Middle East Forum, a "think tank" aimed at defining and promoting "American interests in the Middle East." The Forum holds that the United States has vital interests in the region; in particular, Pipes believes in strong ties with Israel, Turkey and other democracies as they emerge. Author's view.

29 Daniel Pipes, "A New Axis: The Emerging Turkish–Israeli Entente," *The National Interest*, Winter, 1997.

30 Jason Vest, "Turkey, Israel and the US," *The Nation*, August 23, 2002.

31 See Richard Perle, "A Turkish Story," unpublished, The First Annual Robert Strausz-Hupé Lecture, reproduced by *FPRI Wire*, Vol. 7, No. 11, September, 1999. According to Jason Vest, ibid., the *Financial Times* characterized this bilateral US–Turkish agreement as "something of a personal triumph" for Richard Perle.

32 Daniel Pipes, op. cit.

33 In 1989, the IAI was successful in counteracting the Greek Caucus in the US Congress, which tried to pass legislation to keep Turkey's US military aid at a level lower than that of neighboring Greece. The same year, the lobbying firm attained success in defeating the Senate resolution marking the 75th anniversary of the Armenian "Genocide." Jason Vest, op. cit.

34 According to Armenian journalist David B. Boyajian, "Deputy Defense Secretary Paul Wolfowitz, President Bush's chief foreign policy strategist, is fervently pro-Turkish." David B. Boyajian, "The Turkish–Israeli Alliance and Genocide Denial." Available at: www.hairenik.com/armenianweekly/april_2003/politics001.html.

35 Personal interview with Philip Remler, July 7, 2005. Also personal interview with Alan Makovsky, November 11, 2003.

36 United States Congress. House Resolution 437, *Recognizing the Republic of Turkey for its cooperation in the campaign against global terrorism, for its commitment of*

forces and assistance to Operation Enduring Freedom and subsequent missions in Afghanistan, and for initiating important economic reforms to build a stable and prosperous economy in Turkey, introduced July 9, 2002.

37 David B. Boyajian, op. cit.

38 Bulent Aras, *The New Geopolitics of Eurasia and Turkey's position*, London, Portland, OR: Frank Cass, 2002, p. 59.

39 Faruk Logoğlu, "HIRIJW's Conference on Jewish Women in Turkey," Brandeis University, December 9, 2002. Available at: http://my.brandeis.edu/news/item?news_item_id=101090&show_release_date=1.

40 Frederic Encel, "New Geo-Strategic Structure in the Middle East," *Geostrategics*, May, 2001, No. 4. Available at: www.strategicsinternational.com/4enencel.htm.

41 Diane Stone, op. cit., p. 16.

42 Ibid.

43 Ibid., "Introduction."

44 Ibid., p. 2.

45 Ibid., "Introduction."

46 Wolf Blitzer, op. cit., p. 170.

47 Under the US Internal Revenue Services code, the American tax law, this organization should not pursue lobbying activities. See more on JINSA activities at http://rightweb.irc-online.org/org/jinsa.php.

48 Martin Kramer, *Ivory Towers on Sand: The Failure of Middle East Studies in America*, Washington, DC: The Washington Institute for Near East Policy, 2001.

49 It is noteworthy that Martin Kramer served as a fellow of The Washington Institute for Near East Policy.

50 For background on WINEP and its role in policymaking debates, see Joel Beinin, "Pro-Israel Hawks and the Second Gulf War," *Middle East Report Online*, April 6, 2003. For more information on right-leaning Middle East scholars and commentators, see Robert Blecher, "'Free People Will Set the Course of History': Intellectuals, Democracy and American Empire," *Middle East Report Online*, March, 2003. See also Adam Sabra, "What Is Wrong with What Went Wrong?" *Middle East Report Online*, August, 2003.

51 Diane Stone, op. cit., p. 2. I would discount an allegation made by American journalist Jim Lobe that "the WINEP acted as the think tank for the most powerful pro-Israel lobby in Washington, the American Israel Public Affairs Committee (AIPAC)." See "How Neo-cons Influence the Pentagon . . . ," *Asia Times*, August 8, 2003.

52 It is noteworthy that Bulent Aras in his work identified WINEP as a leading Jewish lobby.

53 Diane Stone, op. cit., p. 275.

54 Bahadir Ozgur, "Amerika'nin Son Tabusu LOBI," *Evrensel*, May 5, 2002. Available at: www.evrensel.net/02/05/05.medya.html.

55 Available at: www.washingtoninstitute.org/senior/ross.htm.

56 Richard Holbrooke, "A Statement before the House International Relations Committee," March 9, 1995.

57 It is remarkable that Strobe Talbott used the Washington Institute as the venue for his address: "US–Turkish Relations in an Age of Interdependence," Address delivered at The Washington Institute for Near East Policy, Washington, DC, October 14, 1998.

58 State Department spokesman Nicholas Burns told journalists shortly after Erbakan took office that "secularism" is "not a condition" for good US–Turkish relations.

59 Alan Makovsky, "How to Deal with Erbakan," *The Middle East Quarterly*, March, 1997, Vol. IV, No. 1, p. 12.

60 Personal interviews with Professor Sabri Sayari and Dr. Andrew Mango, May–October, 2005.
61 See headline in the *Turkish Daily News*: "Makovski [sic], Famous American Expert on Turkey: 'Turkey is Concerned about Israeli–Syrian Talks in Respect of Water, Security, Terrorism and Turkish–Israeli Relations,'" *Anadolu Agency*, December 21, 1999.
62 Alan Makovsky, "The Turkish–Israeli–Syrian Triangle," in *Peace Watch*, No. 249, March 15, 2000. Available at: www.washingtoninstitute.org/watch/Peacewatch/peace watch2000/249.htm.
63 Ali H. Aslan, "America's Fears and Turkey," *Zaman*, December 10, 2003.
64 General Çevik Bir, "Reflections on Turkish–Israeli Relations and Turkish Security," WINEP *PolicyWatch*, No. 422, November 5, 1999.
65 Wolf Blitzer, op. cit., p. 73.
66 Available at: www.jinsa.org.
67 Available at: www.jinsa.org/about/agenda/agenda.html.
68 "Turkey and Israel to Cooperate on Security, "JINSA Newsletter, February 1, 1996 in *Information, Analysis and News*. Available at: www.jinsa.org/articles/articles.html/function/view/categoryid/102/documentid/281/history/3,2360,102,281.
69 Ugur Akinci, *An Editorial, Turkish Daily News Report*, February 17, 1997.
70 Sam Vaknin, "Turkey's Jewish Friend," *United Press International*, May 3, 2003. Available at: www.upi.com/view.cfm?StoryID=20030304-052300-9572r.
71 Gökhan Bacik, "The Limits of Alliance: The Turkish Israeli Relations Revisited," *Arab Studies Quarterly*, Vol. 23, No. 3, Summer, 2001.
72 Bulent Aras, "Turkish Foreign Policy and Jerusalem: Toward a Societal Construction of Foreign Policy," *Arab Studies Quarterly*, Fall, 2000; also Gökhan Bacik, "The Limits of Alliance: The Turkish Israeli Relations Revisited," *Arab Studies Quarterly*, Vol. 23, No. 3, Summer, 2001.
73 See "Ambassador's Meeting with the Representatives from Various Jewish American Organizations," Transcript, April 9, 2002. Available at: www.turkishembassy.org/pressreleases/arsiv/200204.htm. See also "JINSA Hosts Israel–US–Turkey Conference," Transcript. Available at: www.ataa.org/observer/obs_may02.html.
74 Personal interview with Daniel Mariaschin, March 10, 2004. The American diplomat, who opened the US embassy in Baku in 1992, expressed the same view. Personal interview with Philip Remler, July 7, 2005.
75 The lack of understanding of the political process in the United States led foreign experts to the confusion in terminology. For instance, Bulent Aras identifies WINEP as one of the "leading lobbying organizations" (see Bulent Aras, op. cit.). Sam Vaknin indicates that JINSA lobbied the US Congress (see Sam Vaknin, op. cit.). In fact, IRS code explicitly states that an organization such as a think tank "may not attempt to influence legislation as a substantial part of its activities and it may not participate at all in campaign activity for or against political candidates." Internal Revenue Service Code. Available at: www.irs.gov/charities/charitable/article/0,id=96099,00.html.
76 Personal interview with Daniel Mariaschin, March 10, 2004.
77 Heydar Aliyev, "Rech na officialnom prieme po sluchayu nacionalnogo prazdnika Gosudarstva Izrail," speech at the official teception on the Occasion of the National Holiday of the State of Israel, Israeli embassy in Baku, May 11, 2000.
78 See "Foreign Aid Conferees Add Safeguards to Presidential Authority to Waive Section 907," press release, the Armenian National Committee of America, November 11, 2002.
79 "2002 Congressional Outreach Campaign Continues with Rep. Berman Meeting," press release, Armenian National Committee of America, January 15, 2002.

80 For a comprehensive discussion of the role of evangelical Christians in the epistemic community, which advocates the "strong Israel" doctrine as a basis of US foreign policy in the Middle East, see Wolf Blitzer, op. cit., pp. 122–4. See also David Newsom, "Foreign Policy Lobbies and Their Influence." Available at: www.cosmos-club.org/web/journals/1995/newsom.html, 1995. For the critical interpretation, see M.A. Muqtedar Khan, "Policy Entrepreneurs: The Third Dimension in American Foreign-policy Culture," *Middle East Policy*, Vol. 5, No. 3, September, 1997.

81 Philip Robins, *Turkish–Israeli Relations*, op. cit., p. 7.

82 Personal interview with Keith Weissman, February 23, 2003.

83 Wolf Blitzer, op. cit., p. 73.

84 See Mehmet Komurcu, "Water Disputes in the Middle East," unpublished LL.M. thesis, University of Wisconsin Law School.

85 See "Ambassador's Meeting with the Representatives from Various Jewish American Organizations," press release, Turkish embassy in Washington, DC, April 9, 2002. Available at: www.turkishembassy.org/pressreleases/arsiv/200204.htm. Also personal interviews with Keith Weissman, February and April, 2003.

86 The Jewish groups stated in the letter that the Israeli actions were "directly comparable" to the Turkish government's armed attacks on the Kurds in northern Iraq. Harut Sassounian, "Despite Turkish Apologies, Ecevit's Words Have Devastating Effect on Jewish Support," *California Courier*, April 18, 2002.

87 Douglas Frantz, "With a Word, Israeli–Turkish Strain Surfaces," *The New York Times*, April 10, 2002.

88 Furuk Logoglu, op. cit., April–May, 2002.

89 Harut Sassounian, op. cit., April 18, 2002.

90 Ibid.

91 Yasemin Dobra-Manco, "Turkey Needs New Strategy for Lobbying in US," *Turkish Daily News*, July 5, 1997.

92 Bahadir Ozgur, "Amerika'nin son tabusu LOBI." Available at: www.evrensel.net/02/05/05/medya.html.

93 By 2010 Azerbaijan is expected to supply about 13 percent of the total Turkish gas imports. Azerbaijan and Turkey are proceeding with plans to construct the Baku-Tbilisi-Erzrum gas (the South Caucasus Gas pipeline) pipeline running parallel to the BTC pipeline.

94 See Manfred Hafner, "Future Natural Gas Supply Options and Supply Costs," *Observatoire Mediterraneen de l'Energie*, 2002. Available at: europa.eu.int/comm/energy/gas/workshop_2002/doc/external_commission/10.pdf; Gareth M. Winrow, "Turkey as an Energy Transit State," Lecture, Conference "Black Sea: Energy and the Environment," Istanbul Bilgi University, Marine Law and Policy Research Center, May 15, 2003.

95 "Mavi Akim projesinin diger projelerin önünü kestigini söyleyen Amerikan–Israil Kamu Isleri Komitesi Baskan Yardimcisi Weismann, projenin Ruslarin basarisi oldugunu belirtti," Istanbul NTV-MSNBC, June 10, 2003.

96 For a detailed analysis of the strategic importance of the East–West corridor, see Necdet Pamir, "Turkey: The Key to Caspian Oil and Gas," IASPS Research Paper in Strategy. Available at: www.iasps.org.il.

97 Bruce Kuniholm, "European Union: Differences in European and American Attitudes, and the Challenges for Turkey's Accession to the European Union," *Working Papers Series*, SANO 1–24, January, 2001.

98 Soner Cagaptay and Nazli Gencsoy, "Improving Turkish–Russian Relations: Turkey's New Foreign Policy and Its Implications for the United States," *PolicyWatch*, No. 942, Washington, DC: The Washington Institute for Near East Policy, January 12,

2005. See also "Outcomes of Gazprom's Delegation's Visit to Israel," available at www.capitallinkrussia.com/press/companies/50010088/28548.html; Andrea R. Mihailescu, "Israel's Ongoing Foreign Energy Dependence," *Washington Times*, August 11, 2004; "Israel Looking to Import Russian Gas," available at http://peakoil. com/printout1848.html.

 99 "International Issues," B'nai Brith International's website. Available at: http://b'nai brith.org/ppolicy/global/index.cfm.

100 Dov Waxman, op. cit., p. 132.

101 Personal interview with Daniel Mariaschin, March 10, 2004.

102 Personal interview with Carol McLelland, August 2, 2004.

103 Daniel Mariaschin, op. cit.

104 Cheryl Halpern and Jason Epstein, "Encouraging Muslim Moderation," *Forward*, November 16, 2001.

105 The American Jewish Committee website, www.ajc.org/WhoWeAre/MissionAnd History.asp.

106 The high-profile celebration of the Quincentennial Anniversary of the admission of Spanish Jews after their expulsion by the Ottoman Empire in Turkey also brought the attention of the American Jewish community to the historic Turkish–Jewish amity. See "An Example to Mankind," by US Congressman Stephen Solarz, Extension of Remarks—September 17, 1990. Available at: http://thomas.loc.gov/cgi-bin/ query/z?r101:E17SE0-25.

107 *Turkish Daily News*, July 29, 1999. Available at: www.turkishdailynews.com/old_editions/07_29_99/feature.htm#f1.

108 "American Jewish Committee Endorses Silk Road Strategy Act," June 24, 1998. Available at: www.charitywire.com/charity11/00406.html.

109 Personal interview with Engin Soysal, a Turkish diplomat in the Turkish embassy in Washington, DC, October 29, 2004; see also Anadolu Agency, October 13, 2004.

110 Ibid.

111 A letter of Support for the Silk Road Strategy Act, June 29, 1999, Personal archive. See also "American Jewish Committee Endorses Silk Road Strategy Act," American Jewish Committee, June 24, 1998. Available at: www.charitywire.com/charity11/ 00406.html.

112 Section 907 of the Freedom Support Act, which took effect in 1992, forbade direct US assistance to Azerbaijan, except for aid for humanitarian purposes and non-proliferation and disarmament programs.

113 A letter of Support for the Silk Road Strategy Act, op. cit.

114 "Silk Road Legislation Passes US Senate Tonight," press release, Office of Senator Sam Brownback, June 30, 1999. Available at: http://brownback.senate.gov/pressapp/ record.cfm?id=175947&.

115 American think tanks especially have thrived in the period after World War II. See above in this chapter.

116 For a good treatment of the subject, see Dilek Barlas, *Etatism and Diplomacy in Turkey: Economic and Foreign Policy Strategies in an Uncertain World, 1929–1939*, Leiden: Brill, 1998; and Zvi Yehuda Hershlag, *Turkey: An Economy in Transition*, The Hague: Uitgeverij Van Keulen, 1958.

117 Suat Kiniklioglu, "Turkey's Think Tank Scene," *Turkish Daily News*, December 27, 2005.

118 It functioned under the aegis of the Turkish Ministry of Foreign Affairs. For example, Yuksel Soylemez, a veteran Turkish diplomat, served as the co-chairman of this institute between 1999 and 2001. The Marmara Foundation was another think tank of note at the time. Ibid.

119 Suat Kiniklioglu calls these epistemic communities in Turkey "virtual actors" because they followed the social trend and Western funding sources for NGOs, which became available under the impact of globalization, rather than being engaged in substantive research. Ibid.

120 Ibid.

121 See, for example, Nazim Cafersoy, *Elcibey Donemi Azerbsaycasn Dis Politikasi (Haziran 1992–Haziran 1993)*, Ankara: ASAM, 2001; *Azerbaycan Ozel, Avrasya Dosyasi* Series, Ankara: ASAM, 2001.

122 They participated in the seminar "Turkey in the 21st Century," Bar-Ilan University, Ramat-Gan, December 18, 2000, and the conference "Ten Years After the Gulf War," Bar-Ilan University, Ramat-Gan, Israel, January 8, 2001. See also Necdet Pamir, "Turkey: The Key to Caspian Oil and Gas," op. cit., August, 2001.

123 David Levi-Faur, Gabriel Sheffer and David Vogel (Eds.), *Israel: The Dynamics of Change and Continuity*, London: Routledge, 1999, p. 166. Cf. Dilek Barlas, op. cit.

124 Israeli Prime Minister Ehud Olmert identified them as "the meeting place for new concepts, new strategies, new theories for those who are in charge of the implementation—and it helps very much." Alan Abbey, "Schools of Thought," *Jerusalem Post*, April 29, 2004.

125 Ibid.

126 MERIA has reached a circulation of around 25,000 in over 100 countries. Available at: www.gloria.co.il.

127 Barry Rubin also serves as the director of the GLORIA-affiliated Turkish Studies Institute that publishes the journal *Turkish Studies*. Ibid.

128 Ofra Bengio, op. cit., p. 92.

129 Personal interview with Efraim Inbar, February 9, 2004.

130 Ibid.

131 Begin-Sadat Center experts are often quoted in *Defense News*, *Dallas Morning News*, *Washington Times*, *Jerusalem Post* and *Haaretz*. See Alan Abbey, op. cit.

132 Sergey Minosyan, op. cit., p. 101; see also *BESA Bulletin*, no. 15, February, 2003, p. 3.

133 In fact, the Azerbaijani President Ilham Aliyev graduated from the prestigious Moscow-based Institute of International Relations, the main center that trains Russian diplomats. See also Vafa Guluzade, *Caucasus Among Enemies and Friends*, Azerbaijan–Turkey: Oka Ofset, 2002, p. 34.

134 Vafa Guluzade, ibid.

135 See Daria Vaisman, "Azerbaijan Creates Diplomatic Academy," *The International Herald Tribune*, July 11, 2007. Prior to that, most Azerbaijani diplomats were trained in other non-related fields. For example, Hafiz Pashayev, the academy's dean and the former long-serving ambassador to the United States, has a doctorate in physics and carried out research in this field as did some other diplomats before Azerbaijani independence. Personal interview with Sultan Malikov.

136 "Azerbaijan: Turning Over a New Leaf," International Crisis Group, ICG Europe Report, No. 156, May 13, 2004, pp. 11–12. See also John Ishiyama, "Political Party Development and Party 'Gravity' in Semi-Authoritarian States. The Cases of Azerbaijan, Kyrgystan, and Tajikistan," *Taiwan Journal of Democracy*, July 2008, Vol. 4, No. 1, pp. 33–53.

137 Personal interviews with Vafa Guluzade and Eldar Namazov.

138 The Public Forum for Azerbaijan published the proceedings of the Conference "Ten Years of Independence," sponsored by the center in 2003. It is a seminal collection of contributions on the domestic and foreign policy of Azerbaijan in 2003. See *Musteqilliyimizin on illiyi*, Baku: Azerbaycan Namine Ictimal Forum, 2003.

139 See Arif Yunusov, "Azerbaijan mezdu Amerikoy y Iranom," in *Rossiya v Globalnoy Politike*, No. 3, 2006.

140 Personal interview with Vafa Guluzade, August 5, 2004.
141 Vafa Guluzade, "Turkey's Foreign Policy," *Caucasus Among Enemies and Friends*, op. cit., p. 103.
142 Ibid.
143 See "Unite into a Single State with Turkey," *Zerkalo*, June 17, 2000; Professor Yahya Tasdelen, "Turkish–Azerbaijan Federation," a letter from Ankara, July 15, 2001, in Vafa Guluzade, *Caucasus Among Enemies and Friends*, op. cit., pp. 110–11; "Turkey and Azerbaijan Must be United," *Exo*, February 7, 2001.
144 During his assignment as a Soviet diplomat in Egypt, Vafa Guluzade served as a personal go-between for Egyptian president Anwar Sadat and the Soviet leaderhip during the Yom Kippur War of 1973. Personal interview, August 5, 2004. See also Samy Rozen, "Strany SNG menyaut svoikh lyudey v Izraile," *Axisglobe analytical agency*. Available at: www.axisglobe-ru.com/article.asp?article=320.
145 "V blizayashhe vremya v Izraile otkroitsya posolstvo Azerbaijana," *Day.az*, May 9, 2006; "Vafa Guluzade mozhet stanet poslom Azerbaijana v Izraile," *Day.az*, May 18, 2006. See also Samy Rozen, op. cit.
146 The BTC project transported the first oil in July 2006.
147 See Saadet Oruc, "Oil Giants and Israel Hold Key to Caucasus Conflicts," *Turkish Daily News*, August 11, 1997.
148 Eduard Shevarnadze, a former president of Georgia who survived several assassination attempts, said at a press conference on January 1, 1998: "The problem of transporting Caspian oil and other energy sources from Central Asia is one of the most sensitive questions of our time." Ursula Beyreuther, "Pipeline Diplomacy," Report, *Deutsche Morgan Grenfell*, January 31, 1998.
149 Mehdi Amineh, *Towards the Control of Oil Resources in the Caspian Region*, New York: St. Martin's Press, 1999, p. 99.
150 Ibid., pp. 9–10.
151 Ibid.
152 Amiheh demonstrates the scale of the domination of the world economy by transnational corporations by pointing to the fact that while in 1988 there were only 20,000 TNCs in the world, their foreign assets amounted to $1.1 trillion and their total assets were appraised at $4 trillion. By the early 1990s these figures reached to 37,000 TNCs with general assets of more than $4.8 trillion in 1991. See ibid., p. 11.
153 Ibid.
154 All of these corporations are enumerated in the list of the top 502 richest business enterprises in the world.
155 Ibid., p. 38.
156 Under EOI, industrial production is oriented toward the world market rather than the protected domestic market. Transnational corporations and multilateral institutions gain relative power compared to the power of governments to affect economic and political outcomes. Traditional functions of the state (e.g. defense, communications, economic management) are now coordinated on a multilateral or intergovernmental basis. See David Held, "Democracy and the Global System," in D. Held (Ed.), *Political Theory*, Cambridge: Polity, 1991, pp. 207–9.
157 In order to make the BTC project feasible, the pipeline depends on Kazakh oil to supply the shortfall of oil needed to exploit the pipeline to its full capacity of 1 million barrels per day. Necdet Pamir calculated that Kazakhstan would need to supply 20 million tons per year, while Azerbaijan needs to supply 25 million tons per year to reach this goal. Necdet Pamir, "Getting Azerbaijan's Oil to the International Market: The Turkish Perspective," *Azerbaijan International*, Autumn, 1995.
158 Turgut Ozal proposed to transport oil and gas from the Caspian region to the world markets in 1991. See Ismail Altunsov, "Turkey Now Has a Voice in Energy Politics," *Zaman*, July 14, 2006.

159 See a detailed account of the role of Georgia in Mikhail Chumalov, *Kaspiyskaya neft y Mezhnazyonlalnye Otnoshenya*, Moscow: The Center for Study of International Relations, 2000, especially pp. 50–3. See also Vladimer Papava, "The Baku-Tbilisi-Ceyhan Pipeline: Implications for Georgia," in S. Frederick Starr and Svante E. Cornell (Eds.), *The Baku-Tbilisi-Ceyhan Pipeline: Oil Window to the West*, Washington, DC: The Central Asia-Caucasus Institute & Silk Road Studies Program, 2005.

160 The Kirkuk-Yumurtalik pipeline delivered Iraqi oil to the Turkish port of Ceyhan. If the pipeline is restored to its full capacity, Turkey stands to gain $500,000 per day in transit fees. See Mevlut Katik, "Turkey Hopes for Oil Windfall in Turbulent Iraq," *Eurasianet*, August 18, 2003.

161 "Country Analysis: Azerbaijan," *Alexander's Gas and Oil Connection*, Vol. 8, Issue 13, June 26, 2003.

162 Ibid.

163 David I. Hoffman, "Oil and Development in Post-Soviet Azerbaijan," in *Energy, Wealth, and Development in Central Asia and the Caucasus*, National Bureau of Asian Research (NBR) Analysis, Vol. 10, No. 3, August, 1999.

164 AIOC includes: BP, 34.10 percent; Unocal, 10.30 percent; State Oil Corporation of Azerbaijani Republic, 10.00 percent; Inpex, 10.00 percent ; Statoil, 8.60 percent; ExxonMobil, 8.00 percent; TPAO, 6.80 percent; Devon, 5.60 percent; Itochu, 3.90 percent; Hess, 2.70 percent. See "Country Analysis: Azerbaijan," op. cit. For more details, see Jonathan Elkind, "Economic Implications of the Baku-Tbilisi-Ceyhan Pipeline," in S. Frederick Starr and Svante E. Cornell, op. cit., p. 43.

165 For an in-depth account of the American strategy in the Caucasus, see Igor Muradian, *Politika SSHA I Problemy Bezopasnosti Regiona Yuzhnogo Kavakaza*, Yerevan: Antares, 2000, pp. 44–52.

166 The dependence on Persian Gulf oil is perceived as breeding "energy insecurity" and wide fluctuations in the international price of oil. See a discussion in Mehdi Amineh, op. cit., pp. 36–7. See also Editorial, *Oil Gas Journal*, November, 1997.

167 S.579, "Silk Road Strategy Act of 1999," *A bill to amend the Foreign Assistance Act of 1961 to target assistance to support the economic and political independence of the countries of the South Caucasus and Central Asia*, available at www.eurasianet.org/resource/regional/silkroad.html.

168 Igor Muradian, op. cit., p. 49.

169 Andrew McAuslan, "Caspian Oil Windfalls: Who Will Benefit?" Conference Report, the Open Society Institute and the Center for Strategic and International Studies, May 13, 2003.

170 Ibid.

171 In retaliation, the Turkish government refused to purchase the oil shipped by these two TNCs in November of 1998. Suha Bolukbasi, "Jockeying for Power in the Caspian Basin," in Shirin Akiner (Ed.), *The Caspian: Politics, Energy and Security*, London: RoutledgeCurzon, 2004, p. 223.

172 According to an American diplomat, it was the CEO of BP, John Browne, who, after his visit to Istanbul, was "converted to this idea" in 1999. At the meeting, Browne became convinced that the BTC was a worthwhile and commercially feasible project. Personal interview with Philip Remler, op. cit.

173 Ibid.

174 See *Baku-Tbilisi-Ceyhan Pipeline Project: Between Two Seas*, a BTC publication, June, 2002, p. 2.

175 *Alexander's Gas and Oil Connection*, op. cit.

176 John Roberts, "Pipeline Politics," in Shirin Akiner, op. cit., p. 84.

177 John Roberts, ibid., p. 82.

178 See David Blatchford, "Environmental and Social Aspects of the Baku-Tbilisi-Ceyhan Pipeline," in S. Frederick Starr and Svante E. Cornell, op. cit., p. 10; also David Blatchford, ibid., p. 119. See also Terence Adams in Shirin Akiner, op. cit., pp. 97, 222.

179 "Shakh-Deniz Drilling Reaches Depth of 5,000 Meters," *Caspian Business Report*, Vol. 3, No. 4, February 28, 1999. The Shakh-Deniz field is developed by a consortium that includes BP, Statoil, SOCAR, LukAgip, NICO, TotalFinalElf, and TOPAS. It is expected to produce 110 mm tons of oil equivalent of natural gas between 2006 and 2020.

180 Other sources estimate the field's reserves as high as 35 trillion cubic feet. "Azerbaijan—The Shah Deniz Venture," *APS Review Gas Market Trends*, July 7, 2008.

181 Shirin Akiner, "Achievements, New Concerns, Future Prospects," in Shirin Akiner, op. cit., p. 366.

182 Gas condensate, or wet gas, contains natural gas, water and other hydrocarbons within gasoline boiling range.

183 See Suha Bolukbasi, op. cit., pp. 218–29.

184 Pepe Escobar, "Pipelineistan Revisited," *The Asia Times*, Part 1, 2B, January 29, 2004.

185 See also Carter Page, "US Involvement in the Caspian Sea Region," in Shirin Akiner, op. cit., p. 271.

186 Pepe Escobar, op. cit.

187 Maia Misheladze, "British and US Banks Rejecting to Finance the BTC Pipeline," *Georgia Times*, May 12, 2003.

188 The EBRD allocated $125 million for the construction of the Azerbaijani and Georgian sections of the BTC pipeline and syndicated another $125 million from commercial banks. "Current Situation in Georgia Won't Disrupt Baku-Ceyhan Project," *Georgia Times*, May 12, 2003. For details of the general activities of branches of the US government (Overseas Private Investment Corporation, Export-Import Bank, and Trade and Development Agency) in the Caspian region, see Mehdi Amineh, op. cit., p. 95.

167 Maia Misheladze, op. cit.

190 Merhav Group, for instance, participates as a part the $80m to $100m enterprise in the infrastructural project to transport water from the Tigris and Euphrates rivers to Southeastern Turkey.

191 See Chapter 5 of this volume. See also Christopher Bollyn, "Same Old Names, Faces Primed to Make Big Bucks Off Tragedy," *American Free Press*, October 15, 2001. Available at www.rense.com/general15/game.htm.

192 Merhav operates a billion dollars worth of contracts in the petrochemical sector of Turkmenistan. "Turkmenistan and Merhav Discuss Upgrade of Large Oil Refinery," *Caspian Business Report*, Vol. 2, No. 7, April 15, 1998.

193 Merhav official website: www.merhav.com.

194 *Turkistan Newsletter* (Turkistan Bulteni), September 5, 2000.

195 See Alexander Murinson, op. cit. Also Michael Lelyveld, "Iran: Contact with Israel May Affect Caspian Oil Countries," *Radio Free Europe/Radio Liberty*, June 23, 1999.

196 Ibid. David Hoffman described Merhav's involvement in Niyazov's political maneuvers surrounding energy exports: "Turkmenistan has joined the ranks of other Caspian countries in turning to US lobbying firms—in their case, through the Israeli company Merhav—to keep tabs on US Caspian policy and to support the visibility of Turkmenistan in the United States." David Hoffman, op. cit.

197 Ibid.

198 David Zev Harris, "Merhav Helps Broker $3b. Gas Pipeline Deal," *Haaretz*, November 3, 1998.

199 Ibid.

200 "Merhav President in Baku to See Aliyev," *Caspian Business Report*, op. cit. See also "Heydar Aliyev Welcomes Idea of Construction of Transcaspian Gas Pipeline," in ibid.
201 Germana Ganzi, "Turkmenistan's Caspian Resources," in Shirin Akiner, op. cit., p. 189.
202 Personal interview with an anonymous employee of energy engineering company Bateman Litwin, April, 2005. See also "Azerbaijan Eyes the West," *United Press International*, June 26, 2006. Available at: UPI/www.wpherald.com.

5 The heart of entente

1 See Mehdi Amineh, "Towards Rethinking Geopolitics," *Central Eurasian Studies Review*, Publication of the Central Eurasian Studies Society, Vol. 3, No. 1, Winter, 2004.
2 For comprehensive conceptualizations of the security complex, see Barry Buzan, *People, States and Fear: An Agenda for Internal Security Studies in the Post-Cold War Era*, Boulder, CO: Lynne Rienner, 1991, pp. 96–107; Mohammed Ayoob, *The Third World Security Predicament: State Making, Regional Conflict and the International System*, Boulder, CO: Lynne Rienner, 1995, pp. 56–8.
3 Meliha Altunisik, "Turkish Policy towards Israel," in Alan Makovsky and Sabri Sayari (Eds.), *Turkey's New World*, Washington, DC: The Washington Institute for Near East Policy, 2000, p. 60.
4 N. Kireev, "Turtsia i Israel-Strategichiskye Soyuzniki na Blizhnem Vostoke," *Xronika Voenno-Politicheskogo Sotrudnichestva v 1994–1997*, op. cit., pp. 105–13.
5 Nadia El-Shazly and Raymond Hinnebusch, "The Challenge of Security in the Middle East in the Post-Gulf War Middle East System," in Raymond Hinnebusch and Anoushiravan Ehteshami (Eds.), *The Foreign Policy of the Middle East States*, Boulder, CO: Lynne Rienner, 2002, p. 78.
6 Ibid., p. 72.
7 Personal interview with Araz Azimov, August 3, 2004.
8 For Arab, Iranian and other Muslim nations' reactions to the break-up of the Soviet Union, see: *The Turkish Daily News*, April 9, 1996; *The Washington Times*, April 10, 1996; *The International Herald Tribune*, April 27–8, 1996; *The Chicago Tribune*, May 22, 1996; *The Wall Street Journal*, May 30, 1996; *The Washington Post*, June 2, 1996; and *The International Herald Tribune*, June 17, 1996. For the Russian reaction, see Vitaliy Demin, "Russkiye Ushli," *Zavtra*, July 23, 1998.
9 Meliha Altunisik, "Turkish Policy towards Israel," in Alan Makovsky and Sabri Sayari (Eds.), *Turkey's New World*, Washington, DC: The Washington Institute for Near East Policy, 2000, p. 69.
10 Ibid. An former Israeli ambassador, Uri Bar-Ner, recently called Turkey the second most important country for Israel in the world (after the United States). Uri Bar-Ner, "Good Friends are Hard to Find," *Jerusalem Post*, July 10, 2001.
11 Personal interviews with Vafa Guluzade, Araz Azimov, Sultan Melikov and Elin Suleymanov. See also Svante Cornell, "Geopolitics and Strategic Alignments in the Caucasus and Central Asia," *Perceptions*, Vol. 4, No. 2, June–August, 1999.
12 Gareth Winrow, "Central Asia and the Transcaucasus," in *Turkey's New World*, op. cit., p. 122.
13 See Svante Cornell, op. cit., p. 119.
14 Bulent Aras, op. cit., p. 59.
15 Heinz Kramer, *A Changing Turkey*, Washington, DC: Brookings Institution, 2000, p. 99; Mikhail Chumalov, *Kaspiyskaya neft y Mezhnazyonlalnye Otnoshenya*, Moscow: The Center for Study of International Relations, 2000, pp. 53–69.

16 Personal interview with Shirin Akiner, November 14, 2005.
17 See the analysis of General Çevik Bir of the transformation of Turkey from a "flank" state into a "frontline" state in Ofra Bengio, op. cit., p. 82.
18 Personal interview with General Çevik Bir, Ankara, May 26, 2004.
19 The Kurdish nationalists had been involved in a long cycle of separatist violence against Turkey since the Sheikh Said uprising of 1925. Gulistan Gurbey claims that there were over 20 Kurdish uprisings. For an account of the Kurdish insurgency in Turkey, see Henri Barkey, "Under the Gun: Turkish Foreign Policy and the Kurdish Question," in Robert Olson (Ed.), *The Kurdish Nationalist Movement in the 1990s*, Lexington, KY: University of Kentucky Press, 1996, pp. 66–8. In the case of Israel, the unresolved issue of permanent boundaries and the absence of diplomatic recognition by the Arab neighboring states, especially before 1979, served the interests of the Palestinian Arab resistance to the existence of the Jewish state.
20 Sergey Minasyan et al., *The Karabagh Conflict*, Yerevan: Nairi, 2005, pp. 47–8.
21 A significant number of Turkish volunteers participated in ethno-religious wars after the break-up of the Communist bloc, including wars in Bosnia, Chechnya and Abkhazia. See "Kaide'nin uzantısı en az 150 Türk var," *Radikal*, July 1, 2004.
22 Generally, ethnic conflicts have a "copy-cat" effect on other zones of ethnic tension. The First Palestinian Intifadah flared up in Israel in 1987; PKK militancy increased dramatically in Turkey in the 1990s. The PKK military wing, the Peshmerga, used bases in Syria, Lebanon, Iraq and Iran to conduct guerrilla operations against Turkey. See Robert Olson, "The Kurdish Question and Turkey's Foreign Policy toward Syria, Iran, Russia and Iraq since the Gulf War," in Robert Olson (Ed.), *The Kurdish Nationalist Movement in the 1990s: Its Impact in Turkey and Middle East*, op. cit.
23 Hrair Dekmejian and Hovann Simonian, *The Troubled Waters: The Geopolitics of the Caspian Region*, London: Tauris Publishers, 2001, p. 125.
24 Emory Bogle, *The Modern Middle East: From Imperialism to Freedom, 1800–1958*, Upper Saddle River, NJ: Prentice Hall, 1996, p. 146.
25 From the beginning of the twentieth century, the most prominent American ambassadors to Turkey were Jewish. The influence on American policy toward Turkey of Ambassador Henry Morgenthau only corroborated this belief among Turkish elites. Personal communication from William Hale, August 4, 2005. Historically the United States appointed as its ambassadors to Istanbul such notable Jews as: Solomon Hirsch, ambassador to Turkey, 1889–92; Oscar Solomon Straus, ambassador to Turkey, 1909–10; minister to Turkey, 1898–9, 1887–9; and Henry Morgenthau, Sr., ambassador to Turkey, 1913–16.
26 In this regard it is important to note that Turkey recognized Israel just a few days before the Turkish foreign minister met with American President Truman. Bruce Kuniholm and Ian Lesser, "Turkish–Israeli Relations during the Cold War," Lecture at the Conference "The History of Turkish–American Relations," Bogazici University, Harran University and Public Affairs Office of the US Consulate in Istanbul, June 4–10, 2006.
27 Harun Yahya, *Israel'in Kurt Karti: Isral'in Ortadogu Stratejisi ve "Kurt Devleti" Senaryolari*, Istanbul: Arastirma Yayincilik, 2002, p. 54.
28 See the text of the letter from Prime Minister Ben-Gurion to the president of the United States of America, *Eisenhower Papers*, International Series, Box 35, Mid. East, July, 1958 (4), Eisenhower Library, Abilene, Kansas. See also a detailed account of the "periphery strategy" formulation in Benjamin Beit-Halahmi, *The Israeli Connection*, New York: Pantheon, 1987, p. 7.
29 Ibid.
30 In particular, the historical support of Israel for the Kurdish resistance fighters *Peshmerga* became a very divisive issue in Turkey in post-Saddam Iraq. Turkey is

naturally inclined to perceive the Kurdish autonomy in contemporary Iraq as the source of irredentism in the Kurdish-populated extensive region of southeastern Turkey.

31 See Amikam Nachmani, *Israel, Turkey and Greece*, London: Frank Cass, 1987, pp. 13–82.
32 Harun Yahya, op. cit., p. 55.
33 When Iranian students seized the archives of the American embassy in Teheran, it came to light that the Trident, the secret trilateral agreement, had been signed between the three countries. See Harun Yahya, op. cit.
34 Ronen Bergman, *The Secret War with Iran: The 30-Year Clandestine Struggle against the World's Most Dangerous Terrorist Power*, New York: Simon & Schuster, 2008, pp. 13–14.
35 Andrew Cockburn and Leslie Cockburn, *Dangerous Liaison: The Inside Story of the US–Israeli Covert Relationship*, New York: Harper Collins Publishers, 1991, p. 100.
36 This cooperation came into being during this decade. According to Harun Yahya, any assassination of the ultra-right and left activists every month was observed closely by the Mossad. Ofra Bengio, however, argues that Turkey froze its intelligence and security cooperation over Israeli "neutrality" in the Cyprus issue in 1966. See Ofra Bengio, *Turkish–Israeli Relationship: Changing Ties of Middle East Outsiders*, New York: Palgrave Macmillan, 2004, p. 64.
37 "Israel Woos Turkey," in *Israel Foreign Affairs*, June 6, 1985. See also Benjamin Ben-Hallahmi, *The Israeli Connection*, op. cit., p. 17.
38 After the military operations of the Caucasian Islamic Army led by the Turkish General Nuri Pasha, the first independent Azerbaijani government was formed in Gyandja, while Baku was the seat of the Bolshevik-supported Dashnaktsun government. See Igrar Aliyev, *Istorya Azerbaijan: Ot Drevneyshih Vremen do Nachala XX veka* ("History of Azerbaijan: From Ancient Times to the Beginning of the 20th Century"), Baku: Elm, 1995, pp. 354–5.
39 The foreign policy concept of Azerbaijan was formulated during perestroika, the period of liberalization under Mikhail Gorbachev (1985–91). The young Azerbaijani intellectuals who later became the leaders of the Azerbaijani National Front, the first party of the government in the independent Azerbaijan, were ideological pan-Turkists. The eruption of the Nagorno-Karabagh crisis became the seminal event that triggered the arousal of Azerbaijani nationalism (pan-Azerism) and Turkism as the popular sentiment. Personal interviews with Qanimat Zahidov, July 30, 2004, Sultan Malikov, May 3, 2005, and Rachilya Geybulayeva, March 4, 2003. See also Igor Muradian, *Geoekonomicheskiye Faktory Razvitya Politicheskich Processov v Kavkazsko-Kaspiyskom Regione*, Yerevan: Antares, 2001, p. 67.
40 Under the Turkish–Soviet treaty of 1921, Turkey retained the right to intervene to prevent threats to the Nakhicevan autonomous region. Ibid.
41 Personal interview with Nariman Gasimoglu, August 5, 2004. Ms. Moqaddam, a deputy from the Iranian Azerbaijan and a Majlis member, called President Abulfaz Elchibey a Zionist agent and condemned his contacts with Israel. *The Echo of Iran*, November 1992, p. 7.
42 *Al-Wassat*, February 16, 1998. See also Vitaly Demin, "Russkiye Ushli," *Zavtra*, July 6, 1998.
43 Ibid.
44 Many external players are involved in attempts to manipulate developments in Kurdistan, such as the United States, Russia, Great Britain, Greece and many others. Many of these countries cynically use the Kurdish problem for their own ends. Throughout the 1990s, the United States played the Kurdish card against Saddam Hussein's regime and the Iranian fundamentalists.

45 Henri Barkey, "Kurdish Nationalist Movement in the 1990s," in Olson, op. cit., pp. 77–8.
46 On October 11, 1993, for example, Iraq denied Turkish allegations that it was selling weapons to the PKK. According to a report by the Turkish national news agency, the Iraqi embassy in Ankara declared that it had never had relations with the Kurdish organization. See: "Iran, Turkey to Strengthen Ties, Fight Drugs," *Reuters*, October 19, 1993; Alan Elsner, "US Terror Report Cites Syria Despite Peace Role," *Reuters*, May 9, 1994.
47 Another account claims that the PKK was formed under Moscow's tutelage in Syria. It was a proxy for Russian interests and was armed by the Czech secret service within the Warsaw Pact framework. There are allegations that Heydar Aliyev, as a former KGB operative in the Middle East and Iran, was personally involved in the formation of the PKK. So the PKK served as an instrument of Moscow to undermine Turkey, an American NATO ally. Personal interview with Rauf Mirkadirov, July 29, 2004.
48 "Protocol against Cross-Border Terrorism Signed with Russia," *Middle East Economic Digest*, February 6, 1995.
49 Personal interview with Boris Trepetin, February 12, 2005.
50 Gulistan Gurbey, "The Development of the Kurdish Nationalism Movement in Turkey since the 1980s," in Robert Olson (Ed.), op. cit. See an alternative view on the Kurdish political agenda in Emine Kart, "'Kurds' Strong Will for a Unitary Turkey Is Assurance of Democratic Future," *Turkish Daily News*, November 13, 2005.
51 Gulistan Gurbey, op. cit., p. 24.
52 Ofra Bengio, op. cit., p. 137.
53 Available at: www.armenianreality.com/.
54 Personal interview with Cengiz Candar, August 12, 2005.
55 Noteworthy is the similarity between the Palestinian and Kurdish militants' ultimate goals. Both perceive the struggle as the struggle for liberation. Like their Palestinian counterparts, the PKK view the Kurdish region as the "colony of Turkish states." See Gulistan Gurbey, "The Kurdish Nationalist Movement in Turkey since the 1980s," in Robert Olson, op. cit., p. 24.
56 "Kurdistan–Kurdish Conflict." Available at: www.globalsecurity.org/military/world/war/kurdistan.htm.
57 Gulistan Gurbey, op. cit., pp. 17–18.
58 Robert Olson, "The Kurdish Question and Turkey's Foreign Policy toward Syria, Iran, Russia and Iraq since the Gulf War," in Robert Olson (Ed.), op. cit., p. 106. The stellar Israeli land- and air-force performance and the effective use of electronic warfare in the Lebanon campaign were major factors that convinced the Turkish military of the need for enhancement of military cooperation with Israel. See Ofra Bengio, op. cit., p. 97.
59 The Turkish military stated that PKK bases needed to be "cleaned out" in order to maintain "security" in Turkey. See Robert Olson, op. cit., p. 107.
60 Stephen Larrabee and Ian Lesser, op. cit., p. 147.
61 According to Ofra Bengio, as late as the summer of 2002, Iran topped the list of regional threats to Turkey. See also *Radikal*, August 1, 2002. Meanwhile, Syria was dropped from Turkey's threats list in 2004, while Iranian nuclear ambitions, terrorist activities and fundamentalism topped it. See "National Security Document to be Revised," *Hurriyet*, November 24, 2004.
62 In 1995 Prime Minister Tansu Ciller threatened to strike at the PKK bases in Iran. In July 1999, the Turkish air force realized this threat. See Stephen Larrabee and Ian Lesser, op. cit., p. 149.
63 Svante E. Cornell, "Iran and the Caucasus," *Middle East Policy*, Vol. 5, No. 4, January, 1998.

64 "Iran Protest to Baku over Oil Activities in the Alborz Area," *Iranian Press Service*, July 23, 2001.
65 The basis for this claim is the administrative division during the Ottoman period, when Palestine was a part of the Syrian Vilayet and ruled by the Ottoman governor from Damascus. See Shlomo Aronson with Oded Brosh, *The Politics and Strategy of Nuclear Weapons in the Middle East*, Albany: SUNY Press, 1992, p. 234.
66 Interview with Israeli non-commissioned officer.
67 *Turkish Daily News*, January 1, 1996. See also Meliha Altusink, op. cit., p. 64.
68 Sam Vaknin, "Turkey's Jewish Friend." Available at: http://samvak.tripod.com/brief-turkeyisrael01.html.
69 Ofra Bengio, op. cit., pp. 153–4. See also Stephen Larrabee and Ian Lesser, *Turkish Foreign Policy in an Age of Uncertainty*, Santa Monica, CA: Rand, 2003, p. 145.
70 The Jordanian track was the most successful, and the parties signed the peace agreement on October 26, 1994. The fact that Israel had secret strategic cooperation with Jordan for many decades only accelerated this process. Given the traditional good relations between Jordan and Turkey, the peace agreement facilitated the official visit to Israel by Turkish Prime Minister Tansu Ciller. See Ofra Bengio, op. cit., p. 80.
71 Tozun Bachcheli, "Turkish Policy toward Greece," in Alan Makovsky and Sabri Sayari (Eds.), *Turkey's New World*, Washington, DC: The Washington Institute for Near East Policy, 2000, p. 134.
72 *Anadolu Agency*, August 4, 1998.
73 Tozun Bachcheli, op. cit., pp. 144–5.
74 Bulent Aras, op. cit., 2002, p. 21.
75 Dekmejan and Simonian, op. cit., p. 89.
76 See Chumalov, op. cit., p. 173.
77 "Turkey to Maintain Military Aid to Azerbaijan," in *Turkish Daily News*, September 25, 2002.
78 Personal interview with Çevik Bir, op. cit.
79 The impact of the American high-tech air and land campaign against the Saddam regime in 1991 put in stark contrast the technological inferiority of the TAF. Turkey had been supplied mostly with decommissioned tanks, airplanes and helicopters by the United States and Germany after the Conventional Armed Forces in Europe Agreement (CAFÉ) cuts. Elliot Hen-Tov, "The Political Economy of Turkish Military Modernization," *Middle East Review of International Affairs*, Vol. 8, No. 4, December, 2004, p. 50.
80 See also Nezih Tavlas, "Turk–Israil Guvenlik ve Istihbarat Iliskeleri," *Avarasya Dosyasi*, Vol. 5, No. 1, 1999, p. 93; *Turkish Daily News*, July 3, 1996.
81 See Hen-Tov, op. cit., p. 53.
82 Ibid.
83 Personal interview with Araz Azimov, August 3, 2004.
84 See "Iran Bullies Israel's Strategic Friends—with Eye on Washington," *Debkafile* Special Report, August 22, 2004.
85 Personal interview with Çevik Bir, op. cit.
86 Ofra Bengio, op. cit, p. 80.
87 Prime Minister Shimon Peres guaranteed that Israel would not sign any agreement with Syria before it renounces terrorism, and specifically the support of Damascus for the Kurdistan's Workers Party (PKK). See "Turkey: Israel Sets Terrorism Condition to Syria," *Turkish Daily News*, January 16, 1996.
88 Alexander Murinson, "Foreign Relations between Israel and the Islamic Newly Independent States," *The Cyber-Caravan*, op. cit.

89 Soner Cagaptay and Alexander Murinson, "Good Relations between Azerbaijan and Israel: A Model for Other Muslim States in Eurasia?" in *PolicyWatch*, No. 982, Washington, DC: The Washington Institute for Near East Policy, March 30, 2005.
90 Personal interview with Vafa Guluzade, August 5, 2004.
91 The Iranian foreign minister said: "Any further rapprochement between Azerbaijan and Israel will harm Islamic unity and those governments themselves." *Agence France-Presse* citing *IRNA*, August 9, 1995.
92 Lowell Bezanis, "Iran to Azerbaijan: No Ties to Israel," *OMRI Daily Digest*, August 10, 1995.
93 Alexander Murinson and Soner Cagaptay, "Good Relations between Azerbaijan and Israel: A Model for Other Muslim States in Eurasia?" op. cit.
94 Araz Azimov called that meeting "the most politically heavy." Personal interview with Araz Azimov, August 3, 2004.
95 In exchange, Heydar Aliyev extracted the Turkish commitment of support to Ilham Aliyev as the successor to the leadership of Azerbaijan. See Igor Muradian, "The Policy of the USA and Formation of Alternative Military–Political Blocks in the Region of Southern Caucasus," in *Politika SSHA I Problemy Bezopasnosty Regiona Yuzhnogo Kavakaza*, Yerevan: Antares, 2000, p. 83.
96 *Ekho*, March 14, 2001; *Turan*, March 15, 2001; *Azerbaijan News Service*, October 1, 2001; *Turkish Daily News*, March 13, 2001; *Zerkal*, April 4, 2002.
97 Interview with Ambassador Ahad Qazaie, *BBC News*, July 25, 2001.
98 "Iran Protests to Baku over Oil Activities in the Alborz Area," *Iranian Press Service*, July 23, 2001.
99 *Turkish Daily News*, September 25, 2002.
100 Elliot Hen-Tov, op. cit., p. 49.
101 The generic term "terrorism" in the title of the agreement was used in order to avoid attracting attention to the seriousness of the Kurdish challenge to the Turkish Kemalist state. Israel also desired not to tip the balance of support for the Jewish state among Iraqi Kurds, Kurdish Jews and the Kurdish Diaspora in Europe. See Ofra Bengio, op. cit., p. 106.
102 The February 23 agreement was leaked by Turkish Islamists to the Islamic magazine *Aksion* on May 18–24, 1996. From there it was reprinted in Israeli and Arab newspapers and also publicized by the United States Foreign Broadcast Information Service. See Ofra Bengio, op. cit.
103 According to Ofra Bengio, David Ivri and Yitzhak Rabin were almost successful in clinching the military agreement with their Turkish counterparts in 1987, but failed due to the eruption of the first Intifada in that year. Ofra Bengio, op. cit., p. 97.
104 Personal interview with General Çevik Bir, op. cit.
105 Ibid.
106 Kfir, a multi-purpose fighter plane, is an Israeli version of the French Mirage V with the powerful American General Electrics J79 jet engine. It has been produced by the IAI since 1968 and was exported overseas, including to the United States, where Kfirs are used for training US Navy and Marine Corps pilots. Available at: www.israeli-weapons.com/weapons/aircraft/kfir/Kfir.html.
107 Gordon Thomas, *Gideon Spies: The Secret History of the Mossad*, New York: Thomas Dunne Books, 2005, p. 337.
108 Personal interview with Alon Liel, April 10, 2005.
109 *Jerusalem Post*, December 10, 1997.
110 Ofra Bengio, op. cit. p. 106. See also *Jerusalem Post*, February 17, 1999. For an account of the Mossad's involvement in the operation to capture Ocalan in November of 1998 at the personal request of Prime Minister Bulent Ecevit, see Gordon Thomas, op. cit., pp. 337–40.

111 "Middle East's 'Phanton Alliance,'" *BBC World*, February 18, 1999; also "Three Kurdish Protesters Die in Shootout with Israelis," *CNN*, February 17, 1999.
112 Igor Muradian, op. cit., pp. 99–101. For information on Israeli–Azerbaijani cooperation, see in "SpetcSluzhby Azerbaijana," available at www.agentura.ru.
113 Personal interview with an Israeli diplomat.
114 Actually, this number is equal to the number of staff in the Iranian embassy in Baku. IDF has special units trained in the Azerbaijani language for potential future deployment. Personal interview with an anonymous security expert.
115 See Bulent Aras, "The Impact of the Palestinian–Israeli Peace Process in Turkish Foreign Policy," *Journal of South-Asian and Middle Eastern Studies*, 1997, Vol. 20, No. 2, pp. 49–72; Mahmut Aykan, "The Palestinian Question in Turkish Foreign Policy from the 1950s to the 1990s," *International Journal of Middle East Studies*, 1993, Vol. 25, pp. 91–110.
116 Ofra Bengio, op. cit., p. 156.
117 Philip Robins, *Turkish–Israeli Relations*, op. cit., p. 6.
118 Stephen Larrabee and Ian Lesser, *Turkish Foreign Policy in an Age of Uncertainty*, Santa Monica, CA: Rand, 2003, p. 142. See also Huseyn Bagci, "Turkish Foreign and Security Policy in 2000: A Retrospective," *Turkish Daily News*, December 25, 2000.
119 See the discussion in Stephen Larrabee and Ian Lesser, op. cit., pp. 142–3.
120 Personal interview with William Hale, August 4, 2005.
121 General Çevik Bir commented that during a trip to a European country he had met a group of European historians and security experts after the conclusion of the 1996 military cooperation agreement with Israel. One European security expert informed him that the agreement "negatively affects security and stability in the Middle East." He countered this opinion by stating that Turkey and Israel, by signing this agreement, transform themselves into the "security-producing" countries from the "security-consuming" countries. Personal interview with Çevik Bir, op. cit.
122 Personal interview with Feridun Sinirlioglu, April 26, 2005.
123 As quoted in Idris Bal, *The Rise and Fall of the Turkish Model*, Aldershot: Ashgate, 2001, p. 96.
124 Ibid. According to Elliot Hen-Tov, however, the Turkish intervention in the conflict and peacekeeping in Nagorno-Karabagh in 1994 was not forthcoming not due to a lack of will on the part of the Turkish military. It was ruled out due to the lack of military capability. See Elliot Hen-Tov, op. cit., p. 52.
125 Personal interviews with Çevik Bir and Brigade General Nogaylaroglu.
126 See Harun Yahya, *Israilin Kurt Karti*, op. cit.
127 See Ofra Bengio, op. cit., p. 125.
128 *Zerkalo*, June 28, 2002.
129 A. Alekperov and N. Aliyev, "Kurdy protiv Azerbaijana," *Zerkalo*, February, 2002. See also Gulnara Inanj, "Mnogie Kurdy podderzivauyt PKK," *Zavtra*, February 22, 2002. The Kurdish leadership in Iraq denied these allegations. See the interview with Yuri Nabiyev, deputy chairman of the Kurdiah Autonomy in Iraq and the representative in the CIS, "Nikakogo Kurdskogo Lobby v Azerbaijane Net," *Obozrevatel*, January 23, 2006. See also interview with Gulnara Inanj, op. cit.
130 See *Monitor*, No. 4, 2002; *Ekho*, January 8, 2002; *Zerkalo*, January 8, 2002.
131 Gordon Thomas, op. cit., p. 338.
132 Less so in the case of Turkey, since it is a fellow Muslim state and a member of such regional organizations as the Black Sea Economic Organization, the Economic Cooperation Organization, and, most importantly, the Organization of Islamic Conference.

133 Political and economic liberalization efforts of Turgut Ozal started to bear fruit.
134 See Stephen Larrabee and Ian Lesser, op. cit., p. 148.
135 Personal interview with Feridun Sinirlioglu, April 26, 2005.

6   Fluctuating zones of influence

1 See Gokhan Bacik, "The Limits of an Alliance: Turkish–Israeli Relations Revisited," *Arab Studies Quarterly*, Vol. 23, No. 3, Summer, 2001; Bulent Aras, "Turkish Foreign Policy and Jerusalem: Toward a Societal Construction of Foreign Policy," *Arab Studies Quarterly*, Vol. 22, No. 4, Fall, 2000; Bulent Aras, "The Impact of the Palestinian–Israeli Peace Process in Turkish Foreign Policy," *Journal of South Asian and Middle Eastern Studies*, Vol. 20, No. 2, Winter, 1997; Hakan Yavuz, "Turkish–Israeli Relations through the Lens of the Turkish Identity Debate," *Journal of Palestine Studies*, Vol. 27, No. 1, Autumn, 1997; Suha Bolukbasi, "Behind the Turkish–Israeli Alliance: A Turkish View," *Journal of Palestinian Studies*, Vol. 29, No. 1, Autumn, 1999; Dietrich Jung and Wolfgang Piccoli, "Turkish Israeli Alignment: Paronoia or Pragmatism?" *Security Dialogue*, Vol. 31, No. 1, 2000; Gregory Burris, "Turkey–Israel: Speed Bumps," *Middle East Quarterly*, Fall, 2003.
2 Personal communication from William Hale, August 4, 2005.
3 "Azerbaijan: Turning Over a New Leaf," *International Crisis Group*, ICG Europe Report, No. 156, May 13, 2004, pp. 11–15.
4 This view is expressed most comprehensively in Bernard Lewis, *The Emergence of Modern Turkey*, London: Oxford University Press, 1961.
5 Svetlana Lourie, *Istoricheskaya Ethnologia*, Moscow: Aspect Press, 1997.
6 K. Poznyanskya, *Staraya i Novaya Turtsiya*, Moscow: Nauka, 1974, p. 105. The Turkish author Makhmut Mekal, in his 1967 essay "Nothing New on the Eastern Front," wrote that when he asked a peasant woman who rules the country, she answered: "Sultan does. He lives either in Istanbul or Ankara." Quoted in ibid., p. 147.
7 Kemal Ataturk signed all official documents as "Gazi Mustafa Kemal Ataturk." Personal communication from Ayala Gol, April 14, 2007.
8 See the detailed discussion in Svetlana Lourie, op. cit., Chapter 10.
9 Hakan Yavuz, op. cit., p. 52.
10 Ibid.
11 Bernard Lewis, op. cit., p. 55.
12 John L. Esposito, *Unholy War: Terror in the Name of Islam*, Oxford and New York: Oxford University Press, 2002, p. 147; see also Sami Zubaida, "Turkish Islam and National Identity," *Middle East Report*, No. 199, April–June, 1996, p. 11.
13 Anthony Shadid, *Legacy of the Prophet*, Boulder, CO: Westview Press, 2002, p. 146; see also Urtugrul Kurkcu, "The Crisis of Turkish State," *Middle East Report*, No. 199, April–June, 1996, p. 5; Gilles Kepel, *Jihad: Ekspania I Zakat Islamizma*, Moscow: Ladomir, 2004 (Russian translation by V. Denisov), pp. 326–7.
14 Muammer Kaylan, *The Kemalists*, Amherst, NY: Prometheus Books, 2005, p. 305.
15 Ibid., p. 22.
16 For details about the switch from the Anavatan core electorate to Refah Party after the death of Turgut Ozal in 1993, see Gilles Kepel, op. cit., pp. 326, 330.
17 AK Party's decision to officially define itself as a "conservative democratic" party is politically expedient. In accordance with the Turkish Constitution, no party can publicly espouse religion. So instead of calling itself an "Islamic democratic" party modeled after European "Christian democratic" parties, AK Party chose the "conservative" democracy label. Cf. William Hale, "The AKP and Christian Democracy," *Turkish Studies*, Vol. 6, No. 2, June, 2005. In fact, Erdogan used the term "Islamic Socialist" to describe his party during the 2002 National Elections. See Zvi Bar'el, "Winner Doesn't Take All," *Haaretz*, November 10, 2002.

18 The 1999 earthquake left 17,000 victims dead and more than 40,000 wounded. The devastation in Central Anatolia left 600,000 homeless.
19 Anthony Shadid, op. cit., pp. 142–5.
20 When participation of the AK Party in the national elections became unavoidable, Turkey's chief of staff, Hilmi Ozkok, declared in Ankara that "an Islamic fundamentalist threat exists in Turkey. But a threat will not be a threat where force exists. Fundamentalism and isolationism have existed since the period of the Ottoman Empire, and they multiply like mushrooms after rain." Quoted in Zvi Bar'el, "Winner Doesn't Take All," *Haaretz*, November 10, 2002.
21 Gökhan Bacik, "The Limits of an Alliance: Turkish–Israeli Relations Revisited," *Arab Studies Quarterly*, Vol. 23, Issue 3, Summer, 2001.
22 Ibid. See also Bulent Aras, "Turkish Foreign Policy and Jerusalem: Toward a Societal Construction of Foreign Policy," *Arab Studies Quarterly*, Vol. 22, No. 4, Fall, 2000, pp. 31–58.
23 Ibid.
24 Ibid.
25 Following the targeted killing of Hamas leader Sheikh Ahmad Yassin, Erdogan condemned Israel's "state terrorism." He has since repeated the charge on a number of occasions. During a May 2004 meeting with Israel's infrastructure minister, for example, Erdogan compared Israel's treatment of the Palestinians to the Spanish Inquisition. As the Israeli army moved to seal Palestinian weapons-smuggling tunnels, Erdogan declared Israel a "terrorist" state. See Michael Rubin, "Shifting Sides? The Problems of Neo-Ottomanism," *National Review Online*, August 10, 2004, available at: www.meforum.org/article/628.
26 Alexander Murinson, "The Strategic Depth Doctrine of Turkish Foreign Policy," *Middle Eastern Studies*, Vol. 42, No. 6, November, 2006, pp. 946–7.
27 Ibid.
28 Graham Fuller, "Turkey's Strategic Model: Myths and Realities," *The Washington Quarterly*, Summer, 2004, p. 59.
29 Personal communication from William Hale, August 4, 2005.
30 Azerbaijan demands an unconditional withdrawal of Armenian troops from all captured territories and restoration of full sovereignty over the Nagorno-Karabagh region.
31 Nagorno-Karabagh, about 12,000 square kilometers of Azerbaijani land, is under Armenian control—that is, about 14 percent of Azerbaijan (not 20 percent, as most Azerbaijanis, including Heydar Aliyev, insist). De Waal argued that it is important to get the facts right. "I don't think the Azerbaijanis would lose any friends if they suddenly started saying fourteen percent instead of twenty percent," he said. On the issue of refugees, de Waal stated that the total number is 750,000, not 1 million (again, as many assert). Tom De Waal, *Interview on the Nagorno-Karabagh Conflict*, July 13, 2003, available at http://bcsia.ksg.harvard.edu/publication.cfm?ctype=event_reports&item_id=75.
32 Personal interview with Gareth Winrow, May 23, 2004.
33 Personal communication from William Hale, August 4, 2005.
34 Personal interview with Elin Suleimanov, July 29, 2004.
35 Personal interview with William Hale, August 4, 2005.
36 Personal interview with Araz Azimov, August 3, 2004. See, for details, Emil Danielyan, "Turkey Nearly Opened Armenian Border in 2003," *Eurasia Insight*, April 2, 2005.
37 Michael Rubin, op. cit.
38 Editorial, *Arab News*, August 25, 2003.

39 Tansu Ciller, "Turkey: Today's Political and Economic Realities," *PolicyWatch* No. 534: Special Forum Report, Washington, DC, The Washington Institute for Near East Policy, May 15, 2001.

40 Ibid.

41 The initial agreement to supply Turkey with Iranian natural gas (or swapped Turkmen gas) for an amount of $21 billion was finalized by the Erbakan government in August 1996. See Philip Robins, *Suits and Uniforms*, op. cit., p. 228.

42 "Turkey's Iranian Relations Unaffected by US," July 29, 2004, available at www.turks.us/article.php?story=2004072906434730.

43 Ibid.

44 See Sami G. Hajjar, "The Israel–Syria Track," *Middle East Policy*, Vol. 6, No. 3, February, 1999.

45 Hilal Koylu, "Suriye ile mutlu gün," *Zaman*, January 7, 2004.

46 Aluf Benn and Amos Harel, "Turkish PM to Israel: Assad Serious about Renewing Talks," *Haaretz*, January 8, 2004.

47 Ibid.

48 Ibid.

49 "Turkey Won't be Israel–Syria Peacemaker," *Al-Jazeera*, February 18, 2004.

50 Lenore Martin, "Turkey's Middle East Foreign Policy," in Lenore Martin and Dimitris Keridis (Eds.), *The Future of Turkish Foreign Policy*, Cambridge, MA: MIT Press, 2004, p. 185.

51 The plan was frozen in November 2005.

52 Personal communication from Rachillya Geybullayeva, May 20, 2003.

53 Personal interview with Azer Rashidoglu, editor-in-chief of *Zerkalo* daily, August 2, 2004.

54 Personal interview with Eldar Namazov, July 29, 2004. In fact, during the 1990s Azerbaijan concluded 22 production-sharing agreements (PSAs) with multinational oil and gas companies. See Rena Safaraliyeva, *The Impact of Corruption on Business: Survey of South Caucasus Countries*, a Transparency International document, available at http://admin.corisweb.org/files/s51067259482.doc.

55 Hans Bodmer, the Swiss agent of the international investment consortium was indicted by a federal grand jury on August 5, 2003 in the Southern District of New York on conspiracy and money-laundering charges and was forced to pay $150 million in restitution. See US v. Bodmer (Cr. No. 03-947) SDNY, August, 2003, in Danforth Newcomb, *Digests of Cases Review Releases Relating to Bribes and to Foreign Officials under the Foreign Corrupt Practices of 1977 (as of November 4, 2004)*, Partner, Shearman & Sterling LLP, New York.

56 Personal interviews with Eldar Namazov, Azer Rashidoglu and Rauf Mirkadirov, July–August, 2004.

57 Interviews with Azer Rashidoglu and Eldar Namazov, July–August, 2004.

58 Personal interview with an anonymous employee of energy-engineering company Bateman Litwin, April 28, 2005. See also "Azerbaijan Eyes the West," *United Press International*, June 26, 2006. Available at: UPI/www.wpherald.com.

59 See Introduction to Dmitry Furman (Ed.), *Azerbaijan and Russia*, Moscow: Letny Sad, 2001.

60 "Azerbaijan: Turning Over a New Leaf," International Crisis Group, *ICG Europe Report*, No. 156, May 13, 2004, pp. 11–15.

61 See *Prayer Profile, The Azerbaijan of Russia*, available at www.global12project.com/2004/profiles/p_code/1019.htm.

62 Ibid. See also "Azerbaijan: Turning Over a New Leaf," op. cit.

63 According to Victor Shirelman, "It was territory, not the history, that until recently was of importance for the Azeris, who identified their homeland with their native

habitat (vatan) . . . Moreover, traditionally the Azeris most appreciated local bonds and associated primarily with some local area ('the minor Motherland'). Both of these factors embedded clans into political structure of the contemporary Azerbaijan." Victor Shirelman, *The Value of the Past: Myths, Identity and Politics in Trans-caucasia*, Senri Ethnological Studies 57, Osaka Museum of Ethnology, 2001. See also Furman and Abasov, op. cit.

64 Theodore Karasik, *Azerbaijan, Central Asia, and Future Persian Gulf Security*, Santa Monica, CA: Rand, 1993.

65 The status of Nakhichevan Autonomous Republic (ASSR) within Azerbaijan SSR was established in 1924. Nakhichevan used to be "connected" to the rest of Azerbaijan by the Zangezur district, which was given to Armenia in December 1920. Effectively, assigning this strip (46 km) to Armenia separated Azerbaijan in two sections, cutting off Turkey from the other Turkic-speaking peoples in Central Asia. Zangezur was continuously emptied of its indigenous Azeri Turk residents.

66 Tadeusz Swietochowski, "Azerbaijan: Perspectives from the Crossroads," *Central Asian Survey*, Vol. 18, No. 4, 1999, pp. 420–1. See also Farid Guliev, "Post-Soviet Azerbaijan: Transition to Sultanistic Semiauthoritarianism? An Attempt at Conceptualization," *Demokratizatsiya*, Summer, 2005.

67 See Rauf Mirkadirov, "Rano Trubit v Fanfary," *Zerkalo*, December 30, 2006.

68 Furman and Abasov, op. cit.

69 Thomas Dye advances a thesis about a relationship between the power elite and policymaking. Dye explains that policy is framed by the values and preferences of the power elite. So-called "decision-makers" knowingly or unknowingly implement policy that is based on the power elite's preferences. See Thomas Dye, Introduction to *Understanding Public Policy*, Upper Saddle River, NJ: Prentice Hall, 1987.

70 Sohbet Mamedov, "Spisok Tridzati: Samye Bogatye Lyudi Azerbaijana—ministry and rodstvinniki Aliyeva," *Novaya Gazeta*, April 28, 2005. Available at: www.ng.ru/cis/2005-04-28/5_spisok.html.

71 See *Azerbaijan*, report published by the Observatoire Geopolitique des Drogues, Paris. Available at www.ogd.org/rapport/gb/RP05_5_AZERBAIDJAN.html. See also Lowell Bezanis, "An Enlarged Golden Crescent," *Transitions*, Vol. 2, No. 19, September 20, 1996.

72 In fact, many members of the Turkish political establishment saw the return to power by Heydar Aliyev as illegitimate. Personal communication of William Hale. Also personal interview with Gokhmaz Asgarov, April 5, 2007.

73 Personal interview with Philip Remler, a US State Department official, who was involved in the opening of the US embassy in Baku in 1992, July 7, 2005.

74 Opposition sources claim that during his tenure as a KGB intelligence officer, Heydar Aliyev was instrumental in founding the PKK. This Kurdish Stalinist-type movement was founded under the Soviet "umbrella" in Damascus in 1978. See Tom de Waal, op. cit; also personal interviews with Rauf Mirkadirov and Qanimat Zahidov, July 30, 2004.

75 Interviews with Azerbaijani journalists, August, 2004.

76 Personal communication from an expert on the ethno-political situation in Azerbaijan, Anna Zelkina, April 19, 2003.

77 Personal interview with Rauf Mirkadyrov, August 5, 2004.

78 Interview with Azerbaijani journalists, Baku, August, 2004. Also interview with Gokhmaz Asgarov, April 5, 2007.

79 "Kurdish Networks in Azerbaijan," *Newswire*, January 22, 2003. Available at: www.anca.org/resource_center/transcaucasus.php?trid=36.

80 Newspaper *Ekho* editorialized: "During this week's visit to Azerbaijan, Erdogan complained that Kurdish militants continued to be based in Azerbaijan under the guise

of various cultural organizations." See *Monitor*, No. 4, 2003; *Ekho*, January 8 and 9, 2003; "Armenia Report," *Radio Free Europe/Radio Liberty*, January 8, 2003; *Zerkalo*, January 8, 2003.

81 Suleyman Demirel promoted interests of Turkish companies using his personal contacts with Heydar Aliyev and his protégés. In particular, Demirel was involved in negotiating the exclusive contract of Barmek, a Turkish energy and electricity supplier that controls a large part of the electric grid of Baku and its suburbs. Interview with Eldar Namazov, July 29, 2004.

82 Interview with Eldar Namazov, ibid.

83 Personal interview with Vafa Guluzade, August 5, 2004.

84 Personal interviews with Vafa Guluzade, Eldar Namazov and Efraim Inbar.

85 Personal interviews with Tahir Taghi-zade (Tagiyev), deputy counsel of the mission, Azerbaijani embassy in Washington, DC, February 23, 2004, and Yakov Finkelstein, deputy counsel of the mission, Israeli embassy, Baku, August 3, 2004.

86 Mirkadyrov stated that in 2004, according to official estimates, 60 percent of energy resources in Azerbaijan, in particular oil, is lost during transportation. He further indicated that according to Azerbaijani oil experts, such a high rate of loss of energy resources is highly unlikely and this oil output in chronically under-reported in official statistics. The atmosphere of widespread graft and corruption is very conducive to such illegal operations. Interview with Rauf Mirkadyrov, July 29, 2004. See also Lala Shoket Gadzjieva, "Gruppa Kurdyukov: V Azerbaijane gosudarstvennaya ideologya est ideologiya korruptsii," May 19, 2007. Available at: http://forums.ng.ru/archive/part/www.ng.ru,cis,2006-12-25,6_aliev/411.

87 Ibid.

88 In fact, the ruling party's own paper, *Yeni Azerbaijan*, editorialized on Ilham's hereditary right and ability to take on the presidential role. According to the paper, the Aliyev genetic code "bears the hallmark of national patriarch." Rustam Seyidov, "Aliev [sic] Succession Race," available at http://lists.partners-intl.net/pipermail/women-in-war/2001-August/000445.html.

89 See Barak Salmoni "Electoral Survival of the Most Corrupt? Azerbaijan, Georgia, and American Regional Goals," *Strategic Insights*, a publication of the Naval Postgraduate School in Monterey, California, December 2, 2003, available at www.ccc.nps.navy.mil/rsepResources/si/dec03/russia.asp.

90 Guliev concludes: "As compared with pure semi-authoritarianism and pure sultanism, the new framework [in the Azerbaijani case] that combines the two has some significant advantages. Semi-authoritarianism is useful to explain more about formal institutions, whereas sultanism can be used to depict the informal dimension." Farid Guliev, "Post-Soviet Azerbaijan: Transition to Sultanistic Semi-authoritarianism? An Attempt at Conceptualization," *Demokratizatsiya*, Summer, 2005, p. 395.

91 Personal interview with Nasib Nasibli, August 6, 2004.

92 Personal interviews with Orxan Gafarli and Taleh Ziyadov, August, 2004. See a detailed account in Bayram Balci, "Between Sunnism and Shiism: Islam in Post-Soviet Azerbaijan," *Central Asian Survey*, June, 2004.

93 Dmitry Furman and Ali Abasov, "Azerbaijanskya Revolyutsia," in Dmitry Furman, op. cit.

94 Personal interview with Eldar Namazov, op. cit.

95 Ibid.

96 Personal interviews with Azer Rashidoglu and Qanimat Zahidov, July–August, 2004.

97 Lowell Bezanis, "Iran to Azerbaijan: No Ties to Israel," *Open Media Research Institute Daily Digest*, August 10, 1995.

98 The Azerbaycan Islam Partisi was founded in September of 1992 and closed down by state order in 1995. See Raul Motika, "Islamskie Seti v Azerbaijane," in Dmitry

Furman, op. cit. See also "ANS: Azerbaijani Security Official Accuses Iran, Some Arab Countries of 'Subversive' Activity," text of report, ANS TV, Baku, May 30, 2001.

 99 Personal interview with Qanimat Zahidov, July 30, 2004.
100 During meetings with their Iranian counterparts, the Azerbaijani officials accused Iran of supporting and financing Azeri Islamist groups aiming at creating a theocracy like the one in power in Teheran. See "Iran Protest to Baku over Oil Activities in the Aborz Area," *Iranian Press Service*, July 23, 2001.
101 Nardaran is a center of conservative Shii Islam in Azerbaijan, which has a medresse and the Rehime Khanim Mosque. The Rehime Khanim *pir*, or tomb, is located in this town. According to the Shii tradition, Rehime Khanim was a sister of Imam Reza. As an important center of the Shii pilgrimage, Nardaran attracted a population that was traditionally very religious and loyal to the religious authorities rather than the state. Interview with Anna Zelkina, April 15, 2003. For the chronology of the Nardaran events see http://mitglied.lycos.de/politzek/news/nardpubl.htm.
102 Personal interview with Qanimat Zahidov, July 30, 2004. Despite later denials, the leader of the Islamic Party of Azerbaijan, Alikram Aliev, reportedly confessed to receiving more than $40,000 in funds from Iranian intelligence operatives seeking to launch an uprising in Nardaran. See also Konul Khalilova, "Government Struggles to Defuse Discontent in Baku Suburb," *Eurasianet*, June 13, 2002. Available at: www.eurasianet.org/departments/insight/articles/eav061302.shtml.
103 Available at: www.anca.org/resource_center/transcaucasus.php?trid=36.
104 "Unrest in Nardaran," Overseas Security Advisory Council, Safety & Security Report, Azerbaijan, Bureau of Diplomatic Security, US Department of State, February 1, 2006, accessed May 1, 2006, available at www.osac.gov/Reports/report.cfm?contentID= 41830.
105 Konul Khalilova, op. cit.
106 Personal interview with Azer Rashidoglu, August 2, 2004.
107 Michael Smith remarked, "The eschatological tension of Maggeram helped to prepare the basis of historical self-conscioussness of Muslim Turks of Baku, their political mass mobilization and new national consciousness." Michael Smith, "Pamyat ob utratax I Azerbaijanskoe obshestvo" in Dmitry Furman, op. cit.
108 Ibid.
109 Personal interview with Azer Rashidoglu, August 2, 2004.
110 Alexander Murinson and Soner Cagaptay, op. cit.
111 "Iran Protest to Baku over Oil Activities in the Aborz Area," op. cit. See also "Azerbaijan Accuses Iran of Caspian Encroachment," *Reuters*, December 14, 1998.
112 "Iran Protest to Baku over Oil Activities in the Aborz Area," op. cit.
113 "Iran Bullies Israel's Strategic Friends—with Eye on Washington," *DEBKAfile Special Report*, August 22, 2004.
114 Irada Huseynova, "Prezidenstvo bolshe zhizni," a radio interview transcript with Tengiz Gudava (Kavkaz I Centralnaya Azia), *Radio Free Europe/Radio Liberty* broadcast, August 7, 2003. Available at: www.svoboda.org/programs/rtl/2003/rtl.080703.asp.
115 R. Gabiboglu, "Osnovniye Batalii Sostoysya v Budushem Godu," *Zerkalo*, January 2, 2003.
116 Ibid.
117 In a personal interview, Eldar Namazov also emphasized the fact of their service in the KGB as an important personal aspect of the relationship between the two leaders. Eldar Namazov, op. cit.
118 See Thomas de Waal, "Heidar Aliev: A Political Colossus," Institute for War and Peace Reporting report. See also Rufat Abbasov and Shahin Rzayev, "Azerbaijan Mourns Aliyev," available at www.mailarchive.com/archive@jab.org/msg55305.html.

119 See Chapter 5 of this volume. For details, see Alan Makovsky, "The New Activism in Turkish Foreign Policy," *SAIS Review*, Winter/Spring, 1999. Available at: www. washingtoninstitute.org/media/amakovsky/alansais.htm.
120 This issue remains the main obstacle today, because Israel is committed to preservation of the Jewish character of the state, which would be impossible if the majority of population of the state became Arab. (Especially after an infusion of 1.5–3 million refugees.)
121 See details "Propositions israéliennes, de Camp David (2000) à Taba (2001), Reconstruction," by *Le Monde Diplomatique*, accessed April 22, 2007. Available at: www. monde-diplomatique.fr/cartes/taba2001. There is controversy surrounding the conditions offered by the Israeli side. See, for example, "Exchange (1. An Interview with Ehud Barak)" and "Camp David and After: An Exchange (2. A Reply to Ehud Barak)," Hussein Agha and Robert Malley, *The New York Review of Books*, Vol. 49, No. 10, June 13, 2002.
122 The completion of the intergoverment agreement (IGA) and host government agreements (HGA) involved the signing of 4,500 pages of documentation. See Summary of the Baku-Tbilisi-Ceyhan Brookings Roundtable Event, The Brookings Institution, March 4, 2003. Available at: www.brookings.edu/dybdocroot/comm/events/20030304btc.pdf.
123 "Clinton Spends a Busy Day in Istanbul and Ephesus," US embassy press release, Tel Aviv, November 17, 1999. Available at: www.usembassy-israel.org/publish/peace/archives/1999/November/me1117c.html.
124 Personal interview with Araz Azimov, August 3, 2004.
125 Ibid. It is quite likely the leaders discussed the issues of strategic cooperation.
126 Sergey Minasian, "Israel–Turkey Strategic Cooperation in the Context of Regional Security Problems," *21 Century*, Vol. 2, No. 4, 2004, p. 100.
127 *Washington Times*, September 30, 1999.
128 This sight is holy to both Jews and Muslims. After Israel captured the Old City from Jordanians in 1967, General Moshe Dayan, as a sign of reconciliation and religious tolerance, left control of this site to the Islamic waqf.
129 Yuksel Soylemez, "A Paradise Lost: Palestinian and Israeli Friends," in *Issues and Opinions on Foreign Policy*, Ankara: Center for Strategic Research, December, 2002, p. 340. In fact, both Israelis and foreign tourists visit the site that in Jewish tradition is known as the Har HaBait ("The Temple Mount"). There is no international or Israeli law barring Israelis from visiting the site.
130 Ariel Sharon, who spent most of his professional career in the military, served as the minister of defense during the war in Lebanon (1982–3). For a detailed account, see Anita Miller, Jordan Miller and Sigalit Zetouni, *Sharon: Israel's Warrior-Politician*, Chicago, IL: Academy Chicago Publishers and Olive Publishing, 2002, pp. 157–77.
131 Ibid., pp. 301–2.
132 Ibid., p. 310.
133 For details of the diplomatic crisis caused by criticism of the Israeli treatment of Palestinians by Prime Minister Bulent Ecevit in 1999, see Chapter 4 of this volume.
134 *Middle East News Agency*, Cairo, October 26, 2000.
135 *Sharon: Israel's Warrior-Politician*, op. cit., p. 356.
136 Yuksel Soylemez, op. cit., p. 340.
137 *Jerusalem Post*, October 22, 2000; *Christian Century*, November 8, 2000.
138 Sharon quoted Bush as saying: "No one would have believed then that I would be president and you would be prime minister." Quoted in Sharon, op. cit., p. 350.
139 According to a *Jerusalem Post* report, when Ariel Sharon visited Ankara in 2001, he was greeted by crowds chanting "butcher of Palestine, go home!" *Jerusalem Post*, August 9, 2001.

140 Sahin Alpay told me: "Turkish people don't have any problems with Israeli people, but we have big problems with Sharon's policies." Personal interview with Sahin Alpay, May 22, 2004.

141 Most of these policymakers were authors of the policy document called "A Clean Break: A New Strategy for Securing the Realm." This document established the priority of building the Israeli–Turkish axis in the Middle East. See Chapter 4.

142 After the Israeli air strike against Jenin's government offices and the Palestinian police station in November 2001, the White House spokesman, Ari Flescher, stated: "Israel is a sovereign country and has a right to defend itself." *Jerusalem Post*, December 4, 2001.

143 Herb Keinon, "Turkish Ambassador to Return Thursday," *Jerusalem Post*, June 10, 2004.

144 Personal communication from Araz Azimov, op. cit.

145 "Turk PM Blames Israel for Rising Anti-Semitism," *Reuters*, June 15, 2004. Jean-Christophe Peuch concluded: "Two years after then-Turkish prime minister Bulent Ecevit accused Israel of conducting a policy of 'genocide' against the Palestinians, relations between the two countries are once again under strain. Prime Minister Ecevit's successor, Recep Tayyip Erdogan, has in recent days condemned as 'state terror' Israel's heavy-handed policy in the Palestinian territories." Jean-Christophe Peuch, "Turkey: Prime Minister's Criticism of Israel Does Not Mark Shift in Policy," *Radio Free Europe/Radio Liberty*, June 10, 2004.

146 Herb Keinon, op. cit.

147 "Turkish Envoys Summoned in Israel," *Sabah*, June 11, 2004; "Turkey Summons Diplomats in Israel for Information," *Turkiye*, June 11, 2004.

148 According to a personal communication from Alan Makovsky, one of the key foreign policy advisors of Prime Minister Erdogan commented slyly to him that "Erdogan's anti-Israeli speech" tipped support of the Organization of Islamic Conference in favor of the Turkish candidate for the post of secretary-general of this organization. Personal communication from Alan Makovsky, September 12, 2006.

149 Personal interview with Soli Ozel, May 24, 2004.

150 Personal interview with Soner Cagaptay, March 17, 2004.

151 Gregory Burris, "The Turkish Israeli Entente and Potential Mines in Its Path," *The Progressive Conservative*, Vol. 5, No. 288, November 29, 2003.

152 See Yigal Schleifer, "One of the Kurds' Leaders Is Jewish? So They Claim in Turkish Newspapers," *The Jewish Telegraphic Agency*, April 7, 2004, available at: www.jta.org/story.asp?id=030407-kurd.

153 In the 1960s and 1970s, Israel supplied Kurdish militants, who waged a guerrilla struggle against the central regime in Baghdad, with military hardware and training in Iraq. However, according to Gregory Burris, after Iraq signed a pact with Iran in 1975, Israel ceased its support of Iraqi Kurds. See Gregory Burris, op. cit.; see also Yossi Alpher, "Hard Questions, Tough Answers," July 21, 2003. Available at: www. bitterlemons.org.

154 See Burris, *The Progressive Conservative*, op. cit.

155 Soner Cagaptay, "Fixing Turkish–Israeli Relations," *Haaretz*, July 22, 2004. Available at: www.Haaretz.com/hasen/spages/454487.html. See also Gokhan Bacik, "The Limits of an Alliance: Turkish–Israeli Relations Revisited," *Arab Studies Quarterly*, Summer, 2001, p. 55.

156 "Israel's Shifting Geopolitical Security Concerns Threaten Its Relationship with Turkey," *Le Figaro*, September 3, 2004.

157 Ibid. See also Sadi Baig, "A Clean Break for Israel," *Asia Times*, June 30, 2004, available at: www.atimes.com/atimes/Middle_East/FF30AK07.html; Justin Raimondo "The Stab in the Back: Israel Plays the Kurdish Card—and Americans Are Caught

in the Crossfire," June 23, 2004; available at: www.antiwar.com/justin/?article4
=2859; Annete Young, "Israel and Turkey Fall Out over Palestinian Crackdown,"
Scotsman, July 4, 2004.

158 Seymour Hersh, "Plan B," *The New Yorker*, June 28, 2004. See also K. Gajendra
Singh, "Turkey and the Great Game in the North of Iraq," *Turkish Daily News*,
July 5, 2004.
159 Gajendra Singh, ibid.
160 Quoted in Singh, ibid.
161 Binnaz Toprak, "Religion as State Ideology in a Secular Setting: The Turkish–Islamic
Synthesis," in Malcolm Wagstaff (Ed.), *Aspects of Religion in Secular Turkey*,
Durham: University of Durham, Center for Middle Eastern and Islamic Studies,
Occasional Paper Series, No. 40, 1990, pp. 10–15; Ely Karmon, "Radical Islamic
Political Groups in Turkey," *Middle East Review of International Affairs*,
Vol. 1, No. 4, December, 1997, passim.
162 *Le Figaro*, op. cit.
163 For example, Mustafa Kibaroglu wrote: "While Turkey fears the emergence of an
independent Kurdish state in northern Iraq, the same possibility seems favorable for
Israel from its security standpoint, vis-à-vis threats posed by countries like Iran,
Pakistan, and beyond. It appears that the 'amazing alliance' is heading toward a
crossroads. Such an eventuality may change the nature of the relationship from a 'win-
win' to a 'lose-lose' situation unless proper steps are rapidly taken with a view toward
rebuilding confidence on both sides." Mustafa Kibaroglu, "Clash of Interest over
Northern Iraq Drives Turkish–Israeli Alliance to a Crossroads," *The Middle East
Journal*, Vol. 59, No. 2, Spring, 2005.
164 See *Le Figaro*, op. cit. See also Ziya Önis and Suhnaz Yilmaz, "The Turkey–EU–US
Triangle in Perspective: Transformation or Continuity?" *The Middle East Journal*,
Vol. 59, No. 2, Spring, 2005.
165 Gregory Burris, op. cit.
166 Tolga Akiner, "Erdoganin ziareti ilerdi," *Radikal*, May 1, 2005; "Diyalog Israil'ile
var," *Radikal*, May 2, 2005. See also an analysis in K. Gajendra Singh, "Erdogan in
Israel to Repair Damaged Relations," *Asia Times*, April 30, 2005.
167 "Turkey's Prime Minister on Landmark Visit to Israel," *Haaretz*, May 1, 2005.
168 On corruption in Azerbaijan, see "The Impact of Corruption on Business: Survey of
South Caucasus Countries," op. cit.
169 For example, former physicist Hafiz Pashayev, who served for 13 years as Azerbaijani
ambassador to the United States, is an uncle of Mahriban Aliyeva, the wife of Ilham
Aliyev. Personal interview with Qanimat Zahidov, July 30, 2004.
170 Igor Torbakov, "Aliyev's Illness Underscores Leadership Conundrum in Azerbaijan,"
EurasiaNet, May 1, 2003.
171 Personal communication from Robert Freedman, May 31, 2005.
172 According to Robert Freedman, "Heydar Aliyev realized that he does not need the
Israeli channel to achieve his foreign policy goals. Personal meeting with President
Bill Clinton at the Istanbul summit [in November of 1999] confirmed his calculations." Personal communication from Robert Freedman, May 31, 2005.
173 Personal interview with Efraim Inbar, April 10, 2005.
174 Personal interview with Sultan Malikov, May 26, 2006. See also Tani Goldstein,
"Israel–Azerbaijan Strategic Alliance in Cards?" *Yediot Achranot*, June 19, 2006,
available at: www.ynetnews.com/articles/0,7340,L-321778,00.html; Fariz Ismailzade,
"Azerbaijanis Take Sides in Israeli–Lebanese War," *Eurasia Daily Monitor*, James-
town Foundation, August 14, 2006.
175 Fariz Ismailzade, ibid.

7 Conclusion

1 Feroz Ahmad, "The Historical Background of Turkey's Foreign Policy," in Lenore Martin and Dimitris Keridis (Eds.), *The Future of Turkish Foreign Policy*, Cambridge, MA: MIT Press, 2004, p. 180.

2 Bulent Aras, "Turkish Foreign Policy and Jerusalem: Toward a Societal Construction of Foreign Policy," *Arab Studies Quarterly*, Fall, 2000, p. 14.

3 Among external factors, I would identify the following: the Islamic Republic of Iran and the Russian Federation with its satellite, Armenia; the domestic actors are radical Islamist movements, e.g. Shia extremists from Iran, Wahhabists (and Salafi networks) and Hezballah in Azerbaijan, Al-Qaeda and other Islamist networks in Turkey, and Hamas and Palestinian Islamic Jihad in Israel; and ethno-national militant movements, e.g. Kurdish PKK in Turkey, the self-proclaimed Armenian Republic of Artsakh (Nagorno-Karabagh), and Talysh and Lezgin separatist movements in Azerbaijan, as well as the Palestinian PLO, which replaced Hamas after the Oslo Peace Accord of 1993, in Israel.

4 Shadow state is defined here as a system of informal networks, which represent security, political, mass media and economic elites, that aggregates interests of different interest groups.

5 Such a situation is not that unusual in recent history, as precedents in France (the period of cohabitation) and the unity government in Israel, when Yitzhak Shamir (Likud) was the prime minister and Yitzhak Rabin (Labor) was the foreign minister, would indicate. See particularly Bulent Aras, "Turkish Foreign Policy and Jerusalem," *Arab Studies Quarterly*, Fall, 2000, p. 125. See also Philip Robins, *Turkish–Israeli Relations*, op. cit., p. 14.

6 Personal interview with George Perlman, executive vice-president, American–Turkish Council, April 12, 2005.

7 According to the estimates provided by Hen-Tov, the Turkish military allocated for this modernization program $25–$30 billion for the first eight to ten years and is expected to spend a total $150 billion within the next 30 years. See Elliot Hen-Tov, "The Political Economy of Turkish Military Modernization," *MERIA*, Vol. 8, No. 4, Article 5, December, 2004, available at http://meria.idc.ac.il/journal/2004/issue4/jv8no4a5.html.

8 Despite the rhetoric of commitment to human rights, the United States remained the main supplier, providing about 80 percent of Turkey's military requirements. Over the past decade (up to 1995), the US Congress has appropriated $5.3 billion in military aid (grants and loans to purchase weapons) for Turkey. Other Western countries, including the UK, Belgium, Netherlands, France, Germany, Italy, Portugal and Spain, supplied Turkey with a variety of advanced weapons systems. See "The Arming of Turkey," available at http://home.clara.net/heureka/sunrise/tr-arms2.htm.

9 Gregory Burris, "Turkey–Israel: Speed Bumps," *Middle East Quarterly*, Fall 2003, pp. 2–3, available at www.meforum.org/article/569.

10 Modern Turkish uses Latin script, which enhances its communication value for the Western world.

11 David Newsom, "Foreign Policy Lobbies and Their Influence," available at www.cosmos-club.org/web/journals/1995/newsom.html. Also personal interview with Charlie Flickner, August 22, 2004.

12 According to Thomas Risse-Kappen, "Transgovernmental networks among states in sub-units of national governments etc. frequently pursue their own agenda, independently from sometimes even contrary to the declared policies of their national government." Thomas Risse-Kappen, Introduction to *Bringing Transnational Relations Back In*, Cambridge: Cambridge University Press, 1995, p. 4.

13 Matthew E. Berger, "Turkish Leader Stresses Strong Ties with Israel in Meeting with US Jews," *Jewish Telegraphic Agency*, December 10, 2002.

14 Obviously, as a relative newcomer, Azerbaijan developed its strategic relationship with the United States later than the other two states. It occurred when the United States advanced a new strategy toward the South Caucasus, approximately in 1995. This strategic commitment by the United States to the independence and security of Azerbaijan was reiterated at the 1999 OSCE Conference in Istanbul on November 8, 1999. "Armenia, Azerbaijan, and Georgia: Security Issues and Implications for US Interests," *CRS Report for Congress*. Available at: www.fas.org/sgp/crs/row/RL30679.pdf.

15 This region includes Russia, the Caucasus and Central Asia.

16 Personal interview with Elin Suleymanov, Baku, August 5, 2004.

17 An international journalist concludes about the Turkish–Israeli relationship: "[I]t is ironic that relations between Turkey and Israel have never been better. The former is ruled by yet another Islamic government—though constrained by secular-minded generals. The latter is increasingly nationalistic–Messianic and theocratic—though its newly elected prime minister, a former army general, Ariel Sharon, has just put together a largely secular coalition government." Sam Vaknin, "Turkey's Jewish Friend," *United Press International*, May 5, 2003, available at www.upi.com/view.cfm?StoryID=20030304-052556-4873r.

18 "Cakmakoglu: Turkey to Modernize M60 Tanks Together With Israel," *FBIS Transcribed Text*. Available at: www.state.gov/g/drl/rls/irf/2003/24344.htm.

19 Zvi Bar'el, "Friend, and Friend of Foe," *Haaretz*, April 1, 2005.

20 Efraim Inbar confirmed this forecast in personal communication in April of 2007. See also Michel Chossudovsky, "'Triple Alliance': The US, Turkey, Israel and the War on Lebanon," *Global Research*, available at www.globalresearch.ca/index.php?context=viewArticle&code=CHO20060806&articleId=2906.

21 Alexander Murinson, "The Impact of American Foreign Policy after 9.11 on the October 2003 Presidential Elections in Azerbaijan," *Insight Turkey*, April/June, 2004.

22 Ozdem Sanberk suggested that if Turkey had realized its "Turkic world" policy and gained a solid foothold in Azerbaijan and Central Asia in the late 1990s, this would have tremendously increased the strategic value of Turkey to the EU. He argues that unfulfilled diplomatic gain in the NIS, in fact, stymied the pursuit of European membership. Personal interview with Ambassador Ozdem Sanberk, May 26, 2004.

23 As quoted in Benjamin Schwarz, "Will Israel Live to 100?" *The Atlantic Monthly*, May, 2005, p. 30.

24 Ibid.

25 Michel Chossudovsky, op. cit.

26 Israel pioneered Harpy UAVs systems. After 1999, Turkey purchased more than 100 Harpies. See Israeli Defense Industry at www.israeli-weapons.com/weapons/aircraft/phalcon/Phalcon.html.

27 Gökhan Çetinsaya, "Turkey's Stature as a Middle Eastern Power," Lecture, Conference, Turkish–Israeli Relations in a Trans-Atlantic Context: Wider Europe and the Greater Middle East, The Moshe Dayan Center for Middle Eastern and African Studies, Tel Aviv University, April 22–3, 2004.

28 Yoav Karny, "Horef Turki," *Globes*, January 9, 2003.

29 Alon Liel, *Demo-Islam: Mishtar Hadash b'Turkiya* ("Demo-Islam: The New Regime in Turkey") (Hebrew), Tel Aviv: Am Oved, 2003, p. 214.

30 Quoted in ibid.

Bibliography and sources

Interviews

Alpay, Sahin, journalist, *Zaman*, May 22, 2004.

Azimov, Anar, an independent advisor to the Ministry of Foreign Affairs, Baku, August 4, 2004.

Azimov, Araz, deputy minister of foreign affairs, Baku, August 3, 2004.

Ben-Ami, Shlomo, former minister of foreign affairs (1999–2000), February 6, 2003.

Benanyarly, Saadat, chairwoman, the Azerbaijan National Group of ISHR, Baku, August 2, 2004.

Bilhan, Murat, chairman, Center for Strategic Research, Ministry of Foreign Affairs, Ankara, August 15, 2005.

Bir, Çevik, former deputy chief of Turkey's general staff, May 26, 2004.

Braun, Peggy, assistant to the ambassador, embassy of the United States, Baku, August 2, 2004.

Bulukbasi, Suha, Professor, International Relations Department, Middle Eastern Technical University, Ankara, August 13, 2005.

Cagaptay, Soner, director, Turkish research program, The Washington Institute for Near East Policy, Washington, DC, May 6, 2004.

Candar, Cengiz, journalist and former advisor to prime minister Turgut Ozal, *The New Anatolian*, Istanbul, August 12, 2005.

Cohen, Gilad, a former spokesman of the Israeli embassy, 3rd political officer in Ankara (1999–2001), March 8, 2003.

Enginsoy, Umit, Washington bureau chief, *NTV*, May 22, 2006.

Erkul, Vakur, head of department, Ministry of Foreign Affairs, Ankara, May 26, 2004.

Flickner, Charlie, former staff member, US Congress, Washington, DC, August 22, 2004.

Finkelstein, Yaakov, second secretary, embassy of Israel, Baku, August 3, 2004.

Gasimoglu, Nariman, Azerbaijani academic and the modern translator of Quran into Azerbaijani language, August 5, 2004.

Gheybulayeva, Rahiliya, Professor of Azerbaijani literature, Azerbaijani National Academy of Science, London, May 4, 2003.

Guluzade, Vafa, former foreign policy chief advisor to three Azerbaijani prime ministers (1992–9) and the head of the American Caspian Political Studies Foundation, Baku, August 5, 2004.

Hashon, Immanuel, deputy counselor of the mission, embassy of Israel, Ankara, Ankara, May 27, 2004.

Habif, Yola, Turkish expert, Jewish Institute for National Security Affairs, Washington, DC, April 14, 2004.

Huseynov, Emin, correspondent, *Turan News Agency*, Baku, August 3, 2004.

Ibrahimli, Haleddin, political expert, former member of the Supreme Council of the Azerbaijani Popular Front and the chairman of the Foreign Relations Commission, Professor of the Kafkaz University, Baku, August 6, 2004.

Ikhilov, Semyon Borisovich, head of Azerbaijani Mountain Jews community, Baku, August 1, 2004.

Inan, Gurkan, admiral (ret.), Ankara, May 26, 2004.

Inbar, Efraim, director, the Begin-Sadat Center for Strategic Studies (BESA), Bar-Ilan University, Ramat-Gan, February 9, 2004.

Jacobs, Barry, director of strategic studies in the Office of Government and International Affairs, American Jewish Committee, Washington, DC, March 18, 2004.

Jafaroglu-Appelbaum, Novella, chairwoman, the Aliyeva Association for the Protection of Women's Rights, Baku, August 5, 2004.

Jenkins, Gareth, journalist, Istanbul, August 11, 2005.

Karny, Yoav, Israeli journalist and author, *Globes*, July 20, 2006.

Rabbi Kishon, Moshe (Israel), Baku, July 31, 2004.

Kodaloglu, Aydan, member of the Turkish–American Business Council, CEO, Akgroup, Ankara, May 26, 2004.

Landau, Jacob, Professor Emeritus of Turkish studies, The Hebrew University of Jerusalem, Jerusalem, April 26, 2005.

Liel, Alon, former chargé d'affaires in Ankara, deputy director of the Middle East section of the Ministry of Foreign Affairs (1984–6), Israeli ambassador to Turkey, policy advisor to Prime Minister Barak (1999–2000), director general of the Ministry of Foreign Affairs (1980–7), April 27, 2005.

Malikov, Sultan, first secretary, embassy of Azerbaijan, Washington, DC, May 3, 2005.

Makovsky, Alan, a senior staff member on the US House Committee on International Relations, Washington, DC, February 28, 2004.

Mamadova, Aybeniz, program assistant, International Republican Institute, August 6, 2004.

Mammedov, Eldjan, journalist, *Express*, Baku, August 6, 2004.

Mariaschin, Daniel, executive vice-president, B'nai Brith International, Washington, DC, March 10, 2005.

McClelland, Caryn, chief, political-economic section, embassy of the United States, Baku, August 2, 2004.

Mirkadirov, Rauf, senior editorial writer, *Zerkalo*, Baku, August 2, 2004.

Mollazade, Asim, MP, chairman, Democratic Reforms Party, Washington, DC, November 20, 2007.

Mollazde, Jeyhun, political analyst, The Cambridge Energy Group, Washington, DC/ Boston, January 23, 2004.

Nachmani, Amikam, Professor, Bar-Ilan University, Ramat-Gan, April 27, 2005.

Namazov, Eldar, former chief advisor to President Heydar Aliyev, president, Public Forum for Azerbaijan, Baku, July 29, 2004.

Nasibli, Nasib, president, Foundation of Azerbaijani Studies, Baku, August 6, 2004.

Nayan, Yekta, deputy directorate, Ministry of Foreign Affairs, Ankara, May 26, 2004.

Nogaylaroglu, Bertan, Turkish armed forces and air attaché, embassy of the Republic of Turkey, Washington, DC, June 2, 2006.

Ozel, Soli, professor, Department of International Relations, Bilgi University, Istanbul, May 24, 2004.

Ozeren, Enver, president, Cag Education Corporation, Baku, August 5, 2005.

Pamir, Necdet, chairman, Strategic Economic Research Center, Ankara, May 23, 2004.

Perlman, George, executive vice-president, American–Turkish Council, Washington, DC, April 12, 2005.

Remler, Philip, former acting ambassador in Azerbaijan and US chargé d'affaires in Tbilisi, Washington, DC, July 7, 2005.

Rashidoglu, Azer, editor-in-chief, *Zerkalo*, Baku, August 2, 2004.

Rubin, Barry, director, Global Research in International Affairs, Herzlia, April 29, 2005.

Ambassador Sanberk, Ozdem, Turkish diplomat and a former secretary-general, Ministry of Foreign Affairs, Ankara, May 26, 2004.

Sayari, Sabri, executive director, Institute of Turkish Studies, Georgetown University, Washington, DC, January 12, 2004.

Shalom, Zaki, Professor, The Ben-Gurion University, Beer-Sheva, Israel, May 29, 2005.

Shlein-Michael, Eynat, first counselor, embassy of Israel, Washington, DC, February 5, 2005.

Sinirlioglu, Feridun, ambassador, embassy of the Republic of Turkey, Tel-Aviv, April 27, 2005.

Soysal, Engin, first counselor, embassy of the Republic of Turkey, Washington, DC, February 16, 2004 and October 29, 2004.

Suleymanov, Elin, currently the Azerbaijani Consul-General, Los Angeles, Baku, August 5, 2004.

Taghi-zade, Tahir, political counselor, embassy of the Republic of Azerbaijan, Washington, DC, June 15, 2004.

Tashan, Seyfi, director, Turkish Foreign Policy Institute, Ankara, May 27, 2004.

Tezel, Yonet, head of Policy Planning Section, Ministry of Foreign Affairs, Ankara, May 26, 2004.

Tezgor, Ertan, deputy plenipotentiary for the Caucasus and Central Asia, Ministry of Foreign Affairs, Ankara, May 26, 2004.

Trepetin, Boris, a former Soviet Azerbaijani academic and a high Communist Party official, Baltimore, February 27, 2005.

Ulsever, Cuneyt, journalist, *Hurriyet*, Ankara, April 22, 2004.

Weissman, Keith, deputy director, Foreign Policy Issues, AIPAC, Washington, DC, May 13, 2004.

Winrow, Gareth, Professor, Department of International Relations, Bilgi University, Istanbul, May 26, 2004.

Zahidov, Qanimat, editor-in-chief, *Azadliq*, Baku, July 30, 2004.

Ziyadov, Taleh, Azerbaijan-American Chamber of Commerce, Washington, DC.

Personal memoirs and biographies

Ben-Gurion, David, *Anachnu ve Skheneinu* ("We and Our Neighbors") (in Hebrew), Tel Aviv: Davar, no date.

Kayalan, Muammer, *The Kemalists: Islamic Revival and the Fate of Secular Turkey*, Amherst, NY: Prometheus Books, 2005.

Mango, Andrew, *Ataturk: The Biography of the Founder of Turkey*, Woodstock, NY: Overlook, 2002.

Pearlman, Moshe, *Ben-Gurion Looks Back*, New York: Simon & Schuster, 1965.

Soylemez, Yuksel, *Issues and Opinions on Foreign Policy, Center for Strategic Research*, Ankara, December, 2002.

Bibliography and sources

Questionnaires

Academics and intellectuals
College students

Reports, unpublished papers and government documents

President Heydar Aliyev's Address to the Buyuk Milli Meclis ("the Great National Assembly"), the Turkish parliament, Ankara, February 9, 1994.
President Heydar Aliyev's Address at the Israeli embassy in Baku, May 11, 2000.
President Heydar Aliyev's Address on the Occasion of the 24th Anniversary of Islamic Revolution in Iran, Iranian embassy, Baku, February 12, 2003.
Armenian National Committee of America "2002 Congressional Outreach Campaign Continues with Rep. Berman Meeting," press release, January 15, 2002.
Kazim Azimov, "Internal and External Dimensions of the Ethnic Conflict in the Caucasus," transcript of an unpublished Event Report, June 28, 2001.
Baku-Tbilisi-Ceyhan Pipeline Project: Between Two Seas, a BTC publication, June, 2002.
General Çevik Bir, "Reflections on Turkish–Israeli Relations and Turkish Security," *PolicyWatch*, No. 422, November 5, 1999, WINEP.
Statement by Prime Minister Tansu Ciller, The Compliment of Directorate General of Press and Information, October 9, 1995.
Ursula Beyreuther, "Pipeline Diplomacy," a report, Deutsche Morgan Grenfell, January 1, 1998.
"Azerbaijan: Turning Over a New Leaf," International Crisis Group (Brussels), *ICG Europe Report*, No. 156, May 13, 2004.
"Silk Road Legislation Passes US Senate Tonight," press release, Office of Senator Sam Brownback. Source: http://brownback.senate.gov/pressapp/record.cfm?id=175947&, June 30, 1999.
Declaration of Establishment of the State of Israel. From Israel Ministry of Foreign Affairs website: www.mfa.gov.il/mfa/go.asp?MFAH00hb0.
Ariel Dloomy, *"Civil–Military Relations in Israel,"* unpublished paper, SOAS, 2002.
US Secretary of State John Foster Dulles's papers of June 1, 1953, J.C. Hurewitz, *Diplomacy in the Middle East and the Near East: A Documentary Record, 1914–1956*, Princeton, NJ: Van Nostrand Company, 1956, pp. 337–42.
Andreas Gross and Guillermo Martinez Casan, "Functioning of Democratic Institutions in Azerbaijan," Report of Committee on the Honouring of Obligations and Commitments by Member States of the Council of Europe (Monitoring Committee), Doc. 10030, January 12, 2004.
Manfred Hafner, "Future Natural Gas Supply Options and Supply Costs," Observatoire Mediterraneen de l'Energie. Source: europa.eu.int/comm/energy/gas/ workshop_2002/ doc/external_commission/10.pdf.
Assistant Secretary of State for European Affairs Richard Holbrooke, Richard Holbrooke, A Statement before the House International Relations Committee, March 9, 1995.
Internal Revenue Service Code, available at www.irs.gov/charities/charitable/article/0,id= 96099,00.html.
"Turkey and Israel to Cooperate on Security: Common Threats to be Met with Complementary Capabilities," Briefing by General Çevik Bir, deputy chief of the Turkish general staff, JINSA, Washington, DC, February–March, 1996. Source: www.jinsa.org/articles/ articles.html/function/view/categoryid/102/documentid/281/history/3,2360,102,281.

"Turks and Jews Enjoy Solid Friendship," The Assembly of Turkish American Associations and the Jewish Institute for National Security Affairs, Newsletter No. 1, May, 2002.

"JINSA Hosts Israel–US–Turkey Conference," transcript. Source: www.ataa.org/observer/obs_may02.html.

A Quarterly Review of Cooperation: US, Turkey and Israel, a publication of The Jewish Institute for National Security Affairs (JINSA) and The Assembly of Turkish American Associations, November 13, 2003.

Mehmet Komurcu, "Water Disputes in the Middle East," unpublished LL.M. thesis, University of Wisconsin Law School.

Bruce Kuniholm, "European Union: Differences in European and American Attitudes, and the Challenges for Turkey's Accession to the European Union," *Working Papers Series*, SANO 1–24, January, 2001.

Bruce Kuniholm and Ian Lesser, "Turkish–Israeli Relations during the Cold War," Lecture at the Conference The History of Turkish–American Relations, Bogazici University, Harran University and Public Affairs, June 4–10, 2006.

Andrew McAuslan, "Caspian Oil Windfalls: Who Will Benefit?" Conference Report, the Open Society Institute and the Center for Strategic and International Studies, May 13, 2003.

Necdet Pamir, "Turkey: The Key to Caspian Oil and Gas," IASPS Research Paper in Strategy. Source: www.iasps.org.il.

A letter of support for Silk Road Strategy Act, June 29, 1999, personal archive.

"The Gülen Schools: A Perfect Compromise or Compromising Perfectly?," Anne Solberg, Conference paper at Religion in Schools: Problems of Pluralism in the Public Sphere, Kotor, April 23–4, 2005, available at www.kotor-network.info/papers/2005/Gulen.Soberg.htm.

"An Example to Mankind" by US Congressman Stephen Solarz, Extension of Remarks, September 17, 1990. Source: http://thomas.loc.gov/cgi-bin/query/z?r101:E17SE0-25.

Study Group on "A New Israeli Strategy Toward 2000," *A Clean Break: A New Strategy for Securing the Realm.* Source: www.israeleconomy.org/strat1.htm.

"A Turkish Story," a lecture by Richard Perle, unpublished text, The First Annual Robert Strausz-Hupé Lecture, *FPRI Wire*, Vol. 7, No. 11, September, 1999.

Turkey and the Southern Caucasus Conference Proceedings, Turkish embassy, London, 2001.

Turkish embassy, Washington, DC, "Ambassador's Meeting with the Representatives from Various Jewish American Organizations," transcript, April 9, 2002. Source: www.turkishembassy.org/pressreleases/arsiv/200204.htm.

US Congress, H.CON.RES.437, *Recognizing the Republic of Turkey for its cooperation in the campaign against global terrorism, for its commitment of forces and assistance to Operation Enduring Freedom and subsequent missions in Afghanistan, and for initiating important economic reforms to build a stable and prosperous economy in Turkey.* Source: http://thomas.loc.gov/cgi-bin/bdquery/z?d107:HC00437:@@@L&summ2=m&.

US Department of State, Overseas Security Advisory Council, Safety & Security Report: Unrest in Nardaran, Azerbaijan, Bureau of Diplomatic Security, February 1, 2006. Accessed May 1, 2006.

"Turkey as an Energy Transit State," Lecture by Gareth M. Winrow, Conference "Black Sea: Energy and the Environment," Istanbul Bilgi University, Marine Law and Policy Research Center, May 15, 2003.

Non-academic periodicals

BBC World Service
Cumhurriyet (Turkish)
Echo (Russian/Azeri)
Economist (English)
Financial Times (English)
Haaretz (Hebrew/English)
Hürriyet (Turkish)
Jane's Defence Weekly (English)
Jerusalem Post (English)
Kommersant (Russian)
Milli Gazete (Turkish)
Monitor (Russian/Azeri)
Nash Vek (Russian/Azeri)
Nezavisimaya Gazeta (Russian)
Novaya Gazeta (Russian)
Turkish Daily News (English)
Radikal (Turkish)
Radio Free Europe/Radio Liberty
The Times (English)
Turan News Service (Russian/Azeri)
Vesti (Russian)
Zaman (Turkish/English)
Zavtra (Russian)
Zerkalo (Russian/Azeri)

Websites

www.caspiandevelopmentandexport.com/
www.bp.com/location_rep/caspian/stakeholder/regional.asp
www.diplomaticobserver.com/english/index.asp
www.ans-dx.com/news.htm#12
www.debka.com
www.mignews.com
http://meria.idc.ac.il/
www2.echo-az.com/index.shtml
http://nashvek.media-az.com/politika.html
http://mediapress.media-az.com/index.html
www.cacianalyst.org/news.php
www.bakutoday.net/
www.lenta.ru
www.zerkalo.az
www.turkishdailynews.com
www.turkishpress.com/turkishpress/
www.anatolia.com/anatolia/
www.Haaretzdaily.com

Selected bibliography

Abadi, Jacob, "Israel and Turkey: From Covert to Overt Relations," *Journal of Conflict Studies*, Publication of Center for Conflict Studies, University of New Brunswick, Vol. 15, No. 2, Fall, 1995.

——, "Israel's Quest for Normalization with Azerbaijan and the Muslim States of Central Asia," *Journal of Third World Studies*, Vol. 19, No. 2, Fall, 2002.

——, *Israel's Quest for Recognition and Acceptance in Asia: Garrison State Diplomacy*, London: Routledge, 2004.

Akiner, Shirin (Ed.), *The Caspian: Politics, Energy and Security*, London: Routledge Curzon, 2004.

Allison, Roy, "Failures of Russia in Post-Soviet Period," in Roy Allison and Christopher Bluth (Eds.), *Security Dilemmas in Russia and Eurasia*, London: The Royal Institute of International Affairs, 1998.

Altunisik, Meliha Benli, "Turkish Policy towards Israel," in Alan Makovsky and Sabri Sayari (Eds.), *Turkey's New World*, Washington, DC: The Washington Institute for Near East Policy, 2000.

Amineh, Mehdi, *Towards the Control of Oil Resources in the Caspian Region*, New York: St. Martin's Press, 1999.

Antoniades, Andreas, "Epistemic Communities, Epistemes and the Construction of (World) Politics," *Global Society*, Vol. 17, No. 1, 2003.

Aras, Bulent, *Palestinian Israeli Peace Process and Turkey*, Commack, NJ: Nova Science Publishers, 1998.

——, "Turkish Foreign Policy and Jerusalem: Toward a Societal Construction of Foreign Policy," *Arab Studies Quarterly*, Fall 2000.

——, *The New Geopolitics of Eurasia and Turkey's Position*, London and Portland, OR: Frank Cass, 2002.

——, "The Caspian Region and Middle East," *Mediterranean Quarterly*, Winter, 2002.

Ashley, Richard, "The Poverty of Neorealism," in Robert Keohane (Ed.), *Neorealism and Its Critics*, New York: Columbia University Press, 1986.

—— and R.B.J. Walker (Eds.), "Speaking the Language of Exile: Dissidence in International Studies," *International Studies Quarterly*, special issue, Vol. 34, No. 3, September, 1990.

Avineri, Shlomo, *The Making of Modern Zionism: The Intellectual Origins of the Jewish State*, New York: Basic Books, 1981.

Azaryahu, Maoz, *State Cults: Celebrating Independence and Commemorating the Fallen in Israel* (Hebrew), Sde-Boker: Ben-Gurion Center, 1995.

Bacik, Gokhan, "The Limits of an Alliance: Turkish–Israeli Relations Revisited," *Arab Studies Quarterly*, Vol. 23, No. 3, Summer, 2001.

Bal, Idris, *The Rise and Fall of the Turkish Model*, Aldershot: Ashgate, 2001.

Baran, Zeyno, "The Caucasus: Ten Years after Independence," *The Washington Quarterly*, Winter Section: Eurasia after Ten Years, Vol. 25, No. 1, 2002.

Barkey, Henri, *Reluctant Neighbor: Turkey's Role in the Middle East*, Washington, DC: USIP Press, 1996.

Barnett, Michael (Ed.), *Israel in Comparative Perspective: Challenging the Conventional Wisdom*, Albany, NY: State University of New York, 1996.

Beilin, Yosi, *A Concise Political History of Israel*, New York: St. Martin's Press, 1992.

Ben-Eliezer, Uri, *The Making of Israeli Militarism*, Bloomington: Indiana University Press, 1998.

Bengio, Ofra, *Turkish–Israeli Relationship: Changing Ties of Middle East Outsiders*, New York: Palgrave Macmillan, 2004.

Beeri, Yadidiah, *What's in the Name: To Whom Belongs the State* (Hebrew), Tel Aviv: Yaron Golan Publishers), 1992.

Bialer, Uri, *Between East and West: Israel's Foreign Policy Orientations, 1948–1956*, Cambridge: Cambridge University Press, 1990.

Blank, Stephen, "Russia's Return to Mideast Diplomacy," *Orbis*, 40, No. 4, Fall, 1996, pp. 517–35.

Blout, Brian, *Geopolitics and Globalization in the Twentieth Century*, London: Reaktion Books, 2001.

Bolukbasi, Suha, "Behind the Turkish–Israeli Alliance: The Turkish View," *Journal of Palestine Studies*, Vol. 24, No. 1, Autumn, 1999.

Brzezinski, Zbigniew, *The Grand Chessboard: American Primacy and Its Geostrategic Imperatives*, New York: Harper Collins, 1997.

Buzan, Barry, O. Waever and J. De Wilde, *Security: A New Framework for Analysis*, Boulder, CO: Lynne Rienner Press, 1998.

Carkoglu, Ali, Eder Mine, et al. *The Political Economy of Regional Cooperation in the Middle East*, London: Routledge, 1998.

Carr, E.H., *The Twenty Years' Crisis, 1919–1939*, Houndmills: Palgrave, 2001.

Caspian Energy Resources: Implications for the Arab Gulf, Abu Dhabi: The Emirates Center for Strategic Studies and Research, 2000.

Cheterian, Vicken, "Sea or Lake: A Major Issue for Russia," *Cahiers d'études sur la Méditerranée orientale et le monde turco-iranien*, No. 23, January–June, 1997.

Chumalov, Mikhail, *Kaspiyskaya neft y Mezhnazyonlalnye Otnoshenya*, Moscow: The Center for Study of International Relations, 2000.

Cohen, Asher and Bernard Susser, *Israel and the Politics of Jewish Identity*, Baltimore, MD: The Johns Hopkins University Press, 2000.

Cohen, Robin, *Global Diasporas*, London: UCL Press, 1997.

Colonomos, Ariel, "Transnational Networks: Old Game, New Rules," in Marie-Claude Smouts (Ed.), *The New International Relations: Theory and Practice*, London: C. Hurst & Co, 2001.

Cornell, Svante, "Konflikt v Nagornom Karabakhe," in Dmitry Furman (Ed.), *Azerbaijan and Russia*, Moscow: Letny Sad, 2001.

Cox, Robert, "Post-Hegemonic Conceptualization of World Order," *Governance without Government: Order and Change in World Politics*, Cambridge: Cambridge University Press, 1992.

Dawisha, Karen, "Imperialism, Dependency and Autocolonization," in Ken Booth (Ed.), *Statecraft and Security: The Cold War and Beyond*, Cambridge: Cambridge University Press, 1998.

Dekmejian, Hrair and Hovann Simonian, *The Troubled Waters: The Geopolitics of the Caspian Region*, London: Tauris Publishers, 2001.

Deudney, Daniel, "Ground Identity: Nature, Place and Space in Nationalism," in Yosef Lapid and Friedrich Kratochwil (Eds.), *The Return of Culture and Identity in IR Theory*, Boulder, CO: Lynne Rienner Publishers, 1997.

—— and Richard Matthew (Eds.), *Contested Grounds*, Albany, NY: State University of New York, 1999.

Dowty, Alan, *The Jewish State: A Century Later*, Berkeley: University of California Press, 1998.

Dunleavy, Patrick and Brendan O'Leary, *Theories of the State: The Politics of Liberal Democracy*, London: Macmillan Education, 1987.

Eickelman, Dale, "Anthropology, the Middle East and Central Asia," in Dale Eickelman (Ed.), *The Middle East and Central Asia*, Upper Saddle River, NJ: Prentice Hall, 1998.

Fuller, Graham and Ian Lesser, *Turkey's New Geopolitics*, Boulder, CO: Westview Press, 1993.

Furman, Dmitry (Ed.), *Azerbaijan and Russia*, Moscow: Letny Sad, 2001.

Gadjiev, K., *Geopolitika Kavkaza*, Moscow: Mejdunarodnye Otnoshenya, 2003.

Gilpin, Robert, *War and Change in International Politics*, Cambridge: Cambridge University Press, 1981.

Gleeson, Gregory, *The Central Asian States: Discovering Independence*, Boulder, CO: Westview Press, 1997.

Goldstein, Judith and Robert Keohane, *Ideas and Foreign Policy*, Ithaca, NY: Cornell University Press, 1993.

Granovetter, Mark, "The Strength of Weak Ties," *American Journal of Sociology*, Vol. 78, No. 6, May, 1973, pp. 1360–80.

Gusterson, Hugh, "Missing the End of the Cold War in International Security," in Jutta Weldes, Mark Laffey, Hugh Gusterson and Raymond Duvall (Eds.), *Cultures of Insecurity States, Communities and the Production of Danger*, Minneapolis, MN: University of Minnesota Press, 1999.

Haddad, George, *Revolutions and Military Rule in the Middle East: The Northern Tier*, New York: Robert Speller & Sons, 1965.

Hale, William, "Economic Issues in Turkish Foreign Policy," in Alan Makovsky and Sabri Sayari (Eds.), *Turkey's New World*, Washington, DC: The Washington Institute for Near East Policy, 2000.

—— , *Turkish Foreign Policy, 1774–2000*, London: Routledge, 2002.

Harely, Shmuel, *Turkiya, mivne arza, toldoteyha, mishtara ha medini, hevrati ve kalkali* ("Turkey: Its Geography, History, Political, Social and Economic System"), Jerusalem: Reuven Mas, 1941.

Hinnebusch, Raymond and Anoushiravan Ehseshami (Eds.), *The Foreign Policy of Middle East States*, Boulder, CO: Lynne Rienner, 2002.

Hoiris, Ole and Sefa Martin Yurukel (Eds.), *Contrasts and Solutions in the Caucasus*, Aarhus: Aarhus University Press, 1992.

Horwitz, Dan, "The Israel Defense Forces: A Civilianized Military in a Partial Militarized Society," in R. Kolkowitz and A. Korbonski (Eds.), *Soldiers, Peasants and Bureaucrats*, London: Allen & Unwin, 1982.

Inbar, Efraim, "Regional Implications of the Israeli–Turkish Strategic Partnership," *Turkish Studies*, Vol. 3, No. 2, Autumn, 2002.

—— , "Turkey's New Strategic Partner: Israel," in Michael Radu (Ed.), *Dangerous Neighborhood*, New Brunswick, NJ: Transaction Publishers, 2002.

Jepperson, Ronald, Alexander Wendt and Peter Katzenstein, "Norms and National Security," in Peter Katzenstein (Ed.), *The Culture of National Security*, New York: Columbia University Press, 1996.

Jouejati, Murhaf, "Water Politics as High Politics: The Case of Turkey and Syria," in Henri Barkey (Ed.), *Reluctant Neighbor*, Washington, DC: United States Institute of Peace, 1996.

Katzenstein, Peter, *The Culture of National Security*, New York: Columbia University Press, 1996.

Keohane, Robert and Joseph Nye (Eds.), *Transnational Relations and World Politics*, Cambridge, MA: Harvard University Press, 1971.

——, and Joseph Nye, "Power and Interdependence in the Information Age, *Foreign Affairs*, Vol. 77, No. 5, September/October, 1998.

——, et al., in Robert Keohane, Joseph Nye and Stanley Hoffman (Eds.), *After the Cold War: Its Meaning and Implications, 1989–1991*, Cambridge, MA: Harvard University Press, 1993.

Kimmerling, Baruch, *The Invention and Decline of Israeliness: State, Society and the Military*, Berkeley: University of California Press, 2001.

Kinzer, Stephen, *Crescent and Star*, New York: Farrar, Straus & Giroux, 2002.

Kotkin, Joel, *Tribes: How Race, Religion, and Identity Determine Success in the New Global Economy*, New York: Random House, 1992.

Kozhohin, E. (Ed.), *Nezavisimyi Azerbaidzhan: novye orientiry* (Russian), Moscow: Rossiiskii Institut Strategicheskikh Issledovanii, 2000.

Kramer, Heinz, *A Changing Turkey*, Washington, DC: Brookings Institution, 2000.

Landau, Jacob (Ed.), *Ataturk and the Modernization of Turkey*, Boulder, CO: Westview, 1984.

——, *Pan-Turkism: From Irredentism to Cooperation*, Bloomington: Indiana University Press, 2004.

Krasner, Stephen, *Defending the National Interest: Raw Materials Investments and US Foreign Policy*, Princeton, NJ: Princeton University Press, 1978.

Lapid, Yosef and Friedrich Kratochwil (Eds.), *Return of Culture and Identity in IR Theory*, Boulder, CO: Lynne Rienner Publishers, 1996.

Liel, Alon, *Turkey in the Middle East, Oil, Islam, and Politics*, Boulder, CO: Lynne Rienner Publishers, 2001.

——, *Demo-Islam: Mishtar Hadash bTurkiya* (Hebrew), Tel Aviv: Am Oved, 2003.

Livneh, Eliezer, "Values and Society in Israel," in Israel Naamani, David Rudavsky and Abraham Katsh (Eds.), *Israel: Its Politics and Philosophy*, New York: Behrman House, revised 1974.

Lochery, Neill, "Israel and Turkey: Deepening Ties, 1995–8," *Israel Affairs*, Vol. 5, No. 1, August, 1998.

McInnes, Colin (Ed.), *Security and Strategy in the New Europe*, London: Routledge, 1992.

Makovsky, Alan and Sabri Sayari (Eds.), *Turkey's New World*, Washington, DC: The Washington Institute for Near East Policy, 2000.

Manisali, Erol, *Turkey's Place in the Middle East*, Istanbul: Middle East Business and Banking Publications, 1989.

Martin, Lenore (Ed.), *New Frontiers in Middle East Security*, New York: St. Martin's Press/Palgrave, 2001.

—— and Demitris Keridis (Eds.), *The Future of Turkish Foreign Policy*, Cambridge, MA: MIT Press, 2004.

Mearsheimer, John, "Back to the Future: Instability in Europe after the Cold War," *International Security*, Vol. 15, 1990, pp. 5–56.

——, "Why We Will Soon Miss the Cold War," *Atlantic Monthly*, No. 266, 1990, pp. 35–50.

Meshkini, Qadir Nasri, "Challenges of Iranian Policy in Central Asia Central Asia and the Caucasus," *Amu Darya: The Iranian Journal of Central Asian Studies*, Vol. 4, No. 5, Spring/Summer, 2000.

Minosyan, Sergey, "Turkish–Israeli Military and Political Cooperation and Regional Security Issues," *Iran and Caucasus*, Vol. VII, Leiden-Boston: Brill, 2004.

Morgenthau, Hans, *Politics among Nations: The Struggle for Power and Peace*, New York: Knopf, 1973.

Muradian, Igor, *Politika SSHA I Problemy Bezopasnosti Regiona Yuzhnogo Kavakaza*, Yerevan: Antares, 2000.

Murinson, Alexander, "Israeli Foreign Relations with the Islamic Newly Independent States: General Overview," *The Cyber-Caravan*, Washington, DC: Publication of the Central Asia-Caucasus Institute, SAIS, August, 1999.

—— "The Impact of American Foreign Policy after 9.11 on the October 2003 Presidential Elections in Azerbaijan," *Insight Turkey*, April/June, 2004.

—— and Soner Cagaptay, "Good Relations between Azerbaijan and Israel: A Model for Other Muslim States in Eurasia?" *PolicyWatch*, No. 982, Washington, DC: The Washington Institute for Near East Policy, March 30, 2005.

—— "The Strategic Depth of Turkish Foreign Policy," *Middle Eastern Studies*, Vol. 42, No. 6, November, 2006.

Nachmani, Amikam, *Israel, Turkey and Greece: Uneasy Relations in the East Mediterranean*, London: Frank Cass, 1987.

Navaro-Yashin, Yael, *Faces of the State: Secularism and Public Life in Turkey*, Princeton, NJ: Princeton University Press, 2002.

Nizameddin, Talal, *Russia and the Middle East*, London: Hurst & Co, 1999.

Noruzi, Mohammad, "Contention of Iran and Turkey in Central Asia and the Caucasus," *Amu Darya*, Vol. 4, No. 5, 2000.

Nye, Joseph, "Soft Power," *Foreign Policy*, Vol. 80, Autumn, 1990, pp. 153–71.

Olcott, Martha, *Central Asia's New States: Independence, Foreign Policy, and Regional Security*, Washington, DC: United States Institute of Peace Press, 1996.

Peres, Shimon, *The New Middle East*, Shaftesbury, UK: Element, 1993.

Pope, Hugh, *Sons of the Conqueror*, New York: Overlook Duckworth, 2005.

Pope, Nicole and Hugh Pope, *Turkey Unveiled*, Woodstock, NY: Overlook Press, 1997.

Radu, Michael (Ed.), *Dangerous Neighborhood*, New Brunswick, NJ: Transaction Publishers, 2003.

Ramazani, Rouhoallah, *The Northern Tier: Afghanistan, Iran, and Turkey*, Princeton, NJ: Van Nostrand Company, 1966.

Robins, Philip, *Turkish–Israeli Relations: From the Periphery to the Center*, The Emirates Occasional Papers, Abu Dhabi: The Emirates Center for Strategic Studies and Research, 2001.

——, *Suits and Uniforms: Turkish Foreign Policy since the Cold War*, Seattle, WA: University of Washington Press, 2004.

Rosenau, James, *Governance without Government: Order and Change in World Politics*, Cambridge: Cambridge University Press, 1992.

——, *Along the Domestic–Foreign Frontier: Exploring Governance in a Turbulent World*, Cambridge: Cambridge University Press, 1997.

Rosenthal, Donna, *The Israelis*, New York: Free Press, 2005.

Ruggie, John, "Territoriality and Beyond: Problematizing Modernity in International Relations," *International Organizations*, Vol. 47, No. 1, Winter, 1993.

Sachar, Howard, *A History of Israel from the Rise of Zionism to Our Time*, New York: Alfred Knopf, 1998.

Scholte, Jan Aart, *Globalization: A Critical Introduction*, New York: St. Martin Press, 2000.

Shankland, David, "Religion," in Brian Beeley (Ed.), *Turkish Transformation*, Huntingdon, UK: Eothen Press, 2002.

Shlaim, Avi, *The Iron Wall*, New York: Norton, 2000.

Smouts, Marie-Claude (Ed.), *The New International Relations: Theory and Practice*, London: C. Hurst & Co., 2001.

Starr, S. Frederick and Svante E. Cornell (Eds.), *The Baku-Tbilisi-Ceyhan Pipeline: Oil Window to the West*, Washington, DC: The Central Asia-Caucasus Institute & Silk Road Studies Program, 2005.

Steinbruner, John, "Can the United States Lead the World?," in Ken Booth (Ed.), *Statecraft and Security: The Cold War and Beyond*, Cambridge: Cambridge University Press, 1998.

Stone, Diane, *Capturing the Political Imagination: Think Tanks and the Policy Process*, London: Frank Cass, 1996.

Strange, Susan, *States and Markets*, London: Pinter, 1988.

Swietochowski, Tadeusz, *Russia and Azerbaijan: A Borderland in Transition*, New York: Columbia University Press, 1995.

Van der Leeuw, Charles, *Azerbaijan*, London: Curzon Caucasus World, 2000.

Walt, Stephen, "Alliance Formation and the Balance of Power," *International Security*, Vol. 9, No. 4, 1985.

—— , *The Origins of Alliances*, Ithaca, NY: Cornell University Press, 1987.

Waltz, Kenneth, *Man, the State and War*, New York: Columbia University Press, 1959.

—— , *Theory of International Politics*, Boston, MA: Addison-Wesley, 1979.

—— , "Reflections on *Theory of International Politics*," in Robert Keohane (Ed.), *Neorealism and Its Critics*, New York: Columbia University Press, 1986.

Watanabe, Paul, *Ethnic Groups, Congress, and American Foreign Policy: The Politics of the Turkish Arms Embarg*, Westport, CT: Greenwood Press, 1984.

Weldes, Jutta, Mark Laffey, et al., *Cultures of Insecurity: States, Communities and the Production of Danger*, Minneapolis, MN: University of Minnesota Press, 1999.

Wendt, Alexander, "Identities and Structural Change," in Yosef Lapid and Friedrich Kratochwil (Eds.), *Return of Culture and Identity in IR Theory*, Boulder, CO: Lynne Rienner Publishers, 1996.

—— , *Social Theory of International Relations*, Cambridge: Cambridge University Press, 1999.

Winrow, Gareth, "Central Asia and the Transcaucasus," in *Turkey's New World*, Washington, DC: The Washington Institute for Near East Policy, 2000.

Yavuz, Hakan, "Turkish–Israeli Relations Through the Lens of the Turkish Identity Debate," *Journal of Palestine Studies*, Vol. 27, No. 1, Autumn, 1997.

Yogev, Ester and Eyal Naveh, *Histories: Towards Dialog with the Past* (Hebrew) Tel Aviv: Bavel, 2002.

Zehfuss, Maja, *Constructivism in International Relations: The Politics of Reality*, Cambridge: Cambridge University Press, 2002.

Index

Abbasov, Namik 20, 21; *see also*
  Azerbaijani Ministry of National
  Security
acquis communautaire 2, 38; *see also*
  European Union
Adalet ve Kalkinma Partisi (Justice and
  Development Party, AKP) 1, 3, 15,
  51–6, 114–18, 137–9, 148–51; new
  political elite 127, 139
AIPAC (American Israeli Political
  Action Committee) 68–9, 73–8
Aliyev, Heydar 5, 7, 19–20, 35, 59, 60,
  65, 87, 92, 128, 129; acknowledgment
  of Turkish assistance 18; authoritarian
  practices 19, 27, 60, 84, 123–5, 127,
  140; and Azerbaijani Constitution 30;
  Azerbaijani nationalism 36; KGB
  general 10, 13, 19, 27, 133; Kurdish
  connection 112, 126–7; plot against
  20, 60, 126; rapprochement with
  Russia 59, 132–3; references to
  Kemal Ataturk 10, 36–7; relations
  with Ankara 95, 108–9, 126–7;
  relations with American Jews 74, 79;
  relations with Israel 107, 127, 134,
  141; return to policy of balancing
  35–6; role of Islam 30, 131;
  secularism 27; Russian sphere of
  influence 105; vision of integration
  into Euro–Atlantic alliance 27–8
Aliyev, Ilham 19, 21, 85, 87, 124, 126,
  128, 132–3; pro-Ilham Aliyev public
  rally 35
Alliance ix, 2, 5, 15, 16, 22, 39, 63,
  66–7, 86, 98, 100, 145–6, 148, 151;
  Azerbaijan, Turkey and Israel

(possibly Georgia) ix, 5, 60, 93, 105,
  113, 115–16, 139; in the expanded
  Middle East ix, 4; model x, 4, 6, 143;
  Russia, Armenia, Iran (possibly
  Greece and Syria) 5, 93; secret
  alliance with Turkey 2, 98; system
  of 11; theory of 3, 4, 7, 10; Western
  alliance 2, 11, 15, 22, 25, 26, 28, 57,
  95, 97; *see also* Periphery Alliance
Alpogan, Yigit 51
Altı Ok (Six Arrows) 31
American Jewish Committee (AJC)
  68–9, 74, 77, 79–80, 81, 146
American Oil Company (AMOCO)
  88–90
Anavatan Party (Motherland, ANAP)
  117–18
Arafat, Yassir 85, 116, 134–6
Armenia ix, 4, 5, 11, 18–19, 20, 22, 24,
  26, 31, 40, 51, 57–8, 59, 100, 113,
  114, 120, 125, 123, 126–8, 131
Armenian diaspora 40, 64, 68
Armenian lobby *see* US Congress 39, 40,
  68, 74–5, 76, 77, 80
Armenian Secret Army for the Liberation
  of Armenia (ASALA) 12, 95, 96, 101
Askeri Is Birligi Koordinasyon Kurulu
  (Council on Military Cooperation) 58
Ataturk, Mustafa Kemal 9, 14, 22–3,
  28–9, 31–2, 36, 37, 47, 97, 108, 116,
  144; *see also* Kemalism
Avrasya Stratejik Arastirmalar Merkezi
  (ASAM) 82
Azerbaijan ix, 1, 2, 18–21, 26–8, 29–30,
  33–7, 39–40, 123–33; armed forces
  18–19, 57–8, 60, 99, 106, 108;